PRAISE FOR *RESEARCH METHODS IN HUMAN RESOURCE MANEGEMENT*

'This book is an invaluable resource. It is clear, succinct and provides a guide to the whole process of developing and completing an HRM project.'
Jannine Williams, Senior Lecturer in Human Resource Management, Queensland University of Technology, Australia

'The fourth edition of *Research Methods in Human Resource Management* is a thorough and up-to-date textbook concerning how to plan and carry out major research projects in human resource management – up to and including dissertations. Equal balance and coverage is given to qualitative and quantitative research methodology. Even though the authors focus particularly on the United Kingdom, this book can and should have international impact. I recommend it highly, and hope that it further strengthens research rigor in human resources management and management education.'
Jon M Werner, Professor of Management, University of Wisconsin-Whitewater, USA

'The latest edition of *Research Methods in Human Resource Management* is an essential resource for any student undertaking research in any area of HR. Each stage of the research journey is covered in significant depth and breadth and the book is written in a highly accessible manner. For students undertaking a CIPD qualification in particular, this text is invaluable.'
Dr Ronan Carbery, Co-director of the Human Resource Research Centre, Cork University Business School, Ireland and Co-editor of *European Journal of Training and Development*

'Human resource management issues in organisations are increasingly complex – and so is HR-related research. This book helps students to break down the complexity into manageable steps. Each of those steps comes with real-life illustrations and questions that trigger further reflection, which ultimately provides the student with the skills to become an independent researcher and critical HR professional. What I particularly value in this book is that students are taught an evidence-based reflex and openness towards very different research methods.'
Nele De Cuyper, Associate Professor, Work, Organizational and Personnel Psychology Research Group, KU Leuven, Belgium

'This is a great go-to textbook for all aspects of a research project. Written in a very practical way, the guidance is relevant to undergraduate and postgraduate students. The focus on HR and the emphasis on the relationship between research and practice will enable students and practitioners alike to make a positive impact from undertaking research. Highly recommended.'
Dr Maranda Ridgway FCIPD, Senior Lecturer in Human Resource Management, Nottingham Business School

'This excellent textbook adopts a structured, student-centred approach to conducting HRM research. With lots of practical examples and insights, the text provides useful advice and guidance to new and developing researchers on how to navigate the contours of a HR research project. The authors demystify the language associated with research and take undergraduate and postgraduate students step-by-step through the stages of completing an HRM research dissertation. It is little wonder that the text continues to remain required reading amongst HRM students of all levels.'
Dr David McGuire, Reader and Deputy Head, Department of Management and HRM, Glasgow Caledonian University

'Evidence-based HR requires a deep focus on method and rigour. This book offers clarity and direction for people professionals looking to increase their capability and improve their impact. It will be an excellent companion for professionals who are looking to learn about the fundamentals of bringing evidence and insights into their practice. Few textbooks are as comprehensive and accessible as this.'
Edward Houghton, Head of Research and Thought Leadership, CIPD

'This fourth edition of an already highly regarded book does not disappoint. The content provides clear and exemplary guidance on all aspects of doing a research project, as well as a wealth of pedagogical features to support learning and teaching. I am confident this book will be a very useful and welcome resource for both students and academics.'
Professor Jim Stewart, Liverpool John Moores University, CIPD Chief Examiner for Learning and Development and President of University Forum for Human Resource Development

'*Research Methods in Human Resource Management* is a timely contribution that covers all the key phases that HRM students need to consider when carrying out research for their studies, whether that be in the form of a project or dissertation. The book is well structured and allows tutors to take students on a journey covering the initial project identification stage, writing a clear literature review as well as offering guidance and clarity on the critical data collection phases. Particularly valuable are the final chapters, which offer practical advice on the write-up stage and how students can really make an impact with their research.'
Dr Martin McCracken, Research Director, Ulster University Business School and Editor-in-Chief, *Education + Training*

Fourth Edition

Research Methods in Human Resource Management

Investigating a Business Issue

Valerie Anderson
Rita Fontinha
Fiona Robson

First published in 2004 by Chartered Institute of Personnel and Development
This edition published in Great Britain and the United States in 2020 by Kogan Page Limited

2nd Floor, 45 Gee Street	122 W 27th St, 10th Floor	4737/23 Ansari Road
London	New York, NY 10001	Daryaganj
EC1V 3RS	USA	New Delhi 110002
United Kingdom		India

www.koganpage.com

ISBNs

Hardback	978 0 7494 9812 2
Paperback	978 0 7494 8387 6
Ebook	978 0 7494 8388 3

British Library Cataloguing-in-Publication Data

A CIP record for this book is available from the British Library.

Library of Congress Cataloging-in-Publication Data

Names: Anderson, Valerie (Principal lecturer), author. | Fontinha, Rita, author. | Robson, Fiona Jane, author.
Title: Research methods in human resource management : investigating a business issue / Valerie Anderson, Rita Fontinha, Fiona Robson.
Description: Fourth edition. | London, United Kingdom ; New York, NY : Kogan Page, 2020. | Includes bibliographical references and index.
Identifiers: LCCN 2019044260 (print) | LCCN 2019044261 (ebook) | ISBN 9780749498122 (hardback) | ISBN 9780749483876 (paperback) | ISBN 9780749483883 (ebook)
Subjects: LCSH: Personnel management–Research–Methodology.
Classification: LCC HF5549.15 .A54 2020 (print) | LCC HF5549.15 (ebook) | DDC 658.30072–dc23
LC record available at https://lccn.loc.gov/2019044260
LC ebook record available at https://lccn.loc.gov/2019044261

Typeset by Integra Software Services, Pondicherry
Print production managed by Jellyfish
Printed and bound in Great Britain by Ashford Colour Press Ltd.

CONTENTS

12   Making an impact: the relationship between research and practice 435

LIST OF FIGURES AND TABLES

Figures

Tables

01
Investigating and researching HR issues

LEARNING OBJECTIVES

This chapter should help you to:

- define what is meant by research in the context of HRM&D and how it can contribute to effective policy and practice;
- identify the different components of an effective research project and the skills needed;
- consider your role and influences as a researcher;
- compare different approaches to HR research and the opportunities presented by an investigation of a business issue;
- reflect upon the key relationships that will support and enhance your project;
- consider how to build on prior learning.

- Writing your research proposal
- Working with your supervisor
- Managing your research project
- Working as a practitioner-researcher
- Summary checklist
- Test yourself, review and reflect questions
- Useful resources

Researching HR issues

This book is aimed at people who are undertaking an HR research project as part of a qualification-related course. You may be a part-time student who is investigating a business issue in the role of a 'practitioner-researcher' or a full-time student who will be researching into an HR issue either inside or outside of a particular organisation or group of organisations. You may be studying in your own country or abroad. At the beginning of the project module some students will already have ideas of what they want to explore whereas others may not; this is fine and this text will help you to explore and plan the possibilities. Different centres also have varying requirements for projects; for example, some will require students to undertake primary research whereas others may direct students to focus on the analysis of data and information that already exists (secondary data).

The ability to undertake good quality research that leads to relevant practical outcomes and contributes to the knowledge base of the HR profession is an important skill. Qualified professionals should be able to research relevant topics and write reports that can persuade key stakeholders in the organisation to change or adopt a particular policy and practice. Most people who make use of this book are likely to be: final year undergraduate students of Management or HRM; students undertaking professional HR courses such as CIPD Intermediate or Advanced level programmes; or students undertaking a 'taught Masters' course (usually an MSc or MA in HRM or a related subject or an MBA).

Using this book to support your work

Making a start with a big piece of work like a research project is a daunting prospect and you may be tempted to 'put off' the moment of making a start. This book is intended to help you make a start and then to see the project through to a successful and rewarding conclusion. The book aims to be practical, accessible and relevant. It should provide you with ideas and resources to apply to your research. We hope that you will use it as a resource to develop knowledge, understanding and the practical skills you need to make best use of the research process you are undertaking and to communicate what you have learned in a convincing and credible way. The book is not a substitute for regular attendance at research methods classes nor does it replace the need to communicate with your supervisor or project tutor.

Research projects are rarely completed quickly and they compete for attention with many other important and urgent matters. Different chapters of the book will be relevant at different stages of your project from initial project idea and research proposal to submission of the final report or dissertation. You may find it useful to reread chapters as you tackle each section of your project.

When research is done well it can provide a 'win–win' opportunity for you and the organisation, or organisations, that have participated in some way. Your organisation(s) can learn from the findings and decide whether to implement your recommendations. You can gain valuable personal and professional development in a wide range of areas. Each chapter in this book ends with a self-test so that you can check your understanding and there is an opportunity to review and reflect on your achievements so far. This can inform any continuing professional development (CPD) record that you will maintain if you are a member of a professional organisation, such as the CIPD. Ideas about further reading are also included at the end of each chapter to enable you to go 'further' or 'deeper' as appropriate.

Why are you required to write a project or dissertation?

A project or dissertation gives you the opportunity to demonstrate all of the skills that you have been developing throughout your qualification. You will use your skills of problem-solving, literature-searching, critical review and data analysis to name but a few. It is also your chance to focus on an area that is of specific interest to you and enables you to be creative in a way that might differ from some of your previous assessments. A good project or dissertation can also be good for your career and gives you something to talk about in future interviews. As projects are usually worth 40 credits or more, they are likely to have a large influence on your final award classification.

Getting started

The research process and the skills you need

 Activity 1.1

Making a critical decision for your future

Think back to when you decided that you would embark on your current studies. This was a big decision in terms of time commitment, cost and the ability to manage your work/study/life balance. You may have had several different push factors – perhaps to support a career change or as a means of getting promoted from your current position.

What were the key questions you asked yourself? Who did you talk to about this? How did you make decisions on where and how to study?

Feedback notes

Your key decisions might have included:

- What are the admission requirements? How do costs vary by centre?
- Which centres offer professional accreditations?
- What is the total duration of the programme? When do the classes take place and how does this fit with my other commitments?
- How many students achieve good degrees and go on to graduate level jobs?
- What do previous students say about each centre?

Information you might have consulted and might have included:

- key performance indicators and rankings;
- publications from your shortlisted institutions, for example, prospectuses and websites;
- talking to current students or alumni whom you know;
- your employer (if your employer has agreed to provide financial support).

As you are digesting this information and data you should have considered the legitimacy of the source. For example, university prospectuses are geared up to emphasise the strengths and positive aspects of their courses, whereas talking to past students may give you more impartial information. There is also a range of useful external benchmarks such as the results of the National Student Survey and ranking tables produced by *The Guardian* and *Times Higher Education* publications.

The research process

Activity 1.1 is, at a basic level, a small and personal research activity. It involves the systematic enquiry into an issue to increase knowledge and underpin effective decision-making. The activities it would involve are, however, indicative of the components of any research process (see Figure 1.1).

Often research is represented as a series of discrete and linear stages and this book is structured in a similar sort of way. However, the reality of organisational research is that each stage is often interrelated with the others and experiences in 'later' stages often leads to reconsideration of earlier ones (Saunders, Lewis and Thornhill, 2019). Some of the best projects are those that are 'messy' and have some backwards and forwards movement from one stage to another. For example, where the data identifies unanticipated results that then leads to a further and extended review of the literature in your topic area.

For research undertaken to meet the requirements of CIPD Advanced level qualifications the current requirements for 'Investigating a business issue from an HR perspective' are:

- Identify and justify a business issue that is of strategic relevance to the organisation.
- Critically analyse and discuss existing literature, contemporary HR policy and practice relevant to the chosen issue.

Figure 1.1 Components of the research process

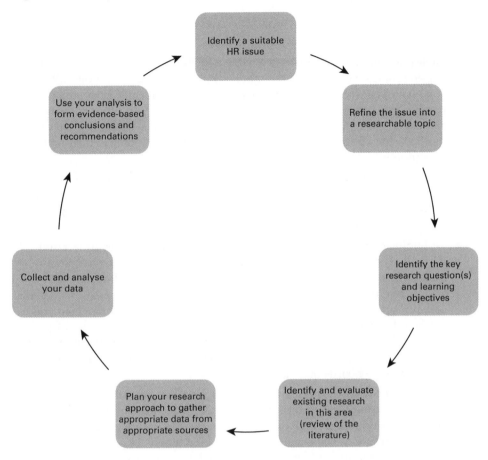

- Compare and contrast the relative merits of different research methods and their relevance to different situations.
- Undertake a systematic analysis of quantitative and/or qualitative information and present the results in a clear and consistent format.
- Draw realistic and appropriate conclusions and make recommendations based on costed options.
- Develop and present a persuasive business report.
- Write a reflective account of what has been learned during the project and how this can be applied in the future.

Each of these stages is considered in more detail in subsequent chapters of the book but an indication of the skills you need to carry out these different elements is provided now.

The effective researcher

Five interrelated skills underpin any effective research project (see Figure 1.2). You will need:

- **Intellectual and thinking skills.** Knowing a lot about your topic is important but other skills will enable you to undertake a more successful project. When you undertake research you have to act as an 'independent learner' and this involves you being able to ask questions, probe deeply into issues and develop and justify your own thinking about the issues involved. We explore later in this book the advantages and challenges for those researching in their own organisation.

- **Personal effectiveness skills.** HR professionals are already aware of the importance of good interpersonal effectiveness in people management; the skills you have developed can be put to good effect in your research project, particularly your skills of time and stress management.

- **Technological/digital skills.** Throughout the duration of your project and particularly at the start, you will need to find information that has already been written on your topic area. Online journals provide a huge number of articles but not all will be relevant so you need to be able to assess usefulness and appropriateness of everything that you read. Technology can help you to record information and data, analyse it and then present it in an appropriate form and also provides useful opportunities to show your creativity. You may use digital resources for your online surveys, carrying out interviews and/or use of message boards or other platforms.

- **Organisational skills.** A research project is very like any other work-based endeavour: it has to be 'project managed'. Knowing how to break down components of a large piece of work, estimate the time requirements for different task areas, undertake more than one task 'in parallel' when appropriate, and keep track of progress are key skills that you can make use of and develop further.

- **Communication skills.** Much of your research project involves you working on your own but high-level communication skills are also necessary. In particular, you will need to orally articulate your ideas to your colleagues and tutors, listen actively (to get advice and also when gathering your data), share your findings within your organisation through effective presentations, and produce a lengthy and well-written research report or dissertation. You will also need to engage with your research participants.

Initial feelings about research

It is possible that you are very excited about getting started with your research project. However, most students have mixed feelings at best or strong doubts at worst about their ability to complete research alongside all the other practical issues and problems facing them in their 'out of study' life. Blaxter *et al* (2010) and Jankowicz (2005) identify some common objections to doing research:

Figure 1.2 The skills of an effective researcher

Intellectual skills
- Thinking
- Evaluating
- Reasoning
- Arguing

Personal effectiveness skills
- Time management
- Stress management
- Social skills

Organisational skills
- Project management
- Arranging access for data gathering
- Multitasking

Communication skills
- Effective writing
- Listening
- Presentation skills
- Explaining your ideas

Technological skills
- Systematic searching for information
- Recording different types of data in appropriate forms
- Analysis of data
- Presenting work in a professional and academic format

- just a way of proving what you already know;
- best left to academics or to experts;
- just a way of justifying what the CEO wants to do anyway;
- too difficult;
- too time-consuming;
- removed from reality;
- unable to change anything;
- too scientific and statistical;
- boring.

Here are some recollections by students about their feelings when they were just starting out on a work-based research project required for their CIPD course.

> I felt overwhelmed; I had lots of good ideas but didn't know which one to pick. (Lucas)
>
> I felt nervous and concerned about how to get started and what I should read. (Caitlyn)
>
> I was looking forward to the challenge but was worried about maintaining a high level of motivation. (Mina)
>
> I was worried that I would not be able to balance my studies with my full-time job. (Jorge)

If these sentiments reflect how you are feeling then read on to find out how much more positive the same students were once their projects had been completed.

> I discovered that I can be very decisive once I have reviewed my task against the assessment criteria. I also realised that I needed to pick a topic that I would find interesting and my knowledge in this area now really helps me in my day job. (Lucas)
>
> I learned that I am actually quite a good project manager, once I had worked out my timescales and factored in my other commitments I felt a lot more confident about the big task ahead. (Caitlyn)
>
> I discovered what I was capable of! Self-determination, dogged enthusiasm and perseverance to achieve a significant challenge. (Mina)
>
> I enhanced my relationship with my line manager as we negotiated a project that would benefit the organisation (and my day job) as well as my academic work, and they were impressed with the result. I also developed strategies to help my work–life balance. (Jorge)

It would be foolish to say that doing research in HR is easy; challenges are likely for even the most confident and experienced practitioners and researchers. Personal qualities like self-motivation, self-confidence and self-centredness will be important for your success (Biggam, 2011):

- **Self-motivation.** You will need to maintain your interest and enthusiasm over quite a long period of time. Choose a topic that you are genuinely interested in and try to tackle all the different stages in the process with a positive attitude and curiosity for what you can learn.
- **Self-confidence.** Self-doubt is an occupational hazard of all researchers at some point in the research process so remember that your ideas are just as valuable as those of an established researcher or a chief executive. If you are

able to learn from the advice of your tutor and student colleagues then there is no reason why your work should not be more than creditable when it is time for your work to be assessed.

- **Self-centredness.** The need to undertake your research over a sustained period means that, from time to time, you will have to turn down requests from family members and friends. Wise judgement is required in these circumstances but it is important to make clear to everyone from the beginning that your project is a priority and you will appreciate their understanding and patience for its duration. Of course, after it is all over you can repay their patience many times over.

Benefits from research

 Activity 1.2

Identifying benefits from research

Imagine that you still have to decide what to do for your project. The chief executive of the organisation for which you work has been to a government-backed seminar on 'reducing sickness absence' and your manager thinks that reducing avoidable absences would be a good project for you to undertake.

If you feel it would be helpful to find out more about absence management before tackling this activity then you might:

- review some of the CIPD resources on absence management (accessible via searching on the homepage www.cipd.co.uk);

- evaluate the latest CIPD annual survey, which is available at: https://www.cipd.co.uk/knowledge/latest-research.

Discussion questions

1 Identify three benefits of tackling a project like this from your own perspective.

2 Identify three benefits from the perspective of your employer.

3 What problems might you foresee if you were to take on this project?

Feedback notes

1 There are a number of benefits that may have occurred to you. Undertaking this sort of high-profile project might be good for your career prospects. Managing sickness absence is a 'hot topic' in HRM and may well sound like an area you could get interested in. There should be a good level of support for you from both managers and employees as both sets of stakeholders may feel they have something to gain. You know the organisation and can have access to a considerable amount of information. Some of the work could be

undertaken in 'work time' rather than at home at weekends (subject to line manager approval).

2   Your organisation also stands to benefit from such a project. Interest in reducing employee absence is high owing to all of the direct and indirect costs that are associated with it. Your work might also look at some of the issues of employee well-being, which is a highly contemporary subject with a relatively small research base. However, it is important to manage expectations as you are unlikely to be able to completely solve the 'problem'.

3   In spite of some benefits there are also some problems that could occur to you in this sort of situation. Practical issues such as your own time constraints may be of concern as well as the extent to which this would be a project that is interesting to you personally. Other questions you might pose may include:

   a   Over what timescale would the employer expect you to work on this project?

   b   Would you be able to gain access to sensitive data around sickness absence and in what format? This might depend on what information you need; that is, you would not need to know about the absence records of individual employees.

   c   If you work within a unionised organisation, what would the issues be around gaining their buy-in?

   d   Is it possible to satisfy both your employer and the requirements for your qualification? If not, how will you approach it?

   e   Given that you are (probably) not a senior manager, how would you go about identifying 'urgent actions' for senior people in the organisation?

   f   Is the organisation 'really' interested in this project?

Perhaps these concerns might be summed up with four questions:

- What exactly would this project involve and what is the required commitment from the organisation?
- Is it feasible as a topic for a student project?
- How would it 'add value' to HR practice in the organisation?
- How might it 'add value' to the HR community beyond your specific organisation?

The purpose of this chapter is to explore these general questions so that you are in a better position to understand the contribution of research to real organisational situations and consider the role of the 'practitioner-researcher'. This should help you to work out how to use this book to plan and execute your own research project.

What is research in HR?

In our daily lives we are exposed to 'research' on a regular basis; when we read our daily newspaper, check our online newsfeed, review what is trending on social media or watch the news on TV many of the features are based on real empirical research. Sometimes this is formal, academic research; for example, to demonstrate the consequences of specified interventions. Sometimes the subject may seem a little more lightweight. Consider, for example, when you read news stories about how researchers explain a mathematical formula for making the perfect slice of toast!

As students you will have been exposed to research within your modules to date; hopefully you will have been encouraged to read journal articles and developed the ability to critically evaluate findings and their implications on theory and practice.

From a business and management academic perspective, there are many different ideas about what 'research' actually is (see, for example, Yin, 2017; Silverman, 2015). A useful and simple definition to start with is: **finding out things in a systematic way in order to increase knowledge**. Research is a key function of higher education and informs much of what goes on in organisations.

As a result universities and colleges as well as professional bodies are increasingly requiring elements of research-based or enquiry-based learning at all levels of study.

HRM involves practical application of up-to-date understanding in the context of 'real world' organisations. Reliable knowledge built on accurate information is needed. In order to undertake effective HRM it is important that good quality information underpins decisions and informs the actions of those involved in the employment relationship, such as trades unions, individual employees, outsourced service providers and professional organisations. The definition of research in HR in this book is: **the systematic enquiry into HR issues to increase knowledge and underpin effective action**. The focus on a 'systematic' approach is critical; through your work the reader needs to be able to understand how and why you have designed and followed your research process and they will be looking for evidence to demonstrate that you have achieved your research objectives.

HR research – the value of applied research

Many writers about research methods distinguish between 'pure' and 'applied' research (see, for example, Saunders *et al*, 2019) although the distinction is not always clear-cut and is best seen as a continuum relating to the purpose and context in which the investigation occurs. The main focus of pure research (sometimes referred to as 'Mode 1 research') is on gaining knowledge to describe and explain phenomena, develop and test generalisable theories and make predictions (van Aken, 2005; Burgoyne and Turnbull James, 2006). Applied research (sometimes referred to as 'Mode 2') by contrast, is more concerned with developing knowledge that can be used to solve problems, predict effects, and develop actions and interventions that are applicable in particular organisational contexts. Although applied research is not always accorded high academic prestige it may require greater skill across a broader range of areas than pure research demands (Figure 1.3).

Most HR research that is undertaken as part of a taught course of study is at the 'applied research' end of the continuum, involving a relatively 'small-scale' investigation in one organisation or using information from a relatively small sample of people or organisations. This book works from the position that, in HR at least, applied research is at least as valuable as pure research. HR research that is carried out in a rigorous way can lead to more effective practice than decisions based mainly on intuition, common sense or personal preferences. Common sense tends to take many features of organisational situations for granted. A systematic process of

Figure 1.3 Pure and applied research

Applied research		Pure research
problem-solving	-------------------------------	gaining new knowledge
seeking to understand	-------------------------------	seeking to change
predicting effects	-------------------------------	establishing causes
concern for action	-------------------------------	assessing relationships between variables
specific	-------------------------------	generalisable
time/cost constraints	-------------------------------	'as long as it needs'
'client' orientated	-------------------------------	'academic' orientation
relevant	-------------------------------	rigorous

(Robson and McCartan, 2016; Easterby-Smith *et al*, 2018; Cameron and Price, 2009; Saunders *et al*, 2019)

research, however, makes it possible to challenge 'taken for granted' assumptions and so generate new ways of understanding situations that can form the basis for innovative approaches to solving complex problems. A key capability for effective HR practitioners is the analysis of HR situations and the use of systematic investigative techniques to underpin decision-making and problem-solving.

The basis of this book is that HR research is about 'advancing knowledge' in a way that is relevant to changing organisational priorities, solution of HR problems and the continuous development of organisations involved in the research process itself. It is important to remember that you are not writing a PhD and the limited word count of a project means that gaining 'new' theoretical knowledge is neither required nor needed.

 Activity 1.3

Web-based activity

Visit the website of an HR magazine such as *People Management* (http://www.peoplemanagement.co.uk), *Personnel Today* (http://www.personneltoday.com), *HR Zone* (http://www.hrzone.com) or *HR Magazine* (http://www.hrmagazine.co.uk). Run a search using the word 'research'. If you can, limit the dates of the search to the most recent one or two calendar months.

Feedback notes

An activity such as this demonstrates how important research is to the development of HR practice. Research evidence is used to justify why certain HR practices are beneficial and is also used to evaluate the success (or otherwise) of HR policies and practices. Research contributes to the development of HR at strategic, policy and operational levels. It also enables new ideas about the 'Future of Work'.

What kind of researcher are you?

Models of the research process and diagrams showing skill requirements can lead to an assumption that there is 'one right way' to undertake research. This is not the case and every individual HR practitioner or student is likely to undertake research in his or her own unique way.

Indeed, research in the HR and management arena is characterised by diversity and it is important, at an early stage in your project planning process, to clarify for yourself a response to the question: 'What kind of a researcher are you?' This will help you to think more clearly about potential topics that you might investigate and how you might go about it (Brown, 2006; Fox *et al*, 2007). It would also be useful to think about your preferred learning style (for example, using Honey and Mumford's learning styles questionnaire) and consider how you can use this information to maximise the effectiveness of your project.

Insider or outsider?

Are you an insider or an outsider? There are two possible types of insider. One type is the person who will be involved in researching their own area of work in their own place of employment. The second type of insider is the researcher who is keen to find out what is going on 'inside' the people whom they are researching; their meanings and understandings. Two types of outsider are also possible. Outsiders are those who will be involved in researching in their own organisation but in a different place or part of it, or those who will undertake research into situations and/or organisations where they truly are outsiders. Your position as an insider or an outsider will have implications for your research. Outsiders may find it easier to establish facts and to discuss 'universals' rather than particulars. Insiders, by contrast, may be led to research that contains more 'narrative' than numbers. Examples of the different ways that a topic might be taken forward by people who are insiders or outsiders are shown in Table 1.1. The examples in this table use the illustration of 'talent management' but the same principles would apply to most HR projects.

Detective, doctor or explorer?

In addition to the distinction between research as insiders or as outsiders, most HR researchers have different mental pictures of the purpose of their research. Brown (2006) characterises three different ideal types, which are depicted in Table 1.2. Many researchers find that they identify with more than one type. Which of these are you **most** like?

Table 1.1   Insiders and outsiders – examples of different options for research projects

Insider/Outsider	Example of Research Project Topic
Insiders – who are undertaking research into their own organisation	An evaluation of employee engagement at XYZ Ltd
Insiders – who want to know about what is 'inside' the people whom they are researching; their meanings and understandings	An assessment of perceptions and attitudes towards an employee engagement programme at XYZ Ltd
Outsiders – who will be researching in a different part of their own organisations	An investigation into the implementation of employee engagement in the Information Systems division
Outsiders – who will research into situations and/or organisations where they have little or no connection	Research into the application of employee engagement programmes in digital service organisations in the UK

Table 1.2   Researcher similes

Researcher as Detective	Researcher as Doctor	Researcher as Explorer
You have a clear idea about the research **problem**; for example, 'employee engagement programmes favour younger workers over older employees'. The researcher as detective gathers relevant information in order to get the clues needed to solve the problem and then marshals the evidence to prove that the solution that the researcher has reached is the correct one.	The researcher as doctor recognises the need to work from the symptoms he or she is presented with in order to diagnose the **cause** of the situation before any appropriate 'treatment' can be prescribed. The researcher as doctor looks for the reasons behind the research issue; for example, 'what factors lead employees to be negative about employee engagement programmes?'	The researcher as explorer loves to enter 'unknown territory' and keep a record about what she or he finds; for example, 'what happens in an organisation that has been acquired and is required to implement the employee engagement programme of the new parent company?'

(Brown, 2006)

Descriptive research

If you see yourself mainly as a detective or perhaps as an explorer then it is likely that you will be interested in carrying out **descriptive** research where you set out to provide an accurate profile of situations, people or events. A descriptive research project focuses on 'what, when, where and who'. Having investigated and described the issue you can then go further and analyse the data to ask, 'why' and 'so what'. Both qualitative and quantitative data are useful in descriptive studies.

Explanatory research

If you see your role as a researcher to be like that of a doctor or perhaps as a detective then it is likely that you will undertake **explanatory research** by setting out to explain a situation or problem, usually in the form of causal relationships. Your focus will be on 'why' and 'how'; seeking to explain organisational problems and, through assessment of the causes, to recommend changes for improvement. Both qualitative and quantitative data may be useful for achieving these research purposes.

Exploratory research

If you see your role as a researcher as more like that of an explorer then **exploratory** research will appeal to you. The purpose of exploratory research is to seek new insights and find out what is happening. There is an attempt to ask questions and assess phenomena in a new light. A more qualitative approach often (but not always) underpins this sort of research and the focus is on obtaining new insights into new or current situations and issues.

***

  Activity 1.4

How real is reality TV?

Reality TV (as distinct from documentaries or other non-fictional TV programmes like sports coverage and news) is a form of television programming that has become prevalent in almost every TV network since the beginning of the 21st century. Examples from UK channels include talent searches such as *The X Factor*, and documentary-type programmes such as *The Only Way is Essex* and *Masterchef*. Reality TV shows claim to show ordinary people in unscripted and real situations. Identify and think about three different reality TV shows that you know about. If you do not watch reality TV shows yourself then you can find out about them from friends or from broadcasters' websites.

Discussion questions

1 How real is reality TV?

2 In what ways is reality TV 'real' and in what ways is reality TV 'not real'?

3 To what extent is heartbreak real?

4 In what sense are dreams real?

***

Feedback notes

Discussion about reality TV can evoke strong reactions. Some people watch reality TV programmes with enthusiasm and commitment; they want to decide for themselves about the qualities shown by those involved and may also identify strongly for or against one or more of the participants. Other people might describe reality

TV as 'tedious', 'worthless' and 'manipulative'. The extent to which the programme that is broadcast is 'contrived' or the effect of the editing process on what we watch might, however, be seen to make reality TV less 'real' than its name would imply. The discussion about the reality of reality TV makes us wonder how we can **know** about **reality** and this is an important issue for everyone who aims to carry out research in the real world.

When discussing the extent to which heartbreak is real your opinion might be different depending on your current emotional circumstances and relationships. For others their view would not depend on their context or circumstances – they would argue that heartbreak is a feeling rather than a real thing. Others might say that they know what is real when they come across it and are able to distinguish between what seems real (dreams and/or heartbreak) and what actually is real as evidenced by the behaviours that they experience. Even those of us who prefer to rely on the evidence of our senses to identify what is real find ourselves challenged by the digital and technological opportunities of the 21st century to 'remaster' or alter what we see and hear. This can lead us to wonder whether reliance on the evidence provided by our senses or on our experience is a sufficient basis from which to know about the real world (Saunders *et al*, 2019).

What is your real-world view?

Work in HR, and this includes research work in HR, takes place in the real world and is about real-world issues (Robson and McCartan, 2016). Most of the time most of us do not trouble ourselves with thinking much about the nature of the real world; we just get on with our lives and our jobs. Before you start with your research, however, you will need to think about your own 'take' on the nature of the real world.

When addressing the question about 'what is real?' there are three prominent options (Brown, 2006; Fox *et al*, 2007). One answer is that reality is **out there** and this corresponds to what is termed an **objective** world view. If your view is that reality is **in here** (ie a feature of your perceptions and feelings) then you may feel more comfortable in what might be called an individually **constructed** world view. You might think that reality is **in here** but influenced by **out there**. This would be represented by what is often called a **socially constructed** world view.

The extent to which you subscribe to an objective, socially constructed or individually constructed world view may well be influenced by your own personal and professional background. Economists, for example, tend to operate within an objective world view; social and care workers tend to be most comfortable with a socially constructed world view. HR researchers are difficult to generalise about: some adopt a socially constructed world view and others work from an objective world view. Your assumptions about these issues, therefore, may well be different from other HR practitioners and researchers whom you come into contact with. The nature of your thinking in response to these issues, however, is likely to be important for the way that you tackle your project.

If you are most comfortable with an objective world view it is likely that you will want to establish objective facts that can be generalised independently of the beliefs, perceptions, culture and language of different individuals and groups. This perspective is often associated with what is termed a **positivist** approach to research, which is outlined in Chapter 2. If you are more comfortable with a socially constructed world view it is likely that you will value information from observation or interviews mostly gathered in the form of words and meanings, pictures and other artefacts and value qualitative rather than quantitative data. This world view is often associated with the **interpretivist** approach, which is also introduced in Chapter 2.

 Case Example 1.1

Research into retention of nurses

Jake was a part-time student working for an NHS Trust in its HR Department. The organisation was concerned that it was losing a significant number of nurses and that its retention rates were lower than others in the region. Anecdotal evidence led Jake to be concerned about the way nurses were being managed and supported by their line managers and that morale in general was very low with weak levels of employee engagement. For his research project Jake decided to measure a number of variables including employee engagement, organisation citizenship behaviour, intention to leave and supervisor–subordinate relationships. He achieved this through the adaptation of existing scales and particularly the work of Shacklock and Brunetto (2011). Jake set out to gather and analyse data from a range of nurses from across the Foundation Trust via a self-completion questionnaire, in order to provide generalised conclusions around some of the key factors associated with turnover.

Ying was also interested in taking forward research into nurse retention after recognising the significant cost to the organisation. However, she took a different approach. She focused on finding out about the experiences and perceptions of nurses through a series of in-depth interviews. Ying wanted to find out about the different feelings people might have even if they worked in jobs at the same level and in the same organisation. Through conducting interviews, therefore, Ying set out to gather information that was grounded in the experiences and perspectives of those involved in order to provide an in-depth understanding of the issues from the different participants' perspectives.

Discussion questions

1   What world view underpinned the approaches to their research adopted by Jake and Ying?

2   To what extent (and why) is it possible to decide which approach is 'superior'?

Feedback notes

The approach adopted by Jake was indicative of the 'objective' world view. He sought to measure variables that are often associated with intention to leave work (and therefore nurse retention) as indicated through generalised patterns of questionnaire responses. Ying's approach was indicative of the 'constructed' world view

Figure 1.4   Factors affecting the employment relationship

and she was interested in the perspectives of different nurses on the basis of their unique experiences and contexts.

The different research world views described here are distinct but you may also have highlighted that there are overlaps between them. No experience (of employee engagement) is wholly individually and uniquely experienced; some aspects will be shared between individuals and groups. Also 'socially derived' views (about executive pay, for example) can become so universally accepted that it can be researched as an objective fact.

You may feel that both objectivist and constructivist perspectives are useful ways forward and research that works from more than one world view is quite common (although not required or compulsory) within HR. The important thing is to be clear about your world view, to yourself and to those who will read your work, so that this can be taken into account in making sense of your research and the conclusions that you draw. This will influence the design decisions that you make (this is explored later in this book). You may well be reflecting at this point that you can see the benefit of both objectivist and constructivist world views and you may be thinking about incorporating both approaches into your research. Within research in HR there is a strong tradition of what is sometimes called a 'mixed methods' approach, characterised by elements of both world views within a project. Such approaches are discussed in Chapter 2. However, bringing insights from both world views together can have implications for your research project that can be very time-consuming and difficult to express within a word limit of 7,000 words (which is often applied for CIPD management or business research reports).

Activity 1.5

What kind of a researcher are you?

Think about yourself: your situation, your world view, your preferences and your interests. Write your comments to the questions on the left in the spaces provided on the right.

About you	Response
Are you likely to undertake research in your own organisation or one where you might be considered an outsider? What are the key issues in gaining access for research purposes?	
Are you interested in general facts and universal trends or are you more interested in getting inside the meanings behind particular issues and experiences?	
To what extent is your preferred research role similar to that of a doctor/explorer/detective (or a combination)?	
Which world view do you feel most comfortable with: objectivist world view or constructivist world view?	
Are you interested in individual stories and experiences or the overall picture of a group or organisation?	

Your responses to these questions might be useful to share with your tutor or supervisor as you discuss potential research topics and the way you might take your research project forward. You will explore world views in more depth later in this book.

The audiences for HR research

 Activity 1.6

Audiences for HR research

1   Use Figure 1.4 as a prompt and write down a list of different groups of people who may be interested in the implications of research into HR issues in your organisation (or one you are familiar with).

2   For each group of people that you identify, try to work out how they might find out about relevant research that has been undertaken.

Feedback notes

Your list of likely audiences for HR research might include:

- individual practitioners;
- individual managers;
- members of trades unions;
- people in central government departments;
- members of your local authority;
- specialist organisations/pressure groups;
- professional associations;
- academics;
- consultants;
- employer/trade bodies;
- trades union members;
- students;
- providers of outsourced HR services.

When it comes to finding out about research, there is an equally wide range of publications and opportunities that different groups might use. These include:

- newspapers;
- web pages;
- specific reports (may be internal or external);
- books;
- trade journals;
- professional journals;
- social media feeds (for example, Twitter and LinkedIn);
- webcasts and YouTube;
- attending conferences/seminars;
- academic journals;
- white and green papers;
- social networking sites;
- unpublished research (dissertations, projects, etc).

Each of these different vehicles for communicating knowledge will do so in a different way in order to meet the needs of its audience. As a result they will engage to different extents with both theory and practice and with the general or the specific.

Figure 1.5 Orientation of different research outputs

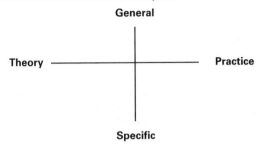

  Activity 1.7

Assessing different research publications

Study one copy of the following types of HR publication:

- academic peer-reviewed journal (eg *Human Resource Management Journal*, *Human Resource Development International* or *International Journal of Human Resource Management*;

- professional journal (eg *People Management* or *Personnel Today*);

- practitioner report (eg IDS Report or a CIPD Research Insight Report (https://www.cipd.co.uk/knowledge/latest-research).

Skim-read the publications and try to plot each of the features of the research articles/reports on the two axes shown on Figure 1.5.

Feedback notes

It is likely that different articles from each of the first two types of publications may need to be plotted differently. Some studies, even within one publication, are very concerned with one specific situation and others are more general. It is easier to characterise the different levels of engagement with theories, models and concepts. Papers in a peer-reviewed academic journal such as *HRMJ*, will be significantly concerned with evaluating theories as well as with practically focused investigations. Practitioner reports, by contrast, are more concerned with describing practice, than with explicitly locating it within any conceptual framework. Feature articles in practitioner journals vary somewhat, although theory is rarely a major feature. This is a factor of the audience or readership of these publications.

Requirements for student projects

If you are working towards a professional and educational qualification then the principal readers of your work will be interested in its academic features as much as the practical outcomes for the organisation(s) in which your research project was

Figure 1.6 Characteristics of a research project in HR

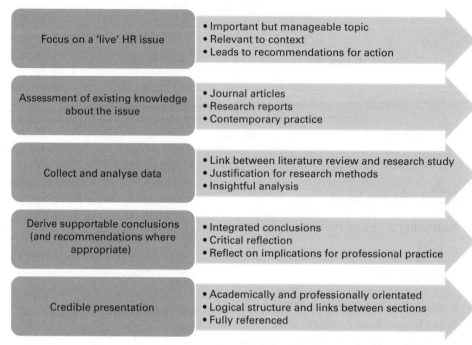

Focus on a 'live' HR issue
- Important but manageable topic
- Relevant to context
- Leads to recommendations for action

Assessment of existing knowledge about the issue
- Journal articles
- Research reports
- Contemporary practice

Collect and analyse data
- Link between literature review and research study
- Justification for research methods
- Insightful analysis

Derive supportable conclusions (and recommendations where appropriate)
- Integrated conclusions
- Critical reflection
- Reflect on implications for professional practice

Credible presentation
- Academically and professionally orientated
- Logical structure and links between sections
- Fully referenced

situated. Therefore, it is important that your work corresponds to the characteristics shown in Figure 1.6.

Focus on a 'live' HR issue

Choosing a topic can be a challenging decision for first-time researchers and this issue is addressed in Chapter 2. A good project will be interesting for you to undertake and will provide the opportunity for 'added value' to those who will read about your results (HR practitioners, student colleagues and academic tutors). Choose something that will be manageable (not too big – your time is short) but something that is challenging enough to merit an academic qualification and be interesting to those who will find out about your work. If you are in need of some inspiration, ask your centre's library if they have any examples of past dissertations or projects that you can review. You can also check out the research page on the CIPD website for details of their most recent research projects.

Assessment of existing knowledge about the issue

Most published HR research, particularly reports that are produced for a practitioner audience, do not engage explicitly with theories, models and frameworks. Research written for an academic audience found in academic journals, by contrast, is **explicit** about theory. If your research forms part of a qualification-bearing course then an explicit use of theory is expected. You must take a constructively critical approach to the current state of knowledge in your topic area and work out how your project fits into the wider context. It is worth finding out now about the expectations of your tutors about the balance between theory and practice for your research report or dissertation. Looking at past projects may also be helpful.

Collect and analyse data

All projects undertaken as part of an HR programme of study usually require the collection and analysis of data. This may be secondary data (that has already been generated for some other purpose) as well as primary data (that you will gather in order to answer your research questions). If you are undertaking a CIPD course then usually you must collect and analyse primary data as part of your research. In many cases your data will come from one organisation but in some circumstances data will be gathered across a range of individuals or organisations. Some HR research involves a new analysis of secondary data sources. A popular example is the use of the dataset from the Workplace Employment Relations Study (WERS), which is regularly analysed by academics looking at different aspects of the work.

Derive supportable conclusions

Once you have gathered your data and analysed it in order to 'make sense' of what you have found you will need to draw some overall and integrated conclusions. This will require you to reflect in a critical way about the limitations of your data as well as the insights you have achieved. You may find it useful to read through the limitations sections of journal articles to understand the range of potential challenges. Most HR research projects fall into the category of 'applied research' and so you will also be able to reflect on the implications of your research findings for professional practice.

Credible presentation

Your research report or dissertation may be the longest document you have ever written and you will expend a lot of time and energy in producing it. The final product must be persuasive to those who read it; academic and professional credibility are important. The way the report is presented; the quality of your written communication; careful proofreading; helpful graphics and charts; and the quality of referencing and citation you exhibit will all make a difference to both the persuasiveness of your report AND to the mark your work achieves. It is crucial to follow the presentation guidelines provided by your centre.

Writing your research proposal

Whether you are undertaking a dissertation, business research report or other form of investigative inquiry it is likely that your study centre will require you to write a research proposal. This is an important but helpful process as it forces you to articulate your plan and consider some of the key issues in order to demonstrate that it is appropriate and achievable within your timeframe. Positive feedback on your proposal will give you the confidence to start tackling your project; it also helps your supervisor to support you in identifying areas for further thought or development. The more detailed your proposal is, the more helpful the feedback will be. The requirements of the proposal will be confirmed by your centre; you should refer to your course information to find the answers to the following questions:

- How long must the proposal be?
- What are the key components?
- Is there a required format for the proposal?
- Is this a formative or summative activity? If it is a summative activity it means you will receive a mark that contributes to your overall grade for your project. Proposals typically account for 10 per cent of the final mark.

Whatever the expected length of the research proposal most students find this a daunting document to produce, but there are good reasons to overcome any natural tendency to put off the moment of writing. Your research project is an independent piece of work. As you undertake it you will benefit from the advice of your tutor as well as others in your study cohort and work organisation.

Table 1.3 provides an indication of issues you will typically need to address in a proposal.

Key stakeholders and sources of support during your project

Working with your supervisor/advisor

A dissertation or a business research report is something for which you take personal responsibility. You will find it helpful to discuss your ideas and your progress with colleagues at work and study-buddies. However, the key source of advice, guidance and encouragement will be your project tutor or research supervisor. Different study centres make different supervisory arrangements and it is important to find out about the practices in your university. The key support your supervisor will provide will be around the process of constructing and writing up your project; the emphasis will usually be on the process rather than your specific subject area. Figure 1.7 depicts the main areas that your supervisor will be able to discuss with you.

Figure 1.7 shows what a crucial contribution your supervisor can make. Establishing a good working relationship can help you to manage the research process in an effective way. The supervisory relationship is different from other tutorial arrangements as, in most cases, supervisors will work with their students on a one-to-one basis. Different supervisors will have their own backgrounds, experiences and preferred ways of working just as you will also have your own preferences. If you want to work effectively with your supervisor then consider the list of 'hints and tips' shown in Table 1.4. It is particularly important that you understand your centre's rules around what supervisors can and cannot do to help you. For example, some centres may allow supervisors to read a draft of only one full chapter.

Table 1.3 Overview of information usually provided in proposals

Topic area; aims and objectives	Provide an overview of the problem or issue you plan to address. Explain why this topic was chosen (What was the catalyst or trigger of the project? What is the value of the project?). Explain what you hope to achieve through the research. You should formulate an initial aim or 'big question' and more specific objectives or questions (see Chapter 2 for help with this).
Literature review plans or progress	This part of the proposal shows how your research is positioned in the existing literature and where your study fits within existing knowledge about the topic. Requirements of study centres vary. Some require you to indicate the main areas for your literature search and key sources of information you are already aware of. Other centres require an initial review of the most important literature sources and an assessment of where your research would contribute to filling a gap in knowledge. At this stage it might be helpful to identify your seminal journal articles.
Research design and methods	This section identifies the way in which you are going to investigate the issue or problem and your world view as a researcher. Your proposal should set out what type of data you intend to collect, your sampling strategy, the research methods you plan to use and your proposed approach to data analysis.
Ethical issues	Indicate here what particular ethical issues or problems you will need to address; in particular obtaining informed consent of any organisations in which you plan to gather data as well as access to individual participants. In particular you will need to explain the approach you will take to issues of confidentiality and anonymity for your research participants. Consider whether there are any additional requirements within the industry or sector in which you work; for example, NHS-based studies are likely to need further external approvals.
Suggested timetable	Present a clear and realistic timetable for the completion of your research and the production of your report. Indicate when important tasks will be carried out. Set achievable targets and time-planning contingencies and build in time for continuous review of different stages by you and your tutor. Consider your personal and professional time commitments.

Managing the research project

A research project is like any other project that you undertake: it has a natural progression, following a series of different stages. To undertake any project successfully you will need to undertake the following steps. Remember that this process will not necessarily follow in such a smooth sequence and you will need to keep continuously evaluating and monitoring progress. However, these stages that are illustrated in Figure 1.8, which also shows the logic of the chapter construction of this book, do act as a reasonable 'road map' and none of them should be left out.

Figure 1.7   Key areas for discussion with your supervisor

Research topic	Have you identified something suitable to investigate? Is it achievable and specific rather than very general?
Research question(s)	Are your initial questions achievable?
Literature	Have you been able to identify suitable literature upon which to base your work? Is there a reasonable balance of academic and practitioner/professional sources?
Research design	Is the chosen research design practical? Is it likely to enable you to answer your research questions? Is it realistic in terms of time and resources that you have available? Is the planned size reasonable?
Collecting data	Do you have a robust plan for collecting data? Have appropriate access arrangements been made?
Ethics	Have you followed the centre's regulations on obtaining ethical consent? Have appropriate arrangements been made to store and process the data? Has appropriate information been shared with the key stakeholders?
Analysis	Has an appropriate means of data analysis been used? Is the analysis presented clearly? Have the data been explored and linked back to the literature?
Conclusions and recommendations	Do the conclusions derive from the findings? Have the research objectives been met? Are relevant and appropriate recommendations offered?

Figure 1.8   Stages in your research project

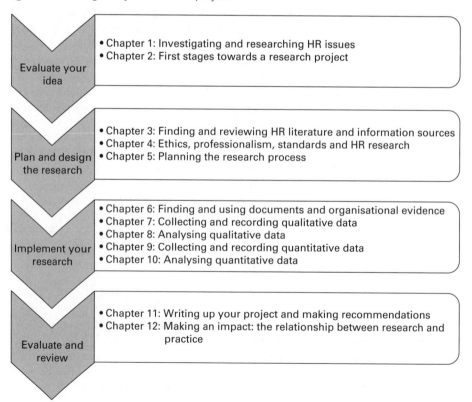

Evaluate your idea
- Chapter 1: Investigating and researching HR issues
- Chapter 2: First stages towards a research project

Plan and design the research
- Chapter 3: Finding and reviewing HR literature and information sources
- Chapter 4: Ethics, professionalism, standards and HR research
- Chapter 5: Planning the research process

Implement your research
- Chapter 6: Finding and using documents and organisational evidence
- Chapter 7: Collecting and recording qualitative data
- Chapter 8: Analysing qualitative data
- Chapter 9: Collecting and recording quantitative data
- Chapter 10: Analysing quantitative data

Evaluate and review
- Chapter 11: Writing up your project and making recommendations
- Chapter 12: Making an impact: the relationship between research and practice

Table 1.4 Constructive working with your supervisor

Establish the format, basis and frequency of meetings	Your centre is likely to have guidelines on how many supervision sessions each student will receive. You may agree to meet face-to-face and have a few long meetings or shorter, more frequent meetings. You may prefer to communicate by Skype, telephone, e-mail, etc if these media are more appropriate. Agree when you need to send the agenda and anything that you would like your supervisor to read.
Identify times when either of you will not be contactable	Check out when your supervisor may be away; let him or her know about your planned absences (holidays, weddings, etc). Don't send work to your supervisor just before any planned leave – your supervisor won't look at it until he or she gets back.
Identify the key areas you feel you will need support with and discuss these at the beginning of the research process	Discuss with your supervisor your strengths and skills that are relevant to the research process and the areas that you feel less confident with. Use feedback from previous modules to identify these areas. Agree an action plan to develop in these areas and seek feedback as appropriate.
Establish project milestones and deadlines by which you will submit draft work for comment	Your supervisor will be able to advise you about realistic time targets. Don't be too ambitious but, once you have established your milestones, make sure you stick to them.
Be honest about your aspirations and priorities for the research project	Discuss what you hope to achieve with your supervisor. If you are aiming for a distinction then commit to this with your supervisor and discuss what will make this more likely to be achieved. Alternatively, if you will be happy with a 'solid' pass then discuss this. If you are hoping to follow up your dissertation with producing a journal article you should definitely discuss this in advance with your supervisor.
If you cannot attend a meeting or meet a deadline then make sure you let your supervisor know in advance	Nothing annoys a supervisor more than waiting around for a student who does not arrive or does not submit work at the agreed date. If you anticipate a change in your circumstances then let your supervisor know sooner rather than later.
Don't prevaricate	Even if you are not fully satisfied with your draft work try to submit it on time and then learn from the feedback you get.
Don't bluff	If you do not understand something or have not actually done something then talking about it means you are more likely to get advice on moving forwards.
Allow time for your supervisor to read your draft work carefully	Although you will undertake a lot of work at weekends do not expect your supervisor to do this as well. If your supervisor is to read your work carefully he or she will need a sensible period of time (there may be many other tasks to fulfil in addition to working with you). Your centre may have agreed timescales for receiving feedback.
Don't ask your supervisor what mark your project/dissertation will achieve	Even if your supervisor will be one of the markers of your report or dissertation the assessment process is different from, and separate to, the supervision process.

It is also wise to reflect upon the feedback that you have received so far on your programme so that you can consider if there is anything that would also be relevant to your project.

 Activity 1.8

Review your most recent feedback and make a list of any learning that you can transfer to your project. For example, if you have received feedback that your work should be more *critical*, this is something that you would need to concentrate on when writing your review of the literature.

- **Evaluate your ideas.** At this early stage you make a research proposal and refine your thinking on the basis of feedback you receive. Issues like the length of time available, any cost implications and achieving necessary permissions to undertake the research need to be considered at this stage.

- **Plan and design the project.** This is where you will think in detail about key activities and tasks within each of your main milestones. Careful planning is required about access to data and ethics, literature searching and literature review, and plans relating to data gathering and analysis. Research projects where the researcher just 'jumps in at the deep end' without careful planning and design are less likely to be successful.

- **Implement your research.** This stage will involve processes of data gathering, review and analysis. This stage will involve you in finding and using documentary and organisational evidence, collecting and recording your data and then analysing them to make sense of them.

- **Evaluate and review.** This is an important stage of any project and with research it is essential that you undertake a careful review of your analysis and formulate meaningful conclusions. At the same time it is important to reflect on learning points to enable you to develop your practice as both a researcher and an HR professional as your career develops.

It is likely that most investigative enquiries will be undertaken within a specific organisational context and will be focused on the solution of a particular HR problem or issue. In this sense an action orientation is more likely and the implications of this for the practitioner-researcher are now explored.

Working with your peers in action learning sets

Many centres formally recognise the support that students can provide to each other when they share thoughts, ideas and experiences. Usually the sets will take the form of groups of six to eight students who will be encouraged to meet on a regular basis to discuss either set topics (related to the stage of the project that the students are in) or to address specific issues from the group. The groups are often facilitated by a project supervisor or tutor who will help students to support and challenge each other and debate potential solutions to problems. Another approach involves students swapping draft chapters and providing feedback to each other based on the marking criteria. Used effectively, this can be a great way of gaining feedback on thoughts and ideas and benefiting from the experience of others. Some centres may allocate a percentage of the projects' final marks to engagement in the process. Participation in the learning sets can also provide some fruitful learning for the reflective pieces that often form the end of the project or dissertation.

Within this section we have looked at the relationship with supervisors/advisors as well as peer groups. In the next section we consider the concept of practitioner-researcher and reflect on how to make this work as effectively as possible.

Working as a practitioner-researcher

A practitioner-researcher is someone who is employed in a job and, at the same time, carries out a research project, which is of some relevance to the person's current role as a practitioner. Some students may choose to undertake a topic that is related to their day-to-day responsibilities or current projects, or they may wish to select a new topic in an area where they can also obtain useful information and data. In the context of this book this definition embraces three types of people:

- Part-time students undertaking research within their employing organisation. In this case the student may be a regular employee or, alternatively, may be someone who is undertaking some form of consultancy assignment in the organisation. Of course, a practitioner-researcher may also be someone who is undertaking an investigative enquiry within the organisation (or that of a client) for which there is no link with the achievement of a qualification.

- Full-time students who have a part-time job in an organisation in which they undertake their research project.

- Full-time students for whom a work placement forms part of their course and they will be undertaking a research project within the placement organisation. If this best describes the situation you are in there are some additional issues for you to consider. Ideally, you will have discussed this with your placement employer prior to the end of your work period and will have agreed what you will research and agree the access arrangements.

Regardless of which type of practitioner-researcher you are, it is important to agree boundaries with the employer at the earliest opportunity.

There are advantages and disadvantages of being a practitioner-researcher. The difficulties that are often encountered relate to:

- **Time.** When the project has to be undertaken in addition to normal workloads it is difficult to give it the attention it deserves.

- **Potential bias.** As you are already familiar with the organisation it can be more difficult to be detached and see things in an objective manner; sometimes you will have a lot of unconscious knowledge so you will need to explore how you can unpick this so that the reader of your work can see the full picture.

- **Status issues.** Often practitioner-researchers are not in senior positions within the organisation. This can make it difficult for their project to be taken seriously. Alternatively, they may have high status within the organisation. This can make it difficult for subjects of the research to express themselves freely.

- **Confidentiality issues.** In the normal course of your day job you may have access to a wide range of data, some of which may be confidential or information that the organisation would not want in the public domain. It is important to agree carefully what can and cannot be referred to within your work; this should be captured as part of the ethics process (which is explored in more detail in Chapter 4).

- **Being critical.** Although undertaking a research project involves adopting a critically evaluative approach to both theory and practice, in some organisations taking a critical approach is not encouraged. This is a particular challenge when researching in your own organisation. Consider what you will do if you uncover information that is challenging for the organisation and how this balances against your ethical obligations.

- **Being instrumental.** A further danger, from the perspective of the organisation, is that where projects are linked with gaining a qualification, research can become more of a vehicle to achieve the student's purposes than being motivated by the resolution of a problem or issue.

There are also significant advantages to being a practitioner-researcher:

- **Insider opportunities.** If you know the organisation and are a part of it, you have access to a range of knowledge and experience that someone from outside would find difficult to achieve.

- **Practitioner opportunities.** As an experienced practitioner within the organisation it is more likely that actions that you recommend can and will be implemented.

- **Synergy between theory and practice.** As a researcher who engages with theory and also knows the context of the organisation it is more likely that you will be able to design and carry out useful studies that contribute to enhancements in both knowledge and practice. A key challenge for students undertaking a project is to provide sufficiently detailed conclusions and recommendations; where you have the inside knowledge of an organisation and its constraints you may find it easier to be able to identify appropriate recommendations.

In summary, undertaking research projects in organisational situations provides a number of advantages but there are also dangers. A key issue for students is avoiding the temptation to merely repeat established organisational 'mantras' and making every effort to ensure that their project leads to new insights. In order to achieve this, practitioner-researchers must endeavour to:

- explicitly consider the wider context of the problem or issue that is being researched, both within the organisation and with regard to practice and developments outside of the organisation;

- manage the expectations of your internal stakeholders right from the start of your project;
- draw clear boundaries around information and data that can be used specifically to inform your project;
- critically engage with theories, models and concepts at all stages of the research process;
- encourage, where possible, the dissemination of the findings of studies so that they can inform the development of practice and understanding in other organisations and contexts.

Some more ideas about how this can be achieved are listed below:

- Where possible, negotiate a time allowance to carry out the research OR agree specific times when you can carry out your research and access the relevant organisational resources.
- Be prepared to pitch the idea of the research within the organisation. Identify the potential benefits and how it might contribute to organisational objectives.
- Try to establish a difference of procedure between activities connected with your research and your normal day-to-day practitioner activities. Be clear to yourself and to others about when you are wearing the 'hat' of a researcher and when you are acting as a practitioner.
- Be explicit in your thinking about methods and sources of information. This will allow you to reflect proactively about the strengths and limitations of your research and so improve on it. It will also enable others to make an appropriate assessment of your work.
- Ensure that your research procedures are systematic and can be justified by more than convenience. If you cut corners (and you probably will) you must be explicit about the impact of the short cuts on your findings and how you have interpreted your information (these issues can be discussed as limitations of your work).

CHECKLIST

- HR research involves systematically enquiring into HR issues to increase knowledge and underpin effective action.
- Most HR enquiry can be characterised as 'applied research' being concerned with solving problems, considering effects, and developing actions and interventions.
- Effective research processes involve: formulating a research topic; evaluating what is already known; obtaining information of good quality; interpreting the information; and formulating conclusions.
- Effective HR researchers require a range of skills including: intellectual and thinking skills; personal effectiveness skills; organisational skills; and

communication skills. Personal qualities like self-motivation, self-centredness and self-confidence are also required.

- Different research world views (eg constructivist and objectivist) can be seen as distinct ways of making sense of the world but there are overlaps between them.
- Projects undertaken to fulfil the requirements of an academic qualification are expected to make appropriate use of theories, models and concepts as well as primary and secondary data.
- Preparing a research proposal allows you to put down your initial ideas in writing: share them with your tutor, and get feedback about the strengths and possible difficulties of your idea.
- Establishing and maintaining a good working relationship with your project supervisor will enable you to benefit from feedback and discussion of your ideas throughout the life cycle of your project.
- There are advantages and disadvantages to being a practitioner-researcher but organisational research, properly undertaken, can lead to new insights into HR issues, problems and situations.

TEST YOURSELF

1 What is the first stage of the research process?

- a Designing a questionnaire.
- b Identifying a suitable topic.
- c Completing the literature review.
- d Evaluating secondary data.

2 When should ethical issues be considered?

- a When you develop your conclusions.
- b Before you start your project.
- c At the same time as you collect your data.
- d When you analyse your primary data.

3 The role of a supervisor is to…

- a Tell you exactly how to get a distinction or first-class mark.
- b Read drafts of every chapter.
- c Organise your time between now and the submission date.
- d Provide advice, guidance and support.

4 What type of publication is CIPD (2019) *Rotten Apples, Bad Barrels and Sticky Situations: An evidence review of unethical workplace behaviour*?

- a Professional journal.
- b Practitioner report.
- c Green paper.
- d Academic peer-reviewed journal.

5 Which of the following describes 'researcher as doctor'?

- a The researcher has a clear idea about the research problem.
- b The researcher likes to enter unknown territory.
- c The researcher likes to replicate existing studies in a new context.
- d The researcher recognises the need to work with the symptoms that are presented.

Review Questions

Carefully study the information your centre provides about the requirements for your research project or dissertation. Look closely at the assessment criteria that are provided. Study the indicative structure that may be described. Make sure that you can answer all the questions below. If you cannot, then make sure you find out the answers from whoever is responsible for projects in your study centre:

1   What is the submission deadline for the final report?

2   What is the indicative word limit?

3   Over what timescale should the project be undertaken?

4   What level of engagement with theories, concepts, frameworks of best practice etc is expected?

5   How important is it to gather primary data?

6   Does the research have to be based in an organisation?

7   Are implementable recommendations a requirement for the project?

8   What support is available to students when undertaking their project and how can that support be accessed?

After you have considered these questions from your centre's perspective, you should also consider your personal and professional constraints by thinking about the following:

9   What are your busiest times at work and how do they coincide with deadlines for your project? How will you manage this process?

10   What personal commitments do you have during the year? How can you build this into your timeline?

11   Are there any time-sensitive elements to your project? For example, in being able to obtain data produced on an annual basis.

Questions for reflection

These questions are designed for two purposes:

1   **Project planning.** Answering these questions should help you to identify actions and priorities that will be important in undertaking your project. The answers you make to these questions may influence:
   - which chapters of this book you need to study particularly closely;
   - which sources of further reading will be relevant to you;
   - the extent to which you need to get further advice on features of the research process.

2   **Demonstrating reflective practice.** If you are a member of a professional body like CIPD then you will need to undertake continuing professional development (CPD). There are many benefits to a process of reflection about your professional development and a commitment to developing your skills and knowledge. Taking this approach to CPD as part of your research process can help you to be more productive and efficient by reflecting on your learning and highlighting gaps in your knowledge and experience. This will enable you to build confidence and credibility, track your learning, see your progress and demonstrate your achievements.

Taking stock

1   What influence might your professional, organisational or personal background have

on the way you approach your research? Do you see your role as a researcher as being like a detective, a doctor or an explorer? Will you be working as an outsider or as an insider? What are the implications of your responses to these questions for your choice of topic and the extent to which your research may set out to achieve a descriptive, explanatory or exploratory purpose?

2 How feasible is it for you to undertake research in one organisation? For how long do you expect to be a part of the organisation in which your research may be based? What other options may be open to you?

3 What access issues might there be in your chosen organisation? What are the likely timescales for obtaining permission?

4 How clear are you about a topic for your project? Who do you need to discuss your ideas with to decide about the feasibility of the project? (Chapter 2 is particularly relevant to these questions.)

5 What resources or expertise and advice are available to you from your project supervisor? How can you make best use of these resources?

Strengths and weaknesses

6 How confident are you about the process of undertaking a literature search to enable you to critically evaluate what is already known about your topic? What are the skills you will need to search and critically review theories, models and concepts within the literature?

(Chapter 3 is particularly relevant to these issues.)

7 How aware are you of sources of secondary data that would be relevant to your project? What skills will you need to obtain and analyse the secondary data you have in mind? (Chapter 7 is particularly relevant to these issues.)

8 What options might you consider to obtain primary data? What are the skill implications of the data generation options that you are considering?

9 What skills and competences have you already developed that you can utilise in the process of undertaking your project?

Being a practitioner-researcher

10 What are the status or 'political' issues within your organisation that may affect the process of undertaking your project? How might you be able to manage these effectively?

11 What are the timescales for your project that are required by: a) your study centre; b) your organisation? What are the implications of this for the process of doing your project?

12 What opportunities can you identify to 'sell' your project ideas to: a) your manager and colleagues; b) others in the organisation?

Finally...

13 Describe how you will feel when you have completed your project. Hold on to that feeling!

Explore Further

It is very important to carefully read any handbooks or guidance notes relating to project work provided by your study centre. Most students skim through these at the beginning of their project process and only read them carefully at the very end of the process, when it is almost too late. Your tutor will usually provide a copy of the detailed marking criteria right at the start of your project – this is an essential document that should be referred to on a weekly basis so that you can understand the requirements of all of the different sections of your project. Use this as a key tool in ensuring your project will meet the criteria.

One of the best ways to learn about research methods is to read and critique good quality, peer-reviewed, research-based articles. You can tell if a journal is peer-reviewed by glancing at its notes for contributors, which will indicate that potential contributions will go through a 'blind peer review' process.

 Useful Resources

Bell, E, Bryman, A and Harley, B (2019) *Business Research Methods,* 5th edn, Oxford University Press, Oxford

Coghlan, D and Brannick, T (2014) *Doing Action Research in Your Own Organisation,* 4th edn, Sage, London

Collis, J and Hussey, R (2014) *Business Research: A practical guide for undergraduate and postgraduate students*, Palgrave, Basingstoke

Gill, J, Johnson, P and Clark, M (2010) *Research Methods for Managers*, Sage, London

Hart, C (2013) *Doing Your Masters Dissertation*, Sage, London

Kirton, B (2011) *Brilliant Dissertation,* Pearson Education, New York

Silverman, D (2015) *Interpreting Qualitative Data*, Sage, London

White, B and Rayner, S (2014) *Dissertation Skills,* Cengage Learning, Hampshire

Yin, RK (2017) *Case Study Research: Design and methods*, 6th edn, Sage Publications, Thousand Oaks, CA

 References

Biggam, J (2011) *Succeeding with your Master's Dissertation*, Open University Press, Maidenhead

Blaxter, L, Hughes, C and Tight, M (2010) *How to Research*, 4th edn, Open University Press, Maidenhead

Brown, RB (2006) *Doing Your Dissertation in Business and Management: The reality of researching and writing*, Sage, London

Burgoyne, JG and Turnbull, JK (2006) Towards best or better practice in corporate leadership development: Operational issues in mode 2 and design science research, *British Journal of Healthcare Management*, **17** (4), pp 303–316

Cameron, S and Price, D (2009) *Business Research Methods: A practical approach,* CIPD, London

Easterby-Smith, M, Thorpe, R, Jackson, PR and Jaspersen, LJ (2018) *Management and Business Research*, 6th edn, Sage, London

Fox, M, Martin, P and Green, G (2007) *Doing Practitioner Research*, Sage, London

Jankowicz, AD (2005) *Business Research Projects for Students*, Thomson Learning, London

Robson, C and McCartan, K (2016) *Real World Research: A resource for social scientists and practitioner-researchers*, Wiley, Oxford

Saunders, M, Lewis, P and Thornhill, A (2019) *Research Methods for Business Students*, 8th edn, Pearson Education, New York

Van Aken, JA (2005) Management research as a design science: Articulating the research products of mode 2 knowledge production in management. *British Journal of Management*, **16** (1), pp 19–36

02
First stages towards an HR project

LEARNING OBJECTIVES

This chapter should help you to:

- develop ideas for a research project;
- focus your project by developing a research aim and research objectives or questions;
- clarify and articulate your research methodology;
- evaluate different research strategies;
- identify potential sources of information for your project and how you might access it;
- develop your skills of project planning.

- Approaches to research methodology
  - Research design
  - Cross-sectional research
  - Comparative research
  - Case study research
  - Action research
- Access to data
- Project planning
- Summary checklist
- Test yourself, review and reflect questions
- Useful resources

How to use this chapter

This chapter is concerned with developing a focused and valuable research project in a practical and organisational context. You may have to produce a research proposal as part of your course. If so, this chapter will help you with your research proposal and/or your thinking about what your research project will involve and what it may be about. The CIPD Advanced level business research project module requires that students 'identify and justify a business issue that is of strategic relevance to the organisation'. Other students undertaking undergraduate or MSc or MA programmes may also carry out work-based research although dissertations in a non-work based context or literature review (theoretical) dissertations are also likely. Study centres may provide a further option of undertaking a consultancy project. This chapter addresses all these forms of research into HR issues with the aim of enabling you to develop a project that has practical as well as academic value to you and to those organisations that may well be involved in your project.

 Case Example 2.1

Thinking about research

In 2017, CIPD published a guide to employer-supported volunteering; a brief overview is outlined below.

The guide articulates CIPD's view that volunteering can be beneficial for a number of stakeholders and that it is a key element of 'social action' (CIPD, 2017). The guide provides a useful introduction to the concept of employer-supported volunteering, shares examples of the types of opportunities and outlines some of their own social action projects. The guide spells out some of the key benefits for individuals, employers and society as a whole. It also outlines 10 practical tips for implementation.

Maria, Arjun and Lena all needed to find a research topic and were considering volunteering as an area they might research. Arjun and Lena were international students. Arjun was studying full-time; his work placement in his course was in a challenger bank that had recently expanded and was interested in supporting the local community. Lena was a mature student studying part-time, outside the United Kingdom, on a distance-learning basis and had a background and interest in HR and talent management. Maria was a part-time student who worked for a large supermarket with a long-term commitment to supporting food banks in their local area. All of these students needed to find a research topic that suited them and their circumstances.

Discussion questions

Listen to one or more podcasts on the topic of volunteering in the United Kingdom or identify some relevant blogs or organisation reports.

Having heard about the topic of volunteering from different perspectives and having reflected on the different circumstances of Maria, Arjun and Lena:

1   What factors might influence the way Maria, Arjun and Lena might decide to take forward 'volunteering' as their research topic?

2   What opportunities might their different backgrounds present to Maria, Arjun and Lena?

3   How might organisations perceive a request to research employer-supported volunteering?

Feedback notes

This case example highlights the range of factors that can influence not only **what** you research but also how you go about doing research. Your choice of project topic will inevitably be influenced by your personal circumstances, the access to data that you can achieve, and your own professional interests and personal research preferences. You will also need to be mindful about your organisation's perception of your proposed topic.

In this case three different, but equally interesting, projects emerged. Maria undertook a critical evaluation of the way that the employer-supported volunteering was currently working in her organisation, and was able to make a series of recommendations about how it could be promoted more effectively and integrated more explicitly into staff development discussions. Arjun's focus was different: he examined the perspectives of different internal and external stakeholders around employer-supported volunteering and analysed some examples of 'best practice' being used by other organisations. Through this work he was able to make a series of recommendations to the challenger bank and outline a detailed cost/benefit analysis. Lena, meanwhile undertook a comparative study of volunteering policies and practices volunteering in her own country and the United Kingdom. This enabled her to identify important issues associated with employer-supported volunteering, which would have value for organisations operating in both countries.

As employer-supported volunteering is likely to be considered a 'positive' topic, it is anticipated that the students' organisations would not have any significant

Figure 2.1 Stakeholders in the research project

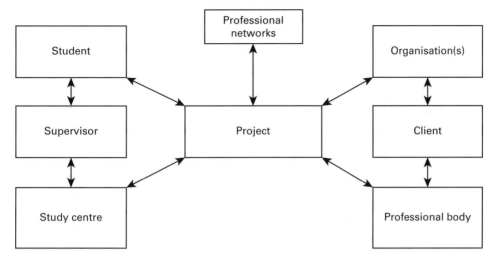

concerns. The students in this example should be able to sell the benefits of the topic, particularly as they should all be able to outline practical recommendations to support their research findings. Sensitive topics may include high employee turnover, sickness absence or investigating poor employee engagement.

Think carefully about any specific requirements (and marking criteria); for example, are you required to select an issue about which you can articulate detailed recommendations? In any research project there are different sets of stakeholders that have something to contribute as well as something to gain (see Figure 2.1). The choice of a topic and the choice of the research methods will be influenced by all of them. If your research is part of a process of achieving membership of a professional body, such as CIPD, then its requirements must also be taken into account. All of these stakeholders have different (and not necessarily complementary) expectations and this chapter should enable you to articulate the key issues you need to address to move forward with the planning of your research project.

Deciding what to research and developing a credible justification for your project

For some students, the choice of a topic for a research project is relatively straightforward; for others, it can be a slow and frustrating process. However, finding an appropriate topic is an important first step in developing a worthwhile research process that has the potential to lead to improvements in organisational practice, and enable you to submit a good quality research report or dissertation. You will need to articulate the justification within the introduction to your project.

Generating ideas for projects

Deciding on a topic to research can be psychologically as difficult as writing the first few sentences of an assignment. However, it is possible to structure the process in order to generate some ideas. Once ideas are generated then it is possible to evaluate them, choose the most appropriate topic and then clarify its focus and objectives.

Starting with the organisation

As Figure 2.1 indicates, the organisational context in which you may be working is an important factor in the choice of a broad project topic and it may be useful for you to 'stand back' from your immediate work context and think about possible issues that would underpin an interesting investigation. Where possible, and where appropriate, part of the topic choice process may involve discussions with relevant managers and colleagues. Many of the suggestions they offer will not be 'right' but listening to them, and considering how you might research into the issues or activities they suggest, will get you thinking. If your chosen organisation has previously supported student research it can be useful to find out further details about the earlier projects.

Key questions that are worth asking in this way are:

- What is currently bothering me/my boss/my department/my organisation?
- Are there any scheduled reviews or new projects in the pipeline?
- Are any organisational policies or systems due to be revisited?
- Have staff groups raised any issues through their forums?
- What projects would the HR team like to tackle if they had spare capacity?
- What HR developments may impact on the organisation in the next few weeks and months?
- What external issues could have an impact on the organisation in the future?

In addition, discussions with customers and clients as well as your friends and family may help. They may not work in HR but the very activity of talking through issues with outsiders can help you to articulate areas of interest and possible research topics.

Starting from journals

If you still have no idea what you would like to enquire into, then the following activity may be helpful.

 Activity 2.1

Getting research ideas from websites and journals

Visit the online pages of an HR magazine or organisation such as www.cipd.co.uk, www.people.management.co.uk, www.shrm. org or the professional association in your home country. Look at the features and comments; check out the main news; skim through the blogs or discussion threads.

1   As a result of your browsing make a list of the main issues that are raised. Summarise what each issue is about in no more than one sentence. Generate a list of at least 12 issues.

2   Each of these issues could act as a 'trigger' to the identification of one or more possible topics for your research. Work through the summaries you have made and list the potential topics they highlight. Give each of the topics a rating for the following

characteristics if you were to consider them as an idea for an enquiry:

– your level of interest in the topic;

– likely value to you;

– likely value to your department/future career prospects;

– any potential ethical issues;

– feasibility as a project (could it be achieved 'on time and on budget'?);

– your data requirements to make the project work.

Starting from past assignments

Another way to generate some research ideas is to look back on work you have already undertaken as part of your course. Perhaps it would be worth rereading coursework that you have undertaken and recalling which topics you found to be most interesting. Is there a potential topic for a fuller enquiry within your previous assignments? Alternatively, it may be that you have been involved in a particular project at work, or on a work placement, that has excited your sense of curiosity, or which you realise you and/or your organisation would benefit from knowing more about. A benefit of this approach is that you will be able quickly to identify some of the key reading from the area.

Starting from past project titles

If all of these suggestions have so far generated no ideas then you might also review a list of past projects undertaken by students to stimulate your imagination enough to generate some possibilities. Your study centre should be able to provide such a list and you may be able to access examples within their library/online portal. An indicative list of project titles is shown in the box below. It is intended as an aid to stimulate your thinking, rather than to suggest that particular topics are more appropriate than others.

- Performance management and the use of appraisals at XYZ County Council
- The effectiveness of XYZ approach to offering postgraduate degree apprenticeship opportunities
- How do employees rate the flexible working practices available at XYZ?

- Factors affecting the success of the Performance Related Pay scheme at XYZ UK
- An evaluation of an employee voice initiative at XYZ
- The impact of the introduction of the living wage at XYZ
- Evaluating the way that L&D is evaluated at XYZ
- The perceived impact of Brexit on staff retention at XYZ
- The effectiveness of training on the General Data Protection Regulations in XYZ
- The management of sickness absence in XYZ
- The effectiveness of LinkedIn as a graduate recruitment tool
- The impact of a pre-induction programme for self-initiated expatriates in Dubai

Starting from a review of the expertise available to support you

If you are still undecided about your topic you could have a look at the expertise of your lecturers and seminar tutors. Your centre's website will usually list staff expertise and provide details of their most recent HR publications.

If your centre allows your work to take the form of a consultancy project you could also review the websites of HR consultancies as well as www.cipd.co.uk.

Deciding between alternative topics

Having identified two or three possible topics it is important to select the one that is most likely to lead to a successful research project. Here again, the expectations of the different stakeholders must be taken into account: the student; the academic institution; the professional association; and the organisation(s).

Your perspective

- **Personal interest.** Choose something that is interesting and you feel passionate about. You will have to work independently on your project for a number of months. If you start on it without much motivation, interest and enthusiasm, there is little chance that you will feel positive about it by the end of the process. You will be doing a lot of reading and spend a lot of time on it!
- **Career plan.** You will be more motivated if you can find a topic that has value to you in the medium or long term. Choose a topic that might make you more 'marketable'; increase your knowledge in a specialised area; or improve your skills and experience. It can be useful to discuss this with your manager at work as well as your supervisor.
- **Time/resources.** The project must be able to be achieved within the specified time limit and in addition to other work and commitments. Avoid any topic

that is so large that it cannot be achieved to a reasonable quality threshold because of time or other resources that are unlikely to be available. You should also be mindful of the word limit.

- **Skills.** Good research topics are stretching to the researcher, but they must also be within your capabilities. A project studying the difficulties of communication in a multilingual organisation would be difficult to undertake, for example, if you can read and communicate in only one language. If the thought of numerical, quantitative analysis fills you with dread then a project that involves qualitative data analysis might be worth pursuing.

Your study centre's perspective

- **Links to theory/potential for fresh understanding.** To achieve academic credit, projects must be capable of being linked in some way to theories, concepts and frameworks of practice. Which of the topics you are thinking about have the most potential for this? It is important to ensure that there will be sufficient academic journal articles on your topic area.

- **Regulations and expectations.** Your study centre will have clear guidelines about what is expected from a research project. Some institutions (and professional bodies) require that primary data are gathered. It is also important to be clear about the expected word count, the relative importance of different features within the project (the marking scheme) as well as the format for presentation. If you are undertaking a course in HR, it will be expected that you will research an issue related with this field (and not principally concerned with marketing or finance, for example). Your centre may have other requirements such as the need to select an international topic if you are undertaking an international qualification. Make sure that you choose a topic that enables you to meet these expectations. The advice of your supervisor is very important as you consider the suitability of your proposed topics.

- **Potential to probe and question.** Avoid choosing a topic that merely replicates a certain form of HR practice and does not provide an opportunity to critically evaluate existing assumptions. If you decide on a secondary data-based project, give careful consideration to how you will be able to add your own analysis of the data.

- **Wider context.** Even if your project is going to be undertaken within one organisation, an appropriate topic will also have some value to one or more of the following interest groups: the business sector; the HR profession; other HR managers; academics with an interest in HR.

- **Expertise in your study centre.** In some colleges/universities you may receive information about the research and/or professional expertise of the tutors who are available to supervise your dissertation or project. You may wish to use this information in guiding you towards an interesting project idea; there may also be a possibility of future involvement in this area of work.

- **Professional institution.** If the course of study you are taking is linked with a professional body (such as CIPD) then choose a topic that meets the criteria that it has established.

The organisation's perspective

- **Organisational relevance.** A project that has potential value to the 'host' organisation is more likely to receive the support that is needed and to be completed successfully.

- **Access to data.** A topic for research will be feasible only if the information you need exists and can be accessed (politically, logistically and ethically) within your time and budget constraints. If it is a UK public sector organisation you may find useful data that has been published as part of their Freedom of Information Act publication scheme.

- **Resources required.** Although basic IT and other resources are likely to be available, requirements for specialist software or other resources (such as particular training and so on) need to be checked out before a topic is selected. For example, it is possible to carry out interviews remotely, and while this poses some challenges, they can be explored within your methodology chapter. If you plan to carry out interviews in person, consider the travel and associated costs. Reflect on how you can make best use of technology.

What if you are unable to find an organisation that will grant you access?

Establish whether your study centre can provide introductions to alumni or corporate contacts who may have projects that you could undertake. If it is not possible to carry out primary research, most institutions will permit a dissertation or management report that does not include primary data; you should discuss this with your supervisor so that you are clear about how to carry out a good piece of secondary research.

It is common at this early stage to lose valuable time in mulling over topics, therefore it is important to try to select a topic, discuss it with your supervisor and then proceed in a timely manner. You can usually make subtle amendments to the title and research question throughout your process, subject to your centre's regulations. Having decided on the broad area of your investigation, it is important to establish a focus for the study.

Establishing the focus of the project

Focusing a research project involves articulating a clearly stated aim, principal research question or hypothesis. For most students there are two ways of going about this. One is to read around the literature to refine your thinking about which features of your topic you are most interested in. The other is to start from the position of the research project as is situated in its organisational context. For the purposes of illustrating the two approaches Case Example 2.1 about the study of employer-supported volunteering will be developed further in this section.

Reading around the subject

Part of the process of refinement from a general idea to a researchable topic is the definition of key concepts, issues and contexts that are relevant for your enquiry. To do this it is necessary to undertake some initial reading. If you are interested in volunteering, therefore, you could make an initial assessment of the literature about volunteering to work out what are the main theories and concepts in this area and to gain an idea about what is already well-researched and where there are some gaps in what is known.

Starting from the research situation

Another way of beginning the process of establishing the focus for your project is to adopt a step-by-step process (Biggam, 2011), which is illustrated in Figure 2.2.

This approach begins when you articulate the one word that defines your topic, for example 'volunteering'. The next step involves identifying other words that are relevant to what you wish to investigate. In the case of this example the other words might include: government policy, corporate social responsibility, employee engagement, employer-supported volunteering, skills development, talent management, employee retention. Already this list is too long and the next stage involves distinguishing between 'must-have' words and 'nice-to-have' words. Stick with the must-have words and let the others go. The third step involves bringing the remaining words together to form a meaningful sentence. In our example here this might be: 'employer-supported volunteering enables organisations to demonstrate social responsibility while engaging employees'. An alternative sentence, reflecting a different research context might be: 'employer-supported volunteering can be a useful tool for managing and retaining internal talent'.

The final stage of this process is to convert the sentence into a statement of: the aim of the research, a principal research question, or a research hypothesis.

Establishing the research aim, principal research question or hypothesis

Opinions vary as to whether your research focus is best expressed through an aim, a principal research question, or a hypothesis, but the key issue is to express in general terms what your research will address. Remember that an interesting project (one that will be worthy of an academic award) must have the potential to provide fresh understanding for HR practitioners and/or academics and ideally have recommendations. Research that sets out to find 'the best way' of one HR practice or another

Figure 2.2 Achieving focus for your research project

(Biggam, 2011)

or to 'prove' the benefits of an organisational initiative is likely to be very limited and will result in an output that will be of little interest to anyone once organisational circumstances change (as they inevitably will). Research that identifies the effect of different contexts on the way HR practices or policies are variously carried out and understood by different participants has the potential to make a valuable contribution. Remember to also cross check against your centre's assessment criteria.

Research aim

A research aim is a broad statement of the general intention of your research. It indicates what you hope to achieve (not how you plan to do it). For example, 'the aim of this research is to evaluate the experiences of employees who have engaged in volunteering programmes'. It is important to write this carefully so that you can be sure that your aim is capable of being met within your work.

Principal research question

Some researchers prefer to articulate their focus through a 'big question' or a principal research question, for example: 'do labour market factors or employer skills demand factors have most influence on the outcomes of apprenticeship schemes?'

Hypothesis

Some supervisors prefer you to articulate the focus of your research through a hypothesis. Opinions vary about the usefulness of hypotheses in action-orientated organisational research (see, for example, Clough and Nutbrown, 2012; Creswell and Creswell, 2017; Fisher, 2007; Fox, Martin and Green, 2007; Maylor, Blackmon and Huemann, 2017; Saunders and Lewis, 2018; Hart, 2013). A hypothesis is a specific type of research question based on 'informed speculation' about something (Robson and McCartan, 2016). It is a statement that asserts that a relationship exists between two or more variables or that particular consequences will follow if a hypothesis (or statement) is true. In some areas of HR research such as in work psychology, the use of a hypothesis to offer tentative propositions as a way of focusing a research project is quite common, although the approach is used less in other forms of HR research. Your research approach will define whether or not a hypothesis is appropriate; they are more common in quantitative work where key variables are already identifiable.

    Activity 2.2

Summarising your research aim digitally

Being able to summarise a research idea succinctly is an important skill and will help you to collate some useful initial feedback.

Twitter is an online social networking and 'microblogging' medium that people use to send and read text-based posts of up to 280 characters, known as 'tweets'. Since its launch in 2006 it has gained worldwide popularity; millions of people send tweets, use search queries and follow twitter content online. Twitter forces users to express their thoughts concisely.

You may also be asked to explain your ideas verbally to an audience of tutors and/or peers, and doing this digitally is a useful way to share information and capture feedback.

Choose one of the following mediums to express your initial research ideas:

Option A – Be a tweeter

1   Articulate your research focus as a tweet. This means that you must express your research aim, principal research question or hypothesis in 280 characters or fewer.

2   Once you have a tweet of your research focus, express, in a further 280 characters, why anyone should care about the outcomes of your research.

Option B – Be a vlogger

1   Articulate your research focus within a 60-second digital recording (audio and/or video) providing the same level of information as the task described above for the tweeters.

2   In a second 60-second recording, explain what the potential impact of your work could be for the organisation.

Option C – Constructing a LinkedIn post

LinkedIn is a valuable networking tool that is used by professionals to identify experts in different areas as well as sharing relevant articles and examples of good business practice. It is also used regularly by recruiters and headhunters who are seeking talent.

1   Consider how you could use a one-paragraph LinkedIn post to summarise your proposed research project and potentially recruit research participants. Be mindful that your current network could view your post so you want it to sound professional as well as encouraging.

Feedback notes

Whether or not you are a tweeter, a vlogger or a LinkedIn subscriber, this exercise demonstrates how difficult and clumsy it can feel to articulate your research focus. However, being able to communicate what you hope to research and why your research has value will help you to achieve the cooperation and assistance that you will require as your project develops. It will also ensure that you stay focused on the key features of your research and stop you from getting distracted from the 'need to know' into other 'nice to know' issues that are related to your topic. It is also important to remember that once information is in the public domain, it exists forever and is attributable to you, so ensure it reflects your personal and professional values.

Case Example 2.2

Moving forward towards a set of research questions

Extracts from: Ridgway, M and Robson, F (2018) Exploring the motivation and willingness of self-initiated expatriates, in the civil engineering industry, when considering employment opportunities in Qatar, *Human Resource Development International*, **21** (1), pp 24–45.

This paper provides empirical and contextual insight into the complexity of Self-Initiated Expatriates' (SIEs) experiences in a unique setting. Factors that influence SIEs in the civil engineering industry, when considering overseas employment, are identified and considered in the context of Qatar as a proposed destination...

Qatar provides a unique setting for this study, due to the region's reliance on foreign workers and the investment into the region's infrastructure and sporting facilities. Building on earlier work, this paper explores the motives for overseas employment with Qatar as a proposed destination... While research into the area of motives and international assignments has been previously conducted (Richardson and Mckenna, 2000; Jackson *et al*, 2005; Dickmann *et al*, 2008; Thorne, 2009; Selmer and Lauring, 2012) there is insufficient research that addresses this topic expressly in the Middle East, and in the particular context of less traditional mobility patterns, such as Self-Initiated Expatriates (SIEs) (Andresen *et al*, 2014; Guttormsen, 2017); a gap which this paper addresses by presenting empirical research that contributes to our understanding of global mobility. This study contributes to knowledge by exploring how the motivation and wiliness of SIEs to

undertake career opportunities in a unique and specific geographic context, particularly, how this is affected by an explicitly proposed destination...

1   To identify the different factors that affect SIEs' consideration of overseas employment opportunities.

2   To understand how the proposed destination influenced these factors, specifically if the proposed destination is Qatar.

This study is grounded in an interpretivist epistemology as the intention is to provide rich and in-depth insights into the issues at hand, thus the research aimed to engage with participants in order to understand their perceptions and understanding, through a qualitative approach. Similar to other studies (Scurry, Rodriguez and Bailouni, 2013; Makkonen, 2016) a qualitative methodology, semi-structured interviews were undertaken to enable investigation of key topic areas while still allowing sufficient flexibility (Aurini, Heath and Howells, 2016) and were conducted at a mutually convenient time and location either face-to-face, or using a voice-over-internet protocol (Iacono, Symonds and Brown, 2016). Interviews enabled the capture of participants' beliefs and experiences, in their own words, and were deemed an appropriate mechanism for data collection.

Adopting a synergistic theoretical position, this study contributes to extant knowledge by expanding our understanding in a new context (Ridder, Hoon and McCandless Baluch, 2014).

At the point of data collection, the first author had been employed in a senior HR position, within the civil engineering industry for over 10 years, which helped to secure interview participants for the research. The participants worked in a professional capacity within the construction and civil engineering industries and were approached directly through the first author's professional network; participants were either already known first-hand by the first author or referred by colleagues.

To meet the criteria for inclusion, participants had to have been employed within a professional capacity, holding either a higher academic qualification or having an established skilled trade, within the construction industry.

Discussion questions

1   What is the aim of the research described in this extract?

2   What is likely to be the value of this research and to which stakeholders?

3   Why is the formulation of a hypothesis inappropriate in the context of this research?

4   What do you think are the key limitations of this work?

5   From an organisation perspective, why and how could this research be useful?

Feedback notes

This extract provides an example of research undertaken outside of one specific organisation but which is concerned with issues of direct relevance to HRM&D in a global context. The research has an **exploratory** aim, setting out to find out more about the career attitudes of self-initiated expatriates. The research has potential value to a range of different stakeholders including employing organisations that operate in different countries across the United Arab Emirates. The work would be of specific relevance to organisations that find it difficult to recruit and/or afford organisational expatriates (ie employees who already work elsewhere for the organisation). The research takes place in a context where knowledge of the issues is rather scant – very little research into these specific issues has been undertaken. This makes the formulation of a hypothesis inappropriate as such a statement would need to be grounded in existing knowledge or theory. The different purposes of research (exploratory, descriptive and explanatory) were discussed in Chapter 1. This case illustrates how a hypothesis is most appropriate for **explanatory research,** which sets out to explain a situation or problem, usually in the form of causal relationships. The focus of **descriptive research** or **exploratory research** (represented in this illustration) is likely to be more effectively articulated through a research aim or a principal research question.

Formulating research questions or research objectives

Having established a provisional aim for your research or a possible hypothesis, it is also necessary to achieve further focus for your project (as in Case Example 2.2) by formulating some research questions or objectives. Research objectives help you to express what you need to do to realise your research aim and begin with a verb (see

Figure 2.3 Formulating a research aim and objective

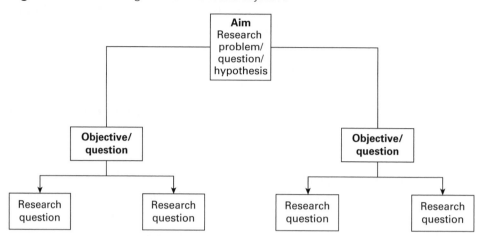

Table 2.1) that indicates what sort of activity you will undertake. Research questions articulate what you need to be able to find out in order to answer your principal research question or to test the propositions that follow from your hypothesis. Most student research projects, which have an appropriately 'scoped' aim or principal research question, will have between two and four meaningful research objectives or questions (see Figure 2.3). If you have more than four objectives then your project may be too big and you will not achieve all your objectives on time, or your objectives are too superficial and some further thinking is required.

The box below shows some example research objectives taken from real-life student projects and Table 2.1 offers some verbs that you may find useful if you are struggling to articulate your research objectives.

Table 2.1 Useful verbs for research objectives

Analyse	Diagnose	Investigate
Appraise	Discuss	Measure
Assess	Establish	Outline
Benchmark	Evaluate	Probe
Classify	Examine	Rank
Compare	Explain	Rate
Construct	Explore	Recommend
Determine	Formulate	Reflect
Derive	Identify	Scrutinise
Develop	Interpret	Test

- To investigate the extent to which XYZ Ltd sickness absence policy aligns to best practice.
- To evaluate how the sickness absence policy is understood by different groups of employees.
- To explore the use of LinkedIn as a recruitment tool.
- To investigate line managers' perceptions of the use of social media in recruitment and selection.
- To examine the current devolution of HRM strategy for Performance Management in ABC council.
- To investigate line managers' perceptions of the effectiveness of devolution of HRM.
- To investigate the current onboarding process within the HR Resourcing division of LMN organisation.
- To evaluate the impact of the onboarding process on employee engagement.
- To investigate current processes and practices used by PQR Ltd to offer degree level apprenticeships.
- To identify improvements or modifications to better align degree level apprenticeships with the organisational efficiencies agenda.
- To evaluate the organisation's current approach to evaluating learning and development activities.
- To establish any gap between what line managers expect their team to gain from learning and development activities and their perceptions of the actual impact.

The style of your objectives will also be influenced by the type of dissertation or report you are writing. For example, in a consultancy report there would be an expectation that key objectives would be formed around recommendations.

You may find that you prefer to articulate the focus of your project through research questions. Research topics at postgraduate level cover many different issues from a range of perspectives and are undertaken in varied ways. What they have in common is that they resemble a puzzle: something that needs to be 'solved' or 'worked out' using careful thought (Hart, 2013) and in a systematic manner. Descriptive research projects tend to set out to solve a 'developmental puzzle' (for example, what factors led to the endorsement of employer-supported volunteering in my organisation?). Explanatory research projects tend to set out to solve 'causal puzzles' (for example, what factors cause an employee to become a volunteer?). Exploratory research projects tend to involve an 'essence puzzle' (for example, how does being a volunteer impact the engagement of employees?).

In all cases, in order to solve the puzzle you need to ask and answer some subsidiary questions, just as you would need to break down any puzzle you attempt to solve into different steps. In research puzzles the subsidiary questions are referred to as research questions.

Research questions or research objectives?

Opinion is divided about whether research objectives are preferable to research questions in expressing the focus of any study. Some study centres (and tutors) may have particular preferences but many will accept research questions, research objectives, or both.

   Activity 2.3

Research questions or objectives?

....

1 Take some of the illustrative research objectives from Table 2.3 and express them as a research question.

2 Discuss whether you think research objectives or research questions are preferable.

Feedback notes

Research questions that you formulate might be something like:

- How does the XYZ Ltd sickness absence policy align with best practice?
- Do line managers understand their role in applying the sickness absence policy?
- How does the HR Department make use of LinkedIn for recruitment and selection?
- What effect does onboarding have on employee engagement?
- How does PQR Ltd recruit to and manage its degree apprenticeship programme?
- How do line managers evaluate the learning and development of their team?

Careful formulation of either research objectives or research questions forms the basis of any good research. When your work is being assessed the marker will look carefully at your research questions or objectives to determine both their quality and the extent to which you have addressed them fully by the time the marker reads your conclusions. In other words, have you delivered what you promised to the reader? If you are undertaking research as a practitioner-researcher it is important to be aware of the danger of formulating research questions that you (or the organisational sponsor of your research project) think you already know the answer to and which will merely serve to reinforce existing personal and/or organisational assumptions or activities. Therefore, as you formulate research objectives or questions, it is worth making explicit what you think the answers may be to your questions **but also** what alternative answers may exist.

In summary, it is important to (Hart, 2013):

- **Articulate your aim and objectives as soon as possible** – The earlier you start the better as you will waste time if you do not establish the focus of your project.
- **Start with the general and move to the specific** – Identifying the focus of your project is a process of refinement. As you discuss your focus with colleagues, tutors and members of your family you will find that it gradually becomes easier and less clumsy to articulate what you hope to achieve.

- **Examine your own motivation (personal and political)** – A good mark for a research project is rarely achieved where it seems you want to prove what you already knew all along (however worthy your cause might be). An HR research project forms part of your course to enable you to demonstrate your ability to undertake a systematic and open-minded investigation into an HR issue. Employers value employees who are able to undertake projects and exhibit these skills in the workplace. In selection interviews, graduates are often asked to give examples of projects they have managed. If you are more motivated by a desire to provide evidence leading to a predetermined conclusion then you are unlikely to get a good mark and your work will be neither credible nor persuasive. Ask yourself the 'so what?' question.
- **Find the line of least resistance** – Choose a topic and develop a focus where you know that data are available and accessible to you and where you are confident that you already have, or could develop in time, the skills you need to analyse the data. For example, if you are confident in analysing numerical data and using Excel and/or SPSS (or equivalents) it would be sensible to carry out a quantitative study rather than having to learn new techniques in qualitative analysis.

 Activity 2.4

Clarifying your topic and focus

Answer the following questions about your research as a way of clarifying its scope and focus.

Question	Answer
What is the central aim, principal research question or hypothesis of your research project? What are you trying to find out?	
What are your research objectives or questions?	1 2 3 4
What do you think the answers will be to your questions?	
What alternative answers might there be?	
What are the unknowns in your topic area?	
Which authors' research will be key for your project?	
Where do you fit into the situation you will be researching?	
What opposition or challenges might you encounter?	

Approaches to research methodology

Whether or not you decide to dwell on this section or move on to the more practical matters outlined in this chapter will depend on your own personal preference and interests, and the requirements of your study centre (expressed in the marking scheme for your research report or dissertation) for a discussion about your methodology. The terms 'method' and 'methodology' refer to different, but interrelated issues associated with research. All research reports, whether produced at intermediate, advanced, undergraduate, postgraduate, or Masters levels or beyond, require a description and justification of the **methods** of your research; the forms of data you gathered (qualitative, quantitative or both); from whom you collected your data (your sample); and how you collected and analysed your data. These are important but tactical issues and are different from the more fundamental positional issues associated with **methodology**. If you need to incorporate a discussion of your methodology then read on – if you are unsure you should confirm with your supervisor.

Key terms

The term **methodology** refers to the **theory** and **philosophy** of how research should be undertaken. The assumptions you make about these issues will have important implications for the research method or methods that you choose to adopt.

It is important not to get scared by these terms. The term **theory** refers to the process of explaining things we experience in the observable world to make them intelligible; to suggest why things are the way they are or to describe the way they happen in the way that they do. Theories make use of concepts, which help us understand why things are. Concepts are abstract: they do not exist in reality; we cannot touch them, but they provide a structure to the way we understand and explain what goes on in the observable world. Within your taught modules you will have learned about lots of concepts. It is highly likely that you will also have had to demonstrate your understanding and application within assignments and examinations. Look back through your notes to remind yourself about concepts. **Philosophy** is concerned with how, as thinking human beings, we make sense of the observable world. Philosophy is concerned with the fundamental nature of knowledge. As researchers we want to extend knowledge and so we cannot avoid philosophy.

Any research philosophy must address two interrelated and fundamental questions (Lee and Lings, 2008): **how can we know the world?** and **how do theories, concepts and experiences lead to knowledge?** Figure 2.4 expresses how philosophy plays a role in the way researchers try to bridge the world we observe and experience, and the intellectual world of ideas that, as thinking human beings, we also inhabit.

If you are working towards a CIPD qualification then these methodological issues need less attention at this stage. However, a discussion about your methodological stance is likely to be necessary if you are undertaking a dissertation leading to an MSc or MA award. If you plan to move towards a research degree (eg MRes, MPhil, PhD, Professional Doctorate) you will need to consider these issues in even more depth and justify decisions taken in the context of your research.

Over many centuries researchers have tackled these questions differently and, as a result, different research traditions have emerged. The next section provides a very

Figure 2.4 Why bother about philosophy?

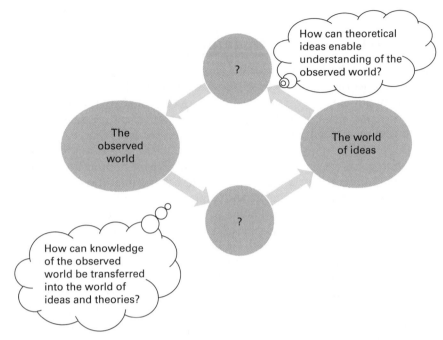

(adapted from Lee and Lings, 2008)

brief overview of the two most prominent traditions in HR research before high-lighting the consequences of these different traditions for your project.

The scientific research tradition

Since the 16th century the scientific tradition has made a huge contribution to the development of what we know and understand about the natural and social world. Researchers in the scientific tradition are concerned with gaining knowledge by gathering facts and observations about the world in order to generate and test theory.

Within this tradition there are many strands of thought; the two most prominent are put forward by **empiricists** who argue that we should rely on the evidence of our senses if we really want to be sure of our facts and **rationalists** who argue that our senses may be deceived and so reason and ideas have a crucial role to play in making sense of the apparently random and even contradictory observable experiences that humans try to comprehend. If you want to go further into this, check out the following research traditions: realism; positivism; post-positivism. These are discussed in more detail in some of the further reading sources at the end of the chapter (see, for example, Lee and Lings, 2008; Bell, Bryman and Harley, 2019; Saunders and Lewis, 2018).

What these approaches have in common is an acceptance of a role for both theories and abstract concepts AND a requirement for robust empirical evidence. Those who work within the tradition of a scientific approach, therefore, emphasise (Lee and Lings, 2008):

- a focus on the objective world that can be observed and measured;
- an acceptance that just because something cannot be seen it might still exist.

The interpretive research tradition

The scientific research tradition remains a very fruitful and dominant one in research throughout the world. In addition to those working in the natural and physical sciences the tradition has been continued by many, but not all, of those who research into the social sciences (including those in management and business). However, since 19th century researchers have increasingly debated the extent to which social or organisational research should make use of the scientific method. Critics of the scientific approach draw on a range of earlier philosophical approaches, particularly romantic and humanist world views that emphasise the importance of 'collective' and 'community' features of social life and emphasise 'natural' and emergent ways of developing knowledge and understanding of the world rather than the 'mechanical' approaches assumed by the traditional scientific method.

An alternative **interpretive** research tradition has developed, therefore, based on the assumptions of **hermeneutics** (the study of the theory and practice of interpretation), which sees human experience as inherently influenced by social context and so less predictable and generalisable than those in the scientific tradition assume it to be. Those working within this interpretive tradition argue that an objective understanding of the world is not possible; instead they focus on interpreting human experience. Just as the scientific tradition is characterised by different approaches so the interpretive tradition contains many different variants. Check out 'phenomenology', 'ethnography' and 'critical research' in the further reading sources listed at the end of this chapter (see, for example, Lee and Lings, 2008; Bell *et al*, 2019; Saunders and Lewis, 2018) if you would like to find out more about these.

In general terms, researchers operating within the **interpretive tradition** (Lee and Lings, 2008) are characterised by:

- a concern for understanding rather than explaining;
- interest in the study of experiences bound up with time and context;
- seeking understanding without 'reducing' variables to what can be measured;
- assumptions that reality is socially constructed in a collaborative and changing way.

You will recognise that this research tradition is based on constructivist world views that were highlighted in Chapter 1. The assumptions about the nature of the world, the nature of knowledge and the role of researchers within this tradition are very different from those within the scientific tradition. In particular, interpretive researchers seek to achieve **reflexivity** (where the role of the researcher, as a feature of the research process, forms an explicit part of the analysis).

Methodological implications for HR researchers

The term **positivist** is often applied to all researchers who work within the traditions and assumptions of an 'objectivist' perspective. This is not strictly accurate but, for the sake of simplicity, the term is used in this book to connote those within the scientific tradition. Positivists emphasise the importance of an objective scientific method (Lee and Lings, 2008). They see their role as collecting facts and then studying the relationship of one set of facts to another. They analyse quantitative data (data that can be counted) using statistically valid techniques and so produce quantifiable and, if possible, generalisable conclusions. This approach stresses the importance of studying social and organisational realities in a scientific way that mirrors, where possible, the research processes used in the natural sciences.

The term **interpretivist** is also used in rather a crude way in this book to connote researchers who are most comfortable with **socially constructed world view** and see information and facts as provisional and significantly affected by the meanings and experiences of different people in different situations of cultural contexts. From this perspective information from observation or interviews in the form of words and meanings (qualitative rather than quantitative data) is often seen to be more valuable for researchers. Interpretivist researchers are concerned to access and understand individuals' perceptions of the world. This is because they see social phenomena (facts) as being the product of human interactions that, because they are the product of shared understandings and meanings, are not always predictable or even formally rational (Remenyi *et al*, 1998; Lee and Lings, 2008). The less quantifiable and the subjective interpretations, reasoning and feelings of people (qualitative data) are seen as a more relevant line of enquiry in order to understand and explain the realities of HR situations. The focus of interpretivist research, therefore, is not so much on facts and numbers but on words, observations and meanings (Creswell and Creswell, 2017). The main differences between the two approaches are shown inTable 2.2. Both research approaches have value and are used by HR researchers as Activity 2.5 illustrates.

Table 2.2 Positivist and interpretivist principles

Positivist Principles	Interpretivist Principles
<ul><li>Work from scientific principles</li><li>Analyse phenomena in terms of variables</li><li>Start with theory and test/refine theory with data</li><li>Data should be collected by 'dispassionate' researchers</li><li>A highly structured research process should be used</li><li>Theories can be used to predict future relationships and behaviours</li><li>Preference for quantitative data</li><li>Validity and reliability of data are important for formulating generalisable conclusions</li></ul>	<ul><li>Knowledge is constructed by human beings as they make sense of their environment</li><li>Analyse phenomena in terms of issues</li><li>Researchers cannot be wholly dispassionate – they are involved and will influence situations to various degrees (often unintentionally)</li><li>Flexibility may be required to allow the emphasis of the research to change as the process unfolds</li><li>Preference for qualitative data</li><li>Generating 'rich' data is as important (or more important) than ability to generalise</li></ul>

Case Example 2.3

Researching into employee sickness absence

Jules was a part-time HR student who worked in a public sector organisation located in the south of England. Jules' employing organisation was struggling with high levels of short-term sickness absence, which was having a negative impact on the direct service users. Jules set about undertaking a literature review and discovered a number of variables that may be associated with sickness absences. This included personal characteristics as well as general work attitudes. Initially, given the grounding of ideas within the HR literature Jules felt that it would be most appropriate to undertake the research on understanding short-term absence with a positivist approach. Jules began by formulating a hypothesis that there was an association between employees' personal characteristics and their levels of sickness absence.

Discussion questions

Find out more about managing sickness by listening to, or reading the text of, some podcasts on the topic, for example https://www.xperthr.co.uk/audio-and-video/podcast-absence-rates-and-managing-sickness-absence/161461/ and review the latest CIPD annual survey at https://www.cipd.co.uk/knowledge/fundamentals/relations/absence/absence-management-surveys.

1 What variables might be helpful to measure and understand reasons for short-term absences?

2 What external factors might influence sickness absence?

3 What data would Jules need to test the hypothesis?

4 How might Jules obtain the data needed?

5 What advantages and disadvantages would this approach provide for Jules?

Feedback notes

Within the scientific approach, a commitment to measurement requires you to **operationalise your concepts**. In this case, perhaps you might come up with variables such as:

- personal characteristics – age, gender, length of service, current job role;
- general work attitudes – job satisfaction, organisation commitment, relationships with others.

As Jules was planning to work in the scientific tradition she wanted to ensure that their data gathering process generated information that was objective, measurable and could be statistically analysed in a rigorous way. As this was a large organisation you may also have suggested that they obtain this data through an electronic survey to employees and/or their managers; the larger the sample size, of course, the more generalisable, and therefore worthwhile, the results of the analysis would be.

If you were to undertake a project in this way you would be able to analyse your data and form a conclusion related to the hypotheses. If the evidence supports the hypothesis then the links between personal characteristics and levels of sickness absence are confirmed. If it does not then alternative links or factors might be examined or the organisation might decide that they need to focus more on employees' experiences of working in the organisation.

Criticisms of the positivist approach

This case shows that it is possible to undertake research utilising a positivist approach. However, having thought through the issues Jules decided against working within the scientific tradition and opted instead to work within an interpretive research approach, which she felt would be more appropriate to her context and would also provide other benefits:

- **Answering the question 'why'.** Although research undertaken in a positivist way might show a relationship between sickness absence and personal characteristics, it would be less helpful in trying to explain why this was the case. In addition, it would not give Jules much information on the types of interventions that could make a difference to levels of sickness absence. To address these questions she wanted to get an understanding of people's perceptions of the issues leading to absences.

- **Problems of categorisation.** Jules was also aware of problems relating to categories and variables. She was conscious that managing absence is a multifaceted issue with many variables that are outside of the control of the organisation.

- **Issues of the data.** The use of quantitative data can provide for broad generalisations but only answers questions posed in a fairly short questionnaire. Jules was concerned to avoid the trap of being too superficial; issues of absence management are complex and she, as well as her manager, felt that 'richer' (more qualitative) data were more pertinent.

- **Relevance for applied research.** In Jules' situation she was aware that the purpose of her research was to contribute to the solution of organisational problems. Although the research that Jules originally considered would have been interesting, it did not really relate with the **management and development** of strategies to minimise avoidable absences.

- **Dealing with complexity.** The basis of the positivist approach is to reduce situations and isolate discrete variables for analysis. Most situations in organisations are rather complex and 'messy' and Jules felt that a more flexible and integrative approach to enquiry would be appropriate.

Criticisms of the interpretive approach

Although Jules opted for an interpretive approach, as she wrote up her research report she discussed a number of limitations that followed from the decision to adopt an interpretivist approach:

- **Loss of direction.** The flexibility of the interpretive approach is attractive, but Jules found she had collected a huge volume of data and, for quite a while, she had no clear idea of what to do with them and she faced a persistent challenge to balance 'flexibility' with 'focus'.
- **Time and resource constraints.** Jules found the time and resource issues associated with data collection and data analysis (arranging interviews, organising focus groups, people cancelling at the last minute and rearrangements needing to be put in place; unexpected events affecting people's responses) very difficult given the time and resource limitations she was faced with.

Mixed methods approach

As indicated already in this chapter, the research approach that you are drawn to may be influenced by your own background and preferred world view. However, many people find that they can 'see the sense' in both the objectivist and the social constructivist world views; equally they wish to benefit from the advantages of research approaches within the positivist and interpretive traditions. The benefits of such a mixed-methods approach have been highlighted by a number of authors in the social sciences and business fields who advocate research grounded in both the positivist and interpretivist approaches either 'in parallel' or on a 'one after the other' basis.

Such an approach often, but not always, underpins both action research strategies and the case study approach, in particular the emphasis on the research questions or objectives as being the driving force between the choice of methods and approach to be used in different research projects; the emphasis on diversity of methods; a willingness to appreciate elements of different methodological approaches; and an iterative, cyclical approach to research (Tashakkori and Teddlie, 2010).

Those who support this mixed approach (Gill and Johnson, 2010; Easterby-Smith *et al*, 2018; Bell *et al*, 2019; Fox *et al*, 2007; Creswell and Creswell, 2017) point out that it:

- reflects the complex and multifaceted nature of work organisations;
- provides opportunities to assess whether different data 'converge' (referred to as triangulation);
- enables one approach to facilitate or provide 'ways into' another;
- enables different research approaches to complement each other;
- offers the potential to investigate both what has happened but also how and why a phenomenon has occurred.

A mixed methods strategy is not for the faint-hearted; it involves trying to forge together two very different sets of assumptions about the nature of knowledge and the social world. Such a project involves achieving a high level of understanding of different research philosophies and approaches (becoming what Tashakkori and Teddlie, 2010 refer to as a *methodological connoisseur*). In addition, each research tradition has its own specialised techniques and, within the time limitations of a student project, you would need to be confident that you are competent enough in both quantitative and qualitative data gathering and analysis. With this in mind remember that more methods do not always lead to better research – it is better to tackle one project in a very competent way from within one tradition than to undertake it poorly from more than one position. There are also time and word-count implications of having more data to evaluate, and a tendency to become too descriptive in order to include all information gathered and analysed.

Research design issues

Your research design enables you to move from your initial idea into a competent research process. The person marking your project will be assessing the thinking behind your approach to design and strategy and you will need to be able to justify your decisions with supporting references. The terms research design and research strategy are used in different ways by different authors. In this book the terms are used as follows:

- Research design – the framework that you devise to guide the collection and analysis of your data. Robson and McCartan (2016) describe research design as being similar to an architect in a building project; it is the general plan that will identify how you will achieve your research aim and answer your research questions.

- Research strategy – the general approach (similar to the main decisions an architect might take about the nature of materials to be used in a building project) that you will take in your research enquiry. This is one of the key components of your research design, but not the only issue that you will need to consider.

- Research methods – the particular choices you will make, having established your overall design and strategy that relate to the specific data gathering techniques you will use.

Research strategies

Books about research methods highlight a range of generic research strategies. Opinion differs about how many strategies there are and what they should be called (see, for example, Saunders and Lewis, 2018; Robson and McCartan, 2016, Bell *et al*, 2019). Here, the strategies that are most appropriate to students undertaking an HR project are described.

Research strategies appropriate for relatively short-term student projects undertaken in organisations are outlined here. These are:

- cross-sectional research;
- comparative research;
- case study research;
- action research.

The choice of strategy for your research will be closely linked to the research objectives/questions of your project. There are advantages and disadvantages with all of these approaches.

Figure 2.5 Some generic research strategies

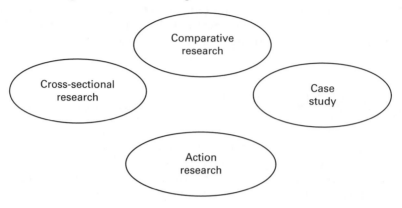

Cross-sectional research strategy

If you adopt a cross-sectional research strategy then you will collect data in a fairly standardised form from groups of people at a single point in time. Some people refer to this as a 'survey' strategy. Postal, telephone, web-based/e-mailed questionnaires or structured interviews may be used to obtain information but the key approach involves establishing a form of sampling to obtain information from a selection of the wider population. The cross-sectional research strategy will help you to establish patterns and comparisons. However, the data will only be 'robust and reliable' if it can offer an adequate representation of the wider population.

 Activity 2.5

Evaluating a piece of cross-sectional research

Visit the CIPD website which lists recent survey reports (http://www.cipd.co.uk/hr-resources/survey-reports/default.aspx). Choose a fairly recent survey and skim-read the report to evaluate its strengths and weaknesses.

1   How many people or organisations received the questionnaire (what was the research population?)

2   What proportion of people or organisations responded to the questionnaire?

3   What are the limitations of the data provided by this survey?

4   What are the useful features of the findings?

Feedback notes

You may have found it difficult to find out how many people received the survey. With CIPD surveys you often have to look towards the back of the report to a

Table 2.3 Survey-based research

Advantages	Disadvantages
Relatively cheap to organise	'Depth' is sacrificed for 'breadth'
Can achieve a broad coverage for comparisons	Poor questionnaire design leads to poor quality data
Can be undertaken within a relatively short timeframe	No opportunity for respondents to query the meaning of questions
Produce a high volume of information	Poor level of responses may make data unrepresentative
Relatively easy to present the data in order to make comparisons	No control over who responds to the questions
Survey can be repeated again at a different location or at a different time to allow for further comparisons	Respondents may be suffering from survey fatigue
Enables use of existing scales and research instruments	Will all the questions be interpreted in the same way by all the respondents?
There are a number of free online tools available to students	What are the motivations of those who respond to the questions?
	What do those who do not reply think (and does it matter)?

(Neuman, 2012; Bell *et al*, 2019)

section titled something like 'Background' where you MAY find out how many people received the survey and what proportion replied. The survey itself may also indicate the extent to which those who replied might be considered to be representative of the overall research population. Survey research offers a range of advantages as it provides a fairly detailed picture 'across the board' about a specific range of issues. However, there are also disadvantages with this strategy (Table 2.3).

Comparative research strategy

This strategy is popular with students who are studying their HR course away from their own country. Comparative research involves examining data from different countries or cultures or organisations in order to achieve a better understanding through comparing meaningfully contrasting 'cases' or 'situations'. It is then possible to gain a deeper awareness of the topic being researched in different national, cultural or organisational contexts and to consider and explain any similarities and differences that are found (Bell *et al*, 2019).

Comparative research strategies can be based on quantitative or qualitative data (or both). Within HR research there is a strong interest in cross-cultural studies as

HR practices are often seen as being significantly influenced by national or societal culture. However, the comparative research strategy may also be appropriate for studies within different parts of organisations or between different organisational sectors. The important issue for the comparative research strategy is the extent to which the distinguishing characteristics of the cases being compared can act as a catalyst for reflection and discussion of theory and practice (Bell *et al*, 2019).

Comparative research may be a particularly attractive research strategy for international students who wish to compare some aspect of HRM practice in their own country with those in their 'host' country. However, a number of difficulties have to be taken into account. First, data access in more than one place is required in a form that will enable an effective comparison. Second, if the research is based on case study data (for example, two or more cases in two or more countries or industry sectors) then it is important to ensure that the cases have sufficient in common, but also sufficient distinguishing factors to facilitate a meaningful comparison. Third, where quantitative data are envisaged there are also challenges to be faced in questionnaire design and administration: will the language of the questions be differently interpreted by people of different countries? To what extent will any linguistic translation alter the original intent of any questions asked? In spite of these challenges, comparative research in HRM offers a range of advantages. It contributes knowledge about HRM practices and frameworks in a range of situations, taking into account specific histories and contexts. In addition it encourages practitioners and academics to take a wider perspective of HR issues by reconsidering the extent to which assumptions about HR theory and practice are appropriate in different situations. It can provide HR researchers with an opportunity to probe into questions about the extent to which their learning about HR in their country of study is relevant in their home country. For an interesting methodological discussion around using datasets from different countries, see CIPD (2018) Part 2 – Indicators of Job Quality, available at: https://www.cipd.co.uk/Images/understanding-and-measuring-job-quality-2_tcm18-36524.pdf.

The case study strategy

Case study research involves a detailed investigation into a situation in a single 'case' or a small number of related cases. It is the term used for research that investigates a phenomenon in context and in depth, and is particularly useful when the distinction between the phenomenon and its context is unclear or disputed (Yin, 2017). The case study strategy is a popular approach for HR students who are in some form of employment, undertaking a project over a limited timescale. Even for full-time students the case study is attractive as it may be easier to obtain access to only one organisation (often where they already have some form of contact) rather than seeking to obtain responses from many companies. This strategy seeks to investigate the interaction of different factors and events that contribute to the focus of the enquiry. A range of types of data, (such as observations, interviews, survey data and the analysis of documents) can contribute to the research to provide the basis for a rounded analysis of the issue or problem. Historical research can also be undertaken to find out about the development of the organisation, or a particular problem, as part of the data gathering process (Farquhar, 2012; Yin, 2017).

Table 2.4 Case study based research – advantages and disadvantages

Advantages	Disadvantages
• One topic can be studied in detail • Interaction of factors and events can be taken into account • Breadth of methods of data collection • Only requires access to one organisation (or a small number of cases) • Case study can focus in depth on one department or group or undertake a comparison between	• Huge volume of qualitative data may be difficult to analyse • How can you cross-check information? • Generalisation is not possible • Researcher may influence and be influenced by the 'case' particularly if the researcher is a member of the organisation

(Neuman, 2012; Yin, 2017)

Case study research involves achieving access to different forms of data over a period of time. It also involves sharing interim findings with stakeholders and analysing data of different types in a way that develops a robust 'chain of evidence'. Data analysis is an incremental and iterative process making it more 'messy' than other research strategies. For HR students ease of access to data is also a limitation of the case study strategy, as in such a situation you may already influence and be influenced by the culture and practices of the organisation in which the research is taking place. Objective detachment may be difficult to achieve.

A summary of the main advantages and disadvantages of the case study approach are shown in Table 2.4.

Action research strategy

The action research strategy represents a radical departure from the scientific research tradition. The term 'action research' was first used by Kurt Lewin (1946), a researcher and writer in change management. He argued that, as organisational change processes are continuous and dynamic, so effective organisational research should be seen as an open-ended and continuous process of planning, acting, observing and reflection.

Most HR research, undertaken within an organisation, occurs in the context of change processes, stimulated by external and/or internal factors. It involves investigating HR problems or issues and making recommendations for change and improvement. In turn any changes that are undertaken will be evaluated, and further changes and recommendations are likely to result. This makes the action research strategy very attractive.

Since the 1940s many researchers have developed and modified the concept of action research (see, for example, Eden and Huxham, 1996; Coghlan and Brannick, 2014, McNiff and Whitehead, 2011) but the assumptions on which it was first developed remain central in that:

- researchers are (and should be) involved in the situations they are researching;
- researchers are (and should be) part of a cycle of improvement.

 Activity 2.6

Action research in practice

Below is an excerpt from the abstract of Sanyal and Rigby (2017).

Advances in technology have reshaped mentoring as a human resource development (HRD) intervention and heralded e-mentoring using online solutions as an alternative to traditional mentoring. This article reports on a unique learning opportunity as a part of the HRD curriculum in a Higher Education Institution (HEI) in which mentoring was offered with pairs separated by not only geographical distance but also by time zone, culture and organisation (Global Mentoring Relationships, GMRs). This empirical study uses an action research approach to aid the programme team's understanding of their own practice and to evaluate 23 GMRs within an e-mentoring scheme in a UK based university. The aim of this paper is to report the evolution of the GMRs and identify benefits and challenges to inform the practice of human resource development (HRD).

The full article can be accessed at Sanyal, C and Rigby, C (2017) E-mentoring as a HRD intervention: An exploratory action research study within an international professional mentoring scheme, *Human Resource Development International*, **20** (1), pp 18–36.

Read the Research Methods section of this article and answer the following questions:

1 Why was the action research strategy chosen for this research?

2 In what ways is the process described here different from a case study research strategy?

3 What skills would the researchers require to carry out this action research strategy?

4 Identify three criticisms of the action research strategy.

Feedback notes

There are similarities and differences between the case study and action research strategies. Both can utilise a range of different types of data (both qualitative and quantitative) to inform the research process. Both research strategies are also grounded in the acceptance of the importance of understanding the situational context of what is being researched. The main areas of difference are that action research is firmly grounded in understanding and promoting change where the researcher is part of a continuous cycle of problem diagnosis, taking action and observing the effects of the action that has been instituted (intervention), followed by reflection and theory-building. As such the researcher is involved in the situations being researched and is part of a cycle of change that may continue indefinitely.

A number of skills are required for effective action researchers (Yin, 2017; Coghlan and Brannick, 2014, McNiff and Whitehead, 2011; Reason and Bradbury, 2006), which include the ability to:

- ask probing questions (and be able to interpret the answers);
- be an effective listener – not hearing only what you expect or assume you will hear;
- be flexible and responsive to new data gathering opportunities that may present themselves as the research process goes along;
- be alert to, and sensitive to the likelihood of, confusing or contradictory evidence from different stakeholders or places within the situation you are researching.

You may have highlighted some problems with action research. For example, focusing on a discrete problem might lead action researchers to uncritically accept the dominant assumptions, theories and ways of thinking within the organisation(s). A further critique of the problem-solving focus forms the basis for an alternative approach known as appreciative inquiry. If you are considering this approach, it is important to discuss this with your supervisor to assess the feasibility for your project.

Appreciative inquiry

Appreciative inquiry was first articulated as a research strategy in the 1980s by Cooperrider and Srivastva (1987) as an alternative to traditional action research. They argued that a focus on problem-solving is too limited if significant change is required. They suggested that a more positive 'appreciative' approach is needed to generate more imaginative responses and innovative practice improvement and knowledge creation processes (Cooperrider and Srivastva, 2017). Appreciative inquiry practitioners argue that their approach is grounded in a range of research positions taking account of insights from a range of research approaches including scientific, interpretive and pragmatic traditions (Cooperrider *et al*, 2008; Hart *et al*, 2008). The aim of appreciative inquiry is to find out the best of 'what is' in an organisation; to establish ideas of 'what might be'; to enable consent about 'what should be' and to foster experience of 'what can be'. Instead of identifying problems, appreciative inquiry practitioners examine areas of strength, both those that are already known and those that may be unknown (Watkins, Mhor and Kelly, 2011) through a process that involves application, practice and collaboration.

Opinions about appreciative inquiry differ widely but the approach has been used in management development, organisation development, adult education and HR settings in a range of sectors, particularly in health and social care. Few systematic evaluations of the approach have been undertaken, however, and it has many critics.

Those within the scientific research tradition are particularly critical of the inclusion of positive imagery and emotive ways of explaining the approach, which focus on its potential to: appreciate, initiate, enquire, envision, dialogue, imagine and innovate. Other criticisms are that it is just another 'management fad' more suited to management consultancy than rigorous academic practice (Grant & Humphries, 2006; Bushe, 2007) as a commitment to work from 'the positive' may lead researchers to overlook tensions and ambiguities inherent in the organisational context for the project. Such an approach might encourage excessive optimism and the avoidance of politically difficult problem areas so that dysfunctional perceptions and behaviours in organisational settings are not examined leading to descriptive rather than analytical outcomes (Grant and Humphries, 2006; Bushe, 2007; Fitzgerald, Oliver and Hoxsey, 2010).

Those who engage with appreciative inquiry, however, have found a number of benefits for both the research process and the organisation. First, the spirit of 'building on the good' encourages more people, particularly those at senior level, to agree to participate as the fear of criticism and negative comment is diminished and higher levels of collaboration are possible both within and outside of the organisation. In addition researchers find the approach liberating in its affirmative but also provocative features.

In common with more traditional forms of action research there are also disadvantages with specific consequences for students undertaking a research project or dissertation.

Practical disadvantages of action research

- **Time duration.** The action research methodology requires continuous involvement in planning, taking action, observing the effects and reflecting (often two or three times round the complete cycle) and many student research projects have to be completed in a matter of months. It may be challenging to record some of the data.
- **Transparency of research process and outcomes.** A key reason for undertaking research in HR is to expand knowledge and understanding of particular organisational phenomena. If the way that action research is undertaken tends to be limited to the pragmatic and common-sense level it may be difficult to justify any 'value' in terms of knowledge and understanding outside of the organisation.

Planning to implement your research strategy

The brief overview of different research strategies provided here shows how, in any one research project it may be appropriate to devise a 'hybrid' approach where you use a combination of strategies. The choice you make at this stage will influence what sort of data you decide to gather and where to obtain your information. Before making a final decision about your research topic and strategy, therefore, it is worth thinking through responses to these questions:

- What will be the main 'level of analysis' in your research: individuals; groups; organisations; societies?
- Will you be able to access the data that you need to implement your strategy?
- Are relevant secondary data available?
- To what extent will the data you gather provide a robust basis to achieve your research aim and objectives/questions?

- Do you have the skills (or can you develop them) to collect and analyse the data you need?
- Are there likely to be any significant ethical issues?
- How might your strategy and methods affect the answers you get?
- How will you (your position in the organisation, preconceptions, etc) affect the research?

Access to data

HR research involves gaining access at three main levels. First, you have to get access to an organisation (or group of organisations). Then you need access to relevant people in the organisation to enable primary data to be gathered. Third, you may require access to sources of secondary data both within 'host' organisation(s) and also from external information sources. Access is a critical aspect of the research design of all projects and the challenges involved are often underestimated. It is important to gain access to participants who are willing to cooperate, rather than those whose initial interest fades away quickly. Access will also present different challenges depending on your position. You may be:

- a part-time HR student in employment in the organisation to be investigated;
- a full-time HR student who also works part-time in one or more organisations;
- a full-time HR student using a work placement organisation for their research;
- an HR student (full- or part-time or 'distance') with no current employing organisation.

You will need to reflect on the perceived impact of your role/position on your project when you are writing it up.

Access as an outsider

Cold calling

Although difficult, this is not impossible but access may be time-consuming to achieve and take many weeks to arrange. Most students find that written requests for access go unanswered and that several telephone calls or e-mail messages, once you have established the identity of the appropriate person to contact, are required. If you are interested in working with a UK public sector organisation, a wealth of information may be available online as part of the Freedom of Information publication schemes (see https://ico.org.uk/for-organisations/guide-to-freedom-of-information/publication-scheme/0 for further details).

Using your networks

Contacting an organisation with which you already have some form of connection is more likely to be successful. Gaining access to organisations through the employers of colleagues on your course, or members of the local branch of your professional association, for example, is often possible. Sometimes it is necessary to ask your existing contact to introduce you to a more relevant contact within their organisation.

Before attempting contact with an organisation it is important to be clear about the aims and purpose of your project and what sort of data you hope to collect (interviews, surveys, observation, etc). Prior to talking to the organisation, it is recommended that you discuss potential ethical issues with your supervisor so that you can provide the appropriate assurances. Once contact has been established you should also be prepared to negotiate on issues like sample size, interview structure and so on. To achieve access you will need to 'sell' the idea of the project in an effective way. Here are some ideas about how to achieve this:

- Communicate clearly about the purpose of your project and the type of access/data that you hope to gather.
- Indicate the time commitment involved. (How many interviews? Of what duration? Who with? How many people to be surveyed? What documents to be analysed?)
- Be aware of organisational sensitivities – if they think you are going to highlight all the weaknesses in the organisation's approach, and none of its strengths, they are unlikely to give permission.
- Be clear about how you propose to ensure confidentiality and anonymity of the organisation and individuals within it.
- Sell the 'benefits' of the research – how will it help the organisation better cope with HR issues in the future? What feedback (copy of your report, production of a summary report, and so on) will you provide?
- Use the language of business, rather than the language of academics.
- Be prepared to develop access on an incremental basis. Perhaps get permission for a short questionnaire first. Provide some feedback based on this and then get agreement for some structured interviews of key people. Then indicate how helpful it would be to be able to read the notes of relevant meetings and so on. If you undertake the first stage in a sloppy way you are unlikely to be allowed to continue. Once your credibility is demonstrated, however, and you are successful in building good relationships within the organisation, there is more chance that you will achieve further access.

A further opportunity is provided through the use of professional networking sites such as LinkedIn (www.linkedin.com), which allow you to either post a message requesting expressions of interest or to identify and contact people directly. With either route to contacting potential organisations and research respondents, be mindful of your own professional networking presence and ensure that it reflects your professionalism.

Access as an insider

Many people will undertake their project in the organisation of which they are already a part, whether on a full- or part-time basis. In this sense, **physical access** is easier, although what is really required for an effective project is **support and acceptance.**

If you are an insider researcher then you have the advantage of knowledge of the politics of the organisation and who best to approach for different types of data. Hopefully you will also have some organisational credibility. There are a number of difficulties, however, that you will have to take into account:

- separating your role as a researcher from your role as a practitioner;
- the dynamics of interviewing colleagues who know you and are known by you;
- handling confidential disclosures that may affect your future working relationships;
- living with the consequences of any mistakes that you make.

Planning and preparing for research in your own organisation requires just as much thought as for one with which you have limited contact. Important features of the access process are:

- Communicate clearly about the purpose of your project and the type of access/data that you hope to gather.
- Indicate the time commitment involved. (How many interviews? Of what duration? Who with? How many people to be surveyed? What documents to be analysed?)
- Be aware of organisational sensitivities – if they think you are going to highlight all the weaknesses in the organisation's approach, and none of its strengths, they are unlikely to give permission.
- Be clear about how you propose to ensure confidentiality and anonymity of the organisation and individuals within it.
- Sell the 'benefits' of the research – how will it help the organisation better cope with HR issues in the future? What feedback (copy of your report, production of a summary report, and so on) will you provide?
- Use the language of business, rather than the language of academics.
- Be prepared to develop access on an incremental basis. Perhaps get permission for a short questionnaire first. Provide some feedback based on this and then get agreement for some structured interviews of key people. Then indicate how helpful it would be to be able to read the notes of relevant meetings and so on. If you undertake the first stage in a sloppy way you are unlikely to be allowed to continue. Once your credibility is demonstrated, however, and you are successful in building good relationships within the organisation, there is more chance that you will achieve further access.

Many of the issues raised with negotiating access also relate to issues of ethics in research and these issues are discussed in Chapter 4. Figure 2.6 highlights how the different factors that have been introduced here might influence your approach to your research.

Figure 2.6 Influences on research design

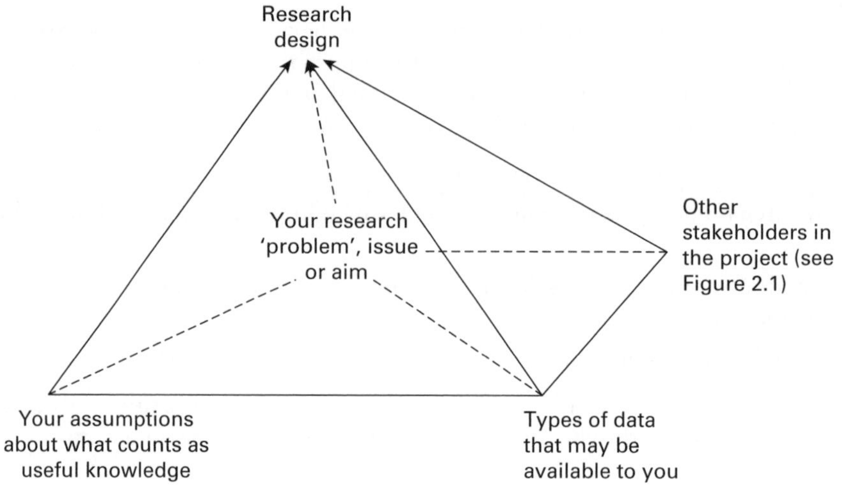

Figure 2.6 highlights the importance of:

- your assumptions about what counts as useful knowledge, factors that are linked with your world view about research and the tradition within which you decide to work; this in turn will influence the purpose of your research;

- other stakeholders in your research who will also influence the design of your study, in particular the expectations of your employing or sponsoring organisation, your study centre (and in particular your supervisor) and your professional association;

- practical issues like access to data that will also influence your research design.

These issues are represented in the form of a decision chart in Figure 2.7.

Final preparations – project planning

Unlike many other features of taught courses in HR, the research project or business research report is a piece of **independent** work, undertaken with the benefit of the guidance and advice of a supervisor or tutor. You may also benefit from participation in action/peer learning sets with fellow students on your programme. Action/peer learning sets give you the opportunity to share and discuss your work with others and to benefit from brainstorming some of the complex issues associated with research projects. A key benefit of being in learning sets is the ability to hear different perspectives on common challenges.

Responsibility for planning your project so that you can be sure to submit work of appropriate quality, on or before the submission date, remains with you. There is more chance that this will be achieved if an effective 'project management' approach is adopted.

Figure 2.7 Research design decision path

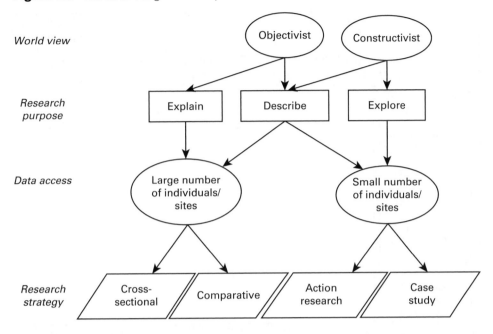

World view — Objectivist, Constructivist

Research purpose — Explain, Describe, Explore

Data access — Large number of individuals/sites, Small number of individuals/sites

Research strategy — Cross-sectional, Comparative, Action research, Case study

As indicated in Chapter 1, important project management skills are: identifying the component tasks and milestones you will need to achieve and then planning a sequence in which to undertake them; identifying which can be carried out 'in parallel' and which must be achieved before other tasks can be started. In addition you need the skill of accurate estimating so that your schedule of tasks is both honest and reasonable. Experience of writing up a coursework assignment might be used to estimate the time required for writing up one section of your final report, for example.

A typical list of tasks that comprise the 'journey' to a completed research project is shown as Figure 2.8.

Having identified the various tasks it is important to allocate appropriate time to achieve them. At this stage it may become clear that other activities, both at home and at work, may be affected, and you will need to discuss this with those involved in order to overcome any potential difficulties. At this stage it is also useful to identify 'pinch points' for your supervisor and research participants so that this can be reflected in your plan. Some tasks can be undertaken in parallel (such as the initial drafting of the literature review and drafting a questionnaire or carrying out some initial interviews) and this is a good opportunity to work out how you wish to proceed.

Many students find that producing a Gantt chart helps them plan and implement their research project in an effective way. A Gantt chart is a type of bar chart used to illustrate the start and finish dates of the different elements of a project. It is a useful tool for analysing and planning your work and it gives you a basis for scheduling when you will carry out the different tasks and to plan ahead for particular resourcing demands (help with software, access to the HR information system, etc) and you

Figure 2.8 The research project journey

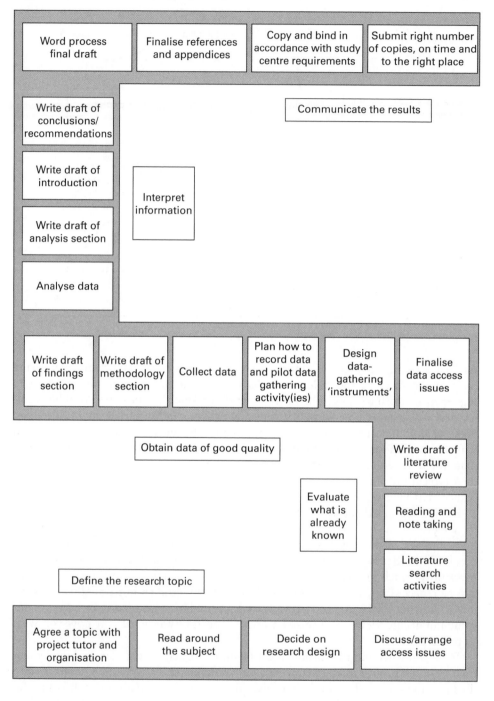

can also work out the critical path (what tasks you must complete by a particular date). Once your project is under way, a Gantt chart can help you to assess whether you are staying on schedule and, if you fall behind, you can identify what you will need to do to put it back on schedule.

There are many different ways of producing a Gantt chart (using Microsoft Project, Microsoft Excel, etc) but it is also possible to produce one using graph paper without the need for a software package by following these steps:

Step 1: List all the tasks you need to complete in your research project. For each of them estimate how long they will take and whether they can be undertaken in parallel with others or in sequence.

Step 2: Head up your graph paper with the time (in weeks) through from the start of your project to the date the research report or dissertation must be completed (these represent the headers for your columns.

Step 3: Draw up a rough draft of the Gantt chart. Allocate each task a row on the vertical axis of your graph paper. Plot each task on the graph paper, showing it starting on the earliest possible date. Draw it as a bar, with the length of the bar being the length of the task expressed in weeks. Above the task bars, mark the estimated time taken to complete each of them. Schedule your tasks in such a way that sequential actions are carried out in the required order. Ensure that dependent activities do not start until the activities they depend on have been completed.

Step 4: Review and redraw. The last stage in this process is to prepare a final (and probably tidier) version of the Gantt chart to show how sets of sequential activities link together, and where critical points occur. You can do this manually on graph paper or, without the need for specific software you can produce one using Excel as in the example shown in Figure 2.9.

 Activity 2.7

Project planning

Critically review the Gantt chart shown in Figure 2.9, which shows a project duration of 16 weeks. What tasks would you consider to have been allocated too much or too little time? Which times of the 16-week period look 'overcrowded' and what might be done to 'smooth out' the tasks? Consider how the chart would look if a more deductive piece of research was being undertaken.

Feedback notes

It may be that you have longer than 16 weeks to undertake your project and this will give more space. If you have a short period of time, however, then the Gantt chart shows how important the early weeks are. There is no time to lose. You may feel that some tasks require more time; where this is the case then make sure that you

Figure 2.9 Example Gantt chart

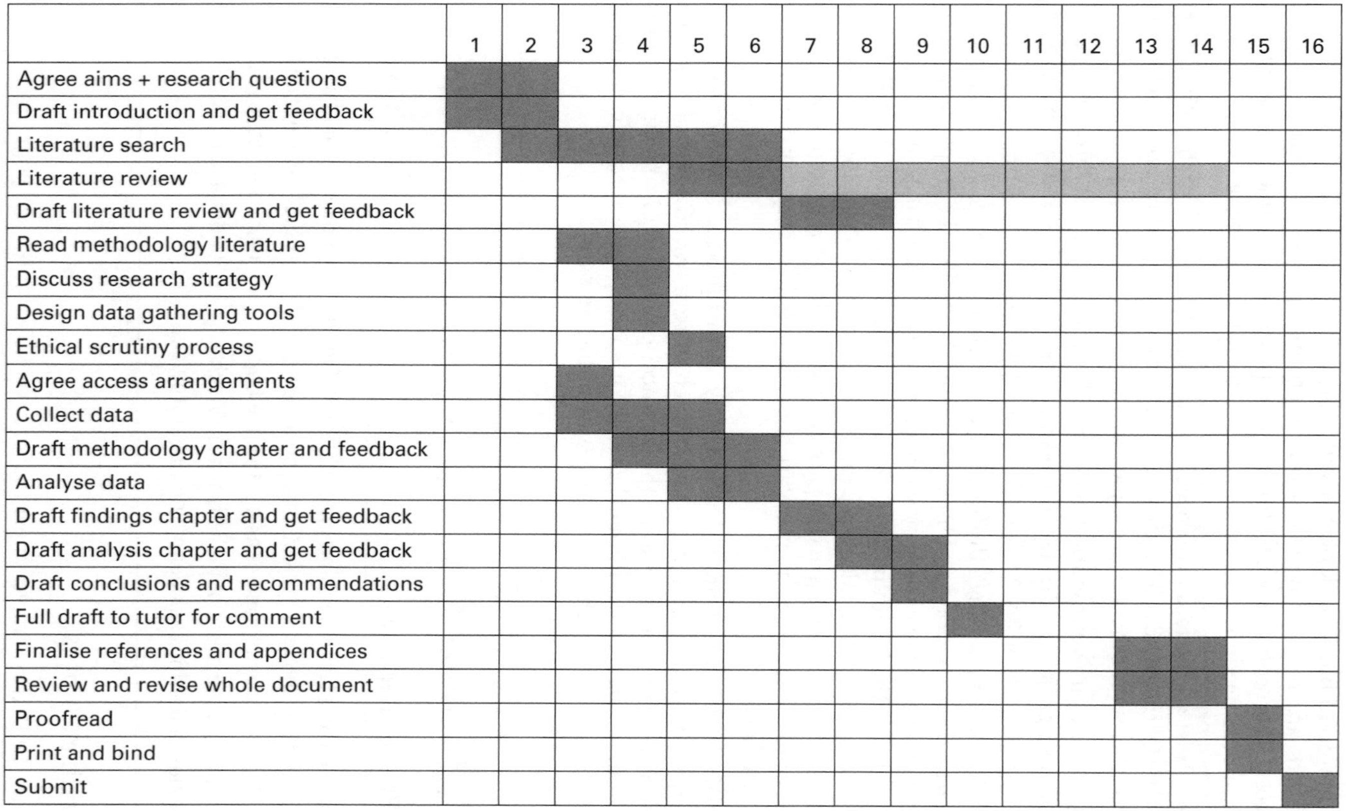

	1	2	3	4	5	6	7	8	9	10	11	12	13	14	15	16
Agree aims + research questions	■															
Draft introduction and get feedback		■														
Literature search			■													
Literature review					■	■	▩	▩	▩	▩	▩	▩	▩	▩		
Draft literature review and get feedback							■	■								
Read methodology literature				■												
Discuss research strategy				■												
Design data gathering tools					■											
Ethical scrutiny process			■													
Agree access arrangements					■											
Collect data						■										
Draft methodology chapter and feedback							■									
Analyse data								■								
Draft findings chapter and get feedback									■							
Draft analysis chapter and get feedback									■							
Draft conclusions and recommendations										■						
Full draft to tutor for comment										■						
Finalise references and appendices													■	■		
Review and revise whole document												■	■			
Proofread															■	
Print and bind															■	
Submit																■

identify where time can also be saved. A further issue not factored in to this illustrative example is the requirement to find out how long your tutor will need to give feedback on different sections or chapters of your project and when she or he may not be available owing to other commitments. Another issue you may have identified is that there is no scope in this Gantt chart for holidays or 'time off'. If your project plan extends over a public holiday, therefore, you will need to factor this in (as well as arrangements for other family celebrations).

Monitoring progress

As with all projects, it is important to 'go public' with the project plan in order that any significant errors of estimation can be discussed, any logistical oversights can be incorporated and those around you, at your study centre, your workplace (where appropriate) and your family and friends, are aware of your commitments. Progress meetings with your manager (where the project is organisationally based) and your project tutor or supervisor will also be an important way to gauge whether you need to revise the plan.

CHECKLIST

- An appropriate research topic will meet the different expectations of: the student; the employing organisation(s) involved; the study centre; and, where appropriate, relevant professional associations.

- Research projects need to be focused such that the aim and purpose of the project are clear and appropriate research questions or research objectives have been formulated.

- The choices you make about what to research and how you plan to undertake your research may be influenced by: your situation at work; your personal and professional interests and background and your world view about what counts as useful knowledge.

- Ethics should be considered throughout the research process.

- Methodology refers to the philosophical framework and foundation upon which research is conducted; the choices you make about these issues will have important implications for the research method or methods that you adopt.

- The positivist research tradition emphasises the importance of a scientific approach to gathering facts and analysing them in order to formulate generalisable conclusions.

- The interpretivist research tradition emphasises the subjective nature of human interactions and focus on the meanings and understandings of those involved in organisational processes.

- There are advantages and disadvantages to both positivist and interpretivist research traditions and some form of 'methodological pluralism' may be appropriate. Many organisationally based HR projects adopt a 'mixed methods' approach to some extent.

- Research design is the general plan that will identify how your research aim will be achieved and how your research questions or objectives will be addressed.

- Research tactics are the particular choices you will make about specific data gathering techniques you plan to employ.

- Four research strategies are popular with student HR researchers: cross-sectional research; case study research; action research or comparative research (or a combination).

- Implementing an HR research design involves gaining access at three levels to organisation(s), people and documents. In addition to 'physical access', support and acceptance is important for effective research to be undertaken.

- Effective project planning and management involves breaking the research process down into stages and tasks, scheduling those tasks; identifying dependencies and critical tasks and dates; and monitoring progress on a regular basis.

TEST YOURSELF

1 Exploring research philosophy involves:

   a Choosing between qualitative and quantitative methods.

   b Considering how we make sense of the world and the implications this has on research.

   c Analysing your primary and secondary data.

   d Identifying your research respondents.

2 Positivist researchers believe...

   a Research should be value-free, utilise a scientific method, and based on empirical observations.

   b Unexpected events and contextual differences prevent researchers from generalising about their research findings.

   c There is no substitute for an in-depth, reflexive understanding of the social world.

   d It is important to establish some positive research findings.

3 Researchers with an interpretivist perspective seek to...

   a Establish correlations between different variables.

   b Make sense of individual experiences.

   c Extrapolate findings across cross-cultural contexts.

   d Triangulate different data sources.

4 A challenge of case study based research is:

   a Findings cannot be generalised.

b   Individuals do not get their own voice.

c   It is suitable only for very large organisations.

d   It requires both qualitative and quantitative data.

5   Cross-cultural studies make use of:

a   A case study research strategy.

b   A comparative research strategy.

c   An appreciative inquiry approach.

d   A longitudinal research strategy.

6   Which of the following is a research strategy?

a   PESTLE analysis.

b   Semi-structured interview.

c   Positivism.

d   Action research.

7   Where a research project is seeking to obtain an accurate picture of something that occurred in a specific organisation, this approach is identified as:

a   Explanatory.

b   Exploratory.

c   Descriptive.

d   Comparative.

 Review Questions

Working in small groups (or within your learning set), each group member should review a recently submitted dissertation or project and share your reflections on the following questions (if you are not part of a group then tackling these questions individually is also possible):

1   What was the chosen topic? Did the author articulate how and why he or she made this choice?

2   Has the author used a research question or objectives? How clearly have they been articulated? Does there seem to be a preference for a hypothesis, a research aim or a principal research question in your study centre?

3   To what extent has the author discussed methodological decisions and what are the implications of this for what will be expected of you?

4   What research strategy has the author used? Does this seem logical for the issue investigated?

5   How did the author get access to the case study organisation(s)? Could you use this approach within your own study?

6   How did the author analyse data? How would you rate the depth of the analysis?

7   To what extent has the author considered ethical implications of the study?

8   Which of the chapters do you think will be the biggest challenge for your own project? What can you do to overcome these challenges?

Questions for reflection

As with Chapter 1 this part of the chapter enables you to reflect about your professional development and develop your skills and knowledge. This will enable you to build your confidence and credibility, track your learning, see your progress and demonstrate your achievements.

Taking stock

1   How much time is left until your project must be completed and submitted? What are likely to be the main stages of your project? How long will you have to complete each of them? How will you measure and record your progress? How much 'slack' is built into your timeline, and is this likely to be sufficient?

2   If you have not yet determined your project, identify three possible research ideas. For each of them write down three advantages/ disadvantages. Make sure you take account of the perspective of yourself, your study centre and (where appropriate) your employing organisation, in the advantages and disadvantages that you identify. Who might you also consult in the process of identifying a research idea?

3   Write a summary (no more than three sentences for each) of the four research strategies (cross-sectional research; case study; action research; comparative research). Which strategy is most attractive to you and why? What are the potential challenges of this approach?

Strengths and weaknesses

4   How clear are you about the aims of your potential project? What are the key concepts that you will need to explore? Who are the key authors in this field? Who might you discuss your research ideas with?

5   What will be the main challenges for you with regard to access to organisation(s), people

and documents? What skills and behaviours will you need to develop to overcome those challenges? What opportunities does your current situation afford for access to people and data?

Being a practitioner-researcher

6   How might your position in the organisation affect, and be affected by, the research project you plan to conduct? What are the implications of your role for the research strategy that you are considering? How will you ensure that you behave ethically for the duration of your project?

7   How might you be able to link your practitioner research with your professional development? To what extent will your position within your professional area or within your organisation affect the extent to which you can probe into and challenge your own (and others') assumptions about HR practices and processes?

Moving forward

Following your reflection it is important to develop an action plan to take your development forward:

• What are the key things you need to learn more about?

• Are there any specific skills you will need to develop?

• How will you achieve this?

• What resources or support do you need?

• What will you do to make sure you gain the maximum benefit from your supervision relationship?

• How will you seek and respond to feedback?

Useful Resources

Bryman, A (ed) (2015) *Doing Research in Organisations,* Routledge, London

Cameron, S and Price, D (2009) *Business Research Methods: A practical approach,* Kogan Page, London

CIPD (2018) *Research report: Part 2 - Indicators of Job Quality,* CIPD, London

Clough, P and Nutbrown, C (2012) *A Student's Guide to Methodology,* Sage, London

Coghlan, D and Brannick, T (2014) *Doing Action Research in Your Own Organisation,* 4th edn, Sage, London

Creswell, JW and Cresswell, JD (2018) *Research design: Qualitative, quantitative and mixed methods approaches,* 5th edn, Sage, London

Easterby-Smith, M, Thorpe, R, Jackson, PR and Jaspersen, LJ (2018) *Management and Business Research,* 6th edn, Sage, London

Eden, C and Huxham, C (1996) Action research for management research, *British Journal of Management,* **7** (1), pp 75–86

Fox, M, Martin, P, and Green, G (2007) *Doing Practitioner Research,* Sage, London

Gill, J and Johnson, P (2010) *Research Methods for Managers,* 4th edn, Sage, London

Maylor, H, Blackman, K and Huemann, M (2017) *Researching business and management,* 2nd edn, Palgrave, London

McNiff, J and Whitehead, J (2011) *All You Need to Know About Action Research,* Sage, London

Saunders, M and Lewis, P (2018) *Doing Research in Business and Management: An essential guide to planning your project,* 2nd edn, Pearson, London

Saunders, MNK, Lewis, P and Thornhill, A (2019) *Research Methods for Business Students,* 8th edn, Pearson, London

 References

Bell, E, Bryman, A and Harley, B (2019) *Business Research Methods,* 5th edn, Oxford University Press, Oxford

Biggam, J (2011) *Succeeding with Your Master's Dissertation,* Open University Press, Maidenhead

CIPD (2017) *Employer-supported volunteering guide,* CIPD, London

Cooperrider, D and Srivastva, S (2017) Appreciative Inquiry in Organizational Life, *Research in Organizational Change and Development,* Emerald Publishing Limited, pp 81–142

Cooperrider, D, Whitney, D, Stavros, J and Fry, R (2008) *Appreciative Inquiry Handbook for Leaders of Change,* Crown Custom Publishing, Brinswick

Farquhar, JD (2012) *Case study research for business,* Sage, London

Grant, S and Humphries, M (2006) Critical evaluation of appreciative inquiry: Bridging an apparent paradox, *Action Research,* **4** (4), pp 401–418

Hart, C (2013) *Doing Your Masters Dissertation,* Sage, London

Hart, RK, Conklin, TA and Allen, SJ (2008) Individual leader development: An appreciative inquiry approach, *Advances in Developing Human Resources,* **10** (5), pp 632–650

Lee, N and Lings, L (2008) *Doing Business Research: A guide to theory and practice,* Sage, London

Lewin, K (1946) Action research and minority problems, *Journal of Social Issues,* **2** (4), pp 34–46

Neuman, W (2012) *Basics of Social Research: Qualitative and quantitative approaches,* 3rd edn, Pearson Education, Harlow

Reason, P and Bradbury, A (2006) *Handbook of action research: Participative inquiry and practice,* 2nd edn, Sage, London

Remenyi, D, Williams, B, Money, A and Swartz, E (1998) *Doing Research in Business and Management: An introduction to process and method,* Sage, London

Robson, C and McCarten, K (2016) *Real World Research: A resource for social scientists and practitioner-researchers,* Wiley, Oxford

Tashakkori, A and Teddlie, C (2010) *SAGE handbook of mixed methods in social and behavioral research,* 2nd edn, Sage, London

Watkins, JM, Mohr, BJ and Kelly, R (2011) *Appreciative inquiry: Change at the speed of imagination,* 2nd edn, John Wiley & Sons Inc, California

Yin, RK (2017) *Case Study Research: Design and methods,* 6th edn, Sage Publications, Thousand Oaks, CA

03
Finding and reviewing HR literature and information sources

- Critical and analytical reading and writing

- The structure of the literature review

- Referencing and citations

- Summary checklist

- Test yourself, review and reflect questions

- Useful resources

How to use this chapter

A literature review is exactly what the name implies: it is a 're-view' of what has been written about your topic by researchers and experts in the area (Lee and Lings, 2008). Students undertaking research at any advanced level are expected to discuss existing literature and contemporary HR policy and practice relevant to the topic of their research. Many students struggle to find the time to keep up with their 'normal' coursework, let alone undertake the additional reading required for a research project. However, a good review of relevant information sources can add value to your research. This chapter focuses on helping you to work in a 'time effective' way to find and read appropriate materials and to construct a literature review section or chapter for your research report. The world wide web opens the door to resources created across the world; this chapter encourages you to think carefully about the reliability and validity of sources. Different parts of this chapter will be relevant at different stages of the research process. The early sections of the chapter introduce the main purposes and benefits of a good literature review. Next, different strategies for literature searching are discussed. If feedback on previous assignments has suggested that your work is too descriptive and/or not critical enough, then the ideas about reading and writing in a critical, analytical and evaluative way will also be helpful. The final parts of the chapter focus on how to structure the literature review and how to ensure that your work is appropriately referenced. Getting to grips with referencing at an early stage is critical. This may well be a section that you skim through at the beginning of your research process but come back to as you begin to draft your literature review chapter or section and then throughout the duration of your project.

 Case Example 3.1

From topic to literature review

Kim was an international student who wanted to explore the concept of work–life balance as this was something that her organisation had asked her to develop and implement a policy on. This review is a response to a recent employee survey where employees identified lack of work–life balance as one of their greatest concerns. Kim's current organisation is based in Singapore but has branches across South East Asia.

Discussion questions

1   What topics would Kim need to 'read up on' in order to make progress with this project?

2   What difficulties might she face?

3   What types of sources do you think Kim should look for?

Feedback notes

The first challenge for Kim was to identify an appropriate focus for her literature search and review. As a result of her previous employment she had collected quite a lot of information about work–life balance and she had downloaded a range of articles and case studies from practitioner journals. Kim had also been able to find some examples of policies from organisational websites. Up until now she had been unable to find any examples from companies in the same industry as her employer. However, these lacked sufficient depth and were written from either a tactical or over-generalised perspective and were too limited for a project linked to an academic qualification. While Kim had found some useful 'best practices' articles and links to a free toolkit, they were written for the UK market and therefore may not be directly relevant to the cultural context of Kim's organisation. To progress her literature review Kim had to search for literature relating to three relevant areas: work–life balance; HR practices in South East Asia; work–life balance policies.

Other challenges facing Kim were:

- Kim had a basic understanding of work–life balance and how it was linked to other areas of HR practice. This was based on some reading she had done for an earlier assignment as well as the new articles. Kim had found a large number of websites with information and some interesting articles from HR magazines; however, she was unsure whether they were suitable sources for a dissertation project.

- The library of the UK Business School where she was based was well resourced with regard to materials related to human resource management and within them a number of articles on work–life balance. So far Kim had not been able to locate many articles looking specifically at the South East Asian context that she wanted to focus on.

- The sources that Kim accessed about work–life balance outlined some frameworks; however, it was more difficult to identify specific theories that could be either tested or explored within her project.

Many practitioners are worried by the requirement to review the literature. The amount of written material around seems to be limitless and assessing its relevance for a potential project seems difficult. The range of different types of material is also extensive and you may feel unsure about what the 'best' types are. This chapter addresses some of these issues.

Why read, when to read and what to read

Why read?

A key feature of any project is to demonstrate an awareness of how your investigation fits into the wider context of theory, policy and practice in HR. The length and extent of the literature review varies depending on the nature of the qualification (intermediate or advanced level, undergraduate, postgraduate, etc) as well as the assessment criteria used by the people who will mark your work. However, for all projects an initial evaluation of what has been published about your topic and where there are areas of uncertainty or a 'gap' in knowledge as well as an assessment of how your findings 'fit' within the general realm of what has been published is a vital component. Your assessor will make a judgement on the type and quality of your sources, and most importantly how you have analysed them and taken forward your learning.

You may feel apprehensive about undertaking a literature review, perhaps because of anxious memories about previous assignments which have not been as successful as you would have liked but there are a range of benefits that you will discover once you start the reading process (Brown, 2006):

- **Getting ideas for your project.** You can gather background information on your topic and get a feel for the sort of perspectives on the subject that are relevant; particularly views that might not be expressed in an everyday work or managerial environment. In this way you can generate 'fresher' or more interesting ideas and you should be able to clarify your initial thoughts about the way forward with your research. Ensuring that there are relevant articles will also give you confidence that sufficient information exists to inform a successful research project.

- **Expand your understanding of your topic area.** If you have an idea about your research topic then your reading about the topic will provide you with useful information about the issues that you will need to consider in your research. You may identify relationships that you had previously not considered.

- **Find out how others have addressed and 'solved' similar research problems to the one you are taking forward.** As you read you can find out not just 'what is known' but also find out how others have researched a similar area or tackled a similar problem. When you make notes on your key articles, highlighting the methodology is also useful. This will help you as you come to think about the research methods that you might use.

- **Identify a way of making sense of your data.** Later in the project, when you have gathered some information, you will have to interpret and analyse it. In order to do this effectively you will need to know what the key issues, concepts and questions are, and how they relate to each other. You will also need to understand how the data were captured and processed and the appropriateness of the approaches.

- **Sources of secondary data.** Reading around the subject might also reveal relevant secondary data. These might include examples of other organisations in a similar position to yours or numerical data that are useful for comparative or benchmarking purposes. The internet provides straightforward access to a large amount of data including policies, strategies and performance indicators, all of which could be used within your work.

When to read

The reading process underpins the planning of your project so it is important not to delay. Start the reading process as soon as you have some ideas about your project topic. This will help you to establish the scope and decide what particular aspects are relevant for your project. It will also reassure you that there are sufficient 'quality' articles for you to construct a good review of the literature. Once you have come up with some initial research questions and/or objectives, further reading will help you to clarify the main issues and concepts. Use this knowledge to make sure you gather primary data that cover all the important aspects.

New sources of information are always becoming available and research into HR operates in a context of development and change and so the literature scanning and reading process will underpin the whole life cycle of your project. You might find it useful to set up new 'content alerts' from key journals, so that you don't miss any useful articles. Brown (2006) points out that, where the literature is concerned, researchers have to be like jugglers, keeping a number of balls in the air at the same time including:

- searching for relevant literature;
- reading the literature that you have found;
- starting to write the literature review section or chapter;
- defining and refining the research objectives or questions;
- planning how to undertake the research.

Depending on your research approach and methodology, your research participants might identify unexpected topics that may open up new areas to explore after you have collected your primary research data. This reiterates the importance of the literature review being work-in-progress for the duration of your project.

What to read

'The literature' is made up of published and unpublished materials often in the form of books, reports, papers and statistics (Hart, 2018). Although you will find yourself reading a range of materials from different sources it is important to ensure that what you read is credible and that you do not waste time and effort reading unattributed sources from internet sites where there is no information about the author and their credentials. Broadly speaking, you can divide the sources of information about what is already known (the literature) into four types:

- **Primary literature sources.** Most of these come from within the organisation(s) you are studying. They will mostly be unpublished, for example, internal reports and e-mail correspondence. If you are working in the organisation you will need to seek ethical clearance to use internal resources as part of your research project.

- **Grey literature.** Documents that are more widely available in the public domain but are not controlled by commercial publishers. Grey literature includes company reports, government publications, technical reports, newsletters, bulletins, white papers, position papers, fact sheets, conference proceedings, dissertations or research reports. Such sources are often produced by the government, academics (and students), professional associations, business and industry. Often, but not always, this has been generated with practitioners in mind.

- **Online-only sources.** The internet provides you with access to a vast wealth of sources, enabling you to access data and information generated from all over the world. These sources may have been written with multiple types of reader in mind and may not always be appropriate for use in academic work. It is sometimes difficult to establish the provenance of some of the information and the validity and reliability. Open-source sites include contributions from multiple stakeholders and can be particularly challenging to rate the usefulness. Your study centre may provide specific guidance about sources that are not appropriate and should not be used.

- **Published literature sources.** What is already known at a more general level about your topic will be found in more widely available published sources such as books, newspaper articles or reports, features and articles in journals. Some of these sources will be written with academic readers in mind and some might be categorised as 'teaching literature', which comprises both textbooks and published case studies (Lee and Lings, 2008).

Although the distinction between these four types of source is not always clear-cut (items from many of them may be available through the internet as well as in print, for example), this chapter focuses mostly on the issues involved in making effective use of published sources and the 'grey literature'. Obtaining and using primary sources are covered in Chapter 6.

Different types of literature

 Case Example 3.2

Different types of literature

Emma was a part-time student who worked in the HR team of an international hotel chain with large properties throughout the United Kingdom and Australia. She was aware from various internal meetings that 'employee engagement' was

something that the organisation was keen to improve upon, but to date this had not been explored in any depth. As the organisation is based in two countries, she knew that any work in this area would need to consider the needs and contexts of both. Emma therefore decided to explore the extent to which their employees in the United Kingdom and Australia were engaged. In order to make a start on the topic (and to create a 'pitch' to the organisation that would enable their consent for her work) Emma knew that she would need to do a lot of reading around the topic so that she could generate an appropriate title and set of research objectives for her project.

Discussion questions

1   In addition to the study of documents available within her organisation, what other sources would be useful to Emma in finding out more about employee engagement in the United Kingdom and Australia?

2   For each of the sources that you identify, list at least one advantage and one limitation of it as a basis for establishing what has been written about these issues.

3   Emma was a student with very limited discretionary time. How might she access the relevant parts of each source without having to read everything?

Feedback notes

You can probably identify a range of different sources that would help Emma to find out more about this broad topic. As 'employee engagement' is still a fairly new concept, which is perceived to be quite exciting, it is explored quite regularly in the written press, particularly when new research or measures are brought into the public domain. In addition, you might suggest Emma consults relevant **trade or professional journals** relating to the areas of business her organisation is involved with as well as those concerned with HRM, such as *People Management*. There is also likely to be some helpful material in a range of **books**. General HR textbooks will provide an introduction to employee engagement and make links to concepts such as job satisfaction, motivation and well-being. Specialist **fact sheets or resources or specialist websites** are also available; in the case of employee engagement, Emma may find it useful to look at sites such as the Global Employee Engagement Index (http://www.employee-engagement-index.com/).

Other important sources of information are relevant articles in **academic journals**, such as the *Human Resource Management Journal*, *The International Journal of Human Resource Management*, *Personnel Review*, *Human Resource Development International*, and *British Journal of Management*. While there are no specific Australian-focused HR journals, Emma might still find it useful to look at publications such as *Asian Pacific Journal of Human Resource Management* to look at how employee engagement has been explored in different cultures. These journals provide information that is the result of careful research and academic consideration and usually incorporate a thorough review of the literature. As a result these articles are useful, not only for their content, but also for the list of references they provide, some of which Emma could follow up for her project. Emma could also explore publications such as the *International Journal of Management Reviews*, which publishes reviews of literature in the areas of organisation and management studies. On the subject of employee engagement, Emma could review the analysis by Bailey *et al* (2017).

Professional bodies may also be a useful source of information in the form of reports, surveys and thought pieces. In Emma's case, she would have access to a range of employee engagement resources through the CIPD website (UK professional body) as well as the Australian equivalent – the Australian HR Institute (AHRI).

Finally, it is possible that another student based in the same study centre or workplace has undertaken a research project for their qualification and the **dissertation, thesis or project report** that they have produced may also be a useful source of information. Of course, care must be taken when reviewing the work of other students to ensure that accidental plagiarism does not occur. An overview of different types of sources (primary and secondary) is shown in Figure 3.1.

Assessing the value of different sources

When evaluating different sources of information, it is important to identify the main audience that they would have been written for and the style of communication that is appropriate for that readership (see Figure 3.2). Newspaper articles, online news items or blog postings, for example, are written to be of interest to a cross section of the general population and will often have been produced in line with an editorial policy or perspective. As a result issues will be covered very generally and the item may not explore all the possible interpretations of what is being described, they are unlikely to cite some of the methodological information that is important

Figure 3.1 Different types of literature

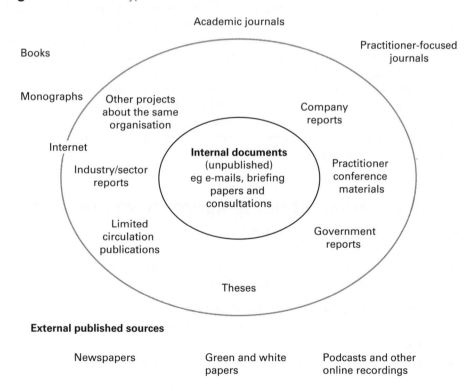

Figure 3.2 Different approaches underpinning different types of literature

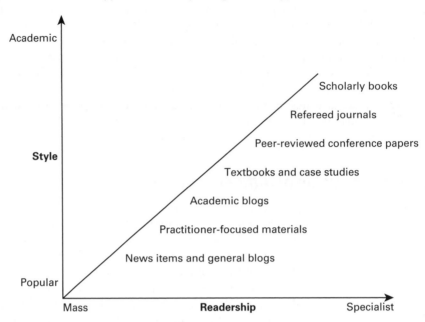

for research projects. Materials from trade or professional journals, while accessible in reading terms, also tend to reflect particular editorial beliefs and priorities and may focus on 'good news' stories or examples from organisations that benefit from large HR departments. Articles in refereed journal articles, by contrast, while providing a good framework of analysis and critique, may seem more remote from your particular interest, and reading them may be hard work as a result of the careful and evaluative style of writing that is necessary if a full consideration of a range of factors is to be included in the discussion. While harder work to read, however, they can provide a useful basis for critical and evaluative thinking to enable you to carry out research that probes and analyses the underlying causes and issues relevant to HR problems or opportunities.

Searching for and finding appropriate literature and information sources

When searching the literature there are some basic questions that need to be addressed when you start on the literature review and these include (Hart, 2018):

- What research and theory is there on my topic?
- Are there likely to be useful research articles from wider social science journals?
- What are the main theories and who are the main researchers in this area?

- What is the 'history' or chronological development of the issue or topic?
- What are the latest debates?

Once you have had a chance to answer these questions then it is important to address other questions that include:

- How has the topic or issue been defined? Which definition will guide your work and why?
- From which countries is the main evidence base? How will you address this within your work?
- What are the key concepts, variables or factors?
- Where do authors and researchers agree and disagree about the topic – what are the debates?
- What are the areas where not much is known in this area or where evidence is lacking? It is not essential that your work fills an existing gap; however, if you are able to do so, this provides a useful opportunity.
- What methodologies and research methods are used?

The volume of available information made possible with the development of digital systems can make the identification of relevant material seem overwhelmingly difficult and an effective literature **search and selection** process is essential. Students in different parts of the world tend to vary in the approach they prefer to use when looking for literature. In some countries or cultures students strongly favour and value information from books and are prepared to invest considerable time and money in libraries or online bookshops looking for as many books on the topic area as possible. A problem here is that the books themselves can vary in quality and may not provide sufficient depth in what they cover. Students from other countries, cultures or educational backgrounds head straight for a general internet search engine to try to find papers and articles, as well as web pages, which deal with their topic. Their difficulty is that they are often quickly overwhelmed with the volume of material that they find and they do not know how to select what will be most useful.

Although the temptation(s) to rush either to dedicated books or to internet search engines can be powerful, a more productive, focused and systematic way to start a literature search for an academic research project is to assess the range of resources of your academic library either by a personal 'physical' visit or through an electronic 'virtual' visit. For student projects the academic library is a more focused place to start. A keyword search of the library catalogue will indicate readily available sources such as: print books and journals; e-books and electronic journals; student dissertations and PhD or MPhil theses. Once you have found the location of some useful looking materials you can identify the main sources that they refer to and see if they are readily available (or can be accessed through the inter-library loan process that your library will be part of). For physical (print) resources all libraries utilise the same 'classmarking' and cataloguing system and Table 3.1 indicates some of the main HRM related classmarks. If you follow the numbering system shown on the shelves of the library and on the spines of the books you will find what you are looking for.

Table 3.1 Library classmarks for HRM subject areas

Subject Area	Classmark	Subject Area	Classmark
Organisation behaviour	302.35 658.402	HRM (General)	658.3
Industrial relations/labour economics	331	Recruitment and selection	658.311
Flexible working	331.257	HR development / training	658.3124
UK employment/labour law	344.4101	Performance appraisal	658.3125
Employee relations	658.315	Reward management	658.32
Cross-cultural management	658.049	Research methods for HRM	658.30072
Coaching and mentoring for business	658.3124	Executive management	658.4
Work and family	306.85	Managing change	658.406

Literature searching: starting from books and other projects

 Activity 3.1

First steps in finding literature

Imagine that you have decided to undertake research into the general area of 'graduate employability'. Undertake a keyword search of your library's catalogue and identify three to four books that are relevant to this subject. Study the 'Further Reading', 'Bibliography' or 'References' sections of those books (or the most relevant chapters) and identify some of the main authors or sources of information that they have used.

1 Produce a list of five to six possibly relevant sources of information.

2 Explain why it might be necessary to read some of these articles and books, rather than relying on the coverage about them in the books where they were cited.

3 Reflect on your preferred learning style; how will you take this into account when planning and carrying out your review of the literature?

Feedback notes

If you have undertaken this activity (which you could do for any topic) and undertaken a first-level 'browse' of the catalogue you might have come across sources such as these:

Tomlinson, M and Holmes, L (eds) (2017) *Graduate Employability in Context: Theory, research and debate,* Palgrave Macmillan, London

Becket, N and Kemp, P (2006) *Enhancing Graduate Employability in Business and Management, Hospitality, Leisure Support and Tourism,* Threshold, Newbury

CIPD (2017) *The Graduate Employment Gap: Expectations versus reality,* CIPD, London

Trought, F (2017) *Brilliant Employability Skills: How to stand out from the crowd in the graduate job market,* Pearson Education, New York

Neugebauer, J and Evans-Brain, J (2017) *Employability: Making the most out of your career development,* Sage, London

A review of the sources that these authors have made use of will enable you to take the next step towards identifying relevant literature and it is likely that they will make reference to a variety of articles, books and websites that reflect the different preferences of those authors. For this topic these might include:

Branine, M (2008) Graduate recruitment and selection in the UK, *Career Development International,* **13** (6), pp 497–513

Cai, Y (2012) Graduate employability: A conceptual framework for understanding employers' perceptions, *Higher Education,* **65** (4), pp 457–69

Collet, C, Hine, D and Plessis, K (2015) Employability skills: Perspectives from a knowledge-intensive industry, *Education + Training,* **57** (5), pp 532–59

Gbadasomi, G, Evans, C, Richardson, M and Ridolfo, M (2015) Employability and students' part-time work in the UK: Does self-efficacy and career aspiration matter? *British Educational Research Journal,* **41** (6), pp 1086–1107

Jackson, D (2015) Employability skill development in work integrated learning: Barriers and best practice, *Studies in Higher Education,* **40** (2), pp 350–67

McCracken, M, Currie, D and Harrison, J (2015) Understanding graduate recruitment, development and retention for the enhancement of talent management: Sharpening 'the edge' of graduate talent, *The International Journal of Human Resource Management,* **27** (22), pp 2727–52

Wilton, N (2011) Do employability skills really matter in the UK graduate labour market? The case of business and management graduates, *Work, Employment & Society,* **25** (1), pp 85–100

These initial sources will provide you with an overview of the main issues in the topic you will need to think about. When you are short of time there is a big temptation not to bother with this process and to 'just' read the information in a few textbooks on the topic you are interested in. However, there are potential dangers with this 'short cut'. Textbook authors and business report writers have to briefly summarise and describe a wide range of material in a generalised way; there may also be a long lead time in the publishing of the book so the subject area may have moved on. In a topic such as graduate employability, there have been many developments over the last five years that may have not been explored within the texts. As a result there is limited scope for a deeper level of examination. You may be tempted to refer to the sources that the textbook authors have used without reading them for yourself but you will potentially miss many important features and perspectives on your topic and it is likely your work would be too descriptive. In addition, too many 'derivative sources' will lead to a disappointing mark for the literature review section or chapter of your research report.

Finding other sources of information: clarifying what resources are available

As you continue with your literature search, find out where information might be most easily available. The main options are listed below:

- **University or college library.** The benefits of using the library have already been indicated and you have paid for the facilities as part of your course fee so it makes sense to use them. Find out what types of books, journals and other collections are held in the main library and what electronic resources are available to you (ask about database facilities, e-books and reference tools). Prepare to be pleasantly surprised. Clarify what user-names and passwords you will need to access material off-site and whether there are time or download restrictions over e-books. Make sure you know how to reserve copies of books, should they not be immediately available.

- **Other libraries and inter-library loan facilities.** Find out if your study centre has any reciprocal arrangements that enable you to use the resources of libraries of other campuses or institutions. Most libraries operate an inter-library loan (ILL) system for students undertaking projects so that the institution can obtain a copy of a book or article from elsewhere for a short period of time (and at a price). Find out in advance what your entitlement might be to the ILL facility (often students have a fixed allocation of ILLs) and what is the usual time period for the library to process and receive resources coming from other locations.

- **Access to professional libraries.** Many HR practitioners, when surveying the literature, will want to make use of a specialised library collection such as that provided for members by the CIPD or the Chartered Institute of Management.

- **Remote access to electronic resources.** All libraries now have facilities enabling registered users to gain electronic access to the full text of materials or to abstracts, summaries or other listings. Once you know how to do this it is easily achieved from within the library itself. It is also possible to access the resources from a PC outside of the institution provided that you can prove you are an academic user from a study centre that is registered with the provider. Universities in the United Kingdom purchase their electronic resources from a number of different publishers who link to an International Access Management System called 'Shibboleth' although often the publishers use other names such as: Athens/Institution Login, Institutional Login/Access, Federated Login, or Academic Sign-in. When you come to a point where you are asked for a password it is important to look for the (often small) link to the institutional login page and do not be tempted with other (often more prominent) user-name and password boxes, which will usually charge you a fee for access to materials.

- **Electronic searching.** Electronic search engines are vital ways of finding further sources of information for projects. There is a range of options, from general searches on the internet as a whole, to more specialised searches utilising academic 'information gateways'. The temptation to start 'broad' and then narrow down the focus of a search is high but this can be very time-consuming, and if time is precious it is better to start with the more specialised search processes and then broaden the search only if you feel you need further information.

Systematic literature search

A systematic and transparent literature search provides the basis for a good literature review and enables your supervisor or tutor to provide effective advice and guidance. Achieving a transparent process requires you to think ahead about how you will record what you find and to cross-reference items as appropriate (Quinton and Smallbone, 2011). The seven-step model shown in Figure 3.3 should provide a basis for a systematic search process:

1   **Identify/generate keywords.** This part of the process is where you think about the topic and those areas in the literature that might be useful. It is worth consulting dictionaries and encyclopaedias at this stage to develop a list of keywords that you can use to inform your search. Aim for 6 to 10 keywords that you can enter in different combinations or 'strings'. Once you find a couple of good journal articles, you can also review the keywords that are provided within their abstracts.

2   **Define the limits (parameters).** A search with the keyword 'performance' is likely to bring a multitude of extracts relating to financial performance and accountancy rather than anything to do with HR. It is important to include the terms 'HR' or 'human resources' within your combination of keywords. Also establish whether you wish to limit your search to sources that are from the United Kingdom and from a specific time period.

Figure 3.3 Seven steps to an electronic literature search

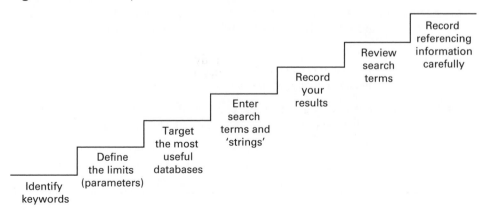

3 **Target the most useful databases.** Find out which electronic databases and electronic journal collections are available to you. Get advice from your tutor on the best databases for your topic. Your library will have information on how to operate these and will also tell you what passwords are required. If you can start the search process on the library premises you can get help from a librarian if you experience any initial problems. Once you know what to do you may prefer to work remotely. Table 3.2 shows a selection of useful databases for HR research purposes. Your centre librarian will be able to advise you if you could benefit from access to any market or sector-specific databases. For example, 'Retail Analysis' provides in-depth company, sector and country reports for the retail sector.

Table 3.2 Some useful databases for HR research

Full Text Databases	Comments
Business Source Premier	This is a full text database with over 8,000 journals, which covers management and international business as well as economics, finance and accounting.
EBSCO	In the UK, the EBSCO database is often branded as 'Business Source Premier, Business Source Complete and Business Source Elite. It is a good all-round database. It holds thousands of online resources including academic journals, periodicals, trade publications, as well as industry and company profiles. As it is so extensive it is important to use 'search limiters' to avoid being overwhelmed with inappropriate 'hits'. If you are a CIPD member you also have access to a wealth of resources via their EBSCO platform, which allows you to view resources from more than 200 journals and magazines.
ABI/INFORM (Proquest)	This database includes full-text journals as well as business press and trade publications, dissertations, conference proceedings and market reports. The focus is on general business and management areas.
Emerald Management	This includes all the journals provided by MCB Press. Abstracts and/or full text articles (depending on the level of subscription) are available and MCB publications contain a fair range of HR related journals.
Euromonitor	An online tool that monitors industry trends and provides strategic analysis. This can be useful when you are exploring the background and context of your selected organisation(s).
Ingenta Connect	This is a general database of papers from a number of publishers, including both academic and practitioner-focused publications.
ISI Web of Knowledge for UK Education	This database provides a route to all the Thomson Scientific products subscribed to by an institution. In addition a range of conference proceedings and papers are held on the database.

(*continued*)

Table 3.2 (Continued)

Full Text Databases	Comments
JSTOR	This is a not-for-profit service that gives access to a digital archive of more than 1,000 academic journals and other scholarly content.
Nexis	This provides access to resources such as company news, financial data and access to national and international newspapers.
Sage Journals Online	This provides a link to Sage products. Sage publishes some good quality journals in business, humanities and social sciences as well as science, technology and medicine. Sage is a particularly good place to look for resources about research methods.
Science Direct	This database, containing articles and e-books published by Elsevier, focuses mostly on the physical sciences but also contains an extensive range of social science (including business and management) titles and sources.
Google Scholar	As part of the Google service, Google Scholar aims to provide an avenue for a broad search for scholarly literature. The database contains a wide range of disciplines and sources including peer-reviewed papers, theses, books, abstracts and articles, from academic publishers, professional societies, preprint repositories, universities and other scholarly organisations. For those students who are 'addicted to Google', Google Scholar may feel like a more familiar way forward. If you are logged onto a computer using your centre's credentials you can make best use out of Google Scholar as you should be able to download and read the full text of your chosen articles directly from the site. You may need guidance from library or IT staff at your centre to confirm how remote access works (for example, through an application such as Citrix Receiver).

4 **Enter search terms and strings.** This is where you use your keywords and 'search strings' to combine your keywords making use of terms such as 'AND', 'OR' and 'NOT'. Also make use of the * (truncation) tool to use word stems to help you find different, but relevant words. *Develop**, for example, should help you select material with 'development', 'developing' and 'developmental'. In addition the ? wild card term will enable the search to include different forms of the same word; for example, *human resourc** should result in a selection of articles with *human resource* and *human resources* in the text and *organi?ation* will select *organization* and *organisation*. Different levels of subscription, resulting in different levels of access to materials, are taken by different libraries. Therefore, to avoid frustration make sure you only choose to know about 'subscribed titles' or 'subscribed content'.

5 **Record your results.** This stage involves making a note of the sources that meet your search criteria. Potential criteria that you may wish to apply include:

- must be published after (say) 2012;
- must be focused on (say) SMEs;
- must be written in English;
- must be full text.

It is a good policy to keep a record of the searches you have undertaken and the results so that you can discuss it with your supervisor who may be able to provide guidance on alternative search strings you may want to try. In addition you can use the results to provide a brief outline of your search process in an early part of your literature review chapter or section. Table 3.3 shows the results of a journal paper search undertaken from two well-known databases. The criteria for the search were:

EBSCO	Emerald
Full text available	Journal article
References available	Published between 2012 and 2019
Peer reviewed articles	
Published between 2010 and 2019	

Table 3.3 Example of search results from two databases

Keywords/string	EBSCO Business Source Complete number found	Emerald Management number found
Recruitment	859	199
Selection	6423	911
Recruitment and selection India	3	1
Recruitment and selection and India and SME	0	1

 Activity 3.2

Refining your selection criteria

Imagine that you wish to conduct research into talent management in Indian SMEs and you have undertaken this initial search.

1 What issues are raised by the different pattern of 'returns' to your search terms?

2 How might your search be further refined?

Feedback notes

You may have highlighted the difference in 'return numbers' for these two databases and you probably noted the difference it makes to search for 'full-text available' – it is possible that your university might not have access to the full text of all the papers in the Emerald database. If you investigate the Emerald database you will also notice that you can specify different types of article (case study, conceptual paper, general review, literature review, research paper, technical paper, viewpoint). The definition of the different types of article can be located in the instructions to authors on each of the journals' web pages. Depending on the focus of your search you may choose to select one or other of these. As you scan the abstracts generated by the EBSCO search you might notice that some of them are concerned with research or practice in different regions of the world so you might also decide to apply regional selection criteria.

A systematic process such as this will enable you to reduce the volume of sources to a level that you can manage and which represents information of appropriate quality. It is important to keep a record of your activities in case your study centre requests to view your 'working papers' and to demonstrate your progress.

6 **Review search terms.** Before you draw the line on your initial search process it is worth reviewing your search terms. Have you missed out any relevant words that might generate important literature sources or are your result rates still too high? This is an area to discuss with your supervisor. You could also have another look at the keywords used in some of the main articles that you have identified.

7 **Record referencing information carefully.** Effective electronic record-keeping is essential for student researchers who do not have time to waste towards the end of the project when they have to compile their list of references and discover they have mislaid some of the information they need. A number of software applications can help you store and organise the information you gather from your literature search and, once you start writing your review, to integrate your references into your Word documents and create a list of references. Commonly used software (check if you can access these for no charge through your study centre) include: EndNote, Reference Manager and RefWorks, and there are also free reference management tools on the web, such as Zotero and Mendeley. Your use of specialist software may be dependent on: a) how much time you have able to learn how to use it; and b) how easily you adapt to using new programs. If time is tight you can create a simple table in Word or Excel.

If your search generates a number of articles that you wish to print, it might be more effective either to save them to a USB, save them to an online dropbox or to e-mail them to a more suitable address from which you can print them at a more convenient time.

If your search generates articles for which the full text is not available electronically, it is likely that you can obtain a hard copy, either through your own library or from another library. If you are a CIPD member, you could also check whether it is available via the resources section of the CIPD website.

Other internet sources

Having searched the journals, you may feel that there might be other resources that would be useful. There are many millions of documents about a variety of subjects, which can be found on the internet. Every medium in digital form can be stored on the internet: text, sound, photographs, cartoons, video images and so on. It is possible that the most relevant sources of electronically stored information can be accessed through specialist HR gateways such as those shown in Table 3.4.

Sources of information derived from official publications can be found from sites such as those in Table 3.5 and sources of information about companies are indicated in Table 3.6. If you are an international student wishing to obtain information for a specific country then the sites in Table 3.7 may be helpful and some sites relevant to international HRM are included as Table 3.8.

If your enquiry requires information about more than one country then you can get country information from sites like those in Table 3.7.

This brief overview of potential sources of information indicates that a wide range of material is available. In order to obtain a suitable breadth of knowledge in an applied discipline area such as HRM, your literature search and review may extend across a range of information types (Quinton and Smallbone, 2011):

- Media sources – newspapers and news pages; general periodicals (eg *The Economist*).

Table 3.4 Some useful HR websites and electronic gateways

Gateway	URL
Chartered Institute of Personnel and Development	http://www.cipd.co.uk
HRM: The Journal	**http://www.hrmthejournal.com/**
biz/ed – Human Resources Management	http://www.bized.co.uk/learn/business/hrm/index.htm
HRM Guide Network – Human Resources	**http://www.hrmguide.net/buscon4.htm**
Work Foundation – part of Lancaster University	**http://www.theworkfoundation.com**
Society for Human Resource Management (USA organisation)	**http://www.shrm.org/Pages/default.aspx**
Workplace Innovation Europe Network	http://www.ukwon.net/
Institute for Employment Studies	**http://www.employment-studies.co.uk/main/index.php**
University Forum for Human Resource Development (UFHRD)	**http://www.ufhrd.co.uk**

Table 3.5 Some sites for sources of information from official publications

Name	URL
GOV.UK	http://**www.gov.uk/government/publications**
UK Legislation Service	**http://www.legislation.gov.uk/**
UK National Archives	http://www.nationalarchives.gov.uk/information-management/
The British Library	**https://www.bl.uk/catalogues-and-collections**
ACAS (Advisory, Conciliation and Arbitration Service)	**http://www.acas.org.uk/index.aspx?articleid=1461**

Table 3.6 Sources of information about companies

Name	Notes	URL
CAROL	Corporate online service with annual reports covering UK, Europe and Asia	http://www.annualreports.com/
Companies House	Basic information available via Free Company Information link	http://www.companieshouse.gov.uk/
Corporate Information	Over 3 million company profiles, research links searches through search engines	**http://www.corporateinformation.com/Country-Industry-Research-Links.aspx**
Financial Times (pay for access)	Key financial data for 20,000 limited companies worldwide	http://**www.ft.com**
Fortune 500	Information on companies in the 'big 500'	**http://fortune.com/global500/list/**
FTSE International	Provides access to 'headline' information on FTSE indices and member companies	**https://www.ftse.com/Analytics/company-reports/search**

Table 3.7 Sites providing country information

Name	Notes	URL
CIA World Factbook	Country profiles that provide geographical and government information as well as key economic indicators	https://www.cia.gov/library/publications/the-world-factbook/index.html
IMF country reports	Full-text access to country reports	https://www.imf.org/external/country/index.htm

(*continued*)

Table 3.7 (Continued)

Name	Notes	URL
International Monetary Fund	IMF statistics and articles, including exchange rates and economic indicators for countries of the world	http://www.imf.org/
Mondaq Business Briefing	Access to world business news pages	http://www.mondaq.com

Table 3.8 International HRM sites

World Federation of Personnel Management Associations	http://www.wfpma.com
American Society for Training and Development	http://www.asd.org
International Federation of Training and Development Organisations	http://www.iftdo.net/
Eurofound, The European Foundation for the Improvement of Living and Working Conditions	http://www.eurofound.europa.eu/

- Practitioner sources – HRM practitioner journals (eg *People Management*); trade journals for your business sector.
- Government sources – eg national statistics; labour market figures, etc.
- Commercial sources – eg commercially published market or labour market reports.
- Company sources – eg publicly available reports, statements, press releases, web pages, etc.
- Academic sources – books and articles written by academics in the higher education sector.

Detective work – cited reference searching

With so many sources available it is possible to feel overwhelmed with the volume of material and selecting the most appropriate sources is important. A good strategy is to try to identify two or three of the most important authors in your chosen topic area. The chances are that subsequent researchers will have made use of their work and so you can follow the development of knowledge that has developed over time by reading the articles that have cited them. In this way you will be able to assess how the 'big ideas' in your topic area have been utilised by other authors and researchers. A useful tool by which you can do this is a 'cited reference search'.

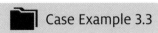 Case Example 3.3

Searching for a focus

Haya was a distance-learning student who wished to undertake research into green HR management but her supervisor was concerned that this topic was too broad and that her research would lack focus. During the course of her initial literature search Haya used Google Scholar and found an article by Renwick *et al* (2016) in the *International Journal of HRM,* which explored contemporary developments in green HRM scholarship, and decided to follow the cited sources link to see which further resources had cited this book. As she scrolled down the list she reviewed the titles of the various papers and books and her attention was caught by a paper: Obeidat *et al* (2018) Leveraging 'green' Human Resource practices to enable environmental and organizational

performance: Evidence from the Qatari Oil and Gas Industry. This gave her an idea as through her LinkedIn network she had connections with organisations in the United Arab Emirates who may be interested in taking part in this research. As a cursory search showed that green HR is still a fairly new field of research it became clear that she might need to look at a wider depth of literature.

Discussion questions

1   If you were Haya's supervisor what advice would you give her at this point?

2   What are the advantages and disadvantages of citation searching undertaken in this way?

Feedback notes

In this instance Haya's supervisor was tempted to advise that she find a different topic with a stronger basis in the published literature. However, Haya and her supervisor soon realised that the gap in the literature might be a positive advantage as this might be an area where Haya could make a contribution. In addition, Haya was able to follow up the references in the paper she had found and she also undertook literature searches relating to HR practices in the UAE and green HR (as separate issues), which provided a robust way forward for her research.

The advantages of the Google Scholar cited reference facility is that it can provide you with an indication of how influential a source or an author may be. Items with a high number of other citations may well be worth following up. The academic database 'Web of Knowledge', which your study centre may also subscribe to, has a similar facility whereby you can see how many subsequent authors have cited the publication and you can follow the links to read their items. Remember that newly published items will not have had the chance to be cited much so don't discount them. Also, the number of citations does not necessarily reflect the quality of the source.

Evaluating your sources

Once you have explored a few search engines, gateways and academic databases you may feel that you have amassed so many sources that there is no time to read them all properly. A great benefit of internet-based sources is their volume and variety. However, there is also no quality assurance built into the world wide web and there are as many out-of-date and poor-quality documents as there are useful and appropriate sources of information. Key questions to ask when you are evaluating web-based documents (Dochartaigh, 2007; Quinton & Smallbone, 2011) are:

- Is there any indication of the date when the document / web page was written? How current is the information? Is it open-source?
- When was the information last updated or revised? By whom?
- Is the author, publisher or organisation responsible for the source clearly identifiable? If so, what are their credentials? What are their affiliations or biases?
- Is the work sponsored or funded by an organisation, group or individual? If yes, what are the implications of this for the findings?
- Are the sources used in the document clearly listed?
- If empirical research has been undertaken, is there clear information on the methodology?
- Has the source been through an editorial process? If so – by whom?
- Are there any published critiques on the source? Have academic researchers referenced this material in their published work?
- How closely related is advertising or marketing with the information that is presented?

Careful selection and evaluation of your sources is required and Table 3.9 provides some tips on the potential value of different forms of web-based documents.

Reading the literature and making notes

Finding the literature is just the start and you may, like many other HR students, begin to feel overwhelmed by the prospect of reading and making notes on all your sources. For this reason it is important to develop effective reading and note-taking processes.

Just-in-time reading and note-taking

Time is your most precious resource when you are undertaking a research project; there is never enough of it and it is important that the reading and note-taking process is undertaken speedily, but effectively. When you are reading material for your research project there are different approaches you can take to suit different requirements (Brown, 2006):

Table 3.9 A hierarchy of web-based resources for research students

Relevance	Document/web-page type	Purpose	Comments
Low	Entertainment sites	Marketing or download purposes	Hard to see any value for HR research.
	Personal web pages/blogs/ wikis (non-experts)	Various	Find out the background of the originator – may provide an insight into a feature of HR that you had not thought of before. Sites like Wikipedia and Businessballs.com fall into this category. Before you go ahead and accept all their content you must validate the information you find there using other sources where you know the credentials of the originator of the materials.
	Business and marketing pages	Promote a company or a product	Will present a biased view and selected information but may be useful if you also supplement with information from other sources.
	Advocacy sites	To promote a particular view on an issue	Published by pressure groups, political parties, NGOs, action groups, etc. May reflect the opinion of only a small minority. Information needs to be assessed against data from other sources.
	Trade press pages	Specialise in information about one business sector or trade	Potentially helpful information but reliant on company briefings and press releases for much of the content. Unlikely to be critical or controversial. Supplement with other sources of information.
	Personal web pages/blogs (experts)	Various	It is becoming more common for academics to share their work via their online pages. There may be a combination of personal thoughts and academic papers so readers will need to be clear about the status of information that they wish to reproduce.
	News pages	Purpose is to 'sell' news	Will be subject to editorial control, which may well be one-sided. Each news organisation will take its own 'slant' and may have different political affiliations that influence their reporting. Ensure you look in several different sites to assess how 'your' issue is covered.

(continued)

Table 3.9 (Continued)

Relevance	Document/web-page type	Purpose	Comments
	Official documents/pages	To provide a news management service and overview data that will attract visitors (investors, tourists, etc)	Can be a rich source of information but may well be one-sided. It may be worth looking in less-prominent parts of websites to find the basis for the data. Try to get back to the 'raw data' behind the announcements in government departments' pages.
High	Academic documents	To 'share knowledge' with other academics and to achieve 'research output' points in academic esteem processes	Quality can vary. Find out the basis for publication if you can: a 'double blind reviewed' journal article will be of higher quality than a 'working paper', for example. Domain names such as .ac or .edu indicate an academic background for the source.

(Dochartaigh, 2007; Quinton and Smallbone, 2011)

- Skim-read – look quickly through the list of contents, headings, introduction and conclusions. If you are looking at a journal article then start with the abstract. Skimming is a good way to get familiar with something on a superficial level. You can do this to check whether the publication is relevant or has the information that you need.

- Scan – this involves a quick search for something specific – a title or keyword. Scanning involves ignoring everything except what you are looking for. This is easier using electronic copies than the printed versions as you can use the 'find' function in most documents and pages.

- Reading to understand – studying the material in detail to absorb the major facts and ideas that are expressed. You may need to read the section(s) more than once and make notes to summarise what you have learned.

Table 3.10 indicates some ideas that may help you to undertake just-in-time reading. Your aim is to be able to undertake an initial reading of any source in just 5 to 10 minutes, in order to identify those sources that will need more careful attention.

Table 3.10 Undertaking just-in-time reading

Strategy	Notes
Decide on your note-taking and filing system in advance	Options include (and preferences vary) for systems such as: - card index system; - word processed notes; - sticky notes; - A4 paper; - collection of photocopies.
Make an accurate note of the author, title and other details about the source	See Tables 3.12 and 3.13 for information on how to reference your work. If you are going to make use of bibliographic referencing software then now is the time to start. Also make a note of where you have saved the article (eg is it saved as a PDF on your laptop?) in case you want to go back to find a direct quote.
If a book – 'speed-read' the introduction and concluding chapter and note down the main points	Read from the author's perspective – don't reject it because it is not the approach you instinctively prefer. If the book is an 'edited by' you may want to look at more than one chapter.
If an article – look for the abstract or executive summary as well as for the conclusion; read them quickly and note down the main points	as above If these sections highlight particularly relevant or interesting issues, you may want to look at one or more additional 'sections'.

(continued)

Table 3.10 (Continued)

Strategy	Notes
If a book or report – look for the contents page and index	Each chapter or section should have an introduction or conclusion so start there each time and note down the main points made.
Speed-read the text, summarising the main text and highlighting any ideas that might be useful to you	Well-written material will highlight key points in the first and/or last paragraphs of each section. The first or last sentences of each paragraph are likely to be the most useful. Use this to speed up your reading. You can also use the 'find' function to look for your keywords.
Make notes on the method as well as the subject	As well as the findings from other research, record the methods used (eg interviews, observation, telephone survey) and where the data came from (the sample) and the context of the article: eg in which country was it carried out?
Identify whether this is a seminal piece of work	Make a note of whether this article is one that has been referred to by many other authors. Also, note what the article notes as its 'original contribution' to knowledge.
Make a clear note of useful quotations	Copy out the quote (or highlight if it is a photocopy) but note down the page number it is on. You will need this to reference the quote when you submit your work.
Note down any other sources that you need to follow up	Make full notes of the author, title, publisher and date. Also, prioritise follow-up sources – you may not have time to find all of them.
Be prepared to read important sources more thoroughly	Make a clear note of the details of all your sources so that you can find and retrieve the ones you need to read more thoroughly without wasting precious time.

Evaluation and analysis

As you undertake your reading, it is helpful to keep in mind the main purposes of the literature review (Gill and Johnson, 2010; Oliver, 2012), which your notes will help you with. These are shown as Figure 3.4:

- **Examining the context.** If you are undertaking a project in an organisation that you know well, it is important to understand the influences on the topic you are investigating beyond its immediate priorities. The literature review will help you understand and explain why your project is worthwhile within HR more generally.

Figure 3.4 Main purposes of the literature review

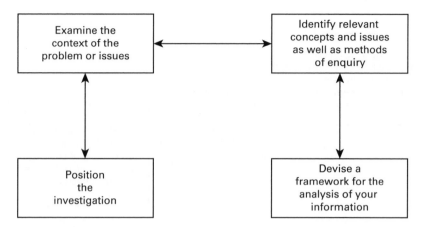

- **Identify relevant concepts, issues and methods.** This provides a basis from which to know what data to look for in relation to your investigation.

- **Devise a framework for the analysis of your data.** Obtaining data is the easy part. Knowing how to analyse and interpret it is much harder. Reviewing the literature will help you to devise a framework for the interpretation of the facts that you gather. For some topics, there may be established frameworks that you wish to try to adapt, for others you may wish to develop your own.

- **Position the investigation.** The literature review can demonstrate how your research can add value in a practical way, in terms of the organisation or business sector, as well as in an academic way, through considering important issues in a different way.

Once you start reading and making notes, you have to consider the information you have found in an analytical way. One way to start this process is to **filter and categorise** the material that you have read and Figure 3.5 provides some ideas about how to go about this.

Reading for a research project involves going further than 'soaking up' and recording facts; the aim is to become an analyst, an evaluator and a constructive critic. Filtering and categorising your literature sources is the first step to becoming an analyst. Create a Word document with a preliminary contents page showing your intended sequence; alternatively if you are a more visual learner you might find sticky notes or a colourful diagram useful to capture your thinking. It is likely that you will rethink some of these as you carry on with the project and you can make amendments as you go. A further benefit of the process is that once you come to start writing your literature review you can tackle one category at a time and the task will not seem too daunting.

You will also avoid the accusation of writing too descriptively if, when you are making notes on what you read, you try to be active in assessing the value of the ideas presented to you; their strengths as well as their weaknesses. These issues are addressed in Activity 3.3.

Figure 3.5 Filtering and categorising what you have read

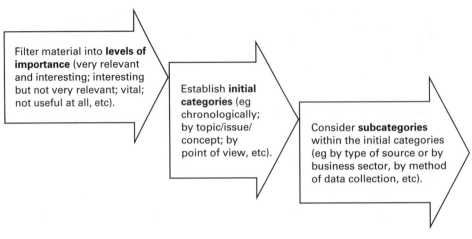

Filter material into **levels of importance** (very relevant and interesting; interesting but not very relevant; vital; not useful at all, etc).

Establish **initial categories** (eg chronologically; by topic/issue/ concept; by point of view, etc).

Consider **subcategories** within the initial categories (eg by type of source or by business sector, by method of data collection, etc).

(Quinton and Smallbone, 2011)

    Activity 3.3

Reading in an evaluative way

Read the following passages, which are extracts from longer articles relating to coaching. For both passages, use some of the tips for just-in-time reading but in addition try to answer the following questions:

- How have key concepts been defined?

- What are the limitations of the scope of the enquiries?

- What assumptions about the issue do the authors seem to work with?

- What data have been used?

- How were the data generated?

Extract 1

Extracts from: Brown, L (2018) Coach Well or Risk Productivity [Online] https://www.peoplemanagement.co.uk/experts/research/coach-well-risk-productivity Reproduced with permission of *People Management*

Helping you get further

While change is never completely predictable, feeling equipped can make transitions easier, according to research by City & Guilds Group.

More than three-quarters (76 per cent) of UK professionals interviewed said they believed coaching was helpful when going through periods of organisational change. For the purposes of the research, 'coaching' was defined as the process of training or guiding an individual to address current, rather than long-term, issues in the workplace.

Of the 1,000 people surveyed, 79 per cent said coaching was useful for adopting new technologies and ways of working. Two-thirds (64 per cent) said coaching had already become important in facilitating intergenerational working.

The research also suggested coaching prevents talent from being wasted. Among those surveyed that had changed role within their company, more than a quarter (27 per cent) said it had taken them four months or more to work to the best of their ability afterwards. However, people who didn't receive coaching at this critical moment were over eight times more likely to say they still didn't feel able to work to the best of their ability compared to those that did.

John Yates, managing director of City & Guilds Group, says: 'With unpredictable times ahead and ongoing change presenting challenges to businesses, employers need to support staff at all levels to maximise their individual performance, as well as that of the business.'

Extract 2

Extracts from: Bickerich, K, Michel, A and O'Shea, D (2018) Executive coaching during organisational change: A qualitative study of executives and coaches perspectives, *Coaching: An International Journal of Theory, Research and Practice*, **11** (2), pp 117–143. © Emerald Group Publishing Limited all rights reserved.

The increasingly complex business world forces organisations to undergo frequent changes in organisational strategies, practices and structures or leadership responsibilities (Oreg, Michel and By, 2013). For successful organisational change, executives must develop their leadership and change management competencies to meet the changing environment (Rafferty, Jimmieson and Restubog, 2013). Emerging research (Bickerich and Michel, 2016; Grant, 2014; Kombarakaran *et al*, 2008) demonstrates that coaching is an effective intervention to develop skills, attitudes and behaviour change among executives during change,

which we refer to as change-coaching from here onwards. However, these studies have not examined the coaching process itself; thus, analysing both executives' and coaches' perspectives is likely to provide new insights...

When we refer to executives in this study, we are including middle managers and project managers. The challenges associated with the responsibility of implementing change mean that this cohort may be especially vulnerable to negative change related outcomes and, thus, could benefit from the reflection and support given by change-coaching. Therefore, the aim of this study was to gain a deeper understanding of how executives experience organisational change and how change-coaching may support them...

Our study is the first to examine the overall change-coaching process from the perspective of both the executive and coach. Using semi-structured interviews, we investigated three main research questions:

– What are the demands executives face during organisational change that may be addressed through change-coaching?

– How do coaches support their coachees during organisational change?

– What are the similarities and differences in the change-coaching results that coaches report and executives expect?

We interviewed both executives and coaches about their experience of organisational change, and the role of coaching as a developmental tool for executives when managing change initiatives... Our sample comprised participants who volunteered for the research by responding to adverts and through personal contacts of the researchers who were contacted and asked if they would participate. We recruited the interview partners through the human resources departments or directly via e-mail and online networking. To address our research questions, we selected participants with first-hand experience of organisational change or change-coaching, who were middle management executives or coaches...

From August to December 2011, we conducted 33 semi-structured, confidential interviews with both executives (N = 15) and coaches (N = 18). Tables 1 and 2 outline information regarding each sample. The executive group included low to middle management executives (5 females and 10 males; averaged nine years of management experience) from nine business organisations such as the automotive or technology industry. One-third (N = 5) of the executives interviewed had 10 subordinates or less; one-third had 10–50 subordinates and one-third had more than 50 subordinates. We deliberately chose individuals, who were not currently being coached because to answer our first research question, the focus in the executive sample was on their demands and needs for a change-coaching...

Thematic analysis revealed distinct perceptions of coaching across the stages of the coaching process, including pre-coaching (phase 1), during coaching (phase 2) and post-coaching (phase 3). Pertaining to the pre-coaching phase, executives spoke of their demands during change and the benefits of coaching for meeting their goals, which motivated the choice to engage in coaching. During coaching, executives' expectations for coaching focused on their reactions to change and their need to engage in leadership behaviour. Referring to the post-coaching phase executives anticipated outcomes of the change-coaching process included both organisational (implementing change) and social (managing others through change) outcomes. Coaches spoke of their role in facilitating the executive to develop behaviours and coping skills to manage the change process (self-management). From the findings, we developed a conceptual model of change-coaching (C-C) across the three phases, which will serve as a guide for future research.

Feedback notes

These two extracts show how literature sources about similar activities can tackle the issues in different ways and with very different stylistic approaches. Both extracts start from the premise that organisations (and their employees) can benefit from coaching. One considers issues from the perspective of organisations in the United Kingdom being able to benefit from coaching during times of organisational change and has been carried out by an organisation associated with coaching. One paper begins with comments from a survey about which there is very little information provided; the other is based on qualitative study undertaken with executive coaches and coachees.

Being critical does not mean being 'negative', but it does involve you in responding to what you have read in a way that is objective and that examines its component parts and assesses the value of the ideas and the evidence. The way that you do this may vary slightly depending on the type of source you are reading. Fisher and Buglear (2010) and Quinton and Smallbone (2011) highlight a number of ways of doing this and Table 3.11 adapts and builds upon their approaches.

Table 3.11 Questions to ask when reading critically

Questions	For sources that use primary data	For sources that are based on theory or opinion
Date/currency	• When was the research carried out? • How current are the results? • If the results are old – is this a seminal piece of research still referred to in contemporary studies?	• When was it written, revised, published? • How current is the discussion? • Is it a classic article still referenced in contemporary studies?
Credentials	• What are the author's credentials? For example; is he or she a researcher or a practitioner? • Was the research funded or sponsored by a third party?	• What are the author's credentials? • What is the author's perspective? Where is he or she 'coming from'? • Was the work funded or sponsored by a third party?
Data collection methods	• What did the author(s) do to collect their evidence? • Who is included in their sample – how does this compare to your project? • What is the scale of their work? • Do the methods seem appropriate to answer the research question? • Are you clear about how they designed their research instruments?	
Provenance	• Does the work build on previous research? • Are the references clearly cited in the text and at the end? • What is the ratio of books:articles in the references? • What types of sources have been used?	• Does the work build on previous research? • Are the references clearly cited in the text and at the end? • What is the ratio of books:articles in the references? • What types of sources have been used?

(continued)

Table 3.11 (Continued)

Questions	For sources that use primary data	For sources that are based on theory or opinion
Position	• In what ways is this material similar to or different from others that you have read? • Does the work present a balanced view of alternatives? • What audience were they aiming for? • Is the work in an HR-focused journal? If not, what are the implications? • Does the work deliver their stated objectives?	• In what ways is this material similar to or different from others you might have read? • Does the work present a balanced view of alternatives? • What audience were they aiming for? • Is the work in an HR-focused journal? If not, what are the implications? • Does the work deliver their stated objectives?
Style	• Is the structure clear? • Can you follow the argument through a logical progression? • Does the use of tables, diagrams and charts add value to the conclusions or the explanations?	• Is the structure clear? • Can you follow the argument through a logical progression? • Does the use of tables, diagrams and charts add value to the conclusions or the explanations?
Analysis	• What is the central issue? • Is there a particular cultural bias? • What assumptions have been made, eg about the generalisability of the results? • What is the evidence supporting these conclusions?	• What is the central issue? • What assumptions have been made? Are they explicit, if so what are they? Are they implicit, if so what are they? • Are the sources drawn from a variety of areas? • Are the sources drawn from a wide range of different authors? • Is there an apparent cultural bias?
Reflection/ evaluation	• How do you respond to what the author is saying? • How do you rate this article (and why?) • How does it relate to other concepts/ideas you have come across? • How can you verify the results? • Where are the gaps? • Does it point to further research in a particular direction? • Is it relevant to your current work?	• How do you respond to what the author is saying? • How do you rate this article? • If this article is purely theoretical, how do you assess its academic quality? • How does it relate to other concepts/ideas you have come across? • Where are the gaps? • Does it point to further research in a particular direction? • Is it relevant to your current work?

Effective reading and writing – the ALT model

The questions in Table 3.11 provide a detailed way forward for evaluating what you read in a constructive way. A more general (and memorable) way of evaluating what you read is the ALT framework (you will have an ALT key on the keyboard of your personal computer), which is illustrated in Figure 3.6 and which is derived from the following key issues:

Argument

Logic

Trustworthiness

You can use the ALT framework to help you evaluate the sources that you read but you should also remember that your tutors will be using a similar framework to assess your research report when it is submitted. Get used to reading other people's work with these issues in mind, therefore, but also be prepared to write in such a way that your work can be seen to adopt the ALT principles.

Follow the tips shown below to ensure that you produce a literature review that meets the criteria of being evaluative, critical and analytical (Hart, 2018; Brown, 2006). What not to do is shown in Table 3.12.

- Include work that supports your ideas but also consider approaches that oppose them.
- Identify and discuss the 'key' sources for your subject.

Figure 3.6 The ALT principles

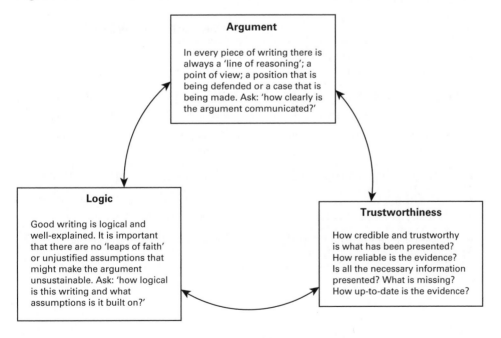

- Define the key concepts and terms you are writing about.
- Include as much up-to-date material as possible.
- Make explicit the values and theories that lie beneath what you are reading about and then consider how successfully the component parts fit together.
- Make clear distinctions between facts and opinions.
- Discuss what you are reading in the light of existing critiques of theories and concepts.
- Relate different readings with each other – look for similarities but also for contradictions or tensions between the opinions and approaches of different authors.
- Support your arguments and judgements about the value of different approaches with reasoned explanations.
- Adopt a writing style that is objective and impersonal. Avoid terms like 'should', 'must', 'this is obviously wrong' and so on. Use terms like '[authors] argue that', '[author] asserts that', 'another perspective is offered by...'.
- Structure your material effectively. While the reading that underpins any project will involve the collection of facts, the project can only really add value if those facts are organised and classified in an effective way. You will need to reorganise what you have read, therefore, and select what is important in each of the sources before putting it together in a way that is relevant to the concerns of your investigation.

Table 3.12 What not to do for your literature review

DO NOT	CHECK THAT YOU HAVE NOT
• Leave out any important publications that relate to your topic	• Discussed ideas without citing or referencing the source of ideas
• Be boring, tedious or descriptive	• Believed everything you have read and reproduced it uncritically
• Use 'pretentious' language, informal language or jargon	• Relied on long quotations by other authors
• Over-rely on a small number of authors	• Used lots of 'as cited in' – go to the original texts
• Cite articles that you have not read	• Ignored key references
• Include tables and diagrams where they do not add value	• Reproduced diagrams without the correct references

(Brown, 2006; Hart, 2018)

The structure of the literature review

A key skill in producing an effective review of the literature is to identify what sources to include and how to make sure that you achieve all the purposes of the review. It is also important to ensure that the literature review 'feeds into' the subsequent sections of the project report, rather than being a stand-alone exercise done to 'keep the markers happy'.

You must include key academic theories that are relevant to your research and you must also demonstrate that you are 'up to date' in your knowledge of the topic. This means that you need to have a balance of classic and contemporary references. Another important aspect of any literature review is a critical assessment of previously published work on the topic. This involves identifying its strengths and weaknesses as well as any areas that may have been left out or handled in a biased way.

Having undertaken a lot of reading you may find it helpful to generate a 'mind map' to start the planning process for the construction of your literature review. A related approach is to generate a concept map: a diagram that illustrates the relationships between the different ideas or concepts that are important for your topic where you 'plot' features of your topic that the literature suggest 'cause' other features or what practices the literature suggests may well 'result from', 'required by' or 'contribute to' particular outcomes (Alias and Suradi, 2008).

Whatever method you use to get started the general structure indicated in Figure 3.7 will enable you to write in an effective way in order to communicate what is already known about the topic.

Figure 3.7 Indicative structure for a literature review

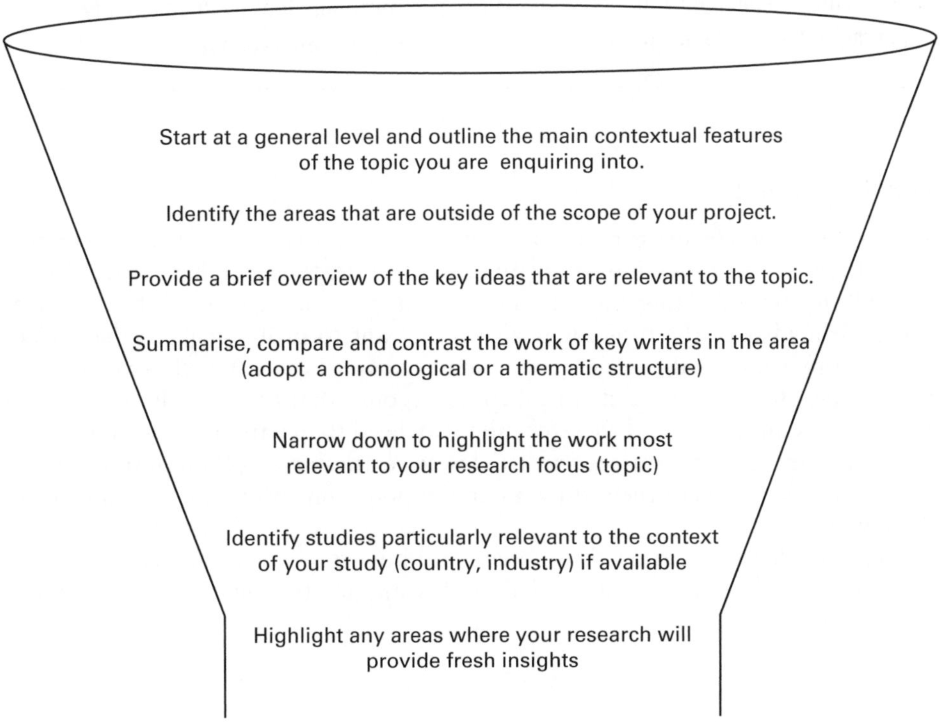

Start at a general level and outline the main contextual features of the topic you are enquiring into.

Identify the areas that are outside of the scope of your project.

Provide a brief overview of the key ideas that are relevant to the topic.

Summarise, compare and contrast the work of key writers in the area (adopt a chronological or a thematic structure)

Narrow down to highlight the work most relevant to your research focus (topic)

Identify studies particularly relevant to the context of your study (country, industry) if available

Highlight any areas where your research will provide fresh insights

Case Example 3.4

Writing in an analytical way

Ingrid was undertaking a business research report into human capital reporting. When she undertook her literature search she found a huge volume of sources including books and journals. A challenge for Ingrid was that there were a number of articles that were published in accounting journals which were quite difficult to comprehend as they focused on numbers rather than interpretation, and the HR implications were not explored. She took careful notes and set about drafting her literature review, focusing on the articles published in HR journals but including a small number of relevant ones from the accounting and general management journals. She then sent the draft work to her supervisor for comment and feedback. When her tutor got back to her Ingrid was somewhat disheartened. Her tutor indicated that she was pleased with the range of sources that Ingrid had made use of but she commented that the review was 'descriptive' rather than analytical and she suggested that Ingrid move away from writing about 'one author at a time' and adopted a more thematic approach to her review. The tutor also felt that Ingrid was using too many direct quotes to report what authors said, rather than providing analysis of the meaning.

Discussion questions

1   How might Ingrid go about revising her literature review to make it more analytical and less descriptive?

2   What structure would help Ingrid to achieve a more effective literature review?

3   What headings could Ingrid use?

4   What criteria should Ingrid use to identify appropriate direct quotations?

Feedback notes

Rather than merely describing some theories or initiatives relating to human capital reporting, it was important for Ingrid to demonstrate her critical thinking abilities by indicating the different approaches and also the difficulties that are associated with the topic. It is also important to probe beneath the surface and identify some of the underlying assumptions of different authors relating to these issues. Ingrid also needs to take into account that the term 'human capital reporting' is quite new and therefore she may need to expand her search terms to uncover other relevant sources and articles. In relation to direct quotations, Ingrid should use them where they illustrate a key point and provide scope for her to show her analysis.

Many students find it hard to understand how to achieve this within a fairly restricted word count. If you feel that this applies to you then have a go at Activity 3.4.

Activity 3.4

Establishing coherent categories and criteria

(adapted from Quinton and Smallbone, 2011)

Organising your work

Imagine that up until now you use three separate computers and each of them holds a variety of files: recent documents, photographs, games, spreadsheets, work from your studies and files from your employment. Your oldest home laptop is now nine years old so holds much of your personal and professional archives.

Now imagine being given a new faster and sleeker laptop, which you can use at home as well as in the office. You recognise that this is an opportunity to condense three separate computer locations into one, which is great news; however, you will need to find a way to combine the content of three separate locations (none of which are well organised individually) so that you can locate resources easily when you want them.

You start off with four main folders:

1   Work – everything related to your employment

2   University work

3   Personal

4   Photographs

You then decide that you would like a fifth folder where you will store all of your apps so that they can be easily accessed from your laptop's desktop screen.

You now have to decide on a structure for each of your folders that will make it easy for you to retrieve the information you need. You begin by looking at your university work documents and giving them consistent titles by using module codes so that you can find things easily.

1   Now you have to decide how to best organise your other folders. How will you do this?

2   On your laptop you can also add 'tags' to files so that they can be easily grouped together even when they are in different folders. How would you organise this?

Feedback notes

This exercise acts as a metaphor: reviewing the contents and organisation of your laptop is quite similar to the process of 'sorting' and reinterpreting the literature. For example, when sorting your photographs folder you could organise it by the dates the photographs were taken. There are many other types of classification you could make, for example: holidays, family, pets.

You can adopt a similar approach with your literature where you sort elements of the literature into categories or themes. However, unlike the example of photographs, the themes and categories that you generate to help you make sense of the literature collection must relate to your research objectives and it is likely that you will then develop one of two alternative approaches to structuring the main body of the literature review (Lee and Lings, 2008): a chronological structure or a thematic structure. A **chronological structure** is helpful if you need to explore how ideas about your topic have evolved over time. This might be appropriate, for example, for discussing how ideas about national culture and the implications on

HR practice. Alternatively, you might decide to use a **thematic structure** where you organise your review around the concepts that you have found in the literature. This might be appropriate for reviews of the literature relating, for example, to national culture.

When researching topics such as national culture you may find that some of the older concepts are still worthy of analysis and use in the present day. Consider, for example, the work of Geert Hofstede. His original work was first published in Hofstede (1980) and then in expanded form in Hofstede (2001) and has subsequently been updated on a number of occasions. A number of critiques have been published including McSweeney (2002) who highlights a number of methodological challenges, yet there are few studies since then that have undertaken work on such a large scale. For a project on national culture it would be difficult to not reference this old but seminal work; indeed it would be very strange to exclude it. Therefore you should ensure that you demonstrate to the reader your awareness of the limitations as well as your justification for its inclusion.

Figure 3.8 Chronological structure

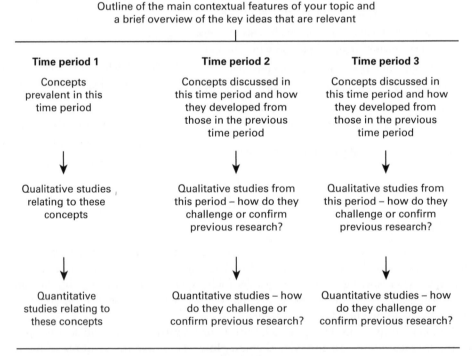

Introduction

Outline of the main contextual features of your topic and a brief overview of the key ideas that are relevant

Time period 1

Concepts prevalent in this time period

↓

Qualitative studies relating to these concepts

↓

Quantitative studies relating to these concepts

Time period 2

Concepts discussed in this time period and how they developed from those in the previous time period

↓

Qualitative studies from this period – how do they challenge or confirm previous research?

↓

Quantitative studies – how do they challenge or confirm previous research?

Time period 3

Concepts discussed in this time period and how they developed from those in the previous time period

↓

Qualitative studies from this period – how do they challenge or confirm previous research?

↓

Quantitative studies – how do they challenge or confirm previous research?

Conclusion

What important concepts are relevant to your research objectives?

What concepts will your research examine? How does your review indicate you should make sense of the data you will gather?

Figure 3.9 Thematic structure

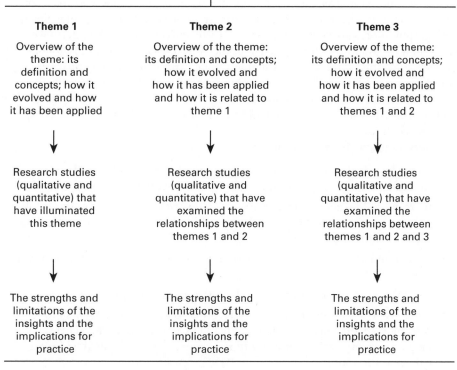

Introduction
Outline of the main contextual features of your topic and a brief
overview of the key ideas that are relevant

Theme 1	**Theme 2**	**Theme 3**
Overview of the theme: its definition and concepts; how it evolved and how it has been applied	Overview of the theme: its definition and concepts; how it evolved and how it has been applied and how it is related to theme 1	Overview of the theme: its definition and concepts; how it evolved and how it has been applied and how it is related to themes 1 and 2
Research studies (qualitative and quantitative) that have illuminated this theme	Research studies (qualitative and quantitative) that have examined the relationships between themes 1 and 2	Research studies (qualitative and quantitative) that have examined the relationships between themes 1 and 2 and 3
The strengths and limitations of the insights and the implications for practice	The strengths and limitations of the insights and the implications for practice	The strengths and limitations of the insights and the implications for practice

Conclusion
What important concepts are relevant to your research objectives?
What concepts will your research examine? How does your review indicate
you should make sense of the data you will gather?

Referencing and citations

There have been a number of occasions in this chapter already where the importance of appropriate referencing has been highlighted. You may think that your tutors' requirements for effective referencing are unnecessarily fussy. However, referencing and citation allows you to get credit for showing what you have read, and how and where you have used what you have read in your project report. Effective referencing also reduces the risk of plagiarism.

Keeping a record of what you have read (reference management)

Maintaining an accurate record of everything that you read is important as you will need to include the references when you come to finalise your research report.

Failure to keep accurate records has led many students to tears of frustration and days lost in 'hunting down' reference information that was not recorded accurately earlier on. You may wish to keep a manual record of what you read. Alternatively, most word processing software systems have a referencing function that can automatically generate a bibliography based on the source information provided in your document, and formatted in an appropriate style. If you think you may conduct more research in the future then a more specialised reference management (or bibliographic) software such as EndNote, Reference Manager or Mendeley would be worthwhile. Most study centres have a licence for at least one form of bibliographic software and others are freely available online. You can use the software as you find references to articles, books and other literature. Such software enables you to import references from online databases, sort them in various ways, retrieve them efficiently, and it automatically generates a bibliography when you have completed the research report.

Important points for referencing are:

- you acknowledge the work by other people that have influenced your thinking and research; this does not just involve the use of direct quotes;
- there should be enough information to allow readers of your work to follow up your reference, and access it for themselves – if it cannot be found again then do not try to reference it;
- you should always try to read the original source before including it in your work;
- you take a consistent approach to layout and punctuation;
- there are many different sources of information that you may wish to reference (media clips, blog posts, e-mail correspondence, etc). There will not be guidance or a 'style' for every type of source so use the nearest format you can to fit the source;
- if in doubt do what your tutor says (not what your librarian or this book says) – only tutors give and take away marks!

In HRM publications the most commonly used format for referencing is the Harvard system, which is based on the surname of authors and date of publication, rather than on any system of footnoting or numbering. This system is briefly outlined below.

Citing references in the text itself (citation)

You can demonstrate how you have used sources through appropriate referencing in the text itself. The Harvard system uses the author's surname and year of publication as the main way to identify documents within the text. Preferred practice varies in different publications as to how to punctuate references, and the order of various pieces of information, but the practical illustrations of referencing within the text shown in Table 3.13 may be helpful.

Quotations

When you quote directly from a source you should place the quotation in 'quotation marks' and the page number should be given in the reference after the year

Table 3.13 Citing your sources in the text

Occasion	Format	Example
For a single author	Family name, year	It has been shown that... (Jones, 2018) or Jones (2018) shows that...
For something written by two people	Family name and Family name, year	The main features of... have been identified as... (Jones and Brown, 2017) or Jones and Brown (2017) have highlighted...
For something written by more than two authors: For three to five authors name all authors the first time, then use *et al* (and others) For six or more authors go straight for the first named author *et al*	Family name, Family name and Family name, year	First time – Smith, Jones and Brown (2019) indicate that... or Key features of... are important within this concept (Smith, Jones and Brown, 2019). Subsequent citations – Smith *et al* (2019) indicate that... Key features of... are important within this concept (Smith *et al*, 2019).
When the author(s) you are referring to are themselves referred to by another author, and you have not read the original work (This is a derivative reference)	Family name, year, cited in family name, year, page numbers	Another view of the issue is... (Brown, 2019, cited by Smith, 2015, p 27) or Brown (2019), cited by Smith (2015, p 27), found...
For corporate authors, eg an organisationally generated document (and the organisation is commonly referred to by an abbreviation)	Corporate name, [Abbreviation] year	Ethical issues to take into account include.... (Chartered Institute of Personnel and Development [CIPD], 2018). Then the next time you wish to cite this organisation – Diversity challenges are reported to be increasing (CIPD, 2019).
For a source that has no author and does not fit into any other clearly defined category	First two or three words of the title, year	Alcohol Concern ('Call to stop', 2018) have proposed....

of publication. For example, Mavin and Grandy (2018, p 4) define self-care as *'an aspect of corporate moderate feminism where women take "proper" care of themselves as valuable, competent and deserving leaders'*.

Referencing in the bibliography or references section

Having provided some information about your sources in the text it is important to provide full details in the section that follows the end of the main text of the report (but comes before the appendices). Strictly speaking a reference list is a list of all sources that you have cited within your text, whereas a bibliography is a list of everything you have read or drawn upon while researching your piece of work, whether you have actually cited them in your text or not. In reality, the distinction between the two is often not recognised and the terms are used interchangeably. If you have been careful to acknowledge all your sources within the report, then the list of references will differ only slightly, if at all, from the list of sources you have drawn upon in your research. It is worth checking with your study centre whether a bibliography is required or a reference list is what is expected.

Whether you produce a bibliography or a references section, the aim is to list the publications in full and in alphabetical order. The following information should be provided to allow anyone to follow up your reference and access it accurately:

- author's surname and initial(s);
- year of publication;
- title of book/article;
- publisher of the book/name of journal in which the article was found;
- if a book, place of publication (eg London, New York, Paris).

It is not difficult to find the information you need for accurate referencing. For books the information will be on the front and back of the title page. Take care to record the name of the publisher and not the name of the printer or typesetter. Ignore any reprint dates and be sure to note down the date when the edition of the book you are referring to was published. The information you need for referencing journal articles should also be easy to find from the contents list of the issue of the journal you have referred to or at some place in the article itself; different publishers position this information in different places.

Some examples of appropriate referencing in the bibliography/references section are shown in Table 3.14.

As indicated already, some publications will show their references in different formats. The final format that you utilise will depend on the preference of your tutor or study centre. The main thing is to reference your work in a consistent format and in an accurate way. If you do not reference appropriately and you utilise material originated by someone else without showing a citation, then you may be accused of plagiarism, which is a form of cheating (passing off the work of someone else as your own).

Table 3.14 Referencing in the bibliography or references section

Occasion	Format	Example
Print book	Name, Initial. & Name, Initial. (year). *Title*. Edition number if not first edition. Place of publication: Publisher.	Edwards, M.R. & Edwards, K. (2019). *Predictive HR Analytics: Mastering the HR Metric*. London: Kogan Page.
Electronic book	Name, Initial. (year). *Title*. Retrieved from...	Bratton, J. & Gold, J. (2017). *Human Resource Management: Theory and Practice*. Retrieved from https://www.dawsonera.com/readonline/9781137586681
Edited book	Name, Initial. (Ed.). (year). *Title*. Place of Publication: Publisher.	Wilkinson, A. & Johnstone, S. (Eds.). (2017). *Encyclopaedia of Human Resource Management*. Cheltenham: Edward Elgar.
Reference to the work of someone cited in a different source (such as a textbook)	Family name, Initial, (year). Cited in Family name, initial. (year). *Title*. Place of publication: Publisher, page numbers of section being referred to.	Neville (2010), cited in Saunders, M., Lewis, P. and Thornhill, A. (2019), *Research Methods for Business Students*. Harlow: Pearson, 210.
Reference to a particular chapter in an edited book	Family name, Initial. (year), 'Title', in Initial, Family name (eds.), *Title*. (pp. x–x). Place of publication: Publisher.	Lain, D. (2017). Employment of workers age over 65: The importance of policy context, in Parry, E. & McCarthy, J. (Eds.). *The Palgrave Handbook of Age, Diversity and Work* (pp 475–497). London: Palgrave Macmillan.
Reference to a journal article. (Use this format if you retrieved the article from the internet as a pdf file and it is also published in hard copy)	Family name, Initial. (year). Title of article. *Journal name, volume number,* (part or issue number), start and end page numbers of article.	Stead, V. & Elliott, C. (2018). Constructing women's leadership representation in the UK press during a time of financial crisis: Gender capitals and dialectical tensions, *Organization Studies*, 39 (1): 19–45.

(continued)

Table 3.14 (Continued)

Occasion	Format	Example
Reference to a paper or report found on the internet that is not also available as a print version	Family name, Initial. (year). *Title of paper.* Retrieved from… (Internet address).	Chartered Institute of Personnel and Development [CIPD]. (2019). *Megatrends: Flexible working.* Retrieved from https://www.cipd.co.uk/knowledge/work/trends/megatrends/flexible-working
Podcast	Last name, Initial (Year, Month Day). *Title* [Podcast]. Retrieved from…	Chartered Institute of Personnel and Development. (2018, November 6). *Are robots stealing our jobs?* [Podcast]. Retrieved from https://www.cipd.co.uk/podcasts/digital-transformation
Blog post. If the author adopts a nickname or screen name, you can use this at the beginning of your reference	Name. (Year, Month Day). *Title* [Web blog message]. Retrieved from…	Martinez, G. (2019, Feb. 5). *How to excel as a young woman entering the workforce today* [Web log message]. Retrieved from http://womenofhr.com/how-to-excel-as-a-young-woman-entering-the-workforce-today/
Intranet document Use this approach for an intranet document (which cannot be accessed by anyone outside the institution)	Author, Initials. or Organisation if no named author. (year, month day if given). *Document title* (policy/report/circular number if given). Unpublished intranet document, Organisation (if not listed first).	Davies, R. (2018). *Internationalisation Strategy 2016-21.* Unpublished intranet document, University of Newcastle.
Interviews and e-mail messages	Interviews and e-mail messages are not 'recoverable data' so you cannot give details in your reference list. You can cite such material within your text as a 'personal communication'.	… and this point was strongly reiterated (C Bradley, personal communication, May 1, 2018).

CHECKLIST

- A critical review of the literature, focused on the issues relevant to your research aim, principal research question or hypothesis, is an important feature of any research project.

- 'Reading around' a topic can help to provide ideas for a project, provide a framework to interpret data, and help to identify worthwhile sources of secondary data.

- A wide range of different types of literature should be included in the literature review, incorporating both 'practitioner', 'teaching literature' and 'academic' perspectives.

- Effective literature search processes will include both manual and electronic methods.

- Finding literature and then not reading it is a waste of your time. Effective reading and note-taking are key skills for effective researchers.

- A good literature review will examine the context of the research problem, identify relevant concepts, issues and methods, develop a framework for the analysis of data and position the study.

- A literature review that is both analytical and critical will include work that supports and opposes your ideas, refers to key ideas within the topic area and uses up-to-date sources. It will distinguish between facts and opinions, establish relationships between different readings, and be explicit about the values and theories that underpin them. It will utilise an objective and impersonal writing style and provide reasoned explanations for arguments and judgements.

- In critically reviewing the literature it is best to start by establishing the broad context, issues, theories and concepts before 'funnelling down' to discuss work that is particularly relevant to the research.

- A good literature review will demonstrate a clear line of argument that links discussion of important concepts in a logical structure and will make use of evidence and sources to establish its trustworthiness or credibility.

- Referencing and citation skills are important parts of any literature review in academic work. Failure to reference properly is evidence of poor scholarship. Plagiarism (passing off someone else's work as your own) is treated as a serious offence in academic institutions.

TEST YOURSELF

1 For the purpose of your literature review, which of the following would be classed as an official document?

  a An organisation's CSR policy.

  b A journal article sponsored by a professional body.

  c A newspaper article in the national press.

  d A personal blog by a credible academic.

2 The ALT principles of being critical stands for:

  a Argument, literature, theory.

  b Assert, list, trustworthiness.

  c Analysis, logic, timeliness.

  d Argument, logic, trustworthiness.

3 A systematic literature search involves:

  a Identifying, reviewing and analysing sources using specific criteria.

  b Identifying the systems that are most important to your research topic.

  c Eliminating research studies carried out over 10 years ago.

  d Only using studies which feature empirical data.

4 Which of the following references is presented in the correct format (in line with the approach shown in this book) for your bibliography?

  a Pereira, V., Fontinha, R., Pawan, B. and Arora, B. (2018) Human resource management and performance at the Indian railway. **31** (1), 47–61.

  b Pereira, V., Fontinha, R., Pawan, B. and Arora, B. (2018) Human resource management and performance at the Indian railway. *Journal of Organizational Change Management*, pp. 47–61.

  c Pereira *et al.* (2018) Human resource management and performance at the Indian railway. *Journal of Organizational Change Management*, **31** (1), 47–61.

  d Pereira, V., Fontinha, R., Pawan, B. and Arora, B. (2018) Human resource management and performance at the Indian railway. *Journal of Organizational Change Management*, **31** (1), 47–61.

5 Which of the following describes a chronological structure?

  a The review is ordered by the impact factor of the journals you have used.

  b The review is ordered by identifying groups of themes.

  c The review is ordered by looking at how concepts have evolved over different time periods.

  d The review is ordered alphabetically.

6 Which of the following is an academic database?

  a People Management

  b European Journal of Training and Development

  c Ingenta Connect

  d www.acas.org.uk

7 Which of the following journals is a 'peer-reviewed' journal?

  a *HR Grapevine*

  b *Human Resource Development International*

  c *The Economist*

  d *Personnel Review*

8 When evaluating the 'position' of authors, you are exploring:

   a Who the lead author is in a multiple-authored publication.

   b How the work is similar to and different from other researchers.

   c The political affiliation of the authors.

   d Whether the author can structure an article in a logical structure.

9 When referencing, page numbers must be shown when:

   a You read any textbook relevant to your project.

   b A source has been written by more than one author.

   c You are using a direct quotation to enhance your argument.

   d When you download a database.

10 Why is it important to analyse the credentials of authors that you read and cite?

   a To ensure only academically qualified sources are used.

   b In case your tutor asks you a question about your references.

   c So you can use the information in your list of references.

   d To demonstrate your critical evaluation of their work.

 ## Review Questions

Take the time to find out about the requirements of your study centre for the literature review.

1 What percentage of your final mark is allocated to your literature review? What sort of word length is expected? To what extent are 'academic' articles and books expected?

2 What literature and information sources are available to you (physically and electronically) from:

   ○ your study centre;

   ○ your place of work;

   ○ any professional institutions of which you or your organisation is a member?

3 What user-name and passwords do you need and where can you get them?

Questions for reflection

This final part of the chapter enables you to reflect about your professional development and develop your skills and knowledge. This will enable you to build your confidence and credibility, track your learning, see your progress and demonstrate your achievements.

Taking stock

1 How familiar are you with HR related internet 'gateways' and other search engines?

2 Which academic journals are you already familiar with and which do you find the most challenging to analyse?

Strengths and weaknesses

3 Reflect critically on your use of literature in previous assignments. To what extent have you relied on ideas 'derived' from other places (usually textbooks)?

4   Revisit assignments you have produced previously for your course. What feedback have tutors made about your referencing technique? How confident do you feel about referencing? What will you do to improve your referencing?

5   What is your preferred learning style? In which environment do you work best? What are the best conditions for you to write your literature review?

6   How effective are your reading and note-taking 'habits' and strategies? In previous assignments how easy has it been to write an overview of what you have read about a topic? How organised is your note-taking system? To what extent do you note down readings that you agree with and tend to skip over those that oppose your viewpoint?

7   To what extent do you adopt a questioning and an evaluative approach when you are reading? How successful are you at making explicit the underlying theories and assumptions in what you read? If you were to create a template for new articles that you have read, what would your criteria be?

8   In your writing are you able to distinguish between facts and opinions? To what extent is your writing style 'objective and impersonal'? What feedback have you received on this in past assignments?

Being an investigative practitioner

9   To what extent is your thinking determined by features like the organisational culture of your employing organisation, your previous work experience, your national cultural background, your political preferences, etc? What steps do you need to take to ensure you consider the issues from a range of perspectives when you are reviewing the literature?

10 What strategies might you adopt to manage the time pressures of organisational and academic deadlines and produce a literature review of good quality?

 Useful Resources

The best way to learn how to write an effective literature review is to read journal articles about your topic. Similarly, the best way to learn how to make notes and to read in an evaluative way is by doing it and learning through practice. The following sources also provide useful tips and hints.

Bailey, C, Madden, A, Alfes, K and Fletcher, L (2017) The meaning antecedents and outcomes of employee engagement: A narrative synthesis, *International Journal of Management Reviews*, **19** (1), pp 31–53

Blaxter, L, Hughes, C and Tight, M (2012) *How to Research*, 4th edn, Open University Press, Maidenhead

Cameron, S and Price, D (2009) *Business Research Methods: A practical approach*, Kogan Page, London

Cottrell, S (2019) *The Study Skills Handbook*, 5th edn, Palgrave Macmillan, Basingstoke

Fisch, C and Block, J (2018) Six tips for your (systematic) literature review in business and management research, *Management Review Quarterly*, **68** (2), pp 103–106

Jesson, J, Matheson, L and Lacey, FM (2012) *Doing a Literature Review: Traditional and systematic techniques*, Sage, London

Ridley, D (2012) *The Literature Review: A step-by-step guide for students*, Sage, London

References

Alias, M and Suradi, Z (2008) Concept mapping: A tool for creating a literature review, in *Third Int. Conference on Concept Mapping; Tallinn, Estonia and Helsinki, Finland 2008,* eds AJ Cañas, P Reiska, M Åhlberg and JD Novak [Online] http://cmc.ihmc.us/cmc2008papers/cmc2008-p048.pdf (archived at https://perma.cc/56W2-JFBW)

Brown, RB (2006) *Doing Your Dissertation in Business and Management: The reality of researching and writing,* Sage, London

Dochartaigh, NO (2007) *Internet Research Skills,* Sage, London

Fisher, C and Buglear, J (2010) *Researching and Writing a Dissertation: An essential guide for business students,* 3rd edn, Pearson Education, Harlow

Gill, J and Johnson, P (2010) *Research Methods for Managers,* 4th edn, Sage, London

Hart, C (2018) *Doing a Literature Review: Releasing the research imagination,* Sage, London

Hofstede, G (1980) *Culture's consequences: International differences in work-related values,* Sage, California

Hofstede, G (2001) *Culture's consequences: Comparing values, behaviors, institutions and organizations across nations,* Sage, California

Lee, N and Lings, I (2008) *Doing Business Research: A guide to theory an practice,* Sage, London

McSweeney, B (2002) Hofstede's model of national cultural differences and their consequences: A triumph of faith - a failure of analysis, *Human Relations,* **55** (1), 89–118

Oliver, P (2012) *Succeeding With Your Literature Review: A handbook for students,* Open University Press, Maidenhead

Quinton, S and Smallbone, T (2011) *Postgraduate Research in Business: A critical guide,* Sage, London

04
Ethics, professionalism, standards and HR research

LEARNING OBJECTIVES

This chapter should help you to:

- discuss the importance of ethical practice for the HR profession;

- explain the development of national and international standards for HR practice;

- examine how your responsibilities as an HR professional are linked to your ethical choices as a researcher;

- identify and address ethical issues arising from your research and the research of others;

- complete any necessary ethical scrutiny processes required by your organisation and/or study centre.

CHAPTER OUTLINE

- How to use this chapter
- Ethics and the HR profession
- Ethics and standards for HR practice
- Ethics, digitisation and data protection
- The ethical responsibilities of the HR researcher
- Research ethics at different stages of your research project
- The positive features of ethical scrutiny
- Summary checklist
- Test yourself, review and reflect questions
- Useful resources

How to use this chapter

This chapter is relevant to everyone involved with HR research. Whether you are undertaking a research project at undergraduate, certificate or Masters level, or considering a proposal for a doctorate, you will need to consider how your project might affect other people: your research participants; organisations involved in your research; wider stakeholders involved in your study centre or community.

Research ethics involves a careful consideration of how the people on whom research is conducted are treated and whether there are activities that we should (or should not) carry out as we engage with the participants in our research projects. All study centres will expect their students to adhere to a code of conduct in relation to the people who become the subject of research work or are affected by it (Bell, Bryman and Harley, 2019). In many study centres failure to achieve a positive outcome from an ethical review process (or failure to participate in ethical review at all) results in an automatic fail at project or dissertation assessment stage. Therefore, time required for ethical scrutiny processes should be an important feature of the project plan for your study and it is important to check with your supervisor, mentor or advisor to find out what the process will be for your research.

Many students find the ethical review process to be frustrating and time-consuming but the experience of those who have been through it suggests that careful thinking through the ethical issues of your project will result in a stronger methodology and a better project outcome.

A CIPD fact sheet (2017) highlights key issues in relation to business ethics and the role of HR, which are that:

- ethics in business is about 'doing the right thing' because it is the right thing to do;
- organisational reputation can be easily damaged if it fails to embed its core values inside an ethics programme;

- HR plays a vital role in facilitating an ethical culture;
- organisations need to adopt a principles-based approach to decision-making if they want to apply and develop ethical values;
- individuals are better equipped to face ethical dilemmas if organisations support a principles-based approach.

The following case example highlights that, in spite of commitments to ethical principles, HR practitioners face many dilemmas and 'grey areas' relating to the ethics of employment and their role in employment relationships.

 Case Example 4.1

The ethics of the gig economy

Edith was a full-time student looking for employment in HR and, at the same time, looking for a topic for her research project. During her studies she found herself undertaking part-time, short-term and freelance work whenever she could to earn money while she was a student. Her tutor pointed out to her that in doing this she had become part of the 'gig economy'. Edith decided that her research project would investigate the ethical issues from an HR perspective, into this increasingly prevalent form of work. As she pursued this research she learned of high-profile legal cases, such as an employment tribunal in 2016 involving Uber drivers who argued that they should be categorised as workers, not self-employed, and therefore be entitled to holiday pay, paid rest breaks and the national minimum wage. Edith's reading highlighted debates between advocates of regulation of flexible work to make it fair for individuals and those who promoted its economic benefits for employers.

Critics of gig-working emphasised tensions in existing arrangements. Although treating flexible staff as contractors can save employers money on tax and other employment-related

responsibilities, nonetheless some workers must still conform to set shift patterns, wear a certain uniform and expect penalties for turning down work. Edith also discovered that companies in sectors associated with delivery services are increasingly using similar work arrangements and imposing high levels of structure, surveillance and control over work practices.

Edith's tutor suggested to her that, while precarious working is often associated with low-skilled, low-paid jobs, she might extend the scope of her research to incorporate the spread of such work practices into other professional areas in sectors such as media content development, legal services provision, care workers and even college lecturers!

Discussion questions

1   What issues relating to 'right and wrong' are raised by Edith's initial research into the topic of the gig economy?

2   What ethical issues might arise for HR practitioners who work for companies that make use of self-employment forms of working as a feature of their business model?

Feedback notes

These questions raise a number of difficult but important issues that are relevant to the HR profession and, therefore, are relevant to issues of HR research. On the one hand you might think that it is appropriate to argue that self-employment forms of contracting provide people with flexibility to integrate their work with other demands on their time. You might also argue that the 'business partner role' often claimed by HR practitioners means that they have a duty to support the organisation to be as profitable as possible provided that no laws can be shown to be broken. On the other hand, you might think that the negative publicity arising from these forms of employment does long-term damage to the reputation and sustainability of the organisation. From a moral basis you may argue that it is not acceptable for those in the HR profession to facilitate a growing trend to insecure, 'precarious' work that is experienced by many low-paid people as exploitative for the instrumental purpose of reducing the costs of employment to the organisation.

Within any business organisation there are difficult ethical dilemmas to be faced. General principles that most people support include values such as respect, honesty, openness and responsibility. However, business values may focus more on profit, growth and efficiency. This makes for a dilemma for many HR professionals about the extent to which the HR function might appropriately be regarded as an important feature of 'the conscience of the organisation' with a duty of care to protect worker rights and the 'employer brand' while at the same time being able to promote HR business partner practices in new and innovative ways.

Dealing with tensions like these is an integral part of HR work so the ethical choices and thinking required for HR research activity should not seem too 'alien'. The HR experience of ethical dilemmas associated with employment means that HR practitioners are also well aware that there are very few 'cut and dried' issues. This chapter builds on the ethical issues faced by HR practitioners and provides a framework you can use to identify the ethical implications of your research and then manage the process in such a way that will achieve a good quality research outcome.

Ethics and the HR profession

Remenyi, Swan and Van Den Assem (2011) define ethics as 'a branch of philosophy which addresses issues of human conduct related to a sense of what is right and what is wrong'. In day-to-day language the terms 'ethical', 'moral' and 'standards' are often used interchangeably and in various combinations. The term 'moral' is mostly associated with the extent to which specific actions are seen to be consistent with accepted ideas of right and wrong. The term 'ethics' refers to general principles as to what people 'ought' or 'ought not' to do. The term 'standard' means something that can be expected to be obligatory as it constitutes a consensual expectation of practice or behaviour in an occupational or professional field.

Case Example 4.2

Unethical behaviour at work

Half of staff 'witness unethical behaviour at work', *People Management* 31 October 2017 [Online] https://www.peoplemanagement.co.uk/news/articles/staff-witness-unethical-behaviour. Reproduced with permission of *People Management*.

More than half (55 per cent) of workers have witnessed, or been asked to do, something unethical at work, a survey published today has found. The poll of 1,000 UK professionals by charity A Blueprint for Better Business also revealed that just 2 per cent would definitely refuse to take part in something that made them feel uncomfortable at work, while almost half (48 per cent) would voice their concerns but go ahead with the activity regardless. A lack of ethical awareness in the office is also taking a toll on staff retention, with more than a third (34 per cent) saying they were tempted to change jobs because of behaviours and actions they witnessed in the workplace, and 15 per cent reporting they had left a role for this reason. Only 9 per cent said that experiencing inappropriate or uncomfortable behaviour would not be a good enough reason to leave a job. 'This poll highlights some worrying common traits of business life, showing that we often find it hard to deal with situations that make us feel uncomfortable,' said Charles Wookey, chief executive of A Blueprint for Better Business... The findings come at a time when a string of high-profile sexual harassment claims have rocked several sectors... [and] last week, a poll published by the BBC revealed that half of women, and a fifth of men had been sexually harassed at work.

Discussion questions

1   Why do people tolerate unethical behaviour at work?

2   What are the implications for HR practitioners of the findings outlined in this case example?

Feedback notes

In discussing these questions you probably highlighted how power relationships and conflicts of interest can result in people tolerating what they perceive to be unethical behaviour at work. You might also have discussed how ethical norms can change over time: patterns of behaviour that may have been acceptable at one point in time have now become ethically and morally unacceptable. Such discussions highlight the important role of HR in initiating policy developments relating to standards of behaviour in the workplace as well as providing policy guidelines and oversight and taking disciplinary action where it is warranted.

These discussions highlight the importance of establishing clear standards for practice. Standards are regarded as a defining feature of reputable professions as they provide the basis for ethical and effective professional activity. Although professional standards are well established in traditional professions, such as law and medicine, to prevent exploitation of potential clients and preserve the integrity of the profession, the HR field lacks such agreed standards of practice leading to criticisms that HR professionals cannot be 'held to account' if they do not practise in an ethical way. Such critiques are, perhaps, somewhat harsh as professional organisations in the HR field in many countries have developed codes of practise and ethics that professionals within their remit are encouraged to subscribe to. However, these codes cannot be enforced to prevent anyone from working within the profession if they do not meet the standards.

Examples of codes of ethics and professional conduct that are published from a range of HR-related professional organisations are shown in Table 4.1.

 Activity 4.1

Ethical implications of CIPD code of conduct

Find the CIPD 2012 code of conduct (https://www.cipd.co.uk/about/what-we-do/professional-standards/code).

1   Review this document and identify the ethical principles that HR professionals are expected to uphold.

2   What standards of conduct are expected?

Table 4.1   Professional institutes – codes of conduct and codes of ethics

Chartered Institute of Personnel and Development (CIPD)	https://www.cipd.co.uk/about/what-we-do/professional-standards/code
Institute of Training and Occupational Learning (ITOL)	https://www.itol.org/wp-content/uploads/2015/06/ITOL-Code-of-Professional-Conduct.pdf
BCS Chartered Institute for IT	http://www.bcs.org/category/6030
European Mentoring and Coaching Council (EMCC)	http://www.emccouncil.org/eu/en/quality/ethics
Society for Human Resource Management (SHRM)	https://www.shrm.org/about-shrm/pages/code-of-ethics.aspx
Association for Talent Development (ATD)	https://www.td.org/about/vision-mission-code-of-ethics
Academy for Human Resource Development (AHRD)	http://www.ahrd.org/general/custom.asp?page=standards_on_ethics

Feedback notes

In relation to Activity 4.1 you may have noticed that the CIPD code of conduct expects that members will challenge others if they suspect unlawful or unethical conduct. In addition you may feel that it is hard to find a clear statement of ethical principles in this code of conduct although the ethical values of honesty, integrity and respect are featured. Across the four areas of behaviour set out in the code there is also reference to obedience (the code says 'compliance') to the law and the expectation that CIPD members will uphold standards to maintain confidence, trust and respect. This suggests that ethical values of transparency, objectivity and confidentiality are also implicit in expectations of HR professions as a feature of professional competence and behaviour. These standards are important for day-to-day HR practice and they also form the foundation for standards of ethical practice in research methods, which are considered later in this chapter.

Ethics and standards for HR practice

Corporate scandals in recent years over issues such as sexual harassment allegations, widespread data confidentiality breaches, admissions about long-term practices of misleading information and so on have led to a range of new developments in the area of ethics and standards. In particular, the HR profession has had to reassess whether minimum standards for the way that people are managed and treated in work organisations should be developed and adopted. This is an emergent area and this section outlines initiatives up to 2018 involving national and international standards bodies such as International Organization for Standardization (ISO) and British Standards Institution (BSI) (CIPD, 2018).

 Activity 4.2

Standards and standardisation: implications for HR practice

Find out which ISO standards your organisation, or an organisation with which you are familiar, has adopted. In addition to highly technical standards related to design, process efficiency or manufacturing it is likely that the organisation may be accredited against one of the general 'management' standards (referred to as management system standards) listed below:

ISO 9001 – Quality Management System
ISO 14001 – Environmental Management System

ISO 27001 – Information Technology
ISO 22000 – Food Safety Management System
ISO 5001 – Energy Management System
ISO 31000 – Risk Management System

1   Once you have identified a general standard that the organisation has adopted, or you have identified a standard that you would like to know more about, then use your internet or intranet-based research skills to find out the

evidence requirements to show compliance with the standard you are considering.

2   Make a list of the implications for the HR function that are contained in the standard you have chosen. These may not be the responsibility of the HR function but look out for items such as: training and education; management reviews; qualification and competence; record-keeping and so on.

3   Write down a list of the potential advantages of management system standards such

as these as well as a list of the potential disadvantages. If you have access to those people whose work is affected by the requirements of this standard then you might like to find out their opinions in response to this question.

4   Write down reasons why management system standards for HR could contribute to ethical practice. Identify the potential difficulties of developing and implementing national and/or international standards for HR practice.

Feedback notes

In the process of researching these issues and discussing them with colleagues inside and outside of HR it is likely that you will have come across two differing perspectives about management system standards. Supporters of standards argue that they increase efficiency and consistency of management practices in organisations and enable cross-organisational working and synergy (International Organization for Standardization [ISO] nd). However, critics suggest that they inhibit organisational flexibility and lead to a 'box ticking' and bureaucratic 'compliance' mentality (Corbett and Yeung, 2008).

Discussion of these issues in relation to the HR field raises a number of further issues (Anderson, 2017). First, the purpose of such standards requires discussion: should HR standards be directed at improving the performance of the organisation or should their focus be on the quality of the work–life experience of those who work on behalf of the organisation? A second area of debate concerns the extent to which HR practices 'travel' – that is to say whether HR practice relevant in (say) large corporates in the United States are also appropriate to organisations of different sizes and types across different geographical locations. A third issue concerns the time horizon of HR activities. While operational and transactional processes focus on the short term so that practices can be recorded and monitored, strategic HR work relating to organisational development or strategic change processes are more difficult to standardise and record. Finally, you might also feel that having to abide by standardised expectations of practice would compromise flexibility, change and development.

The debate about whether national or international standards for HR are necessary continues. Critics of the HR profession contrast it with other management professions such as accountancy, where there are clear and accepted standards of competence and ethical behaviour that might be expected of a professional. In this context, work was initiated by the International Organization for Standardization (ISO) in 2011 to develop agreed standards for HR practice and by 2017, 49 countries were involved with the ISO standards-setting process. National-level standards development processes have also been initiated in the United Kingdom and elsewhere. In 2015 in the United Kingdom, the first National Standard for HR, with clear links to ethical standards of practice, was published: *BS 76000:2015, Human resource. Valuing people. Management system* (BSI, 2015). In contrast with 'traditional' rules-based standards, this document makes clear that it is 'principles based', each principle having equal importance:

- The interests of staff and other stakeholders are integral to the best interests of an organisation.
- The organisation is part of wider society and has a responsibility to operate in a fair and socially responsible manner.
- Commitment to valuing people should come from the most senior leaders of an organisation.
- The people who work for an organisation have rights over and above those in law or regulation, and these rights and legal protections are respected by the organisation.

Subsequent standards issued by BSI in the 'Valuing people' theme include: *BS 76005:2017, Valuing people through diversity and inclusion* (BSI, 2017) and *PD 76006:2017, Guide to Learning and Development* (BSI, 2017).

In related developments a number of ISO standards have been issued that include: *ISO 30400: HRM: Vocabulary*; *ISO 30401 HRM: Knolwedge Management Systems*; *ISO 30405: HRM: Guidelines on recruitment*; *ISO 30406, HRM: Sustainable employability management for organizations*; *ISO 30407: HRM: Cost Per Hire*; *ISO 30408: HRM: Guidelines on human governance*; *ISO 30409: HRM: Workforce Planning*; *ISO 30410: HRM Impact of Hire*; *ISO 30411: HRM Quality of Hire*; *ISO 30414: HRM Guidelines for internal and external human capital reporting*; (CIPD, 2018).

Ethics, digitisation and data protection

A further significant change in the global environment that has transformed HR practice and the ethical implications of HR is the increasing dominance of digital technologies as an important part in employment (Parry and Strohmeier, 2014). Almost every feature of HR recruitment and selection and 'employer brand' activity is managed through technology. In addition, work tasks have been increasingly automated or adapted to take account of the opportunities of digital tools and media. New organisational designs increasingly rely on virtual workplaces and groups.

However, the area of digitisation with most implications for ethical practice in HR is the digitisation of HR processes and transactions such as pay roll processing, attendance management, pay and performance management, which are increasingly undertaken through digital self-service platforms. These developments provide operational advantages of cost reduction, increased speed of processing and greater consistency in HR transactions but there are also ethical implications for the relational aspects of HR work.

Activity 4.3

Digitisation and employment

Undertake a 'digital stocktake' of your own organisation or one with which you are familiar.

1   How does digital technology currently affect HR work?

2   How are new digital technology innovations likely to affect work generally in your organisation in the next five years?

3   What ethical issues arise from digital technology developments?

Feedback notes

The first issue that usually arises in discussions about the impact of technology in HR work is data protection. Although the HR function has always been responsible for the management of data about employees, data security is more challenging to ensure when it is held in a digital form. There are considerable benefits to the organisation to be obtained through knowledge-sharing processes that draw, in part at least, on data held about employees but digitisation makes possible the gathering and storage of a wide range of sensitive data. Managing the balance between knowledge-sharing, decision-making grounded in HR analytics, and data security requires a high level of transparency about data sharing protocols to clarify what personal data can be subject to digitised analytical tools and how this links with organisational governance rules. A second issue that you may have identified relates with the appropriate use of social media for HR processes. Social media often features in recruitment and screening applicants as well as with monitoring behaviours (both inside and outside of work-time). This scrutiny can lead to performance management and/or disciplinary procedures (Lam, 2016) but ethical issues are also raised about potential discrimination as well as invasions of privacy.

Other longer-term ethical issues also arise as a result of digital technology. First, social and other digital media are increasingly forming an important feature of workplace learning and workplace communication. There are many advantages to this such as: just-in-time learning; peer-to-peer support; opportunities for self-directed and virtual learning and working. Cost savings are possible through appropriate 'curating' of online learning and development resources. Such initiatives are under-researched (Li, 2013) but, in terms of ethics, it is possible that learning with and from others outside of the organisation through digital platforms may present risks to individual or corporate confidentiality. HR practitioners concerned with the ethical issues arising from digital technology, and particularly the use of social media have an ethical duty to ensure that social media and confidentiality policies are clearly communicated so that people in the organisation know what it is appropriate to share online and what is inappropriate. A further issue relates with behaviours on social media platforms that might constitute harassment so clarity is needed about what social media behaviours are acceptable inside as well as outside of work-time. Finally, any conditions and restrictions that the organisation deems appropriate to ensure proper use of organisational IT equipment, software or social media accounts must be communicated in a clear way by those people who are responsible for HR in the organisation.

In the United Kingdom, until 2018 the Data Protection Act 1988 was the main statutory reference point for the protection of the privacy for individuals in relation to the data held about them. However, since 2018, European Union (EU) General Data Protection Regulations (GDPR) have come into force with important implications for the way any organisation with either clients or workers in the EU collects, stores, manages and uses personal data. Personal data is defined in the regulations as anything that can be used to identify a person; this includes locational information, biometric data and so on. For HR practitioners, and for HR researchers the GDPR requirements mean that personal data must only be processed for legitimate reasons that are both relevant and must only be held for as long as is necessary. It also means that 'active' rather than 'assumed' consent is needed from workers, contractors, job applicants and others who may undertake work on behalf of the organisation for each specific purpose that information may be used for. These regulations also mean that data-retention policies are required and careful contractual arrangements are made with any third-party agreements that may involve data transfer.

Although the GDPR applies to those who undertake business in Europe or employ people in Europe, many other parts of the world have also enacted laws to regulate how data concerning people may be collected, transferred, stored and processed. Legal regulation varies in different countries but the main concerns are:

- Who could access information?
- How accurate is the information?
- What precautions are there to prevent data copying?
- How do people find out what information is stored about them and what happens if they object to this data about them being held?

These provisions have clear implications for 'insider research' projects undertaken within one or more organisations as:

- It would be regarded as not only unethical but probably illegal for individuals' personal data to be used except for the purpose for which they were collected.
- The regulations mean that personal data may not be disclosed to other parties who are not connected to the original purpose for which the data were collected.
- Data should only be held for the time required to achieve the stated purpose.
- Data must be stored in a secure way.
- People have a right of access to any data held about them.

Activity 4.4

Implications of the GDPR

Imagine that you are planning to undertake research utilising a case study research strategy that will involve secondary data from the organisation as well as primary data (interviews and a questionnaire-based survey). What are the

GDPR implications for the way you undertake your research using:

1   Secondary data?

2   Primary data?

Feedback notes

The first and most obvious point about the implications of the GDPR is that you cannot assume, just because the organisation holds secondary datasets relating to workers, that you can obtain permission to use these data for your research project. Although the GDPR makes exceptions for public health research, statistical research, historical research and scientific research, organisational data controllers are not permitted to authorise the processing of sensitive (personal) data unless the 'data subjects' have provided explicit consent. When you gather your primary data it is important that you obtain the active consent of all your research participants and that they freely consent in full knowledge of how the data will be gathered, stored, utilised and ultimately, destroyed.

In addition, if you plan to gather data that cannot be fully anonymised (qualitative data often cannot be fully anonymised) then it is important that you communicate this clearly to those who will be participating and that they understand any plans for 'pseudomisation' as well as the intended purpose and subsequent use to which your research will be put. If you say that you will use the data for your dissertation or research report then you are not entitled to assume that you can also use it for any other forms of communication (organisational newsletter items, journal article, conference paper and so on). Therefore, if you think you may wish to use the data after the end of your project you must make this clear when the data are gathered and those people about whom the data will refer must give their explicit consent.

A second issue concerns the length of time you retain and store the data; it is important that you set out the length of time you intend to hold the dataset (10 years is often the norm) as well as explain the secure methods that will be used to destroy the data at the end of that period. A third implication relates to data security and you have an obligation under the GDPR that data should be stored securely and be password protected. A fourth implication relates to an individual's right to see what data you hold about them. If you are creating a transcript of your interview the interviewee has a right to request a copy of the transcript and to request that any inaccuracies are changed.

HR research and research ethics

This chapter has discussed a wide range of issues that affect ethical practice and standards within the HR profession in general. Ethics is now acknowledged as an area that has been overlooked for far too long in the HR profession and also in the practice of researchers in the business and management field generally. The remainder of the chapter now focuses specifically on issues that relate to research in the HR field.

 Case Example 4.3

Employee survey ethics

Stephanie was a Masters level student employed by a large multinational company involved in the production and marketing of consumer goods. In discussions with her manager she learned of a large-scale culture change project that the top team had decided to implement. The aim of the culture change process was already established and would involve not just cultural but also structural change for the organisation. As a feature of this change process the company wished to undertake a wide-ranging employee survey, to be completed by all employees across the world, to find out how the existing culture was perceived and also to identify issues that might both encourage and inhibit the planned change process. A consultancy firm had been employed to design the survey but an 'insider' was needed to act as the liaison point with the consultants. Stephanie's manager suggested to her that she might fulfil this role and could then use the survey data as the basis for her Masters dissertation. In making this suggestion it was made clear to Stephanie that if the company was pleased with the results of this process then she might expect to achieve some career advantage through further involvement with the culture change project.

Discussion question

What ethical issues should Stephanie consider and discuss with the organisation in relation to integrating the planned employee survey with her research project?

Feedback notes

One issue that you might immediately highlight is whether Stephanie's project or dissertation-focused research questions would be addressed by this survey. An issue here, therefore, would be the extent to which she would be able to influence the wording of the questions or, perhaps, have her own questionnaire items added to the survey. Aside from this research design issue there are other points that Stephanie needed to consider that specifically relate to research ethics. First, although the organisation might have no qualms about 'serious encouragement' for its workers to complete the survey, from Stephanie's position as a researcher, this would contravene the ethical principles of the rights of any individuals to decide not to participate in a research project with no fear that they would suffer disadvantage as a result of their decision. Linked with this, survey respondents would need to know that the data would be used, not just for corporate purposes, but also for her Masters studies. A third issue, which often arises when research is carried out at the place of employment of the researcher, relates to conflicts of interest. The organisation had a vested interest in the outcome of the project and Stephanie needed to consider whether this might challenge her integrity in the approach she took to data presentation, data analysis and the formulation of conclusions. Indeed, an issue that Stephanie had to think hard about was whether, in the long term, she wished to be associated with what was likely to be a radical structural and cultural upheaval within the organisation.

In this circumstance Stephanie's study centre insisted that, if she were to pursue this project then the survey questionnaire must be 'double badged', with both the name of the organisation and also the name of the university. It was also important that the purpose of the study (for both organisational and research purposes) be made clear in the information provided to survey respondents. Third, 'ownership' of the data generated by the survey had to be clearly explained in the information provided on the survey. Fourth, no participant should feel any obligation to participate as part of his or her work duties.

Case Example 4.3 highlights how research in HR, like business and management research more generally involves thinking carefully about your social responsibilities in the way you conduct your project and the extent to which your work maximises benefit for individuals and organisations while also minimising risk of potential harm to those who participate in the research process. Therefore, it is important that you design your project so that you can be seen to respect the privacy, values and dignity of individuals, groups and the community or organisations that are involved without risk of discrimination against the needs, experiences and beliefs of different people. In tackling such issues, for research purposes it is important that lines of responsibility and accountability are clearly defined. For academic research projects the person accountable for the students' ethical behaviour is likely to be the research supervisor or the programme leader. As the case example indicates, it is important to maintain appropriate independence through the research process. Where conflicts of interest cannot be avoided then they should be made explicit. As indicated already in this chapter, confidentiality, if it is promised, must be respected and careful attention must be paid to data security.

To summarise, research ethics requires you to consider carefully some fundamental questions about your research project that include:

- the purpose and intent of your research;
- the way in which you intend to answer your research questions;
- your own safety and well-being as well as the safety and well-being of those with whom you come into contact (your research participants);
- issues associated with honesty and openness with those involved in your research;
- what your research outcomes will lead to (how your findings will be applied and to what end).

These issues are also features of the longer-term management of your research project. A key principle of research ethics is that the interests of participants should be protected. In general, people from whom you gather data should be no worse off at the end of your research than when you started. However, the next case example indicates some of the 'grey areas' in this field.

 Case Example 4.4

Suspicions are aroused

Hamid was a full-time HR student who undertook his research project while on an unpaid internment in a large not-for-profit organisation operating in a social care setting. The organisation's work focused on delivering medical supplies to people suffering from a range of chronic and life-limiting conditions, mostly supplying organisations within the UK NHS funding system. For his internship Hamid was assigned to a project involving a review of training and development provision in the organisation. During the course of his internship, and with the encouragement of the organisation, Hamid designed his research project to evaluate learning and development provision at the organisational level and to consider how e-learning might contribute to the development of the organisation. As a part of his research Hamid examined organisational data relating to course bookings for training programmes delivered by outside consultants. Once he had gathered these data Hamid's analysis suggested that, alongside a range of very cost-effective training programmes delivered by outside consultants, there was also evidence of a pattern of activity where the Operations Director was booking courses delivered by a freelance consultant for quality management training at a volume that was beyond the requirements of the organisation. When he checked his data Hamid found that

half of the courses were booked and paid for in advance but then cancelled as a result of a lack of sufficient staff being available to attend. When he was undertaking analysis of the financial data associated with training expenditure Hamid was surprised to find that, although other providers had issued credit notes to the organisation when their sessions had been cancelled there was no evidence of any credit notes provided by the consultant who undertook the quality management training.

Towards the end of his internship Hamid was asked by the Operations Director to make a booking worth £2,000 for him at a spa hotel using a voucher code. The director explained that this was for the purpose of evaluating the venue as a possible location for training programmes in the future. The voucher Hamid used clearly indicated that it was provided by the quality management training consultant about whom Hamid had concerns. Indeed, Hamid's understanding was that the organisation had recently upgraded its in-house training accommodation in order to reduce spending on outside venues. Hamid was concerned. He was an unpaid intern and the spa visit was to be undertaken by the Operations Director during the working week. Hamid began to wonder if his research project had uncovered fraudulent practice by the Operations Director.

> **Discussion question**
>
> In this situation what ethical concerns might Hamid need to take into account? Consider the issues from the perspective of:
>
> - the organisation in which he was working;
> - ethical assurances of confidentiality of information that Hamid had made.

Feedback notes

When he commenced his project Hamid did not feel that his research would raise any particular ethical issues but, as his suspicions about misuse of the organisation's funds were aroused, so difficult ethical dilemmas arose. From the organisation's perspective, some discrete communication of his concerns might be justified but Hamid had to balance this against the ethical principle of confidentiality, especially as he could not be 100 per cent certain that any fraudulent activity was occurring. Hamid was also aware that ethically, individuals who participated in his research project should not be 'worse off' as a result of it. Nonetheless fraud is an illegal activity and the misuse of public funds is a serious ethical matter and a further ethical principle, of CIPD as well as of research ethics, is the duty to report criminal activity or serious breaches of professional misconduct.

In this case Hamid waited until the end of his internship and then, with the support of his study centre, raised his concerns with a director (not the Operations Director) at the organisation who conducted a discrete investigation of her own. Hamid's suspicions were right: ultimately the Operations Director and the training consultant pleaded guilty to stealing a significant sum of money from the organisation.

Case Example 4.4 highlights how even the most uncontroversial looking projects might become more sensitive as a result of factors outside the control of the researcher. There is a range of possible issues that have ethical implications in almost all research projects that involve human subjects either directly or indirectly.

Anonymity – the extent to which the identity of research participants is concealed

In your project you must consider issues of both individual participant anonymity and organisational anonymity. If your research is to meet the code of conduct set by CIPD relating to the maintenance of relationships based on trust, confidence and respect then it is important that you respect people's rights to know whether you will achieve **anonymity** when you undertake your research. If your research involves a small number of interviews with high-profile people in one organisation it might be impossible to achieve anonymity as identities could be 'deduced' by those who know the organisation even if they have not been formally named. Some participants may be happy to accept this situation and some may not see anonymity as something that must be achieved in their case (the individual or organisation may be willing to be named in your research or to be given an appropriate pseudonym) particularly where they are sponsoring your project in some way. However, this is something that should be established at the planning stage and before information collection begins.

Confidentiality – the guarantee that data will not be shared with unauthorised people

A second important issue relating to the professional standard of maintaining relationships of trust is **confidentiality**. Here it is important that those who participate in your research are aware of and agree to arrangements you will make relating to any communication of information that you gather. They need to know, before they participate, who will be able to read and scrutinise the information that they have provided.

Data storage

A further expectation of the CIPD professional code is the safeguarding of confidential and personal or commercially sensitive information and so **data storage** arrangements that you make are also important. Individuals and organisations have become increasingly aware of the potential dangers of the loss or theft of confidential information. A further ethical principle is that arrangements for the secure storage of any data you gather are made and communicated to potential participants before the information is gathered. At some point the data will also need to be disposed of and so your plans (and timescales) for this should be clearly communicated to those who participate in your research.

Dignity and well-being of research participants

A fourth general ethical principle is that research should not cause distress, embarrassment or harm to anyone involved with it. However small your group of respondents, it is likely that there will be differences between them (and you) relating to gender, employment experience, ethnicity, language and educational background. Any research process that makes someone feel 'stupid', for example, is inconsistent with the principle of not causing distress or embarrassment.

 Case Example 4.5

Cultural sensitivity

Noura was an international student from Saudi Arabia studying on a distance-learning basis and undertaking her research project in her home country. Noura's research design was based around a staff satisfaction questionnaire and she obtained permission to gather data from staff at a hospital close to her home. Noura prepared a paper-based survey instrument and she was aware that most of the survey respondents who were working in care roles in the hospital would never before have been part of a survey process. In order to assuage any possible doubts about the confidentiality and anonymity of the survey process Noura achieved permission to attend the hospital in person and conduct face-to-face briefing sessions about the research she was undertaking for groups of potential respondents in the staff rooms. Sealed boxes were also arranged in the staff room areas for people to place their completed questionnaires and Noura planned to remain on site during the data-collection process to ensure the security of the boxes. This process worked well to start with as Noura began her data collection but challenges arose in the second week of her fieldwork process.

In the second week of fieldwork, cultural issues connected with gender arose. Although the healthcare sector is one of the few places of employment in her country where men and women who are not related 'by family' have the ability to be in contact with one another, in common with many other hospitals in her part of the world, the site was separated into female only and male only sections. Female 'wings' of the hospital, staffed by female nurses and other staff did not present a problem for the data collection. However, Noura had to take account of the problems that would arise if she were to attempt to visit the staff room areas in the male wings of the hospital as strict traditions of gender segregation were in force in these areas.

Discussion question

What ethical issues arise in relation to collecting data from male staff working in the male only parts of the hospital?

Feedback notes

This case illustrates ethical issues that may arise when research in different cultural contexts is being undertaken. It is important to be sensitive to different values, attitudes, social customs and religious beliefs. Noura was aware of the cultural sensitivities but this was not something that her distance-learning supervisor had anticipated. After some discussion with the health sector sites for her research Noura found a way to conduct her research with male respondents but it involved changing the location of data collection in order to avoid causing offence or embarrassment. Her solution was to be accompanied by a senior male official and to hold the briefing meetings in an area that was not designated as 'male only'. While being accompanied by a senior male member of staff enabled the fieldwork to be undertaken in the male only wing of the hospital Noura found that a smaller proportion of male respondents than would be expected from the survey population of the hospital had completed a questionnaire, although this was not the case for the female respondents.

This case example highlights how 'drawing the line' between ethical and unethical practice in research ethics can be difficult; something that Noura included in the 'limitations' section of her dissertation.

Potential for conflicts of interest

 Case Example 4.6

Action research into work engagement

Jack was employed in a senior role in the police service and decided to undertake his HR research project into the topic of work engagement among serving police officers. He considered a research design that used a quantitative survey such as the Utrecht Work Engagement Scale (Schaufeli, Bakker & Salanova, 2006) but subsequently decided to undertake a mixed-methods case study research approach to examine key issues in the specific context of policing. His purpose ultimately was to use his research findings as the basis for the design of HR interventions to try to improve levels of work engagement within his specific operational setting. Jack designed a fieldwork strategy that involved a combination of methods.

First, he gathered data through 'non-participant observation' with patrol officers as they went about their duties. Second, having generated an initial model from his findings from the observation phase he undertook face-to-face interviews. Third, he made use of large amounts of secondary data sources that were relevant to work engagement.

Discussion question

Jack was undertaking research with the explicit aim of improving employee engagement and in a context where his senior role was well known. What conflict of interest can you identify for this case?

Feedback notes

The situation described in this case example is not uncommon in HR research projects where they are encouraged or supported by the employing or sponsoring organisation. In such instances the organisation will expect that the research will lead to benefits and will be very interested in what you do, how you do it, and the eventual outcome. Conflict of interest issues that Jack had to resolve were: to what extent could he conduct his research without interference by the organisation? How should Jack communicate with research participants (who in this case were the interviewees and the operational teams whose day-to-day work he wished to observe)? Did Jack's interview questions need to be 'authorised and approved'? How confident was Jack that the organisation would respect the need for him to formulate research conclusions in an open-minded and independent way?

In Jack's case he discussed in advance with his employer that it would be inappropriate for him to observe people that he had line management responsibility for; instead he observed (with permission of all team members) teams who reported to a different senior officer. He also decided that he would wear 'plain clothes' rather than his police uniform while conducting the observations and the interviews. In the pre-briefing and discussions with potential participants that formed part of gaining consent from the teams that would form his research sample he took care to always use his student rather than his work e-mail account. In addition, all consent forms used the study centre logo and made clear that his role in these instances was as a student rather than as a police officer. The same approach was taken with the interview processes and Jack gained organisational permission for these to take place during working hours but in locations that were not associated with operational duties. Nevertheless Jack's reflections on this process were that some interviewees were less 'open' in a recorded interview environment than they had been when he had interacted with them during the observation processes.

In addition to these sorts of issues it is important that, as part of gaining organisational consent for the research, you clarify whether they wish to receive a full copy of your final research report (more usually, an abridged summary is preferred). Other issues for discussion relate to your plans for the dissemination of your findings after the project has been completed. Some organisations and sponsors might be very comfortable with the idea of an article or paper being published in a professional, practitioner or academic publication that draws on the research data but these matters should be established early on (at least in principle) so that both parties are clear about their rights and responsibilities and so that clear and documented organisational consent has been achieved before any fieldwork or data gathering is commenced.

Ethical issues from different stakeholder perspectives

As these case examples have suggested, a number of different stakeholders will have an interest in your research project and each of these may have a different perspective about ethical issues. In addition, the rights of those involved as research subjects, participants or respondents are very important. Table 4.2 offers a brief summary of the issues from the different perspectives, which are then discussed more fully later in the chapter.

HR researchers who are undertaking organisationally based research in their own employing organisation also have particular tensions to take into account. In addition to being a 'researcher' they may also be closely involved with individuals in a range of other organisational 'real life' situations. This involves a careful consideration of power relationships within the organisation. While the research process may be a project for you, those who have been researched will have to live with the consequences of it in the longer term. Throughout the research process it is important to recognise that being a researcher is quite different from being a practitioner. It may be difficult for you, and those around you, to distinguish between the two roles. Practitioner-researchers need to be aware that the involvement of colleagues in any research project may impact on the work relationships that they have. Particular issues can arise where an HR researcher wishes to invite someone that they line-manage to be included in their research. To what extent might the person feel that they could decline the invitation? To what extent will the person feel that they can provide 'truthful' information? Key principles that may be helpful in this context are:

- make sure that all relevant permissions have been gained before commencing the project;
- involve participants – encourage them to shape the form of your enquiry;

Table 4.2   Ethical perspectives of different stakeholders

Stakeholder Group	Ethical Issues to Consider
Individual respondents; 'research subjects'; participants	• To what extent might the research process affect their well-being? Is there any risk of distress, embarrassment or inconvenience? How disruptive will the research process be to their work or home life? What time commitment would be involved? Is this their 'own time' or 'work-time'? • Confidentiality and anonymity – to what extent will any information given to you be treated as confidential and to what extent will they be assured of anonymity? • Privacy and consent – to what extent will they know and understand what is involved and feel that they can freely choose to take part or not to take part?
Organisation(s) in which research is undertaken	• To what extent might the research process affect the reputation of the organisation? Is there any risk of disruption to working patterns as a result of the data gathering processes? • Does the organisation have its own ethical policy or framework that must be taken into account in any research process? • Would the research process comply with wider organisational policies (eg data protection, health and safety and so on)? • Consent – has someone with appropriate authority been informed about the research and given permission in advance for the information to be gathered? • Anonymity and confidentiality – is the organisation willing to be named and what information must be treated as confidential?
Study centre	• To what extent might this research affect the reputation of the study centre? • Does the research comply with wider study centre policies (eg data protection; equal opportunities and diversity; ethics)? • Would the data gathering process pose any risk to the researcher (eg travel at night in a remote area to interview employees on a night-shift)?

- be prepared to negotiate access with individuals, don't assume it will be given;
- be open about your progress so that any concerns can be taken into account;
- never undertake observation without the explicit permission of 'the observed';
- get permission before you examine or copy files, correspondence or other organisational documents;
- report back to participants your accounts of interviews and observations of them and allow them to suggest amendments which enhance fairness, accuracy and relevance;
- take responsibility for maintaining confidentiality.

Online research

As indicated earlier in this chapter, the extension of internet-enabled technology into every aspect of our lives creates an opportunity and a challenge for those undertaking HR research projects. The internet can be a tool for data collection but also a site of data collection. Some HR researchers undertake research using traditional methods but through some form of web-enabled platform (for example, soliciting responses to an online survey or conducting face-to-face interviews using Skype). However, other options are open to researchers such as making use of social media platforms for recruiting research participants and/or gathering data.

 Activity 4.5

Using online sources for research

Imagine that you have been asked by your manager to undertake research into internships as this is something that your (small) organisation is thinking of taking forward. You have undertaken some initial research and have identified a number of different perspectives about the issue connected with pay, career development, work experience and so on. However, you want to find out more about the issues from the perspective of the HR practitioners responsible for sourcing interns and also from the interns themselves.

Visit an employer-focused online community (the CIPD community may be appropriate – http://www2.cipd.co.uk/community) and see if you can find any discussions that would be pertinent to your research.

Visit a student-focused online community (the NUS website might be a place to start – https://www.nus.org.uk/) and see if you can find any discussions that would be pertinent to research in the experience of interns.

Discussion question

What ethical issues arise with informed consent and confidentiality relating to the use of data taken from online or social media sites?

Feedback notes

The prevalence of social media platforms developed for people with different interests and experiences means that an increasing amount of data are available that could contribute to research projects (Association of Internet Researchers, 2012) but ethical issues arise where data from such applications that have been placed there for one purpose may be used, without prior knowledge, to achieve different (research) purposes. In such situations ethical and legal issues may arise relating to copyright, data protection and deception. Although research ethics principles apply in the same way to online as to other forms of research there are further issues that warrant particular attention. Issues of anonymity arise as contributions to discussion threads, for example, are made on a 'named basis' (although some people may falsify their names or use a pseudonym). Confidentiality issues may also arise if the data gathered in this way are then used by the researcher in some form of public dissemination. The names might be removed in your project report, for example, but 'verbatim' views expressed in a 'discussion thread situation' could be tracked back using online search technology and so the identity of one or more participants could be found.

Table 4.3 sets out a range of ethical issues that different forms of online research might pose:

Table 4.3   Online research and ethical practice

Online Form/Venue	Indicative Ethical Questions
Direct communication (text, audio or video) real-time or asynchronous	• How is informed consent obtained? • To what extent might participants be considered vulnerable? • Are the data subject to 'open data' regulations meaning that they can be freely used and redistributed by anyone? • Can privacy be achieved through anonymisation of e-mail content and/or header information?
Special interest discussion forums and chat-rooms	• How do terms of service (TOS) articulate privacy of content? • What are community or individual norms and/or expectations for privacy? • Does the author/subject consider personal network of connections sensitive information? • Are the data easily searchable and retrievable? • Would harm be likely to result if the content of a subject's communication were to become known beyond the confines of the discussion forum? • How will the profile location or other personally identifying information be used or stored? • How is informed consent and protection of privacy achieved? • To what extent might participants be considered vulnerable?

(*continued*)

Table 4.3 (Continued)

Online Form/Venue	Indicative Ethical Questions
Social networking platforms	• How do terms of service (TOS) articulate privacy of content? • Does the author/subject consider personal network of connections sensitive information? • Are the data easily searchable and retrievable? • How will the profile location or other personally identifying information be used or stored? • Does the 'participant' understand and agree to interaction that may be used for research purposes? • Does research purpose and design balance possible conflicts between participant and researcher perceptions of public/private and sensitive/non-sensitive? • Does the dissemination of findings protect confidentiality?
Personal spaces/ blogs/YouTube/ multimedia presentations and so on	• Could analysis, redistribution or dissemination of content harm the person in any way? • Does the author consider personal network of connections sensitive information? • Does the author consider the presentation of information or the channel to be private or public? • Do the terms of service conflict with ethical principles? • Is it likely that the author is under the age of adult-hood?
Avatar-based/virtual worlds/online gaming spaces	• Should the virtual world be considered 'public'? What constitutes 'privacy' in this space? • Should avatars be afforded the same protection as a human research participant? • How and when should consent be sought? Will the process of requesting consent cause harm? • Do users consider their interactions in this space to be private or public? • How do terms of service (TOS) specify anonymity of users and privacy/confidentiality? • To what extent could research activity compromise a user's play or outcomes in the game? • Could data be used to identify a user's location or other sensitive demographic information?

(*continued*)

Table 4.3 (Continued)

Online Form/Venue	Indicative Ethical Questions
Commercial web services such as Google; Survey Monkey; Cloud Storage	• What are the participants' and authors' expectations of privacy? • Are the data easily searchable and retrievable? • Are the data subject to 'open data' regulations meaning that they can be freely used and redistributed by anyone? • Does the service's privacy policy align with ethical principles? • How will cross-border data be handled if IP addresses are considered by one country to fall under specific privacy regulations?
Databanks and repositories	• Where are the data stored? How long will they exist in the repository? • What consent is needed for subsequent data use? • Does the analysis of data enable identification of individual or group identities? • What conditions were placed on data use by the original compiler of the dataset? • How will images/audio be effectively anonymised?

(Association of Internet Researchers, 2012)

If part of your project involves drawing on social media as a basis for your research data then it would be advisable to include explicit discussion in any ethical approval process that you make (and also in your methodology section or chapter) of the following issues (Hooley, Marriott and Wellens, 2012):

- **Privacy** – in a context where levels of self-disclosure by individuals has increased on social media platforms what ethical stance have you taken about what are public and what are private data?
- **Informed consent** – what steps will you take to negotiate and achieve informed consent for research conducted online? What links to further information or 'frequently asked questions' information will you provide?
- **Anonymity and confidentiality** – will your data gathering platform (for example, your online survey platform) collect the IP addresses of participants and what are the implications of this? What steps will be taken to anonymise qualitative data from social media sites?
- **Legal issues** – what Terms of Service (ToS) have participants in different social media platforms signed up to? What are the implications for who owns the data on the platform?

- **Participant vulnerability** – although a particular advantage of online research is the opportunities it presents to access 'hard to reach' or otherwise stigmatised research populations (for example, people suffering from mental health disabilities) what ethical issues arise from data drawn from individuals that could be considered to be 'vulnerable' (for example, young people; elderly people; those with serious health problems)?

To summarise, there are no easy or 'cut and dried' ethical answers in the domain of online research. Ethical decisions will be contextualised and situated within research project design and methodological issues. Therefore, continuous review is needed to take into account the intersection of legal and ethical issues, particularly relating to privacy, consent and confidentiality (Hooley *et al*, 2012).

Freedom of information

Freedom of Information (FoI) legislation is another important ethical issue for researchers to consider that has risen to prominence in the last 15 to 20 years. FoI has been incrementally developed in the United Kingdom and fully enacted since 2005 and Access to Information (ATI) mechanisms exist in a number of other countries (Walby and Larsen, 2012). FoI provides for public access to information held by public authorities in the United Kingdom such as government departments, local authorities, the NHS, state schools and police forces. One feature of the Act is that public authorities are obliged to publish information about some of their activities. Another is that members of the public are entitled to request information from public authorities (this includes universities). Within the FoI legislation access requests are 'motive-blind', which means that anyone can request information and, once they have received information under the legislation, the information is considered to be in the public domain (Birkinshaw, 2010).

For researchers FoI issues are complex although the impact on student projects is fairly small. A benefit of FoI is that enquiries made to an organisational FoI officer in a constructive way can be a useful tool for obtaining information to answer your research question from a public authority (Savage and Hyde, 2014). However, as most student projects are undertaken through affiliation with a publicly funded organisation (a university) there may, in some circumstances, be a case when an FoI request for your research data may be made, although this is a most unlikely scenario.

Research ethics at different stages of your project

Three stages of the research process have ethical implications (Saunders, Lewis and Thornhill, 2019; Oliver, 2010) and these are shown in Figure 4.1 and considered in more detail in the following sections.

Figure 4.1 Ethical issues through the research process

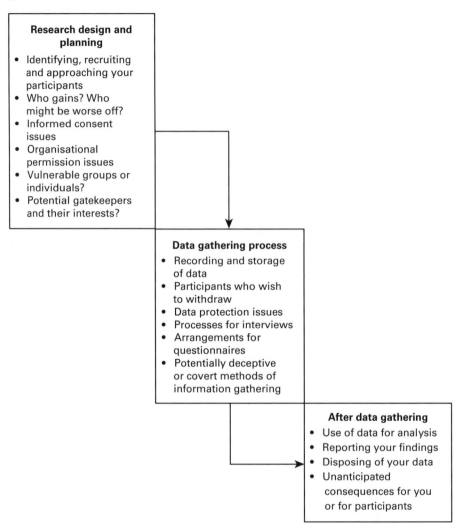

During the planning stage

 Case Example 4.7

Research into whistle-blowing

Charlie was a distance-learning student who was out of work but who hoped to specialise in employee relations. She became intrigued by issues associated with 'whistle-blowers' – situations where a person informs on another person or organisation whom they regard as engaging in an unlawful or immoral activity. She read around the issues and identified important features including: whistle-blower protection and public interest disclosure; issues that do and do not 'count' as whistle-blowing and organisational policies about whistle-blowing. Charlie wanted to understand more clearly the situations that most often led to whistle-blowing; the HR issues arising from whistle-blowing incidents and how organisations might formulate and implement policies relating to whistle-blowing.

With this in mind she felt that a multiple case study research design would be appropriate and she set about contacting a range of organisations in the public and private sectors that she hoped would allow her to conduct research in their organisations.

Discussion question

Write down a list of about five concerns that an employer might have regarding giving Charlie permission to carry out this research in their organisation.

Feedback notes

It is possible that you could list far more than five concerns that you might have as an employer in this situation. These might include:

- What would this project involve? Who would be required to provide what sort of information?
- Why has the organisation been chosen? Is there a problem that the organisation should be aware of? Would you have to release sensitive data?
- How much 'poking around' would this person want to undertake?
- Could some employees be 'unsettled' and consider whistle-blowing if the subject was 'out in the open' in this way?
- What difficult public relations issues would be likely?
- How confidential would the information be?
- How competent is the person to undertake such a sensitive project?
- Who would get to read the findings of the research?

Concerns like these represent some of the ethical issues that have to be considered as part of the planning of any research project. Key issues are related to the ethical themes of privacy (individual and organisational) and consent. All of the people and organisations you wish to involve in your research have the right to know how and why you identified them for inclusion. Privacy and data protection issues are also relevant.

It is important, right from the planning stage of your enquiry, to ensure that potential participants are able to give **informed** (rather than implied) consent to be involved. It is insufficient to assume that consent has been implied just because an interview, focus group or some other intervention has taken place.

Informed consent

Ethical research must fulfil criteria of 'informed consent' (Saunders, Lewis and Thornhill, 2019) whereby all participants, regardless of the way data are gathered, give their consent freely having received full information about their participation and the use to which the data will be put. Implied consent, where you infer consent as a result of participation or completion of a survey instrument, is not sufficient. A lack of consent, where deception may have been used or where participants have no knowledge about the project, is rarely if ever, justifiable in HR research projects. An important principle is that people have the right to give or withhold consent on the basis of full information about what the data they provide are for and how they will be stored, used and ultimately disposed of. Informed consent involves clearly communicating the scope and intention of the project to potential participants so that they are clear about:

- the nature of the research – its purpose, who is undertaking it and who should be contacted if they have any further questions;
- what participants can expect – the type(s) of information to be collected and methods of collection, the time commitment involved, their right to withdraw without repercussions;
- arrangements with regard to anonymity and confidentiality;
- subsequent use of data – who will have access to it, how results will be communicated, what will happen after the project has been completed;
- compatibility with organisational or other relevant professional codes or policies.

To achieve these standards it may be necessary to develop an information sheet or briefing note for potential participants that clearly sets out, in the language of the participant (rather than in academic jargon), what is involved.

 Activity 4.6

Informed consent

Imagine that you plan to collect data from within one organisation about perceptions of the gender pay gap. You anticipate gathering data through some form of questionnaire to be completed by a sample of the organisation's employees (all types of staff) and also through semi-structured interviews with senior managers and HR practitioners. Complete the relevant sections of the information sheet below to ensure that any individuals would be able to give informed consent to their participation.

Research into your view of gender pay gap issues at XYZ Ltd

Please read the following information. You should feel able to ask any further questions you may have about the project. Contact details are provided as part of this information sheet.

1. Who will undertake this project?	Your name(s) and contact details
2. Which study centre is supervising the research project?	Your affiliation
3. What is the title of the research project?	
4. Who can the participants contact if they wish to complain about any feature of the research process?	
5. What is the purpose of the project?	If your research aim and objectives are rather 'technical' make sure that this explanation of your research purpose can be easily understood by the people whose participation you are requesting.
6. What contribution am I requesting from you?	What sort(s) of data? What time commitment? How many times? Over what time period?
7. Why have you been asked to participate?	
8. How will I gather information?	Be clear about the method or methods you will use.
9. How will the information be recorded?	
10. When will the information be gathered?	Be clear about whether this is the participant's own time or work-time.
11. What arrangements will be made regarding confidentiality of information?	
12. What arrangements will be made regarding anonymity of participants?	
13. What if you do not want to participate?	
14. What will happen to all the data when they have been gathered?	Be clear about data storage and data disposal.
15. How will the findings be reported?	Explain your procedures relating to confidentiality and anonymity in what you report. Explain your plans for your business research report/dissertation. Indicate if you plan to provide other reports/ accounts of your findings in any other format.
16. What are the possible disadvantages?	You may foresee no negative consequences so don't be afraid to say so.

(continued)

17. In what way will the project be beneficial and to whom?	Indicate who can benefit and in what ways.
18. Who has reviewed the research study to ensure that it complies with appropriate ethical standards?	Say here who has reviewed the study at the university/study centre and, if the organisation has its own ethical scrutiny processes, explain how this has been undertaken.
19. Can permission be withdrawn having previously been granted?	Indicate how and when a participant can withdraw from the study but also indicate if there is a point in time when the data cannot physically be disaggregated from the overall dataset.
20. Can you refuse to answer a question?	

Feedback notes

As a result of completing this activity you may be feeling that working out the answers to all these informed consent (and other ethical) questions as a feature of the research planning process is particularly time-consuming. Many students get impatient with the requirements for 'advance thinking' before they are close to commencing their research. However, by tackling these questions as part of your research planning you will find that you have a stronger and more robust research design and you are then able to undertake better quality research and increase your chances of achieving a good assessment grade.

Cross-cultural research

As alluded to already in Case Example 4.5, when research is carried out in different cultural contexts with different ethnic groups there may also be ethical implications arising from cultural and language differences and these can arise when research is carried out at home or abroad.

 Case Example 4.8

Cultural differences and ethical research

Hui-Hsien was a full-time international student from China studying in the United Kingdom.

He became very interested in the study of employability for international students and decided to undertake his dissertation on final-year students' self-perceived employability, thinking forward to their return to their home countries at the end of their studies. In order to answer his research questions Hui-Hsien decided to use a semi-structured interview approach and to recruit a sample of international students from his own university. Hui-Hsien wanted to explore perceptions of internal employability characteristics such as psychological and personal development features that students might associate with employability as well as their views about external signals of employability characteristics such as skill and qualification outcomes of their studies associated with their qualifications and other academic credentials obtained in the United Kingdom although work would be sought in their country of origin.

Discussion questions

1   What ethical and research design issues can you identify that Hui-Hsien faced with this project?

2   To what extent were cross-cultural issues appropriate to consider in this project as it was undertaken entirely in the United Kingdom?

Feedback notes

Although this project was undertaken at a UK institution, cross-cultural issues became an important issue for Hui-Hsien to address. The first issue that he faced was that of linguistic confidence and fluency. Although all students were studying in English and it was anticipated that the interview process would be carried out in English, Hui-Hsien had a distinctive accent that sometimes made it difficult for others to fully understand what he was saying. Some respondents, from both China and Taiwan indicated that they would consent to undertake the interview only if it were conducted in 'Standard Chinese'. Others indicated that they would only participate if they could receive the interview questions in advance. After discussion with his supervisor Hui-Hsien agreed that the questions could be given in advance, in English, but that responses to them could be in the students' own language. This involved obtaining ethical permission for an appropriate bilingual colleague to be present at the interviews to assist with translation or explanation as necessary. However, this also alerted Hui-Hsien to the need to take additional precautions in seeking informed consent (Remenyi *et al*, 2011) and after discussion with his supervisor he decided to arrange for language translation of his project information sheets and to seek advice about whether the words used had 'resonance' with the proposed participants.

A further ethical principle relevant in this case is that of sensitivity for customs, practices, culture and beliefs of others and it was important to ensure that interviews were not scheduled to clash with religious observance or national holidays for potential participants. A third issue that arose for Hui-Hsien was that of 'cultural obligation' and peer pressure for participation that would have meant that some participants might not have fully and freely given their consent to be interviewed. In this context a key ethical principle is that researchers should guard against possible harmful consequences for participants, and the risk factors of (implicit) coercion to participate in research must be avoided.

When undertaking this project Hui-Hsien was advised by his supervisor to keep a 'reflexive diary' to keep track of the progress of his study and to enable him to reflect on cultural and ethical issues that arose which he had not anticipated. This was wise advice as one such unexpected event occurred when some interviewees from cultures where semi-structured interviews are rarely used in research arrived for their interviews (having received the questions in advance) with their answers preprepared and read them aloud without the scope for 'probing' or follow-up questions. Indeed one respondent e-mailed his answers to Hui-Hsien one hour in advance of the scheduled time of the interview and informed him that she would not be present in person.

The data gathering phase

Once your research project is underway it is important to keep basic ethical principles in mind such as:

- participants' (and organisations') right to withdraw at any time;
- the importance of scoping out (and then sticking to) the purpose of the project and the data gathering methods you plan;
- collecting and recording data accurately and fully;
- ensuring that you keep to any promises made about participant (and organisational) confidentiality and anonymity;
- fair treatment – making sure that you do not put participants in a position where they feel undue pressure or which might diminish their self-esteem.

 Case Example 4.9

Research into e-learning in SMEs

Heather was a full-time PhD student who wanted to undertake research into e-learning in small and medium enterprises (SMEs). Her review of the literature led her to realise that SMEs are an under-researched sector in the HR field and that most learning in smaller organisations is informal and rarely involves formal 'learning platforms or systems'. Heather realised that exploratory research was appropriate for her project and, after evaluating a number of options she decided to use ethnography as the basis of her research design. Ethnography involves the study of groups of people (in this context employees) and their interaction using a number of qualitative approaches, including observation, intensive involvement, interviews, documentary analysis, case studies and so on to study naturally occurring phenomena. To undertake this the researcher lives/works in the environment being studied. Heather was able to gain permission to work on a voluntary basis for up to five days per week in each of three different small organisations. The first organisation constituted her pilot study and then she worked in each of the other two organisations over a six-week period. The data she collected was in three forms: data from participant observation, interviews (both semi-structured and informal) and photographs, which helped to ensure that as much data as possible was captured, by evoking memories and reminders of features of the use of e-learning in the organisation that might otherwise have been overlooked.

Discussion questions

1   What ethical issues might be raised by the use of participant observation as a way of gathering data?

2   To what extent would 'covert' (ie secret) observation be justifiable in any HR research project?

Feedback notes

Given the potentially intrusive nature of ethnography in people's (work) lives it is important that there are good reasons for conducting the research and managing the trust relationship between researchers and participants is vital. Key ethical principles are that researchers have a responsibility to prevent doing harm to participants as well as to the research community. Poorly conducted research will undermine future work planned by other researchers. Specifically the use of observation as a way of gathering information raises a large number of ethical issues. The principles of informed consent meant that Heather had to ensure that anyone being observed as a part of her study had the right to know in advance about her plans and could withhold consent if they wished. In addition, Heather also had to plan in advance to ensure she would enact another ethical principle: that of the objectivity of the observation process. This required her to address an important question: to what extent might one observer 'see' a behaviour and describe it in one way and another observer see the same behaviour and describe it differently?

Therefore, before Heather could commence her work it was important that all those in the organisations she gained access to knew why Heather was there and gave their consent to the observation process. It might be argued that their behaviour might be different as they knew they were being watched. However, Heather's reflective account suggested that after a relatively short time people relaxed and behaved in a relatively natural way.

In some situations researchers might argue that 'truer' or 'fuller' data would be available through covert observation. However, it is unlikely that this would accord with the ethical policies of your study centre, and it was prohibited by the university ethical approval process in Heather's case. Such a strategy would need a detailed justification in advance to ensure the ethical legitimacy of data gathering plans. The issue of covert observation is also relevant where HR practitioners are undertaking research into their own organisations and have particular opportunities to observe interactions in (say) meetings or on training courses but without declaring the real purpose of their interest. The ethical questions below would need to be addressed whether any planned observation was 'overt' or 'covert' (Saunders, Lewis & Thornhill, 2019; Zikmund *et al*, 2013):

- Are you proposing overt or covert observation? If the latter, can you justify the use of covert rather than overt observation?
- How will informed consent be gained?
- Are the processes for data recording objective and accurate?
- Will your research observation have a detrimental effect on your relationships with those whom you will be treating as research participants?
- How might the process of observation 'fit' with the organisational culture in which it will take place?
- What time and opportunity is required through which to establish the trust and cooperation of those who will be observed?
- Would it be appropriate to undertake a debriefing with the participant(s) after any observations?

When thinking through these issues it is important to consider the level of trust and confidence that your intended participants will have of you. This will be affected by the nature of the power-relationship you have at present with them as well as the organisational culture and management style of the organisation in which your research is to be conducted.

Ethical issues after the data have been gathered

Once data have been collected you will be involved in interpreting them; formulating conclusions and then communicating your findings by writing and submitting a research report or dissertation. Many students assume that the main research ethics 'challenges' have been dealt with once your data have been collected. However, in addition to continuing concern about participants' anonymity and data confidentiality (which span all parts of the research project life cycle) the time that you spend after the data have been collected also has ethical implications.

First, the ethical responsibility of collecting data in an objective and accurate way 'carries forward' to the phase of the research where you are interpreting the information you have gathered and formulating conclusions (Zikmund, 2009). Here again it is important that your analysis honestly represents the data and that you **report fairly and accurately** on the information (rather than editing out the parts that are inconvenient).

Second, it is possible that some of your research participants (a line manager or the HR director, for example) are sufficiently interested in your research that they request some of the results. Perhaps an **interim report** is sought to gain some idea of the conclusions that might be drawn. Here the type of research project with which you are engaged and the relationship with any project sponsor or manager involved will influence the extent to which such requests could be met. For organisationally based projects where organisational sponsorship and support has been provided it is reasonable to provide a summary of the findings. However, if you hurry to meet an organisational deadline it is important that you do not fall into the trap of presenting partial results that may be misinterpreted as the **final** conclusions of your analysis.

A third issue with the reporting of findings revolves around **permission to iden-tify** any organisation(s) that participate in your research. If you have entered into a commitment to maintain organisational anonymity then you must abide by this unless the organisation agrees to a change. Where the organisation (or any individ-ual) agrees to be named it is possible that this will depend on them being able to read relevant parts of your report to assess the context within which their name will appear. They may also insist on some revisions.

Disposal of data is another issue that has ethical implications. Where data have been gathered for a student project there are few occasions when it will be needed after the successful assessment of the dissertation or research report. Disposal in such circumstances should be undertaken thoroughly and carefully: shredding paper rather than leaving documents in your organisation's waste paper bin and ensuring that files are deleted or 'wiped' from the storage devices on which they were held. However, there may be circumstances where the data you gathered are to be used for further purposes. You may, for example, have devised an attitude survey for the organisation as part of your project and follow-up surveys are to be undertaken in subsequent years. Alternatively, in addition to your research report, you may be hoping to disseminate your findings in other ways (presentation at a conference or in a journal article, etc). This may involve subsequent reference to your dataset. Another circumstance might be that your data might be donated to a data repository, which may then be accessed by subsequent researchers so that they can undertake some comparative research. Where there is a case for data retention it is important that the principles of data privacy are maintained and all references to names or other forms of identification are removed. It is also important that such issues are anticipated well in advance and that the permission of those who provided the data in the first place (the participants) is obtained.

The positive features of ethical assessment processes

 ## Case Example 4.10

Ethical assessment and scrutiny – another factor for delay?

Alexa was a part-time, self-employed, student who planned research into coaching using an action research method. In order to undertake her research Alexa had to find a client organisation that was willing to be the site for her research project. The process of securing such an organisation was lengthy but eventually Alexa

found an organisation where the research would be permitted and the process of action research was welcomed.

The organisation, having agreed to 'host' the research wanted the process to start quickly but Alexa's university supervisor indicated to her that she must complete an ethical scrutiny form to assure the institution that appropriate standards would be adhered to. This required Alexa to formulate her research objectives; be specific about the reasons for choosing this organisation, and identify how the participants would be selected. The ethical form also required a copy of her informed consent form, a detailed explanation of the action research process, a copy of the interview schedule that she planned to use and detailed information about how she would record and analyse her data. The form also required detailed information about her plans for data storage and security; the extent to which she would be able to achieve confidentiality and anonymity given the action research process and her plans for when and how she might

dispose of any of the data she had gathered. Alexa was worried. She was concerned that the organisation might change its mind if too much delay occurred but had not yet formulated her information sheet, interview schedule or research-gathering plans in sufficient detail.

Discussion questions

1 What objections might Alexa have to the requirement to complete an ethical application before beginning her action research fieldwork?

2 What positive features might result from the requirement for a thorough assessment and approval of ethical issues?

Feedback notes

When Alexa's supervisor confirmed to her that she could not begin any fieldwork without a successful submission of an extensive ethical assessment form her objections were somewhat similar to some of those expressed (usually in private) by other students. The most pressing objection was that unnecessary delay might result in the withdrawal of the organisation. A further objection that might be raised was that 'it is only bureaucracy'. While ethical assessment is often seen to be important for large-scale and significant pieces of research there might be the view that such a process is too extensive for a relatively small-scale applied research project. However, once Alexa had invested the time in the ethical assessment process she recognised its benefits. First, it enabled her to go forward with her research with confidence that she had thought ahead about any possible implications for her research participants and was in a better position to be able to answer any questions they might have about the research process. In addition, the process encouraged her to discuss the sampling strategy and methods for recording data with the client organisation, which meant that she was better able to plan a good quality research enquiry and avoid mistakes that she might have otherwise made.

Many student researchers (not just in HR) are tempted to want to move ahead quickly without undue delay with their data gathering processes. However, for good reasons, the requirement for ethical scrutiny in the planning and execution of research is becoming more prevalent in many higher education institutions. Managed appropriately this can lead to better research being undertaken.

Activity 4.7

Ethical assessment processes

1   Find out the ethical assessment requirements for your study centre and obtain a copy of any forms that you must complete. Identify: a) the main issues behind the questions that are asked; and b) the level of 'permission' you will require for your planned research.

2   If you are a student researcher planning to undertake your research in your own organisation then find out if your organisation has any ethical policies or forms of assessment and identify how you should go about obtaining ethical approval to enact your plans.

Feedback notes

Ethical assessment forms and processes are all structured and organised in different ways but the principles on which they are based are those outlined in this chapter. Key issues that relate to both individuals and organisations are privacy, anonymity and confidentiality. The dignity and well-being of research participants and the management of any issues involved in the relationship with organisations, sponsors or 'gatekeepers' are further important issues. Even with small-scale research it is becoming increasingly likely that your research plans will be scrutinised by someone (perhaps your supervisor or an ethics 'champion' within your study centre). Many educational institutions are developing different levels of scrutiny to reflect the different scope of research activities; perhaps distinguishing between undergraduate or postgraduate level studies; staff and research degree projects. In some institutions the research tutor or course leader may be responsible for ethical scrutiny of your proposals. In other instances, however, you may be required to submit your plans to the scrutiny of an ethics committee and this can be a slow process.

There are both advantages and disadvantages to the increased level of ethical scrutiny that has been developed in research in HR (and business and management more generally) over recent years. Timescales for research projects are increasingly difficult for students to achieve and so you may feel that this is yet another burden. However, there are important benefits to be achieved. If you take the time to address all the ethical issues in the planning stage of a project then it is likely that your project will achieve better quality outcomes. You will also find that you are better prepared to write the 'methodology' or 'methods' section or chapter in your dissertation or business research report (see Chapter 5) and it may well achieve more marks than it might have if the ethical issues had not been considered early on. Explicit concern with ethics is no longer an optional extra in HR investigative enquiries; rather it is now seen as a fundamental feature of good research.

CHECKLIST

- Research ethics is about adherence to a 'code of behaviour in relation to the rights of those who become the subject of your work or are affected by it'. Explicit concern with ethical issues is a fundamental feature of good research in HR.

- Standards are a defining feature of reputable professions as they provide the basis for ethical and effective professional activity. Initial work to develop national and international standards of practice by accredited standardisation organisations is at an early stage but is likely to become increasingly important for HR practitioners.

- Key ethical principles that are relevant to any research involving 'human subjects' at both individual and organisational levels are: privacy, confidentiality and anonymity; the dignity and well-being of research participants; and potential conflicts of interest with sponsors and/or organisations.

- HR practitioners operate within a professional code of ethics and conduct. HR research should be undertaken in a way that is professional, honest and characterised by integrity and sensitivity for customs, practices, culture and beliefs of others and which safeguards confidential, personal and commercially sensitive information.

- Ethical issues arise throughout the research process and need to be taken into account at the project planning stage, during the data gathering processes and after data gathering has been completed.

- There are a number of ethical issues to be considered where personal data held in a digital form may comprise part of a data gathering strategy, particularly relating to compliance with data protection regulations.

- Online methods of research require particular attention to ethical issues associated with: privacy; informed consent; anonymity; legal compliance and participant vulnerability.

- Ethical scrutiny is increasingly required for student research projects. Although this can be time-consuming it can lead to a better investigation than might otherwise have been the case.

TEST YOURSELF

1   Why are ethical considerations an imperative in HR research?

   a   Because the ends justify the means.

   b   Because research, like HR, is an inherently bureaucratic process.

   c   Because adherence to a professional code of conduct and ethics is important for the development of relationships of trust and integrity.

   d   Because it is a requirement to get a good mark in any qualification.

2   Which of the following is a purpose of standards in management and HR?

   a   To provide the basis for ethical and effective professional activity.

   b   To increase efficiency and consistency of HR practices in organisations.

   c   To ensure cross-organisational working and compliance with accepted norms of good practice.

   d   All of the above.

3   HR researchers have a duty of care to minimise any risk to research participants of:

   a   Physical discomfort or injury.

   b   Stress or anxiety.

   c   Coercion to participate.

   d   All of the above.

4   Why is it important that research data are stored in a secure way?

   a   So that you can track down your respondents at a later date if you want to get more data from them.

   b   So that people will not know what you have written about them.

   c   So that the external examiners can see the data if they want to.

   d   To prevent research participants from potential harm through identification or disclosure of confidential information.

5   Which method of data gathering is associated with a lack of informed consent?

   a   Structured interviewing.

   b   Questionnaire survey.

   c   Covert observation.

   d   Focus groups.

6   Which of the following approaches to organisational data gathering goes against the principles of organisational informed consent?

   a   Taking internal organisational documents without permission.

   b   The researcher pretending to be a job applicant in order to find out how the process works from an applicant's perspective.

   c   Telling the organisation you wish to research one thing when, in reality, you are interested in something else.

   d   Failing to ask permission to interview someone.

7   A gatekeeper is:

   a   A pathway to continuing access to a group of people or organisation.

   b   Gaining acceptance for your research from someone who can arrange access to research participants and other forms of data.

   c   Someone who requires money to 'let you through' into an organisation.

   d   The person in charge of ethical approval for student research projects.

8 Which of the following is **not** part of the principles underpinning the Data Protection Act?

 a Data may only be used for the purpose for which they were collected.

 b Data must be stored in a secure way.

 c Data must be kept for five years.

 d People have a right of access to any data held about them.

9 The purpose of the Freedom of Information Act in the United Kingdom is to:

 a Ensure data privacy and protect personal data.

 b Increase the transparency and accountability of public authorities.

 c Enable anyone to get information for any reason from any organisation.

 d Ensure that people who request information explain why they want it.

 ## Review Questions

Take the time to find out what the requirements are for the ethical scrutiny and assessment of your research.

1 What are the ethical scrutiny requirements of your centre?

2 If you are undertaking your research in an organisation then does it have any ethical policies or procedures you must adhere to?

3 What is the ethical code of conduct of your professional organisation?

4 Are there questions on any of the ethical forms you need to complete that you do not understand? Is it possible to access guidance for the completion of the forms and for a successful ethical review process?

Questions for reflection

This final part of the chapter enables you to reflect about your professional development and develop your skills and knowledge. This

will enable you to build your confidence and credibility, track your learning, see your progress, and demonstrate your achievements.

Taking stock

1 How might the professional standards of your professional association impact on the research project you are planning to undertake?

2 In the research context in which you will be working who has an interest in the findings, conclusions and outcomes of your project? Might there be a potential conflict of interest between your role as an objective investigator and the expectations of your line manager? A 'gatekeeper'? A project sponsor? What actions might you consider to clarify your role as investigator and as colleague/employee/supervisor/internal consultant, etc?

3 To what extent is your research idea a 'sensitive issue' for any organisation(s) and for any individuals who participate? What influence might this have for your ethical choices about informed consent and respect for dignity and well-being?

Strengths and weaknesses

4   How clear are you about the type of data you propose to gather? Can you articulate the sampling strategy that you propose and explain how you would recruit and select your research participants? Who might help you to clarify these issues?

5   How clear are you about what information to provide on an information or briefing document that would ensure informed consent has been achieved? Who might help you to clarify these issues?

6   What plans do you have for the secure storage of data? Think about: a) paper based data; and b) electronically stored data. Can you access locked storage in the workplace? Would you be permitted to remove data gathered at work and store them at home? Do

you know how to add password protection to any electronic files that you keep?

7   What expectations might your sponsor or organisation have about the retention of any data for subsequent use after your research project has been completed? Who do you need to discuss this with and what steps would be required to ensure data confidentiality and anonymity?

Being a practitioner-researcher

8   To what extent will it be possible for you and those with whom you work to be able to distinguish between your role as a researcher and your 'usual' work role? What steps might you take to maintain this distinction during the research process?

9   What organisational sensitivities will you need to take into account in your research to ensure the dignity and well-being of all those who are involved and in relation to any potential unintended consequences?

 ## Useful Resources

Ackland, R (2013) *Web Social Science: Concepts, data and tools for social scientists in the digital age*, Sage Publications, London

Anderson, V (2017) HRD standards and standardization: Where now for Human Resource Development? *Human Resource Development International*, **20** (4), pp 327–45, DOI: 10.1080/13678868.2017.1321872

Association of Internet Researchers (AoIR) (2012) Ethical Decision-Making and Internet Research: Recommendations from the AoIR Ethics Working Committee (Version 2.0) [Online] http://www.aoir. org/reports/ethics.pdf (archived at https://perma.cc/ C3K4-RRDS)

BSI (2017) Webinar on PD76006 – Guide to Learning and Development [Online] https://www.bsigroup. com/en-GB/our-services/events/2017/2017-09-13— Webinar-PD-76006/Webinar-PD76006-live/ (archived at https://perma.cc/X99Q-5HYC)

BSI (2017) BS 76005:2017 Valuing people through diversity and inclusion, Code of practice for organizations [Online] https://shop.bsigroup.com/ ProductDetail/?pid=000000000030338898 (archived at https://perma.cc/R9A8-GRK6)

BSI (2017) PD 7006:2017 Guide to learning and development [Online] https://shop.bsigroup.com/ProductDetail/?pid=000000000030350673 (archived at https://perma.cc/7FFW-H6KH)

CIPD (2017) Business Ethics and the Role of HR, CIPD Fact Sheet [Online] https://www.cipd.co.uk/knowledge/culture/ethics/role-hr-factsheet (archived at https://perma.cc/97X2-LY3A)

CIPD (2018) HR and Standards, CIPD Fact Sheet [Online] https://www.cipd.co.uk/knowledge/strategy/hr/standards-factsheet (archived at https://perma.cc/LJY4-3NAP)

EthicsWeb.CA (nd) Applied Ethics Resources on WWW [Online] http://www.ethicsweb.ca/resources/ (archived at https://perma.cc/SHM3-5GB7)

Fielding, NG, Lee, RM and Blank, G (2008) *The Sage Handbook of Online Research Methods*, Sage, London

Iphofen, R (nd) Research Ethics in Ethnography/Anthropology, *European Commission* [Online] http://ec.europa.eu/research/participants/data/ref/h2020/other/hi/ethics-guide-ethnog-anthrop_en.pdf (archived at https://perma.cc/233N-NGRU)

Institute of Business Ethics, Codes of Ethics: Introduction to ethics policies, and programmes and codes [Online] https://www.ibe.org.uk/ethical-values-and-codes/102/52 (archived at https://perma.cc/NPT7-7FP4)

ISO (nd) [accessed 9 February 2017] ISO/TC 260 Human Resource Management, *ISO website* [Online] http://www.iso.org/iso/standards_development/technical_committees/other_bodies/iso_technical_committee.htm?commid=628737 (archived at https://perma.cc/8JMK-KYJH)

MacDougall, AE, Bagdasarov, Z, Johnson, JF and Mumford, MD (2015) Managing Workplace Ethics: an extended conceptualization of ethical sensemaking and the facilitative role of human resources, *Research in Personnel and Human Resources Management*, **2015**, pp 121–89

Naden, C (2016) Improve the Bottom Line With a New Range of Human Resource Management Standards [Online] https://www.iso.org/news/2016/09/Ref2111.html (archived at https://perma.cc/WJ8G-7AK2)

Taylor, M (2017) Good Work: The Taylor Review of Modern Working Practices, *Department for Business, Work and Industrial Strategy* [Online] https://www.gov.uk/government/publications/good-work-the-taylor-review-of-modern-working-practices (archived at https://perma.cc/B2W4-62EG)

Trevelyan, L (2018) The GDPR: Everything you know about data protection is changing, *People Management* [Online] https://www.peoplemanagement.co.uk/long-reads/articles/gdpr-data-protection-changing (archived at https://perma.cc/4EA2-C2W4)

 References

Bell, E, Bryman, A and Harley, B (2019) *Business Research Methods*, 5th edn, Oxford University Press, Oxford

Birkinshaw, P (2010) *Freedom of Information: The law, the practice and the ideal*, Cambridge University Press, Cambridge

BSI (2015) BS 76000:2015 Human resource, Valuing people: Management system - Requirements and guidance. Retrieved from https://shop.bsigroup.com/ProductDetail/?pid=000000000030298954

Corbett, CJ and Yeung, ACL (2008) Special Issue on Meta-Standards in Operations Management: Cross-Disciplinary Perspectives, *International Journal of Production Economics*, **113** (1), pp 1–2. doi:10.1016/j.ijpe.2007.02.044

Hooley, T, Marriott, J and Wellens, J (2012) *What is Online Research?* Bloomsbury, London

Lam, H (2016) Social media dilemmas in the employment context, *Employee Relations*, **38,** pp 420–37, DOI: 10.1108/ER-04-2015-0072

Li, J (2013) Web-based technology and the changing landscape of HRD, *Human Resource Development International*, **16** (3), pp 247–50, DOI: 10.1080/13678868.2013.799401

Oliver, P (2010) *The Student's Guide to Research Ethics*, McGraw Hill, Maidenhead

Parry, E and Strohmeier, S (2014) HRM in the digital age – digital changes and challenges of the HR profession, *Employee Relations*, **36** (4), DOI: 10.1108/ ER-03-2014-0032

Remenyi, D, Swan, N and Van Den Assem, B (2011) *Ethics Protocols and Research Ethics Committees*, Academic Publishing International Ltd, Reading

Saunders, MNK, Lewis, P and Thornhill, A (2019) *Research Methods for Business Students*, 8th edn, Pearson, London

Savage, A and Hyde, R (2014) Using freedom of information requests to facilitate research, *International Journal of Social Research Methodology*, **17** (3), pp 303–17, DOI: 10.1080/13645579.2012.742280

Schaufeli, WB, Bakker, AB and Salanova, M (2006) The measurement of work engagement with a short questionnaire a cross-national study, *Educational and Psychological Measurement*, **66** (4), pp 701–16, DOI: 10.1177/0013164405282471

Walby, K and Larsen, M (2012) Access to Information and Freedom of Information Requests: Neglected Means of Data Production in the Social Sciences, *Qualitative Inquiry*, **18** (1), pp 31–42. https://doi. org/10.1177/1077800411427844

Zikmund, WG, Babin, BJ, Carr, JC and Griffin, M (2013) *Business Research Methods*, Cengage Learning, Kentucky

05
Planning the research process

LEARNING OBJECTIVES

This chapter should help you to:

- decide what data to gather and when;
- identify the main types of research studies in HRM research;
- highlight key differences between qualitative and quantitative data;
- examine the implications of using a mix of qualitative and quantitative methods;
- clarify the relationship between research, theory and practice;
- evaluate the quality of your data;
- write about your research methods.

CHAPTER OUTLINE

- How to use this chapter
- HRM research
- Qualitative, quantitative and mixed methods research
- Research, theory and practice
- Data quality issues

- Planning to gather data

- Writing your methodology chapter or section

- Summary checklist

- Test yourself, review and reflect questions

- Useful resources

How to use this chapter

This chapter draws together some of the themes and issues that have been introduced in Chapters 1 to 4 to help you to clarify the overall approach and the different types of data that will be most appropriate for your research. By the time you read this chapter you should have a fairly firm idea about the focus of your topic and some ideas about the overall research strategy that you will adopt. Now you need to make further decisions about how you will put your ideas into action and take the project forward in a coherent and justifiable way.

An explanation and justification of your research methods is required for projects at all levels, whether you are undertaking a small-scale research project for an intermediate level qualification, a dissertation for an undergraduate course, a CIPD advanced level investigation into a business issue or a dissertation for a taught Masters-level qualification in HRM. You may need to provide a justification of the research methods you intend to use in your research if you are asked to submit a research proposal at an earlier stage of your qualification. This chapter will help you to develop that justification. If you are in a hurry to get on with your project, you may be tempted to skip this stage and launch straight into some form of data gathering. However, the investment of a small amount of time and thought now will reap significant rewards in the quality of the research that you carry out and prevent costly mistakes that you may come to regret when you begin your data analysis.

 Case Example 5.1

From research idea to research plan

Vivienne was a student undertaking a distance-learning course in her home country in Central Europe. She worked at an HR service centre that provided HR advice, support and processes for all of her organisation's many European operations. For her research project Vivienne gained permission to study communications and knowledge management in one of the divisions in her organisation where some problems about 'mis-communication' had recently arisen. When she read her course materials Vivienne noticed that before she undertook any research she had to produce a research proposal for her supervisor to scrutinise and also complete a fairly detailed form about issues associated with research ethics. However, the manager of the division where Vivienne was due to be undertaking her project was impatient: he wanted the data NOW and some recommendations for action VERY SOON. He told Vivienne he had already decided which staff she could interview and had set up some of the appointments for her. The first appointment was scheduled for the following week.

Discussion questions

1   What are the opportunities and the dangers of proceeding quickly into a data collection process as described in this case example?

2   What would you do if you were in the same circumstance?

Feedback notes

You may have guessed that, in the circumstance in which she found herself, Vivienne felt confused and anxious. On the one hand she was lucky to be given the opportunity outside of her normal service-centre work role to undertake a piece of research with the support of a divisional manager. Gaining permission to conduct research in an organisational setting is a very relevant achievement and will allow her the collection of primary data for her research project. The collection of this data will also be very important for practice in her organisation, since Vivienne will provide feedback and recommendations for action. On the other hand, Vivienne had several concerns. The risk of losing the support of the manager and permission to undertake the data collection for her research project was a big worry. This made her inclined to proceed gratefully in the way the divisional manager had arranged. However, his concern for haste could lead to a range of problems. First, Vivienne was anxious that the manager seemed to have already decided her research method (interviews) and her sample respondents. Vivienne did not know the basis on which they had been chosen but felt it was unlikely that they would be a representative sample of people in the division. Second, in her course materials Vivienne had been reading about the importance of informed consent, anonymity and confidentiality for those involved in her research and she had no idea about whether such issues had been taken into account when the manager arranged the interviews for her. She knew that these ethical concerns were extremely relevant when one conducts any type of research involving people, and her distance-learning course required that all students follow rigorous ethical procedures when they conduct this type of research. Third, Vivienne was not even sure that interviews would be the most appropriate way to gather data. She was very nervous about his request for recommendations within a month; as a distance-learning student working part-time Vivienne was conscious that she could not work full-time on this project and that a full analysis of the data and completion of her research report would not occur for three to four months. Her distance-learning course workbooks were very clear about the importance of thinking through methods to formulate an approach capable of generating meaningful and valuable conclusions. She knew that, whatever methods she used, they must be clearly explained and justified.

After an e-mail exchange with her tutor Vivienne arranged an urgent meeting with the divisional manager. At this meeting she reassured him that she acknowledged the urgency of the issue he had asked her to investigate but also explained the requirements of her course. In this context Vivienne proposed that she undertake some initial interviews (as planned by the divisional manager) to take the form of a 'pilot study'. This would help identify any other issues that were pertinent and allow for some initial thoughts to be fed back to the management team in an aggregated and generalised form and for the development of a fuller research strategy to take forward a study. The manager accepted these proposals and the study centre was also in agreement so Vivienne had a good basis on which to proceed.

The aim of this chapter is to help you develop and articulate a credible rationale for the method or methods that you decide to use to answer your research question or questions. This is a focal chapter of the book; many of the issues about approaches to research that were introduced in earlier chapters are brought together in this one. Many of the issues about types of data that are introduced in this chapter will also be considered in more detail in the chapters that follow.

HRM research

Hart (2013) points out that all research needs data. Research data in HR can be very diverse and it depends on the type of research question or questions we want to answer. Some studies focus on what HR practices are adopted by an organisation and on how they are implemented. For this type of study, we may wish to conduct some interviews with HR managers and use a more qualitative approach. Some other studies are more concerned with how HR practices relate to the perceptions, attitudes, behaviour and well-being of employees in the organisation. For this type of study, we can use either a qualitative approach or a quantitative approach, or even a mixed methods approach. For example, if we want to understand how employees form their opinions about their managers we may wish to interview them. Another example is if we want to identify the major predictors of turnover intentions in an organisation, then we may want to use a quantitative approach, where we provide surveys with previously validated scales and test the effect of different employee attitudes on turnover intentions. Additionally, there are studies that focus on more objective aspects related to HRM, such as the budget allocated to specific HR practices and their link with organisational profit. The methodological approach for this type of study is likely to be quantitative, since we are dealing with readily available objective data in this case.

Wright and Boswell (2002) revised the research done in the HRM field and proposed a typology of HRM research based on two dimensions: level of analysis (individual/group or organisation, that is the micro or the macro level) and number of practices (single or multiple). Figure 5.1 presents Wright and Boswell's (2002) typology of HRM research.

According to Wright and Boswell (2002), traditionally micro HRM research has explored the impact of HR practices on individuals. This type of research is associated with industrial/organisational psychology and is usually interested in assessing the impact of specific HR practices (Q4) or bundles of HR practices (Q3)

Figure 5.1 Wright and Boswell's typology of HR research

Number of HRM Practices

	Multiple	Single
Organisation	Q1. Strategic HRM Industrial relations High performance work systems	Q2. Isolated Functions (ie, research aimed at demonstrating a relationship between a particular functional area and firm performance)
Individual	Q3. Psychological contract Employment relationship	Q4. Traditional/functional HRM Industrial/organisational psychology

Level of Analysis

Reproduced with permission.

on individuals (skills, abilities, attitudes, etc) and their ultimate impact on some performance measure (productivity, absenteeism, turnover). In contrast, more recent macro HRM research uses the organisation (corporation or business unit). This type of research usually assesses variables through asking an informed respondent about their organisation. This type of research usually focuses on how different are variables across organisations, assuming relative uniformity in the variable within the organisation. In this type of research there are studies that ask HR managers about an overall HR strategy and a combined set of multiple practices in a high-performance work system (Q1), whereas others focus on specific practices (like training, recruitment, selection, performance appraisal) that are investigated individually (Q2).

This section aimed to give you an overview of the type of research that can be done in the HR field. As you can see, there are many different approaches you can take and the choices you make will depend on your own personal interests, your professional goals, the access you may have to organisations and the type of research philosophy and methodological approaches you identify the most with. The following section will help you explain and justify your methodological choices for your research project.

Qualitative, quantitative and mixed methods research

The type of data that researchers gather in order to answer their research questions tends to vary depending on the research tradition they are working within. Chapters 1 and 2 considered the different approaches to thinking about knowledge that affect how researchers undertake their investigations. The world view associated with positivism underpins an objectivist research approach grounded in an attempt to use the scientific method that originated in the physical sciences. This includes collecting facts or indicators and testing for relationships between them in order to make generalisable conclusions. The constructivist world view underpins the interpretivist research approach, which examines the meanings and experiences of people in different situations or cultural contexts in order to understand and explain their particular situations in detail. As indicated already, researchers within these traditions tend to find different forms of data more meaningful. Those within a positivist tradition tend to value **quantitative data** (the term given to data that can be quantified and counted). Interpretivist researchers value **qualitative data** (the term given to data based on meanings that are expressed through words and language).

 Case Example 5.2

Researching apprenticeship schemes

Carly was a mature student who had been very involved in running apprenticeship schemes in her organisation. She was passionately committed to the ideals of vocational education and training and apprenticeship processes but became increasingly aware that, even with UK government support of apprenticeship schemes and the introduction of a 'levy', HR practitioners and organisations seemed to lack a common view of the purpose and benefits of work-based apprenticeships. She decided to compare different understandings of apprenticeships for her business research report and had to decide what data to collect and how to do it. She contacted a number of local organisations and eight of them agreed to participate in the research. She offered them a summary of her findings in return for their help. Having achieved the involvement of these organisations Carly had to decide how to gather data and which groups of the workforce within each organisation she needed to access. She considered using focus groups, interviews and a questionnaire.

Discussion questions

1   What are the advantages of a questionnaire survey method for measuring expectations of apprenticeship schemes?

2   What value might interviews or focus groups add to the research?

3   Which method of gathering data is best for Carly's research project, and why?

4   If Carly were to opt for gathering both qualitative and quantitative data what challenges would she face?

Feedback notes

There was a range of methods that Carly could use to find out what people think about apprenticeship schemes. It would be possible to interview those responsible for recruiting apprentices and also to interview a sample of the apprentices. Alternatively, a series of focus groups could be organised or, perhaps, people could be encouraged to keep a diary, in which their understanding of the apprenticeship scheme could be recorded in their own words and over an extended period of time.

Carly also felt that an attitude survey might be a useful way of collecting data from the apprentices. She was keen on this idea as a questionnaire provides a structured approach with pre-validated measures, meaning that her results could probably be replicated. Therefore, she felt that it would be possible to compare the results from surveys at each of her eight participating organisations. The anonymity afforded by a questionnaire would also mean that apprentices could respond in a more honest way. As a result of both of these factors (structure and detachment) Carly felt that data generated in this way could be analysed to identify relationships between different variables such as different educational backgrounds, different employment sectors, differences in age and gender, and so on.

On the other hand, however, it might be possible that people's opinions about the apprenticeships may include more elements than the ones they are being asked about in a questionnaire. Where the researcher is more involved in interviews it would be possible to probe for meanings and interpretations and to ask why the respondents feel the way that they do in relation to a question.

Consideration of these issues might lead you to suggest that a mixture of methods would be appropriate to generate data to help Carly answer her research questions. You might suggest that she undertake some quantitative research first to establish the 'broad trends' in terms of attitudes and then utilise qualitative data to probe into the underlying reasons and meanings behind these trends. She could perhaps undertake quantitative research, asking apprentices to reply to surveys and identify their main trends in terms of attitudes, guaranteeing anonymity, and also conduct some interviews with those responsible for recruiting apprentices.

Mixed methods research can also bring difficulties, however, and Carly was very conscious that her time was limited. Undertaking one form of data gathering and analysis in a systematic and competent way is time-consuming enough. Using more than one method, particularly when the skills required in collection and analysing data are so different, would present major challenges to her in terms of a lack of time and expertise.

The main differences between qualitative and quantitative approaches to research are shown in Table 5.1.

Figure 5.2 provides an overview of the different methods in relation to the extent to which they are structured/unstructured and the level of involvement that the researcher has with the process of gathering data.

Mixed methods research

As indicated in Case Example 5.2, many HR researchers, particularly those who are undertaking case study research, find that they can see the value of both qualitative and quantitative data. The term 'mixed methods' research is often used to describe research that makes use of both data types in a way that enables the insights to be mutually illuminating (Bell, Bryman and Harley, 2019; Saunders, Lewis and Thornhill, 2019). Mixed methods research provides a number of advantages to HR researchers:

- **Triangulation:** this term is used to describe the process whereby data from different sources are used to 'cross-check' the findings. In this way you can add credibility to your conclusions (Saunders, Lewis and Thornhill, 2019).

Table 5.1 Qualitative and quantitative approaches to research

Quantitative Data	Qualitative Data
Hypotheses created based on theoretical assumptions and results from empirical research	Research questions aiming to explore a specific real-life context or situation
Analysis of a predetermined number of variables to be measured	Analysis of themes that are suggested by a range of sources
Concern to verify the existence of significant relationships between the variables that are being measured	Concern to understand the meanings and associations between different factors
Variables are expressed in the language of the investigation	The particular language of informants is valued and utilised
Seeks to achieve abstraction from repeated observations and understand the effect of different variables on people's opinions and actions	Seeks to find out how a smaller number of people understand a situation and how their understanding influences their actions

(Neuman, 2012)

Figure 5.2 Different methods of gathering data

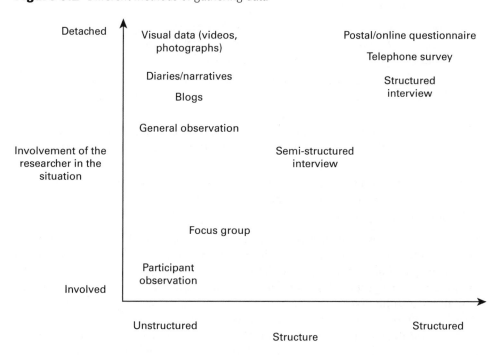

- **Facilitation of alternative methods:** in some cases, qualitative data might generate an interpretation about a number of important variables and a quantitative approach might then enable you to examine the extent to which the relationships between these variables applies across a wider research population.
- **Interpreting the relationship between different variables:** in other cases, quantitative analysis may have established that relationships between variables are significant and did not occur 'by chance' and qualitative data may then help you to establish 'why' such relationships are occurring.
- **Moving between different stages of a project:** some researchers start with a broad research question. Once they have made use of data from a quantitative survey they find they are better able to refine the focus of their research for the next stage. Other researchers invite people who have participated in a survey to provide access information so that they can participate in a second, more qualitative, phase of research.

Although there is no consensus on these issues, mixed methods research is advocated by an increasing number of business and HR researchers (see, for example, Gill and Johnson, 2010; Bell, Bryman and Harley, 2019; Fox *et al*, 2007; Creswell, 2018). In some cases, qualitative and quantitative data are gathered and analysed 'in parallel' and in others the data are gathered on a 'one after the other' basis. However, mixed methods research should not be confused with 'messy-methods' research. A systematic and rigorous approach is required, regardless of the range of the different data types that are gathered and analysed. Key issues for the quality of mixed methods research are (Bell *et al*, 2019):

- Ensure a competent and justified research design and execution. Poorly designed and implemented research will generate dubious and unreliable findings even if more than one method is used.
- 'More is better' is not an appropriate justification for mixed methods research. The rationale for choice of method(s) must follow from your research questions or objectives.
- Ensure that you have the time to engage in different data gathering and analysis methods within the constraints you are under for your student project.
- Ensure that you have the expertise to gather and analyse different types of data. Mixed methods data gathering followed by poor quality analyses will not lead to a valid outcome.

In organisational research, particularly when it is part of a qualification process, there are also other practical issues that influence decisions about methods. Operational issues, time pressures and the preferences and imperatives of others who will be involved in the project, such as the employees, line managers and the project sponsor will all have to be taken into account. In the particular case of a student research project, the research supervisor's view in terms of research philosophy and associated methodology will also influence decisions about methods. Part of the planning process of any project, therefore, will require discussion and negotiation about the methods to be used, the participants who will be available, and the timescale over which the research must be undertaken.

A number of different factors will influence the choice of methods that you make and these are briefly outlined below:

- **Nature of the topic.** The nature of your research objectives and questions are a fundamental starting point for deciding on appropriate methods. Key things to ask are: what are my research questions? What data will enable me to answer those questions? What is the most appropriate way to obtain the data? If you find that your initial data gathering plans have changed for some reason it is a good idea to review (and consider amending) your research questions or objectives if the changes may have resulted in a lack of alignment between your research aim and questions and the type of data you will be analysing.

- **Extent of literature.** If you know that there is a lot of literature already about your topic, then it is likely that you will choose methods that enable you to build on what is already known. If, however, your area is relatively new and 'unexplored' then this will also influence your choice of method(s).

- **Timescale.** Another issue to take into account is the time available to you. Some methods might be able to be undertaken over a shorter timespan than others. You may also need to learn new skills to analyse your data, and the time needed for this type of learning should also be accounted for.

- **Resources.** Some methods require specialist resources (perhaps facilities to generate transcripts of unstructured interviews or the availability of quantitative data analysis software) and it is important that you find out if these are available in your study centre.

- **Issues of access and permission.** Some project sponsors, in organisational research, have clear preferences for different methods, and these must be taken into account in deciding which methods to adopt and whether the nature of the research questions/objectives might need to be reviewed.

These aspects should be discussed in detail with your supervisor, who will help you organise your research ideas and assess how feasible your choices are given the time-frame you have.

Research, theory and practice

In chapters 1 and 2 the different purposes of research (do you see yourself as an 'explorer', a 'detective', a 'doctor'?) were discussed. Regardless of the way in which you see your role while you are undertaking your research and whether you intend to undertake descriptive, exploratory or explanatory research, you will need to position your work within a broad body of theory. You will be able to start shaping your decisions concerning theory by finding different resources, as described in Chapter 3. The way you use theory will affect your reasoning process and the way that you take your research forward. This affects decisions about what data to gather and where to look for the data, and how you will make sense of data. This section considers the issues about theory and practice-based research in 'plain English' so that you can: work out an appropriate reasoning process; be clear about your own use of theory; and work out your data gathering and data analysis intentions in a justifiable way.

Activity 5.1

Web-based activity

Imagine that you want to study the motivations behind individuals' career choices. Go to a general search engine (such as google.co.uk or yahoo.co.uk) and type in the search words 'motivation theory'. Glance through the first five links that are given as a result of your search. What are the first results you get when you search for 'motivation theory'?

Feedback notes

Theory is the foundation on which almost all HR practice and research is based and your research project needs to be 'grounded' in a theoretical perspective; it needs a theoretical 'home'. Even if the term is a difficult one for you, theory is useful in all credible research processes. Theory provides ideas about how different HR relevant phenomena are related to each other and why these things are related. People make use of theories (often in an implicit way) to make sense of what is happening. For example, in your web-based search, it is likely that your first results were about Maslow's theory of motivation (Maslow, 1943). This theory still provides something of a basis for a range of career or personal development processes undertaken within organisations. One of the important outcomes of research is to find out which theory is better at explaining what is happening in practice and help people make sense of data to refine and develop professional practice.

As theory plays an important (if implicit) part of effective HR practice it is important that professionals working in HR are able to evaluate different theories, models and frameworks to provide a clearer understanding of what is going on in organisational situations. From there it is possible to plan and implement HR interventions that have more chance of achieving their objectives.

What is theory? What are models? What are frameworks?

In everyday conversation people tend to use the word 'theory' to mean 'opinion' or 'conjecture' (Lee and Lings, 2008) and it is true that many HR practitioners often seem to base what they do on intuitive opinions or propositions. HR research, however, involves making use of, and refining, explicit theory, defined as: **a logical model or framework of concepts (ie abstract ideas) that describes and explains how phenomena are related with each other and which would apply in a variety of circumstances.**

Theory is particularly useful for HR practitioners for three reasons:

- **Theory helps us understand what is happening.** In HR departments or functions people come from all over the organisation to ask about people-related situations and problems. However, in order to contribute to the solution of those people-related problems or issues HR professionals cannot just rely on '**know about**' knowledge; they need to have an equivalent body of '**know why**' knowledge in order to effectively communicate organisational messages. Theory provides that know-why knowledge.

- **Theory helps us to understand issues from more than one perspective.** Anyone who works, or aspires to work, in HR comes to realise that people issues are never simple; they always invoke the need to see things differently and through more than one 'lens'. Knowledge of theory equips us to do this as HR practice draws on a wide range of different and often overlapping areas of theory or disciplines such as systems theory, complexity theory, psychology, sociology, economics and anthropology. Therefore, theory helps us to diagnose and understand what is going on and evaluate credible approaches to address HR situations and opportunities.

- **Theory provides a basis for models and frameworks of practice.** Much of day-to-day HR practice is dominated by models and frameworks. **Models** are derived from theories; they make use of theoretical concepts (abstract ideas) to represent and describe what is (or could be) going on in organisational situations. Performance related pay is an example of an HR model of reward that is guided by concepts about performance and behaviour derived from economic theory. However, an understanding of some of the potentially dysfunctional consequences of performance related pay might come from theories of human action and development grounded in other areas of the social sciences. **Frameworks** are also linked to both models and theories. They describe the underlying structure of the way that work-based practices are carried out. Kirkpatrick's (1959) four levels of training evaluation are a good example of a framework (or structure) through which the value of training interventions can be assessed. Although Kirkpatrick has never made this explicit, his approach is grounded in systems theory.

Where do theories come from?

Having established that everyday life for HR practitioners, at both individual and organisational levels, would be difficult to sustain without the use of theory it is interesting to ask where theories come from in the first place. Gill and Johnson (2010) use Kolb's Learning Cycle (Kolb *et al*, 1979) to illustrate the point that theory and practice are like 'two sides of a coin' and that it is possible to understand the relationship between theory and data in terms of how people learn to make sense of the world.

Kolb suggests that learning involves a number of different stages. Each stage feeds into the others and Kolb suggests that the learning process can begin at any part of the cycle. This can be illustrated by referring to the learning experience that many HR practitioners go through when they develop their skills in recruitment interviewing. Some HR professionals, in the early stages of their careers, are asked to carry out interviews with no formal training. They undertake their first interviews in a state of nervous tension, armed only with the company's forms and procedures, which they have, hopefully, read in advance. They undertake the interview(s) and, afterwards they reflect on 'how it went'. There will be some features of their practice that they are pleased with and some that they will want to improve. They will devise for themselves some general guidelines (the dos and don'ts of interviewing) and they will try them out the next time that they interview. In this way their learning process involves **HR practice** (doing the interviews), **reflection/evaluation** (what went well and not so well), **generalisation** (personal/organisational dos and don'ts) and **implementation** (applying the dos and don'ts the next time that they interview). This cycle will, of course, repeat itself many times and, over time, HR practitioners may be able to go on a course or read some books on effective interviewing to enhance the quality of their practice.

This example illustrates how, at an individual level, generalised concepts and principles (theories) form part of the normal process of developing practice in HR and there is a link between theory and research based on our experience and practice. It also shows how 'theory-building' can occur as a result of different reasoning processes that researchers refer to as 'deduction' and 'induction'.

Deduction and induction

A key point to make is that any theory is always provisional (Lee and Lings, 2008). No theory can ever be '100 per cent proved'. **Deductive** reasoning involves refining and reconsidering theories through a process of testing propositions (what should happen as predicted by a theory) in different contexts or situations. Research is needed to generate the evidence about what happens in these conditions and on the basis of the evidence the theory can be provisionally confirmed or amended (and in extreme cases it may be discarded altogether).

Inductive reasoning starts at the level of practice. Through a process of gathering data through research the inductive researcher will develop some general propositions about what is happening and start to 'theory-build'. In many cases theory that has been developed from an inductive approach will go on to be further developed through empirical testing in a deductive way. Therefore, both inductive and deductive approaches to research are rooted in practice and in theory. It would be unrealistic to think that your research (or ours!) will ever develop a 'new' theory; most HR research, particularly that which is carried out by practitioner-researchers, works at the 'margins' of theory. Nonetheless, it is important to be clear about the theoretical 'anchor' or starting point for a project so that it is possible to add new ideas to it, expand its power to explain what is happening or highlight areas of weakness within it.

 Case Example 5.3

Choosing a research approach

Pavlin was a part-time HR student who worked in an education ministry in his government outside of the United Kingdom. A key issue for all government departments in Pavlin's country was to try to develop a more performance orientated and less bureaucratic style of management. In addition, government policy was to base HR decisions on employee competence rather than relying on employees' family connections and other networks associated with traditional patronage processes. Pavlin was given responsibility for finding an objective and reliable process that would help managers identify appropriate people for appropriate job roles. He decided to make this the focus of his dissertation research.

Pavlin did some reading around the topic and found very little reference to theory although he found many lists of different methods to identify which people might be appropriate for different roles in organisations. He also noticed that most authors recommended a mix of methods to increase reliability. Pavlin came across a lot of literature about scientific methods such as psychometric testing and assessment centres. Pavlin decided to focus his research on an evaluation of psychometric methods for future use within the education ministry.

Discussion questions

1   To what extent would a deductive or an inductive approach be most appropriate for this research?

2   On what type of theories could this research project be based?

Feedback notes

You may have noticed that it is not possible to rule out either the inductive or the deductive approach in this sort of situation. Pavlin considered using an inductive approach. His reading had alerted him to the way in which a number of different factors, such as employee expectations, management style, clarity of expectations, initial training and employee reward make a difference to employee performance. Therefore, he wondered about exploring these issues by asking newly appointed staff and their managers to describe their experiences and the factors that both inhibited and encouraged performance in order to make a rounded set of recommendations about selection and induction processes to enhance performance. Pavlin also had to think hard about the extent to which he could utilise a theoretical perspective in his dissertation as so much of the literature in this feature of HR involves descriptions of models and frameworks with very little reference to theory.

On the other hand, Pavlin also considered using a deductive approach. His idea was to take a sample of existing staff comprising a mix of those considered to be very effective in their roles as well as those whose performance was less good. He thought that he would then give them a number of different psychometric tests and assess which tests were associated with results that offered the best prediction for work performance. If he had undertaken his research this way, then Pavlin's research would involve gathering data to analyse the propositions concerning the predictive ability of different psychometric tests.

In this instance Pavlin had to make a choice. If he decided to explore the different organisational factors influencing employment performance, then he would need to ground his work in systems theory and try to add on to this theory in his context. On the other hand, if he decided to pursue the approach of testing different psychometric tests he would need to position his work within the many psychological theories about personality traits, attributes and work performance.

Figure 5.3 Inductive and deductive reasoning

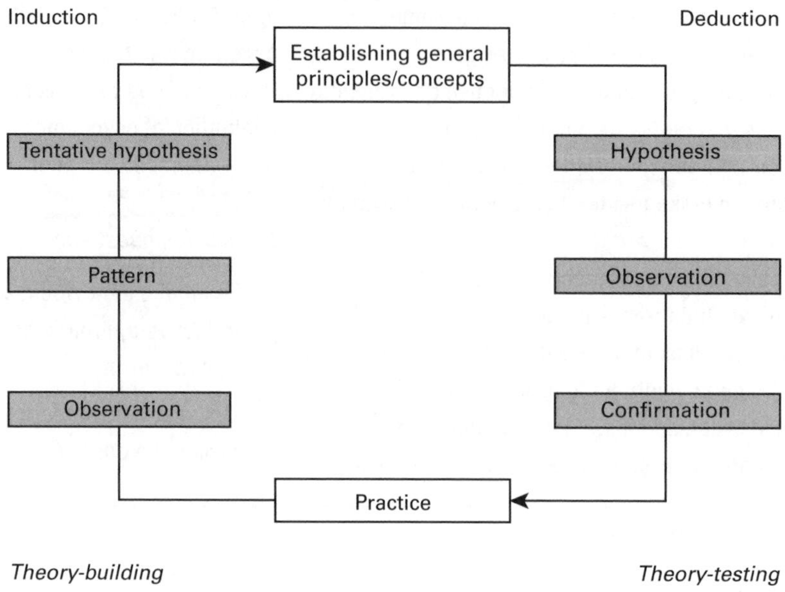

Induction   Deduction

```
                    ┌─────────────────────┐
                    │ Establishing general │
                    │  principles/concepts │
                    └─────────────────────┘

┌─────────────────────┐                    ┌─────────────────────┐
│ Tentative hypothesis │                    │     Hypothesis      │
└─────────────────────┘                    └─────────────────────┘

┌─────────────────────┐                    ┌─────────────────────┐
│       Pattern       │                    │     Observation     │
└─────────────────────┘                    └─────────────────────┘

┌─────────────────────┐                    ┌─────────────────────┐
│     Observation     │                    │    Confirmation     │
└─────────────────────┘                    └─────────────────────┘

                    ┌─────────────────────┐
                    │      Practice       │
                    └─────────────────────┘
```

Theory-building   *Theory-testing*

The main features of the inductive and deductive approaches to research are shown in Figure 5.3. This indicates the different relationships with theory of the two approaches (theory-building and theory-testing, respectively). It also indicates how an inductive approach is sometimes associated with the constructivist and inter-pretivist understanding of the research process and the deductive approach can be informed by an objectivist and positivist approach. Both deductive and inductive approaches have value in HR research. The points summarised below (Robson and McCartan, 2016; Saunders, Lewis and Thornhill, 2019) represent ends of a continuum rather than a hard-and-fast distinction. Where a mixed methods approach is being adopted there is also likely to be an interaction and overlap between them.

Deduction

- Involves the formulation of **propositions to be tested,** which are derived from theory.
- Concepts are **operationalised** such that the variables involved can be identified and measured in an objective way and this measurement process could also be repeated by others in different situations.
- The strength and significance of the relationships between variables can be established.
- A predetermined set of variables can be identified as antecedents or consequences of another set of variables.

Data gathering takes place to test the evidence against the propositions. As a result of the analysis process it is possible to identify weaknesses in the theory or to show ways in which the theory may be slightly modified.

Figure 5.4 Inductive and deductive approaches

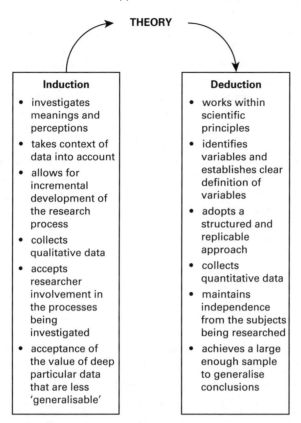

Induction

- Involves observation and investigation into variables that are not necessarily identified through deductively based propositions in complex situations.
- Occurs without prior assumptions about propositions, categories and measurement.
- Incorporates the context of the situation into the analysis process.
- Develops an analysis process to build a credible explanation of the phenomena that have been observed.
- Is less concerned with the need to generalise although further avenues for research may be identified.

Data quality issues

Regardless of whether you take a broadly inductive or deductive approach to your research it will lack credibility if you are not able to ensure that your data are relevant and trustworthy. Key concepts in the traditional scientific research tradition are **reliability and validity**. In general terms, reliability refers to the repeatability of findings, meaning that if the same study were to be repeated a number of times, it should still yield the same results in order for the findings to be considered reliable. Reliable research is research that is accepted as trustworthy, fair and objectively undertaken (Biggam, 2018). Validity refers to the credibility and believability of the research. Valid research uses research strategies and data collection processes that are appropriate to your research question and are implemented properly; validity means that your research is sufficiently robust to allow confidence in your conclusions. This section of the chapter addresses these issues.

 Case Example 5.4

How trustworthy is the research?

Abigail was a full-time student who was passionate about issues associated with violence in the workplace. She had worked for many years in 'front line' public sector occupations and had been threatened on more than one occasion by angry members of the public. In her HR course she was determined to undertake research to show without doubt the level of violence faced by casual employees on low wages in many public-facing occupations. However, she was running short of time and she was unable to get any work organisations in her area to give her permission to approach their staff with a questionnaire designed to measure their exposure to violence as a result of their work roles. Abigail was active on social network sites and had been involved with one or two networks that focused on supporting people who had suffered from aggressive behaviour and she had some friends with similar interests. In order to take her research forward and to meet the fast-approaching deadline Abigail devised

a very short web-enabled questionnaire using a free online survey provider. Money was short so she limited herself to a few questions in her survey about the extent to which people worried about violence at work. There was no space to ask biographical or demographic questions. In addition, she reproduced the questionnaire into a paper format. Then she set up a specific e-mail address that could not be traced to her personally and posted invitations on various websites and forums inviting people to contact the e-mail address to get a link to the online questionnaire. Next she and her friends set off and stood outside public places, such as the library, the job centre, the train station, the citizens advice centre and the bus station. They approached people who were passing and conducted short 'structured interviews' based on the online survey questions. Abigail was disappointed with the number of responses that she got although, one way and another, she and her friends managed to get the number up to 50. When she looked at the questionnaire responses she felt able to show that workplace violence was a prevalent issue for many people and employers were not doing enough to deal with it.

However, when Abigail paid a fleeting visit to her supervisor to reassure her that the somewhat late-in-the-day data collection had been completed she was upset to find that her supervisor did not praise her for her quick work but instead asked her to discuss the validity and reliability of her data.

Discussion questions

1   Why do you think Abigail's supervisor may have had concerns regarding the validity and reliability of her data?

2   What could Abigail have done differently in order to have more valid and reliable data?

Feedback notes

You may feel that the basis for the concerns about Abigail's approach to data gathering related to the rather 'ad-hoc' basis on which she collected her data. The survey instrument that she devised was very short and her supervisor was anxious about whether the questions were measuring levels of anxiety about violence at work or the extent to which respondents had actually suffered from violence. Another issue connected with validity was the way in which 'violence' was defined and whether all of the survey respondents would have understood it in the same way. It is possible that, without a careful explanation by those who were administering the survey about the definition of the term 'violence at work' (physical harm and contact; psychological abuse; shouting?) people may have responded in different ways making it hard to know whether the research really was measuring what it set out to measure. You may have also noticed that Abigail recruited her friends to try to help with the data collection and her supervisor was certainly concerned about the extent to which they were all briefed to behave in the same way (not to 'put answers in people's mouths', for example). Here the issue is one of reliability: did the different ways that the data were gathered and by different people make the study unrepeatable? In addition, you might be wondering how representative her sample was and how reliable in their responses people might be who had been recruited at train and bus stations and through special interest sites set up to support those who are concerned about violence at work. The lack of any demographic data also made it hard to assess the extent to which the 50 responses Abigail managed to achieve were spread across different demographic groups and different employment sectors.

What could Abigail have done differently to increase validity and reliability in her research project? Survey research can be a very good source of quantitative data and Abigail could have had valid and reliable data if she followed some important guidelines for survey research:

- An important aspect to consider when conducting quantitative survey-based research is to thoroughly search the literature for existing measures of the variable that we want to study. For example, if Abigail wanted to research violence at work, her first step would be to search for books and research articles that have pre-validated measures of workplace violence, such as Schat and Kelloway's (2003) workplace violence scale.

- Second, she would verify if there were any newer versions of this scale, validated in the country where she aims to conduct her research. If Abigail were to apply her questionnaire in a country with a different language, she would need to be extra careful and follow further steps to validate the measure she wants to use. More detailed information on how to validate a study in a different cultural context can be found in Beaton *et al* (2000). The validation of a scale is crucial, because it allows researchers to determine if the great majority of people would interpret the same questions the same way – an important validity concern. One important aspect to consider when conducting survey research is that your first decision should never be to create your own questions – pre-validated questionnaires should always be prioritised and you can only create your own questions if a pre-validated questionnaire does not exist (although this is unlikely).

- Third, Abigail would seriously need to reconsider her data collection strategy. The use of a convenience sample with the questionnaires being shared on social network sites, combined with short 'structured interviews' to people passing can lead to concerns regarding reliability, as well as validity. People who replied to structured interviews could have been helped by the interviewers, and this may have influenced their responses. This means that the combination of different data collection methods is not desirable in survey-based research.

- Fourth, after following the steps that were recommended, Abigail would have to start pre-analysing her data and assessing whether her data are normally distributed or not. You will find more information on data distribution in Chapter 9.

Important questions about data quality to ask in relation to any research project are (Easterby-Smith *et al*, 2018; Robson and McCartan, 2016):

Questions relevant to assessing reliability

- Would similar observations be reached by different observers?
- Is it easy to understand how raw data have been collated and analysed?
- Would the methods used generate the same results on other similar occasions? (Are the results generalisable?)

Not all research sets out to produce conclusions that are generalisable (Hart, 2013); indeed statistical generalisation is rarely possible in HR research and is very difficult even in randomised scientific experiments. However, it is possible to evaluate the normality of the distribution of a sample and conduct statistical analyses that indicate significant relationships between variables. Furthermore, it is possible to consider the extent to which 'comparative generalisation' between two or more different types of 'case' is possible. You might also consider the extent to which an analysis of concepts important to explaining an HR phenomenon in one context might also be helpful to understanding what is going on in other situations (this is known as concept generalisation).

Questions relevant to considering validity

- What difference might the context of the investigation make to data that have been collected?
- To what extent has the enquiry process itself influenced the possible answers?
- How easy is it to separate cause from effect in the data (the chicken and the egg scenario)?
- How sure can you be that other factors (intervening variables) have not affected your data?

The concepts of validity and reliability are most frequently used by researchers who make use of quantitative data and they are less easy to apply in a direct sense to mixed methods studies or research making use of qualitative data. It is equally important (some researchers argue that it is **more** important) to undertake a careful assessment of data quality if your approach does not make use of a 'traditional' randomised sampling approach and if your pursuit of in-depth, less structured, data makes generalisation less possible. If your research is based around a qualitative approach then other assessments of data quality and trustworthiness may be more appropriate (Lincoln and Guba, 1985) and you should consider the following issues:

- **Credibility** – have your respondents had a chance to validate that you have made an accurate record of their data? Can you cross-verify from more than two sources?
- **Transferability** – have you offered a rounded picture (often called a 'thick description') that draws on a range of perspectives incorporated into your data to make a judgement possible about the possible transferability of your findings to another context?
- **Dependability** – have you provided enough information about the research procedures you have used to enable an 'audit' of the process?
- **Confirmability** – have you reflected on the extent to which your own personal bias or that of some of your respondents has been discussed or acknowledged?
- **Authenticity** – can your research outcomes be judged to be genuine through the inclusion of a range of data sources?

Activity 5.2 provides an opportunity to consider how these questions would apply in a practical situation.

 Activity 5.2

Assessing data quality

Imagine that you are undertaking a project to investigate the effectiveness of performance management processes in an organisation. You will be obtaining information through interviews from a range of people in different departments and at different levels within the organisation. Using the criteria for data quality (credibility; transferability; dependability; authenticity; confirmability) try to identify what the main practical issues might be with regard to data quality.

Feedback notes

Important questions you would need to consider in a project such as this might include:

Reliability/data credibility – how replicable is the research process?

- Would interviews about performance management that took place just **prior** to the annual pay review process generate different findings if they were undertaken just **after** the pay awards had been announced?
- Would interviews carried out by someone from the HR function within the organisation generate the same data as interviews that were carried out by an external researcher?
- To what extent might two different people make sense differently of the same raw data generated by the interviews?

Validity/trustworthiness – do the data give evidence about what you are trying to examine?

- To what extent do data generated in interviews just after the pay review process actually reflect opinions about performance management or might they really provide opinions about pay awards by interviewees?
- To what extent will interviewees give you the answers they think you want?
- If an interviewee has recently been subject to a disciplinary procedure and he or she is negative about performance management in the organisation, can you be sure whether the process leads to negative perceptions of performance management, or have problems with managing performance then led to the employee performing his or her role in an unacceptable way?
- How confident can you be that what you have found out about performance management would also be applicable in different types and sizes of organisations, as well as different individuals?

No one project is going to be able to produce findings that are 100 per cent reliable, trustworthy, valid and credible. It is, however, necessary that you address these issues so that you are able to determine an approach to data gathering that indicates you have attempted to take an 'open minded' approach to gathering data and that you have taken steps to minimise the limitations of your study and maximise its credibility. This means taking a planned approach to gathering data and being able to justify the decisions that you make. This will be done in the **methodology** section of the report that you write.

Planning to gather data

Preparation is very important in any research project and your data gathering procedure needs to be thought out in advance. As you plan your data collection process, therefore, it is important to be clear about **what** data you plan to collect and **why**. Make sure you are clear about how your proposed data will help you to answer your research questions and have reasons to justify the particular methods you propose to use and the sample of respondents you plan to invite to participate.

Planning also extends to the data gathering instruments you develop (your questionnaire or interview questions) and it is important to plan to run a small 'pilot process' for your methods so that you can find out if any of your questions are ambiguous; how long the interview really does take; whether your questions are likely to generate data that you can analyse in a relevant way.

Important points for planning a research project likely to enable persuasive conclusions to be drawn are (Hart, 2010; Bauer and Gaskell, 2000):

- Ensure that the methods you use are transparent, ethical and justifiable.
- Make sure that your own position, in relation to both the topic and those from whom you will gather data, is clear and open.
- Fully inform participants in your research about what you are setting out to learn and the implications for them of their participation.
- Take into account alternative theories and interpretations of the data you gather.
- In addition to reflecting on the data, develop your ability to reflect about your role in the research and the implications of this.

The methodology chapter is where you address these issues and explain: the basis for your research design; your specific methods of data gathering; and the piloting process that you undertook. This is the chapter of the dissertation or section of the report that will help your tutor assess the quality of the data you have gathered and is crucial to the mark you will get. Poor quality data always lead to conclusions that lack credibility.

The term 'methodology' is used differently by various authors but in this book it is taken to mean the philosophical framework or orientation within which your research is based (for example, positivist or interpretivist). Methodology is important as it provides the rationale for your particular method or methods of data gathering. The methodology section of your report, therefore, should address what world view underpinned the approach you adopted to gathering and making sense of data. Although some study centres, for some qualifications, do not require a discussion of these features in your project report they are still worth thinking through as they will form the basis from which you can take consistent action and gather and analyse data of good quality. If your study centre requires you to consider these issues in a methodology then three, interrelated issues require explanation as indicated in Figure 5.5.

Figure 5.5 Key issues to establish in your methodology

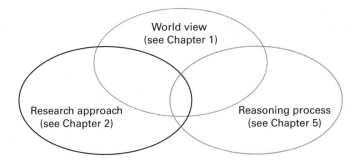

Having established your initial position with regard to your own world view, your research approach and whether your reasoning is inductive or deductive it is also necessary to explain and justify the way you have designed and executed your research. Increasingly, study centres require a full explanation of the more philosophical features of your research approach as well as a full justification of the methods of data collection and analysis that you have used and your approach to accessing a sample and your sampling strategy. Key points that are helpful in determining these features are indicated below and further illustrated in Figure 5.6.

In order to make sure that your methodology is as credible as possible it is important to:

Clarify the research questions/objectives and research approach first. Planning the methods for any study is a logical sequence of judgements taking into account what is reasonably possible. Your first decisions relate to the research questions or objectives. These decisions will involve discussion with other stakeholders in the project (the organisation(s) and your supervisor, tutor or advisor etc). It is also necessary to be clear about what approach will be adopted (inductive or deductive etc) as this will affect the way you organise your reading and the data gathering methods that you choose.

Carefully consider what information you need in order to answer your questions and achieve your objectives. Many students obtain information that is easy to find but it is not always sufficient to answer their research questions. Work out what data you need and where to find the information. Then decide the extent to which this is feasible. Consider the ethical aspects you need to comply with when conducting research involving people – it is important to read any ethical norms that both the organisation and the study centre may have available. Again, discussions with the project sponsor in the organisation(s) and your supervisor are likely to be important.

Consider what different sources of information and data are available to you and make use of as wide a range of sources as possible. Many students rush to collect some form of primary data (for example, from a questionnaire, from interviews or from a focus group) and they do not utilise other available information such as documentary evidence that already exists within the organisation or secondary data from a range of published sources. Ideas about this are in Chapter 6.

Clearly identify and justify the research population and your sample selection. The research population is all the units of analysis (people, departments, organisations, etc) within the scope of your research. Is your study to be concerned with all employees in the organisation, one particular business unit or department or one specific staff grouping? It is unlikely that you will be able to gather data from the whole population (unless it is very small) so some form of sampling will be required and you will need to consider, and justify, how you will choose the people who will form your sample. This may also need to be discussed with the project sponsor at organisational level and with your supervisor. Issues of sampling are considered in more detail in Chapter 7 (qualitative data) and Chapter 9 (quantitative data) and you will be able to classify your chosen sampling strategy.

Decide on the type(s) of primary data that you will gather and allow time to devise and pilot effective data gathering 'instruments'. Many people choose to use a questionnaire method because they think it will be quick or the interview method because they think it will be easy. Many then find that their questionnaire had a lot of missing data or that their interviews did not provide sufficient information to answer their research questions. All forms of data gathering require considerable

Figure 5.6 Factors influencing research methods

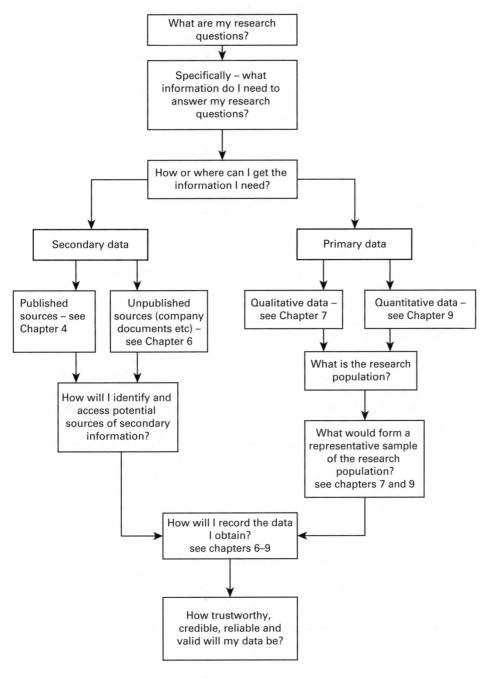

thought in the design process and it is also important to allow time to pilot the instrument and procedure (and then make amendments in the light of the pilot) prior to launching into the full-scale data gathering process. See chapters 7 and 9 for more on this.

Decide in advance how you will record the data that you gather and then how you will perform the analysis. As part of the planning and design process for any primary data gathering instrument it is important to be clear about how you will record and analyse the data. These issues are discussed in chapters 7 to 11.

Consider issues related with data quality. If you can, get someone to act as a 'critical friend' and try to expose areas where the validity, trustworthiness, reliability and credibility of the approach you are planning to adopt could be questioned. As noted already, no study can ever be wholly valid and reliable but being critically evaluative at this stage will enable you to address any issues that you can resolve. You will also be better placed to discuss the advantages and limitations of your study within the report that you produce.

Writing up the methodology

Study centres tend to have different expectations about the methodology section and the level of the qualification you are undertaking also has implications for what you should explain and justify about your research methods. Therefore, it is very important to find out in advance how long your methodology section should be and the issues you are expected to explain and discuss. All project reports must explain and justify how data (primary and secondary) were gathered and analysed. The points below indicate the key issues to address, as a minimum, for any HR research project:

- **Appropriateness of the methods.** What was the context for the research? For research in one organisation, what was the organisational context? What was the nature of the relationship of the researcher with the organisation(s)? What were the research questions? What approach to data gathering (qualitative; quantitative; both?) was adopted and why?

- **Quality and quantity of data collected and analysed.** How secondary sources were identified (literature search as well as any organisational documents, etc) What primary data were gathered? How was the sample of respondents selected? How were data gathering instruments (questionnaires, interview questions, etc) developed? What were the main sources of measures/survey items? What were the response rates and what are the implications of the response rates? How were the data analysed?

- **Management of access and cooperation.** In what way did the context of the study influence the research process as it actually occurred? What ethical issues were raised by the project and how were they handled? How were non-returned questionnaires or other refusals to provide data taken into account?

- **Evaluation of methods.** What issues of data quality were there? What were the advantages and limitations of the methods and research process used?

CHECKLIST

- There are many different ways of tackling research projects in HR and it is important to formulate an approach that is contextually appropriate and will generate data and conclusions that are meaningful and valuable.

- Existing research in the HR field can be categorised in terms of the number of practices being investigated, as well as on the level of analysis (organisational and individual). Choices about level of analysis and number of practices should be discussed with both your contacts in the organisation and your research supervisor, as they will greatly influence your choices regarding the methodology and the methods to be used.

- Quantitative data (data that can be quantified where predetermined variables can be related) and qualitative data (data based on meanings and expressed through language) are both relevant to HR research. Both approaches can form part of research projects that generate useful knowledge. Mixed methods approaches may also be utilised effectively within HR research.

- Triangulation is the process of using data from different sources to analyse a phenomenon from different perspectives and to cross-verify data from more than one source.

- Organisational research and decisions about methods of gathering data will be influenced by contextual factors such as operational issues, time pressures and the preferences of organisational stakeholders.

- Theory and practice are related. People use theories in everyday life to generate expectations about the world and to make sense of things. Theories are refined through practice so that everyday experience informs the generalisation process.

- Theories can be evaluated by testing them empirically (in practice) or by analysing their component parts to establish the extent to which they make sense.

- Theories are developed through the processes of induction and deduction. Induction (theory building) involves observing facts, behaviours and meanings to form a generalised interpretation of what is occurring and why. Deduction (theory development through testing) involves identifying propositions from existing theories and testing them in different situations and contexts in order to refine and amend them where appropriate.

- The value and credibility of an investigative enquiry can be assessed by considering the quality of the data on which the conclusions are based. Reliability is the extent to which similar results would be obtained in all similar occasions and validity is a judgement about whether the data really provide evidence of what the researcher claims they are about. Qualitative researchers will also need to consider issues of data credibility and trustworthiness.

- All project reports require a section that explains and justifies the method or methods that were used. Different study centres have different requirements for this section.

- The methodology section of any report should evaluate the appropriateness of the method for the particular enquiry; the quality and quantity of data collected; the appropriateness of the analysis processes; and the management of access and cooperation.

TEST YOURSELF

1 Which of the following is a data collection method?

  a Case study.

  b Positivism.

  c Focus group.

  d Social constructivism.

2 Which of the following is associated with quantitative data?

  a Analysis begins as data are collected.

  b Is associated with interpretivism.

  c Research process takes full account of the research context.

  d The emphasis is on 'thick description'.

3 Which of the following is associated with qualitative data?

  a Meanings and words.

  b Pie charts.

  c Randomised sampling strategy.

  d Positivism.

4 A study based on 12 in-depth interviews with people from different departments in an organisation is:

  a A longitudinal study.

  b A structured study.

  c A quantitative study.

  d A qualitative study.

5 Issues of data credibility and transferability are particularly relevant to:

  a Experiments.

  b Cross-sectional research.

  c Case study research.

  d Positivism.

6 Inductive reasoning involves:

  a Refining and reconsidering theories through testing propositions in different conditions.

  b Maintaining independence from the subjects being researched.

  c Incrementally developing theory from the research process.

  d Adopting a structured and replicable approach.

7 One of the advantages of mixed methods research is:

  a Facilitation of different methods in order to answer a research question.

  b Focus in depth using open interviews.

c   Theoretical purity.

d   Eliminating different perspectives.

8   Theory is important for HR research because:

a   Tutors give a bad mark if there is no theory.

b   Theory relates to 'know-about' knowledge.

c   There is a general theory of HR.

d   Theories provide a basis for understanding issues from different perspectives.

9   Which of the following approaches to data enable a consideration of change over time?

a   Cross-sectional 'one moment in time' survey.

b   Secondary data analysis.

c   Longitudinal data.

d   Literature review.

10 Data quality issues involve thinking about:

a   The sampling strategy.

b   The data gathering instrument.

c   Data recording processes.

d   All of the above.

 Review Questions

1   Find out about the requirements of your study centre for the methodology section of your report. What sort of word length is expected? What headings or key issues should be discussed?

2   What are the expectations of the organisation(s) with which your research will be concerned? What organisational issues or priorities might affect the methods by which you gather data or the timing of your data gathering activities?

3   What secondary data sources (organisational documents, etc) are available to you? What level of permission will you need to obtain company information? Who are the 'gatekeepers' of such information?

Questions for reflection

This final part of the chapter enables you to reflect about your professional development and develop your skills and knowledge. This will enable you to build your confidence and credibility, track your learning, see your progress and demonstrate your achievements.

Taking stock

1   How clearly articulated are your research questions/objectives? To what extent have your research questions informed your decisions about the research design and data gathering process?

2   How has your review of the literature informed your thinking about methods of data gathering? How satisfied are you with your review of the existing literature?

Strengths and weaknesses

3   What is your level of expertise in designing of data collection instruments (questionnaire design; interview design; facilitating focus groups and so on)? What development might be helpful in this area and how might you undertake it?

4 What knowledge and understanding do you have of sample selection processes? Where might you obtain effective advice about this?

5 What experience and level of expertise do you have in recording and analysing quantitative and/or qualitative data? Where can you learn more about these activities?

Being a practitioner-researcher

6 What skills will you require to obtain access to organisational information (primary and secondary) and to achieve the cooperation of participants in your research?

7 To what extent have organisational stakeholders got firm ideas about the methods you should use? What skills will you need to manage these expectations and ensure the validity and reliability of the data that you gather?

 ## Useful Resources

One way of finding out about the advantages and disadvantages of different methods is to read literature sources about your topic for method as well as for content. Every general textbook on research methods will cover issues of methodology. The following list indicates a selection of them.

Creswell, J (2018) *Research Design: Qualitative, quantitative and mixed methods approaches*, Sage, Thousand Oaks, CA

Fox, M, Martin, P and Green, G (2007) *Doing Practitioner Research*, Sage, London

Jankowicz, AD (2005) *Business Research Projects for Students*, Thomson Learning, London

---

 ## References

Bauer, MW and Gaskell, G (eds) (2000) *Qualitative Research With Text, Image and Sound*, Sage, London

Beaton, DE, Bombardier, C, Guillemin, F and Ferraz, MB (2000) Guidelines for the process of cross-cultural adaptation of self-report measures, *Spine*, **25** (24), pp 3186–3191.

Bell, E, Bryman, A and Harley, B (2019) *Business Research Methods*, 5th edn, Oxford University Press, Oxford

Biggam, J (2018) *Succeeding with Your Master's Dissertation*, 4th edn, Open University Press, Maidenhead

Easterby-Smith, M, Thorpe, R and Jackson, PR (2018) *Management and Business Research*, Sage, London

Gill, J and Johnson, P (2010) *Research Methods for Managers*, Sage, London

Hart, C (2013) *Doing Your Masters Dissertation*, Sage, London

Kirkpatrick, DL (1959) Techniques for Evaluation Training Programs, *Journal of the American Society of Training Directors*, **13**, pp 21–26

Kolb, DA, Rubin, I and McIntyre, J (1979) *Organizational Psychology: an experiential approach*, Prentice-Hall, New Jersey

Lee, N and Lings, L (2008) *Doing Business Research: A guide to theory and practice*, Sage, London

Lincoln, YS and Guba, EG (1985) *Naturalistic Inquiry*, Sage Publications, California

Maslow, AH (1943) A theory of human motivation. *Psychological Review*, **50** (4), pp 370–396.

Neuman, W (2012) *Basics of Social Research: Qualitative and quantitative approaches*, Pearson Education, Harlow

Robson, C and McCartan, K (2016) *Real World Research: A resource for social scientists and practitioner-researchers*, Wiley, Oxford

Saunders, MNK, Lewis, P and Thornhill, A (2019) *Research Methods for Business Students*, 8th edn, Pearson, London

Schat, AC and Kelloway, EK (2003) Reducing the adverse consequences of workplace aggression and violence: The buffering effects of organizational support, Journal of *Occupational Health Psychology*, **8** (2), 110.

Wright, PM and Boswell, WR (2002) Desegregating HRM: A review and synthesis of micro and macro human resource management research, *Journal of Management*, **28** (3), pp 247–76

06
Finding and using documents and organisational evidence

LEARNING OBJECTIVES

This chapter should help you to:

- identify documents or organisational evidence that will help to answer your research questions;
- evaluate the use of different types of evidence (written and visual) in designing and implementing a research project;
- differentiate between materials that can be used as part of the literature review and materials that can be used as part of the research;
- determine how to make use of data from management information systems;
- identify sources of secondary data across organisations;
- identify the most appropriate and relevant forms of organisational evidence for your research;
- think about different ways of analysing documentary and organisational information.

CHAPTER OUTLINE

- How to use this chapter
- Different forms of documentary and organisational evidence
- Using data from organisational management information systems
- Finding and selecting secondary data sources
- Analysing documentary and organisational information
- Summary checklist
- Test yourself, review and reflect questions
- Useful resources

How to use this chapter

If you are planning to carry out an organisationally based piece of research, there is likely to be a range of information that already exists in or about the organisation that can help you to answer your research questions. Many people invest considerable time generating new data and overlook sources of valuable data that already exist within the organisation or are to be found in both physical and electronic formats. While some existent data may be more suitable to address as part of the literature review, some other sources of secondary data are extremely valuable for the research itself, either on their own or in combination with primary data.

 Case Example 6.1

Researching the cultural consequences of an organisational relocation

Poppy was a distance-learning student who had recently joined the head office of a large retail organisation and was responsible for the HR provision for the head office staff. The staff at the head office had recently moved into new purpose-built premises where 'open plan' working had featured strongly in the design. The idea was to facilitate a culture change headquarters of the organisation from functionally separated subcultures to an approach characterised by flexibility and cross-functional communication. Poppy decided to focus her research project on the leadership style consequences and challenges of the new environment. Poppy thought that a questionnaire to staff would be a good way of finding out the extent to which they thought leaders' behaviours had changed as a result of the move to new premises. Her supervisor was also very keen that she find and make use of organisational data that might also provide relevant and useful information.

Discussion questions

1   In addition to the data from the questionnaire that Poppy planned for her research, what other forms of organisational evidence might

be relevant for this study? Try to list about four sources of evidence.

2   What difficulties might Poppy have in trying to locate and utilise the information you have identified?

Feedback notes

Poppy found that internal documents such as management handbooks and policies had not been updated since the move and so were not particularly helpful. However, she did find records of management meetings and documents issued to staff to keep them updated about the progress of the move and the opportunities that the new 'architecture' presented. In addition, Poppy made use of visual information: she took photographs of the old building and some of the offices prior to the move and also took photographs of the new office layouts immediately prior to the move as well as at a point three months after it had taken place once things had become more 'embedded'. These enabled her to show how offices 'worked' in reality as well as in the vision of the architects and planners.

There is a huge range of potential sources of information that can add value to any organisationally based research project. Much of this information is 'unobtrusive' and easy to overlook. Sometimes students opt for time-consuming data generation methods that add little extra value to data that are already available within the organisation. However, there are some difficulties with the effective use of organisational documents and sources of evidence. It might be the case, for example, that organisational policy documents give a view of things that are not implemented in practice. In addition, detailed reports from computerised information systems requiring many hours of time to obtain access and to get the report in an understandable format might not add much value to the findings of the project. This chapter seeks to highlight different forms of organisational evidence that may be relevant. It discusses different approaches to finding documents about organisations, selecting what is most relevant and useful, and then making sense of the information they provide.

Different forms of documentary evidence

    Activity 6.1

Sources of information about an organisation

Imagine that you know absolutely nothing about an organisation. It is not possible for you to contact any of the people (either verbally or in

writing) who are involved with the organisation although you can access documents within the company. Produce a list of all the sources of information that might help you to know something about the organisation: its purpose; culture; business operations and so on. Include different kinds of evidence in your list, not just written forms of information.

Feedback notes

There are a wide variety of sources of information that can help you to learn about any organisation (see Table 6.1). Your list of evidence might include external marketing

Table 6.1 Different types of organisational evidence

Examples of Evidence Produced Internally for Internal Use	Examples of Evidence Produced Internally for External Use	Examples of Evidence Produced Externally Using Internal Sources of Evidence
Administrative sources • HRM audits • Safety records • Production/service records	**Organisational internet site(s)**	**Newspaper cuttings**
Business records • Agendas • Notes from meetings • Progress reports • Project proposals • Intra-organisational surveys	**Corporate brochure(s)** (for clients/potential investors etc)	**TV/radio transcripts/ recordings**
Operational records • Letters • Memos • E-mails • Handwritten notes	**Corporate video streaming** (for PR purposes)	**Books and journal articles featuring the organisation**
Policy documents and procedures • HR • Procurement and supply • Finance and accounting • Marketing	**Marketing information**	**Internet hosted 'postings' about the organisation; 'blogs' etc**
Other internal 'artefacts' • Briefing notes • Induction presentations • Maps, plans and drawings • Process diagrams	**Published diaries/ memoirs of key people**	**Company profile about the organisation**

information, such as company website information as well as internal documents such as hard copies of e-mails, agendas, minutes of meetings, reports submitted to working groups, proposals for business projects and also progress reports. In addition, it is possible that there may be information about the organisation to be found in newspaper clippings, online news items or articles about the organisation in trade journals or business related books. It would be possible to get more knowledge of the type of organisation and its type of business if you could access generalised information about its client or customer base and about its market share. Information about employees (numbers; skills; length of service; turnover and so on) would also be useful as well as financial information through its published annual accounts. You may also be able to access an existing dataset such as a large-scale survey or a commercial database. As a general note, if someone else has collected the right data and you can gain access to it, you should make use of it if you can.

In addition you may be able to find out about the organisation by accessing publicly available documents. For example, CIPD members and students whose library subscribes to the Business Source Premier database can access Datamonitor Company Profiles. In addition it is possible to find case study based articles from electronic database collections such as Emerald Full-text and Web of Knowledge.

Other non-written sources would be valuable in helping you to understand about the organisation. This might include maps (also available electronically) showing the sites of different parts of the organisation; architectural plans of some of the buildings; diagrams showing the production or workflow processes and so on.

 Activity 6.2

Making use of published diaries, autobiographies and memoirs

Imagine that you are undertaking some research into HR issues about entrepreneurship. As part of the background research you are reading diaries and autobiographies of prominent 'self-made' figures in business. There is a huge range of these and you are not sure how useful such sources will be. If you have the time (and the interest) skim-read one such book. You may already be a 'consumer' of biographies of business leaders but if not, and you are not close to a bookshop or library, then you can read limited previews of books from any e-book collection that your study centre may subscribe to or through the Google Books search engine (use a search term such as 'business autobiography'). You will need to choose 'full or limited preview' to ensure you choose a book that you can actually browse inside the cover and you will need to scroll down the list of titles that are presented to find an entrepreneur's autobiography.

Discussion questions

1   Why do business leaders (and others) publish their diaries and autobiographies?

2   What are the advantages and disadvantages of evidence from sources such as these?

3   How do I differentiate between materials that can be used as part of the literature review and materials that can be used as part of the research?

Feedback notes

Sources such as these, produced by the people involved, are helpful to researchers in finding out about the background of issues they are interested in. An advantage of this sort of account is that they have come into existence within a close proximity to the people or the events you are interested in and have been produced by or authorised by those who were involved. However, the motivation to write such documents must be taken into account. This will include the commercial incentive for well-known and influential figures to publish their autobiographies or some form(s) of memoir. They are also likely to have been motivated by the desire to ensure that the most flattering side of their story is available. In some ways, therefore, such forms of evidence have been produced for the attention of future readers and must be read with this in mind. In addition, none of them will have been produced for the purposes of your research and so it is important to remember that they are 'inadvertent sources' (Bell, Bryman, and Harley, 2019), which are the result of someone else's interpretation.

Nonetheless, this sort of information and these documents can be very useful. Although those who already work within an organisation in which their research is based will feel that much of the evidence they may have to hand merely replicates their existing 'tacit' knowledge this will not be the case for the people who will read and mark your research report. They will be less knowledgeable about the organisation and reference to this sort of evidence enables you to justify the context and the particular characteristics that you highlight in your report. In addition, data generated within the organisation may also enable you to challenge 'taken for granted assumptions' about 'the way things are around here'.

There are also more reasons for the use of documentary evidence in HR research. First, documentary evidence can provide specific details about particularly relevant events (Yin, 2017). Interviews with those involved in a culture change process, for example, might suggest that those involved felt that the need for a major change was triggered by significant factors (such as loss of key accounts; acquisition of a new business; financial and budgetary difficulties within the organisation and so on). However, people make sense of events in different ways and their interview data may not fully reflect the actual chain of events. Study of relevant documents from the time of the decisions might enable you to pinpoint whether the factors that are cited by those involved really did occur prior to the change process.

Second, documentary evidence can corroborate and augment evidence from other sources. For example, research into appraisal interviews may indicate that those being appraised feel their objectives are unachievable and unrealistic. Analysis of a sample of the appraisal forms themselves might yield further evidence about the quality of objective setting by managers and provide a further justification (or otherwise) for this conclusion.

Third, documentary evidence can provide 'inferences'. Research into the management of a redundancy process, for example, would be enhanced by analysis of news cuttings, blog entries and other public documents relating to the months before any formal announcements were made as well as the process itself once the redundancies were communicated and then enacted.

What is referred to here as documentary evidence can take many forms, including films, photographic images, videos available through social media (such as YouTube), web pages, as well as collective, electronic 'administrative' data (such as that deposited in an HR information system). This sort of information is often overlooked in research projects although it requires as much thought and planning as other forms of primary data so that you do not waste time dealing with organisational evidence that is inappropriate. Organisational sources such as these will usually be supplementary to other forms of primary and secondary data but for some research projects they will form an important part of the data that are analysed. In some cases the data for a research project may come entirely from documentary or other evidence about one or more organisations.

One important question to address is how to differentiate between materials that can be used as part of the literature review and materials that can be used as part of the research. Let us follow up on the idea of conducting research into HR issues in entrepreneurship. Using biographies or memoirs of entrepreneurs could be a relevant way to contextualise the topic when you are doing a study involving primary research. These biographies or memoirs could be case studies that could help support your literature review in the sense that they are good examples to add to the contextualisation of literature on entrepreneurship. For example, if you would like to focus on HR issues on entrepreneurship in the information technology sector, it could be a good idea to include biographies such as those of Steve Jobs (Isaacson, 2015), Bill Gates (Wallace and Erickson, 1993) or the more recent case of Elon Musk (Vance, 2017) in your literature review.

Using biographies and memoirs in a literature review may seem like a straightforward logical strategy but, as mentioned above, they can also be valuable sources of information to analyse as part of your research. For example, you may wish to use the biographies of Steve Jobs, Bill Gates and Elon Musk as a source of qualitative data on the topic or entrepreneurship. In this case you would probably analyse the content of the biographies with a content analysis, just as you would do when analysing an unstructured or a semi-structured interview. These biographies could provide relevant information that you would now analyse qualitatively and draw conclusions from your results.

Using data from organisational management information systems

All organisations collect information relating to the people whom they employ. These records can form a valuable source of information and it is important at the planning stage to determine how information from this type of source can help you to answer your research questions. Prior to electronic datasets most of this information existed in the form of card index systems or collections of paper records in filing cabinets. Perhaps it will be possible to compare data over different time periods or for different parts of the organisation, as a way of identifying priorities for further probing in your research. However, such administrative records are unlikely to provide direct answers to your research questions and it is important not to waste time with pages of descriptive statistics that carry little meaning in their own right.

Activity 6.3

Research issues with management information systems

Imagine that you are undertaking a project into the employment of disabled people in your organisation. The organisation has an HR information system that contains details about disabilities that employees have declared as well as historical data on pay, grading and disability for the last 10 years. Five years ago the HR information system was linked with the organisation's payroll system to ensure a consistency of data. Subject to many rigorous security and data protection safeguards, the organisation has agreed that you can have access to the system, but only for the audit-related purposes of obtaining aggregated quantitative reports and not for the study of the records of any individual employee. Anonymity, confidentiality and data protection are extremely relevant aspects when gaining access to data from HR information systems.

Discussion questions

1   What reports from the HR information system would help you to evaluate the employment experiences of disabled people in the organisation?

2   What challenges will you face in obtaining this information?

3   What issues should you bear in mind assuming that you are able to generate the reports that you need?

Feedback notes

The development and utilisation of HR information systems has enabled research to be undertaken that would have been almost impossible 10 or 20 years ago and research into employees reporting disability is one such area. Reports that you might decide to generate could include:

- number of male and female staff on each grade who have declared a disability;
- bonus payments or other discretionary awards achieved by employees with disabilities over the last 10 years;
- average pay for disabled employee (per year; per month or week; and per hour) in the organisation;
- proportion of disabled employees working on a part-time basis;
- a comparison of average pay for disabled and non-disabled employees;
- length of service for disabled employees.

One of the challenges in obtaining these sorts of data, which also applies to requirements to publish gender pay gap data, relates to the functionality of the system. To what extent is the system itself capable of generating these reports? Many HR information systems are very good at taking in information but generating reports in the form required by those who use them is more difficult. Establishing whether the system could generate these reports may well require liaison with local 'system experts'. Assuming that the system is able to generate the reports that you require, a further challenge may be the development of your own skills with the system in order to obtain and interpret the reports. Here again it would be necessary to allow sufficient time for you to develop such an expertise.

You may also have highlighted a further range of issues that you would need to take into account and these are outlined below:

- **Access.** Irrespective of whether the information is in paper or electronic form, if it shows people's names or other means of identification there are data protection regulations that will affect what data you can access and how you utilise the information.

- **Quality and reliability of the data.** How thoroughly and regularly have records been updated? Have some data been re-coded when system upgrades have been implemented, making time comparisons difficult? System experts should have access to code books or data dictionaries that can clarify these issues. Are there areas of ambiguity in the way the system is set up that might allow for different responses to reflect the same situation? Are the recent data more reliable than the information that is five years old? To what extent have all relevant employees declared a disability?

- **Focusing on research questions.** The range of information included in digital databases can encourage a rather addictive process of devising and running queries but valuable time can be lost scrutinising information that is 'nice to have' but not really 'need to have'.

In spite of these issues many practitioner-researchers find that data from the HR information system of the organisation in which their research is based can help them to answer (and in some cases to formulate) meaningful research questions. This sort of data can also help you to judge how representative information from survey data you subsequently obtain may be.

Finding and selecting appropriate secondary data sources

 Activity 6.4

Using online community contributions as a form of data

Imagine that you are a full-time student interested in researching into the HR implications of stress at work and mental health. You want to find out about the key issues surrounding stress from the perspective of HR practitioners. You want to probe further into questions that you might address in your research. Visit a discussion thread section of any HR practitioner internet site, for example: http://www.cipd.co.uk/community; or https://www. hrzone.com/community-voice/discuss. Navigate your way to relevant opinions or discussions. Select what looks like a promising discussion thread (make sure you assess this on the basis of the number of postings rather than the number of 'hits'). Open the site and skim-read the contributions.

Discussion questions

1   Identify the ways in which this sort of information would assist your research.

2   What problems might arise from study of these postings 'in isolation'? What do these postings **not** tell you?

Feedback notes

There are many ways in which these postings might be helpful to your study. They will provide an overall indication of the immediate concerns of the practitioners who made contributions. From this basis you could devise a study or formulate meaningful research objectives or questions that build on this starting position. Such sources can be valuable, although a study that was based only on these contributions would be only partial, as you do not know about the background or context of the contributors whose words you are reading. Also, they might not consider the issues in much depth. The postings that you have seen are unlikely to be representative of all HR practitioners, being confined to those who engage with activities such as blogging and engagement with other social networking opportunities.

It is always necessary to take a critically evaluative approach to the use of evidence generated in this way. It would be naive to believe that something that has been recorded in written form provides evidence that is not biased in any way. All organisational documentary sources of evidence are partial and require critical assessment and comparison with other forms of evidence generated in different ways. An overview of the strengths and weaknesses of documentary sources is shown in Table 6.2.

In order to maximise the advantages of organisational sources of evidence and minimise the difficulties it is necessary to think systematically about how to locate and select appropriate information and it is also important to take data quality issues into account.

The first stage in an effective process to make use of appropriate organisational evidence is to **identify and categorise** the types of evidence that would be helpful to your research. Having done that, it is necessary to **locate** where such sources might be and then to **select** the material that will be most relevant to the aims and research questions underpinning your project. In particular, it is important not to choose sources that will merely reinforce the conclusions you expect to draw, but to look for evidence that might develop your thinking, and therefore the value of your study.

Once you have selected and obtained the evidence, it is necessary to evaluate it against the following criteria (Saunders, Lewis and Thornhill, 2019):

- **Authenticity and credibility.** The accuracy of what is described in one source of information would need to be assessed by comparison with other sources

Table 6.2 Advantages and disadvantages of documentary and other organisational evidence

Advantages	Disadvantages
Not time constrained – repeated study of the documents is possible	Identifying and accessing all relevant sources of evidence can be difficult
Unobtrusive – those in the organisation are not inconvenienced and their work is not disrupted. Also, you can 'observe' without being observed	Partiality – incomplete information may lead to exaggerated bias in the information the sources provide
Level of detail – sources can provide exact details of names and details of particular events or initiatives as well as quantitative data about organisational processes	The bias or perspective of the author/ producer of the document is not known
Coverage – documents can show trends over time, incorporate many events, and include many locations	Access – the organisation may not be willing to allow access to some forms of evidence for confidentiality reasons
Time – there are opportunities for an element of longitudinal analysis when the timespan available to undertake other forms of data gathering is very limited	Analysis – it may be difficult to say whether the documents you are studying 'caused' the phenomenon you are interested in or resulted from it

(Robson and McCartan, 2016; Yin, 2017)

of data about the same issue. For example, is there consistency between the data found in HR information systems and the information present in the organisation's website or social media outlets?

- **Representativeness.** To what extent are the views expressed in sources from one part of an organisation (say the HR function) also reflected in the views of other functions such as marketing or finance? Alternatively, if you are studying sources related to the activities of a trades union, to what extent does the information you are reading about reflect all members of the union, or is it more reflective of the union activists? Additionally, to what extent does the information gathered from employee representatives reflect the overall perception of employees?

- **Meaning and significance.** This may be the most challenging area, particularly if you are unfamiliar with the culture and language (jargon) used within the organisation that you are studying. This difficulty is most apparent where sources may have been generated in a different country with a different cultural context. Words used in HR in the United Kingdom, for example, may mean different things when used by the HR function based in Germany. This is not only related to translation, but it happens when multinational firms have the same words in English, as the common organisational language, but they are interpreted differently across different subsidiaries of the firm, for example. Titles of different jobs are also expressed and understood differently in different countries. Organisational cultures also can lead to different interpretations of the same language. The term 'strategy', for example, is understood in somewhat different ways in different organisations.

To make best use of organisational evidence it is necessary to undertake a deliberate evaluation of it. This will involve asking questions such as:

- What kind of 'source' is it?
- What does it actually 'say'?
- Who produced it and for what purpose?
- What was the context of its production?
- Is it typical or exceptional for its time?
- Is it complete – has it been altered or edited?
- What is known about the background and experience of the people who generated this source?

    Activity 6.5

Social media policy

Imagine you came across this document on the internet site of a large university as part of your research into social networking and social media issues in employment in the United Kingdom.

Introduction and scope

The university recognises that the internet provides unique opportunities to participate in interactive discussions and share information on various topics using a wide variety of media such as Facebook, Twitter, blogs and wikis. The use of such online media sites has become a significant part of life for many people as a way of keeping in touch with friends and associates and can be used to exchange ideas and thoughts on common interests, both from a personal and employment perspective.

However, the use of social media by students and employees of the university can pose risks to the university's confidential information, reputation and overall compliance within the law. To minimise such risks, the university expects its students and employees to comply with this policy in relation to the use of social media. This policy is intended to apply to personal use of social media by students and employees of the university. If such personal use does not make any reference to the university and the university cannot be identified, then the content is not likely to be of concern to the university.

If students are encouraged to use social media as part of their study, in the absence of a formal policy being put in place, such use should be conducted in line with the spirit and intent of this policy.

Guidelines for students relating to use of social media

If you wish to have a social media presence, or already have a presence in place, which refers to the university or from which the university can be identified, please make sure it is clear that you are speaking on your own behalf, for example by writing in the first person and using a personal e-mail address.

You are personally responsible for what you communicate in social media. Remember that what you publish may be readily available to the public (including the university, prospective future employers, the media and social acquaintances) for a long time. Keep this in mind when posting content. Inappropriate posting of content can damage your career potential, since potential (and current) employers often screen social media sites when considering applications.

Social media should not be used to verbally abuse or intimidate staff or students. Respect should be had at all times for other people's privacy and feelings. Care should be taken to avoid language that may be deemed as offensive to others. For example, you should not:

- say defamatory things about people or organisations;

- say anything that is or could be construed as discriminatory;

- engage in any criminal activity;

- tell lies or mislead people; or

- post inappropriate pictures or videos.

Before posting pictures or details of another person you should obtain their consent.

Any member of staff or student is free to talk about the university on social media sites. However, please be aware that disparaging or untrue remarks that may bring the university, its staff or students into disrepute may constitute misconduct and disciplinary action may be applied. You should avoid posting any

communications that might be misconstrued in a way that could damage the university's goodwill and academic reputation, even indirectly.

If you are approached by a media contact about content on a site relating to the university you should contact the Director of Communications before taking any action. If you wish to complain about any inappropriate posting of content, which identifies the university, you should contact the Head of Registry who will investigate the matter on behalf of the university to ascertain what action, if any, may be appropriate.

Social media should not be used for accessing or sharing illegal content.

Compliance with related policies and agreements

All of the university's other policies that might apply to the use of social media remain in full force and effect. Social media should never be used in a way that violates any other university policies or obligations relating to employees or students. If your post would violate any of the university's policies in another forum, it will also violate them in an online forum. If there is any conflict between this policy and any of the other relevant university policies, then the more restrictive policy shall take precedence.

Discussion questions

1   Evaluate this document using the questions shown below:

   a   What kind of 'document' is it? Is it authentic and credible?

   b   Who produced it and for what purpose? What is known about the author(s)' background and experience?

c What was the context of its production?

d Is it typical and representative of such documents or exceptional for its time?

e To what extent is its meaning clear?

f Is it complete – has it been altered or edited?

2 In what ways is this a useful document and what other information would you require if you were researching into social networking and social media issues in employment in the United Kingdom.

Feedback notes

Your evaluation of this document would probably highlight the following issues. There seems to be very little doubt about the authenticity of the policy statement as it 'reads' like the policy of a large university and it was accessed on the internet site of a large, reputable organisation. In this sense its 'espoused' meaning is clear but what is not known is the extent to which those in the organisation know about and comply with its statements and intentions. It is also not clear who 'authored' the statement and the extent to which other stakeholders had an opportunity to contribute to it. Further information is required, therefore, on these points and it is also necessary to access other organisational evidence.

In addition, this source relates to a university and may not be typical of policies in other employing organisations, particularly those in the private sector.

 Activity 6.6

Identifying sources of secondary data across organisations – large surveys

Imagine you want to study the relationship between employee skills and pay among employees working for organisations in the United Kingdom. In this particular case, you want to access information from a large number of respondents in multiple organisations. The effort of collecting data from multiple organisations yourself would probably be a very challenging task for the aims of your research project. It is a very large endeavour and it has several implications in terms of time and costs. For this reason, you might consider accessing secondary data from large surveys. These large surveys are often conducted by large organisations or universities aiming for an overarching analysis of the labour market. One example would be

the Skills and Employment Survey, which is part of a research project led by Professor Alan Felstead and is funded by the Economic and Social Research Council. You could access the survey by clicking on the following link: https://esrc.ukri.org/research/our-research/skills-and-employment-survey-ses/.

You will need to be logged in and a member of a British university in order to access these results.

Discussion questions

1 Identify the ways in which this sort of information would assist your research.

2 What are the main sources where I can find this kind of secondary data from large surveys?

Feedback notes

Secondary data from large surveys are useful for subjects that rely on public or corporate financial data or statistics, such as economics, finance, strategy and international business. However, it can be equally applicable in HRM research, specifically if we want to compare organisations on more objective HR data, such as payroll, turnover rates, recruitment numbers, sources used to attract candidates, as well as formal interactions with trades unions. The advantage of research using secondary data like this is the exploration of new relationships and patterns within these existing sources of data (Easterby-Smith *et al*, 2018).

These large surveys can often be accessed by multiple researchers, and there is a danger in you trying to analyse relationships between variables that are already being tested by someone else. However, large surveys often have a large diversity of variables, which may indeed not have been addressed in relation to other variables yet. For this reason, when focusing on large surveys, it is important to carefully read all other published studies that make use of that specific dataset.

Some of the main large datasets from where you could retrieve HR related data are:

- Skills and Employment Survey (https://esrc.ukri.org/research/our-research/skills-and-employment-survey-ses/);
- The Workplace Employment Relations Study (http://www.wers2011.info/welcome/4587719945);
- The British Household Panel Survey (https://www.iser.essex.ac.uk/bhps);
- CRANET – The Cranfield Network on International Human Resource Management Survey (https://learn.som.cranfield.ac.uk/cranet);
- The European Social Survey (http://www.europeansocialsurvey.org/);
- Labour Market and Labour Force Survey – Eurostat (http://ec.europa.eu/eurostat/statistics-explained/index.php/Labour_market_and_Labour_force_survey_(LFS)_statistics).

You could also access employment and labour market-related data from the Office for National Statistics. Some examples of useful links are:

- Earnings and Working Hours (https://www.ons.gov.uk/employmentandlabourmarket/peopleinwork/earningsandworkinghours);
- Employment and Employee Types (https://www.ons.gov.uk/employmentandlabourmarket/peopleinwork/employmentandemployeetypes);
- Labour productivity (https://www.ons.gov.uk/employmentandlabourmarket/peopleinwork/labourproductivity);
- Public Sector Personnel (https://www.ons.gov.uk/employmentandlabourmarket/peopleinwork/publicsectorpersonnel);
- Workplace Disputes and Working Conditions (https://www.ons.gov.uk/employmentandlabourmarket/peopleinwork/workplacedisputesandworkingconditions);
- Workplace Pensions (https://www.ons.gov.uk/employmentandlabourmarket/peopleinwork/workplacepensions);

- UK Business Register and Employment Survey (https://www.ons.gov.uk/ employmentandlabourmarket/peopleinwork/employmentandemployeetypes/ bulletins/businessregisterandemploymentsurveybresprovisionalresults/ previousReleases).

On the examples mentioned above, you can access a so-called 'raw' type of data, meaning that you are accessing actual databases and you can statistically analyse the data yourself. However, you may also be interested in secondary data in the form of reports or fact sheets. For example, when accessing the CIPD's Knowledge Hub, you are accessing the main descriptive figures of an analysis made by other researchers/ consultants. Given that this type of report and fact sheet is mostly descriptive, you may still use some of these data, not only to include in the literature review, but also to perform some type of *a posteriori* analysis. For example, when looking at the CIPD's Resourcing and Talent Planning Survey https://www.cipd.co.uk/knowledge/ strategy/resourcing/surveys, in partnership with Hays, one can have access to relevant resourcing data in the United Kingdom for each year. Using these data, you could perhaps correlate the information on the most common resourcing and talent management practices for each year and the median average cost per hire for each year. Some other examples of useful HR-focused sources of secondary data in the form of reports or fact sheets are:

- The Deloitte Human Capital Global Trends (https://www2.deloitte.com/ content/dam/insights/us/articles/HCTrends2018/2018-HCtrends_Rise-of-the-social-enterprise.pdf);
- CIPD's Workforce Trends (https://www.cipd.co.uk/knowledge/work/trends);
- CIPD's UK Working Lives (https://www.cipd.co.uk/knowledge/work/trends/ uk-working-lives);
- CIPD's Human Capital Analytics and Reporting (https://www.cipd.co.uk/ knowledge/strategy/analytics/human-capital-analytics-report);
- CIPD's Reward Management Survey https://www.cipd.co.uk/knowledge/ strategy/reward/surveys.

Analysing documentary and organisational information

 Activity 6.7

Comparing sources

Researching harassment and bullying

Go to a general web-based search engine (such as Google or Yahoo) and enter the search terms 'Harassment and Bullying'.

1 From the 'hits' for this sort of search you are likely to be able to access the harassment and bullying policies of a range of different public sector bodies. If you were interested in

researching into harassment and bullying, as part of your topic, what steps would you take to make sense of the information contained within these documents?

2   Navigate to the 'images' part of the site and select two or three images that represent harassment and bullying. How might you include an analysis of these images as part of your research?

Feedback notes

Making sense of the documents is at the heart of the analysis process and you need to do this in a systematic way. You may wish to assess the similarities and differences between the different sources you have found. You might also try to find out how harassment is defined in different organisations and the different routes open to a victim of bullying in different situations. In this way, therefore, you will need to engage in a categorisation and comparative process.

Information from policy documents alone, however, is partial and may be an unrepresentative selection of how harassment and bullying is managed in practice in different organisations. Much of the significance of the information is only apparent when considered in relation to other documents and evidence from within the organisation(s). Analysis of documents, therefore, tends to be comparative, and involves abstracting elements of relevant information, grouping these elements and comparing them with other relevant evidence.

Analysing images presents different challenges. Images can capture different aspects of issues or situations; these can also be categorised and analysed. This process can supplement other evidence you are analysing or, if you ask research participants to describe their reactions to images that you show them it can help you to explore meanings in more depth. The advantage of making use of pre-existing images is that it may be possible to show historical changes, for example to capture how the portrayal of bullying and harassment has changed over time and to assess how this relates to changes in social or economic concerns of the time. However, if you are making use of pre-existing images you will not necessarily know the intentions and purpose of the person who created or generated the image and it is difficult to know what has been excluded. For example, the context surrounding a photograph may be difficult to understand and it is possible that the image may have been 'photoshopped' or cropped in a way that distorts the original picture (Banks and Zeiltlyn, 2015).

An important first step in analysis of an image is a cataloguing of 'seen' elements (Banks and Zeiltlyn, 2015) something that requires you to look for details in the image and to take the context of its production into account. When assessing the image you have selected, for example, you will need to make detailed notes about the layout of the image, the activities depicted, facial expressions and so on. Items in an image or set of images can then be counted and compared in a similar way as word frequencies may be counted in an analysis of the text of policies and procedures. Alternatively, it is possible to identify and compare key issues, patterns and themes that are evident in images. The examination of images from corporate websites, for example, as well as 'messages' from company newspapers or copies of written communications relating to a particular topic, for example, might be qualitatively analysed, establishing and examining themes and categories in chronological order or some other sequence.

Induction and deduction

The analysis of organisational evidence can be undertaken in one of two different ways, which are illustrated in Figure 6.1, and which link to the different approaches of relating theories and evidence that are discussed in Chapter 5.

A deductive approach towards the analysis of documents would make use of a theory or framework of practice that has already been established and consider the extent to which the organisational evidence indicates that this theory is occurring in practice. Thus the basis on which the evidence is analysed (the analytical framework) is derived from the literature.

Alternatively, it is possible to analyse the information from the context of the organisation from which it has been generated. In this way data from the evidence are organised utilising contextually appropriate categories and further detailed

Figure 6.1 Categorising and analysing organisational evidence

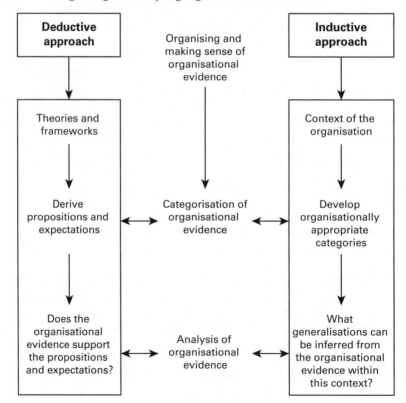

interpretation, on the basis of which conclusions are drawn, takes place from this more inductive approach to analysis. Yin (2017) argues that researchers should choose one or the other of these analytical strategies. However, as different types of organisational evidence may lend themselves to different analytical approaches, and the boundaries between the inductive and deductive approaches may not be as clear as Yin's approach would suggest, the use of both could be appropriate (Gill and Johnson, 2010; Saunders, Lewis and Thornhill, 2019; Bell, Bryman and Harley, 2019).

Qualitative and quantitative analysis

A key theme of this chapter has been the diversity of organisational evidence and the potential of these forms of information to add value to research projects provided that there is a clear rationale underpinning the data gathering and evaluation process. In addition, it is necessary to ensure that data are analysed in a systematic and rigorous way and treated with as much care as would be accorded to other forms of data. Given that organisational evidence is characterised by diversity there are also a range of different approaches to analysis. Qualitative analysis may be appropriate for some of the organisational data and quantitative analysis may be required for other forms of information. Some of the evidence you have obtained may be suitable for both qualitative and quantitative analysis processes.

The following activity demonstrates how both qualitative and quantitative analysis may be utilised. It also provides an illustration of a situation where an HR issue can be researched without access to any one organisation and through making use of organisationally generated documents (job advertisements).

 Activity 6.8

Categories for analysis

Visit an online HR jobs site and go to the section that advertises training and development posts (for example, http://hr-jobs.peoplemanagement.co.uk/jobs/training-learning-and-development/). Imagine that you are undertaking research into the effect of contemporary economic conditions on learning and development job roles. The site will provide you with information about a range of posts, with specific job descriptions, as well as potential salary information.

Discussion questions

1 Decide how you would go about analysing the information about role expectations for training and development professionals.

2 What opinions might you have about the sampling strategy for this approach to research?

Feedback notes

To begin the analysis, you will need to generate some categories. Possible categories that you might try to use when undertaking your analysis of the role expectations of training and development professionals might include:

- responsibilities of the job;
- range (and types) of work;
- levels of qualification expected;
- job title;
- salary.

In addition, it is likely that when you start to compare the texts of the different advertisements you notice particular words that seem to be significant (such as 'strategic', 'results orientated', 'complex problems' etc). However, you might also wonder whether choosing a 'random' week in which to assess the advertisements would be representative (suppose you undertook your search on a different week or month?). For example, what would be the impact of macro contextual elements such as Brexit debates on the way job advertisements are presented? Equally, you might ask whether the choice of one source of job advertisements is representative; why not use other online sites or paper-based journals?

This activity highlights a range of key issues for the use and analysis of documentary forms of data (Bell, Bryman and Harley, 2019):

- **Sample selection.** If you propose to find documents from the public domain, then which media will be chosen and why? If you propose to find documents from within the organisation, then what selection criteria will you use? In both cases what time period will you select from?

- **Subjects and themes.** Having identified the documents you will select, what subjects or themes do you wish to focus on? You can possibly anticipate main themes before considering the above-mentioned questions about sample selection. How will you go about this (qualitative or quantitative approach or both)?

- **Evaluating the sources.** None of the information referred to in this chapter is likely to have been generated with your research project in mind. Key questions to ask will be: what kind of person produced the item (eg HR director; news reporter; online blogger)? Who or what is the main focus of the item you are considering? What is the context in which the document was generated (annual report; redundancy announcement, etc)?

- **Coding and categorising.** Having identified the key issues or themes you wish to investigate using organisational or secondary sources it is important to assess how you will make sense of your data. You are likely to need to simplify and summarise what you have found (which may well amount to many pages of written words and/or numbers). Some thought needs to go into establishing a set of categories and a method of cataloguing and recording the data you have gathered so that you can get a sense of (and communicate about) the 'intensity' or prevalence of your themes within the selection of data that you have gathered.

CHECKLIST

- The range of sources of information about any organisation or HR issue includes materials produced within organisations for internal or external use, materials produced externally about organisations, and administrative records and data.

- The term 'organisational evidence' refers to artefacts, films, images and websites as well as those things more usually referred to as documents.

- Secondary data from large surveys on HR-related topics may be useful especially when comparing multiple organisations or determining general trends.

- These sources of information can add value to any organisational research project. These can help you to establish the context of the organisational situation that you are investigating, provide specific details about relevant events and corroborate and augment evidence from other sources.

- Most, but not all, organisational evidence is inadvertent – it will not have been generated for the purposes of your investigative enquiry. It will contain 'witting' and 'unwitting' evidence that may be useful to you.

- Key issues when evaluating organisational sources are: access and confidentiality; data quality and reliability; and relevance of the data to the research questions.

- Effective utilisation of organisational sources requires identification and location of evidence that is relevant to the research questions and effective sample selection.

- Key issues when evaluating organisational evidence are the authenticity and credibility of the sources; how representative the sources are; and the meaning and significance of what they contain.

- Organisational evidence and secondary sources can underpin an inductive and/or a deductive approach to analysis.

- Documentary evidence is diverse in its form and nature. To make sense of the information may require qualitative and/or quantitative analysis.

TEST YOURSELF

1   Which of the following are documentary forms of evidence about any organisation?

   a   Minutes of executive committee meetings.

   b   E-mail exchanges between an employee and his or her manager.

   c   Newspaper articles about the organisation.

   d   All of the above.

2   What are the disadvantages of using organisational sources within your research project?

   a   Provision of contextual information about the situation or issue that is being researched.

b Difficulties of achieving access within data protection regulations.

c Provision of specific details about relevant events.

d Difficulties in determining whether data are passable of analysis or better fitted to the introduction/literature review.

3 What issues need to be considered when evaluating sources of evidence about an organisation?

a The hand-in date of your research report.

b Whether the organisation is well known or not.

c Whether you are an employee of the organisation.

d Access and confidentiality; data quality; relevance to the research questions.

4 What criteria are helpful for assessing the quality of organisational sources of evidence?

a Objectivity, subjectivity, accuracy, significance.

b Authenticity, credibility, representativeness, significance.

c Credibility, reliability, pictorial clarity, ease of access.

d Meaning, subjectivity, volume, validity.

5 What issues should you take into account if you decide to make use of evidence from published diaries, memoirs or autobiographies?

a They were produced for commercial intent.

b It is likely that they will describe, flatter and justify rather than evaluate.

c They may have been 'ghost-written' by an author who was not present at the time of the events being described.

d All of the above.

6 What problems are presented by analysing photographs as a form of visual data?

a They capture different features of what you are researching into.

b They can supplement other evidence that is available to you.

c They can show historical changes in work organisations.

d The context of the photograph's production may be difficult to understand.

7 What challenges are presented by making use of evidence about organisations taken from website sources?

a They are difficult to reference in a dissertation.

b Website data are always less reliable than proper data.

c The visual images are distracting.

d The motivation of the author and the context of his or her contribution may be unclear.

8 Qualitative analysis of organisational sources of evidence involves:

a Counting the number of times a word or feature appears in artefacts.

b More creativity and imagination than other forms of analysis.

c Engaging in an interpretive understanding of the source in the context of its production.

d Deciding in advance what to look for and making sure you find it.

❓ Review Questions

1   What sources of organisational evidence (primary and secondary data) may help you to answer your research questions?

2   What are the views of your supervisor about the use of organisational sources of evidence?

3   Who might be helpful in arranging access to organisational forms of evidence?

4   What are the implications for confidentiality and ethics if you make use of internal information sources?

Questions for reflection

This final part of the chapter enables you to reflect about your professional development and develop your skills and knowledge. This will enable you to build your confidence and credibility, track your learning, see your progress, and demonstrate your achievements.

Taking stock

1   To what extent are you so familiar with the organisation that your knowledge of many of its features is 'tacit'? What sources of evidence would justify your understanding through making your knowledge explicit?

2   To what extent might images and photographic evidence help you to answer your research questions or provide a useful context for your analysis?

3   In what ways may data from any HR information system be useful to achieving your research objectives? What would be the most helpful format for the data?

4   To what extent might large institutional surveys provide useful information about multiple organisations? Would these data be useful for benchmarking?

Strengths and weaknesses

5   What level of skills would you need to generate specific queries and reports from information management systems? How might you develop the skills you need? Who would be the best person to help with this?

6   What information search skills do you need to identify and select appropriate documentary sources? How might you develop these?

7   To what extent are you interested in, and able to contribute to social media-based interactions such as blogs, social networking sites, podcasts and so on that may provide information and ideas for your research project?

Being a practitioner-researcher

8   What level of permission will you require to utilise data from an HR information system (whether paper-based or electronic)?

9   How can you check on the meaning and significance of some of the terms and expressions used within any organisational sources that you study?

10 How might you ensure that you take into account any biases (such as a management perspective) in the documents that you analyse?

Useful Resources

Bauer, MW and Gaskell, G (eds) (2000) *Qualitative Research with Text, Image and Sound,* Sage, London

Isaacson, W (2015) *Steve Jobs*, Simon & Schuster, New York City, NY

Maylor, H, Blackmon, K and Huemann, M (2017) *Researching Business and Management*, Palgrave Macmillan, London

Vance, A (2017) *Elon Musk: Tesla, SpaceX, and the quest for a fantastic future*, Ecco, New York City, NY

Wallace, J and Erickson, J (1993) *Hard Drive: Bill Gates and the making of the Microsoft empire*, HarperBusiness, New York City, NY

 References

Banks, M and Zeiltlyn, D (2015) *Visual Methods in Social Research*, Sage, London

Bell, E, Bryman, A and Harley, B (2019) *Business Research Methods*, 5th edn, Oxford University Press, Oxford

Easterby-Smith, M, Thorpe, R and Jackson, PR (2018) *Management and Business Research*, Sage, London

Gill, J and Johnson, P (2010) *Research Methods for Managers*, 4th edn, Sage, London

Robson, C and McCartan, K (2016) *Real World Research: A resource for social scientists and practitioner-researchers*, Wiley, Oxford

Saunders, MNK, Lewis, P and Thornhill, A (2019) *Research Methods for Business Students,* 8th edn, Pearson, London

Yin, RK (2017) *Case Study Research: Design and methods*, 6th edn, Sage Publications, Thousand Oaks, CA

07
Collecting and recording qualitative data

LEARNING OBJECTIVES

This chapter should help you to:

- consider how qualitative data can add value to your research;
- assess how participation or observation might provide some data for your project;
- highlight how to collect and record interview and diary based data;
- discuss the use of focus group and other group interview techniques in HR research;
- consider the use of electronically obtained qualitative data;
- determine an appropriate sample of respondents to provide trustworthy data.

CHAPTER OUTLINE

- How to use this chapter
- The value of qualitative data in HR research
- Observation and participation

- Data from individuals

- Focus groups

- Sample selection for qualitative research

- Making sense of the data

- Summary checklist

- Test yourself, review and reflect questions

- Useful resources

How to use this chapter

Nearly all HR research projects undertaken in work organisations make use of qualitative data of some sort and this chapter sets out some of the options. Many HR practitioners find they need to ask questions in depth of one or more 'key individuals' when they are conducting research and so you may be tempted to go straight to the material about interviews or focus groups. However, if your project is likely to incorporate your own observations of the work environment then you should consider the issues involving participation and observation.

The aim of qualitative research is to gain an understanding of situations from other people's perspectives. Researchers can never directly access other people's realities but, through the process of your interaction with your research participants, you can find out other people's accounts of their experiences, thoughts and meanings. Therefore, undertaking qualitative data gathering is a shared process. The depiction of reality that emerges will be something that you and your research participants have produced together. This means that, to get the best out of qualitative data it is important that, before you start the process of interviewing or collecting other forms of data, you think carefully about how you will gain access to your research participants and how you will subsequently analyse your information (Riese, 2018). In addition to this chapter, it is well worth reading Chapter 8 before you make final decisions about your data gathering process. The materials in this chapter are also relevant to writing the methodology section of your report as it covers sampling decisions as well as data gathering processes.

 Case Example 7.1

E-learning and social technologies in a not-for-profit organisation

Jeremy was a part-time student who was undertaking his research project in his employing organisation. The company was a medium-sized charity that undertook development projects to support people in different parts of the world. People who worked for the organisation regularly used online video conferencing software to meet with others based at the organisation's headquarters. The HR director was aware that many learning and development priorities were difficult to meet for those employees who were based overseas. She began to devise a new learning and development strategy based on an e-learning training delivery which would be supported and reinforced through 'social learning' across the organisation, making use of social media platforms. Jeremy's project was to investigate the opportunities and come up with recommendations. He started reading around the topic of e-learning and technology in learning and this led him to appreciate the many opportunities for sharing learning and discussion and for benefiting from reflection with others through using social media platforms. However, he also came across consistent evidence about the challenges of 'technology acceptance' as a factor that might inhibit people from accessing and making use of social learning opportunities through mobile technology (Šumak, Heričko and Pušnik, 2011). With this in mind, Jeremy wanted to find out about perceptions and attitudes towards social media and other e-learning technologies among the people in his organisation. He considered organising a questionnaire survey to ask about these issues. However, Jeremy wanted to try to get 'underneath' general attitudinal trends towards social media so that he could better understand people's perspectives as a basis for considering what the organisation might be able to do to make learning opportunities timelier and more widely available.

Discussion questions

1   What sort of information would Jeremy need to gather to find out about the different perceptions of learners working in different areas of the world about their experiences of, and attitudes towards, and use of, e-learning delivered through social media platforms?

2   How might he gain access to the people he needed to hear from?

3   What issues might impact on the quality and persuasiveness of the qualitative data that Jeremy would gather?

Feedback notes

In order to find out about perceptions about attitudes to e-learning, Jeremy needed to explore different factors that influenced the views of employees who worked in different parts of the world in relation to their attitudes towards e-learning and social media usage. He wanted to know about how people in different contexts currently used social media (if at all) and their levels of confidence in both technology and in its use for learning purposes. He also needed to find out how people who were not initially confident with the technologies learned how to use them when they needed to.

Jeremy knew from his own experience that regular users of social technologies are familiar with a range of expressions (hashtags, twitter-feed and so on) that have no meaning to non-users. He was determined to access the words and language of his colleagues in an inclusive way, whether or not they regarded themselves as regular, occasional, or non-users of technology. He decided to interview the managers responsible for work in the different parts of the world. In addition he 'reached out' by e-mail to invite colleagues to volunteer to take part in focus groups. He decided to have one focus group of each of the categories of 'confident user; moderate user; non-user'. In addition, to gain as diverse a 'picture' as possible, Jeremy decided to interview the project lead who was promoting the e-learning initiative to identify the specific programme design features that were being considered.

In thinking about his data gathering Jeremy was concerned that managers might 'overstate' their perspectives – either positive or negative – towards the strategic change that was being considered. As he considered the focus groups he worried that people might be reluctant to 'admit' their non-use of social technology – or that the 'occasional user' category would be difficult to define. Focus group members also worked in different time zones. This was a logistical issue and Jeremy also worried about how he would facilitate the online focus groups: some members might feel inhibited from expressing their views and experiences and others might be dominant.

The value of qualitative data in HR research

The issues highlighted in this case are common for many HR research projects, particularly those that are organisationally based. While quantitative data can identify the extent to which things are, or are not, occurring in organisations, it is less helpful in answering the question 'why' things are the way they are. Most organisationally focused HR projects, therefore, will include the use of some qualitative data. This chapter considers the key issues with gathering and recording qualitative data. Chapter 8 considers the data analysis process.

Qualitative data can be broadly categorised as encompassing **information about meanings, expressed in words, language and visual images** from:

- observation and participation;
- one-to-one interviews or conversations;
- individual accounts or diaries (digital, 'virtual' and paper-based) of events and/or activities;
- focus groups and other forms of group interviews;
- visual representations – drawings/illustrations/photographic images and so on.

As such, qualitative data are often generated through a process that is emergent rather than structured and where questions posed are not standardised. Success in collecting data of this type requires that researchers suspend their own assumptions, preconceptions and categories and encourage and value the language and expressions of their 'informants'.

Although in-depth, unstructured and semi-structured interviews are shown in Figure 7.1 as methods to gather qualitative data it is important to note that structured interviews are not included. This is because structured interviews, like highly structured observations of work activity, are likely to generate standardised forms of quantitative, rather than qualitative data. Such data can be useful, but they are considered in Chapter 9 (quantitative data). The focus in this chapter is on gathering and recording qualitative data.

Figure 7.1 Types of qualitative data

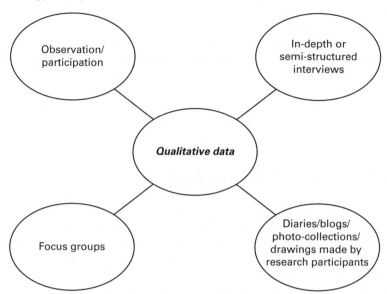

Working with qualitative data as part of your project is not an easy undertaking. Although proficiency in maths and statistics is not required, there are a lot of other skills you will need if you are to credibly reflect the information gathered from your sources. Qualitative data analysis involves working with small sample sizes but, in order to obtain information of good quality, it is important to establish mutual trust with your participants. Good quality qualitative data is detailed, rich and extensive. Qualitative analysis also requires an in-depth and 'open-minded' approach to interpret the data; to 're-present' them in an appropriate way. This means being open to the possibility that your own background may influence your prior understanding of the issue you are researching into and taking care that you limit the influence of your 'positionality' on your collection and analysis of data (Levitt, *et al*, 2018).

Qualitative data can add value to your research in different ways and can support both inductive and deductive research approaches (O'Reilly and Parker, 2013). You may choose to keep a direct (empirical) record of your observations or the experiences of those included within your research sample for the purposes of analysing the evidence to answer clearly defined questions within an established theoretical or conceptual model. Alternatively, you may work within an interpretivist 'world view' (see Chapter 5) to 'get beneath' a 'situation' or issue. This requires the development of an informed awareness of research participants' (and your own) 'pre-understandings' of what is going on. You will need to make sense of what you see, hear and read through a reflective process of becoming familiar with the data; seeing issues as part of a 'whole' rather than breaking them down; and 'making sense' of events through offering new descriptions and provisional explanations of the events that you have examined.

Qualitative data helps you to explain or understand issues in their organisational context. The aim is to develop a 'rich picture' of situations and events that are taking place. If you are undertaking an action orientated approach, where your project forms part of a wider change initiative, then you can use a qualitative approach to help you interact with different stakeholders as part of your data collection strategy and so explore some of the issues that emerge over time. Alternatively, you may choose a qualitative approach in order to develop a case study based understanding of an HR issue from the (perhaps multiple) perspectives of those who have to participate in it.

One thing is clear: qualitative research is unlikely to add value if the only reason you choose to undertake it is because it seemed like an 'easier' option.

Observation and participation

An obvious way of finding out information about people's behaviours and actions at work is to watch and listen to them. If you are undertaking a project in an organisation in which you already operate – either as an employee, as an intern, or as part of a paid work placement – there are likely to be plenty of opportunities for participation in, or observation of, organisational processes. However, if these practices are to be used as part of a research project, it is important to distinguish between different types of observation and participation and the uses to which data gathered in this way may be put.

 Case Example 7.2

Multidisciplinary team working in the care sector

Melani worked for a large healthcare organisation and part of her responsibilities were to support healthcare professionals working in children's community mental health services. A key feature of work in community mental healthcare is the need for multidisciplinary team working. The purpose behind policies promoting multidisciplinary team working is to enable professionals from different specialisms to work collaboratively together to provide evidence-based care to client families. However, this policy proved difficult to enact in Melani's organisation and professionals from different occupational backgrounds (administration, nursing, psychology, medicine, occupational

therapy, social work and peer support workers) found it difficult to 'let go' of primary loyalty to their own professional field and have only limited experience of, and no training in, effective team working.

At her performance appraisal meeting Melani's manager set her the objective of developing appropriate training support for multidisciplinary teams. For her research project, therefore, Melani decided to probe into the challenges and opportunities of such team working. She decided to gather data about different team members' attitudes towards their work, the team situation they were expected to enact, the influence of their professional training and so on. She also decided that it would be useful to observe two multidisciplinary teams when they met together.

Discussion questions

1   In what ways might observation of team members 'add value' to the findings of the research? List what you think are the advantages and the disadvantages of using observation as part of a research project in HR.

2   What problems might emerge for the researcher, the situation being observed, and the organisation in which observation is being undertaken? What issues need to be taken into account in such situations?

Feedback notes

A major advantage of gathering data by watching people's behaviour is its directness. Rather than asking people about their feelings, you can watch (and make notes or other forms of record about) what people do and say, and also reflect on your own experience as part of the analysis of the situation. What people say about their experience at work is valuable but new insights can often be achieved through direct observation of, and reflection about, the experiences of those who are being researched. Melani also found that, as she reflected on observations she made, she found herself thinking differently about some of the issues and so an additional 'loop' of (self-reflective) data was generated by this method.

However, there are important ethical and legal issues that must be taken into account if observation is used, particularly if it may be interpreted as covert surveillance (see Chapter 4). There are also practical disadvantages. One such difficulty is the time commitment. Although Melani was already involved in HR provision for these groups of staff, she had other pressing duties and the time commitment involved in working 'alongside' people in their work roles in order to achieve observational data is difficult to fulfil. In addition, it is possible that your presence as a researcher might influence behaviour one way or another and so it is still difficult to know what would have happened if you had not been part of the situation.

Other issues that are important to take into account are (Iacono *et al*, 2016):

- **Bias.** Being a participant watching and listening is easy but, as you have been part of the situation, how can you be sure that the data you record are not biased in some way? This leads to further questions:
  - **What to record.** When you are observing a situation how will you know what to look out for?
  - **How to record.** Another question is the format you will use to record your data. Many HR students claim to have undertaken some observation but are less clear about how they recorded and then analysed their data. Relying on your memory and on anecdotes is insufficient and effective methods of recording data are essential. Robson and McCartan (2016) recommend noting down 'memory sparkers' within a few hours of the event that will help you recall and record more details of what happened.

Other researchers keep some form of diary that they update on a daily basis. Records not made within 24 hours of any observation are rarely reliable.

- **Ethics.** As discussed already in Chapter 4 there are a number of ethical concerns relating to observation. Being explicit about the purpose of your observation and obtaining informed consent overcomes many of the difficulties, but may also influence the nature of your findings. For these reasons it is important that you discuss any plans to utilise some form of observation with your supervisor or tutor.

Although there are difficulties, observation and/or participation, in the context of your research project, can provide opportunities to record, describe and interpret people's behaviour. It is important, however, to be clear about the purpose of any observation and the way in which it will be carried out. Robson and McCartan (2016) describe a range of different approaches to participation and observation (see Figure 7.2) and these are briefly described now.

Complete participation. The observer becomes as full a member as possible of the group or organisation being studied. Employment within an organisation provides many opportunities to undertake this (Easterby-Smith *et al*, 2018) although the ethical implications of concealing the purpose of your participation need to be clearly thought through and discussed with your supervisor.

The participant as observer. The observer makes clear to those involved that research is their explicit role although they may also participate in the activity in one way or another, perhaps through some form of voluntary activity. This is not an easy option and it is important to gain the trust of those involved. It does, however, provide opportunities for you to ask people to explain what is going on and why. Some students use an approach of 'interrupted involvement' (Easterby-Smith *et al*, 2018) and complement it with in-depth interviews of key participants after the activities that have been observed.

Figure 7.2 Participation and observation

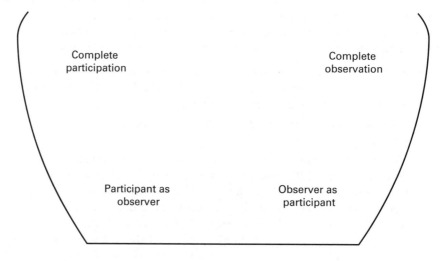

The observer as participant. This approach (referred to in Robson and McCartan, 2016 as the 'marginal participant') occurs when your main role is 'merely' to observe but, to some degree, you unavoidably become a participant in the situation as a result of your very presence. Researchers who wish to find out the extent to which new corporate values really have become 'embedded', for example, may 'loiter' or spend time near a coffee machine or a photocopier to observe what issues people really do discuss when not at their desks. The very fact of their presence, however, may mean that the researcher becomes drawn into conversation, or may influence in some way, the conversations of those around them.

The complete observer. This is someone who takes no part in the activity but the research purpose and the role as an observer is known to the participants. In many ways there is little distinction between this end of the spectrum and being an observer/participant as it is hard to see how the presence of someone to 'observe' would not affect the behaviour of those being observed.

If you are considering some form of participation or observation, it is important to adopt a methodical and justifiable approach to what you plan to do. Recording data appropriately is one of the key challenges of this approach. DeWalt and DeWalt (2010) indicate three broad types of data that may be generated:

- **Primary observations.** Those 'field notes' made at the time, or very near to the time, usually in some form of jot-notes, diary or journal.

- **Secondary observations.** How other people who were there 'saw it' – generated through asking participants as closely to the time of the events as possible.

- **Experiential data.** How you 'felt' about what you were observing and experiencing as time passed. Here a reflective format can help you to record how your feelings or values have developed or changed as a result of the research process.

Observation and participation are valuable ways of obtaining qualitative data but it is important to think ahead to ensure that time invested in this approach is productive. Key issues that underpin the planning process are summarised in Table 7.1.

Video methods

Video technology is increasingly available. If you use a 'smartphone' then it is likely that you are familiar with creating and sharing digital video footage to attach to messages and send to others using social media platforms. Many organisations make extensive use of video technology, including video recording, for video conferencing, quality control, internal knowledge sharing, training and so on. Video footage, for marketing and public relations purposes, is readily available on many corporate websites and recordings of meetings undertaken through video conferencing platforms are increasingly common. Given this prevalence it is surprising that video methods for HR research have received so little attention. Video methods can be used as a feature of both quantitative and qualitative data. In this part of the chapter their use as a feature of qualitative data gathering is considered.

Table 7.1 Preparing for observation

Clarify what you need to know	What are your research questions? What information do you require to answer them?
Is observation the most appropriate way of obtaining the information you need?	Consider alternative ways of data gathering?
What aspects of the situation(s) do you need to find out about?	Are you interested in **process** or **content**? Are all subjects equally interesting?
What times are most appropriate to carry out your observations?	Will the timing of your observations affect what you find out?
Access and permission	What permission do you need to undertake this observation? What level of authority is required? With whom should you discuss any plans for observation?
'Blending in'	How 'visible' will you be? Will what you wear, your gender, your age, etc affect how people behave when you are observing them?
Recording data	How will you record what you observe? Will the data be sufficient to enable you to form conclusions?
Roles and responsibilities	If you are going to participate as well as observe, how will you balance the demands of both activities?
Pilot your methods	Observation is an 'unrepeatable method' so mistakes cannot be rectified. Pilot your approach first before committing yourself fully to it.

(Robson and McCartan, 2016; Bell, Bryman and Harley, 2019; Iacono *et al*, 2009)

An obvious characteristic of video is that it combines both audible and visual channels, enabling you to record and analyse the behaviour and activities of people by both watching and listening. Although video methods are not appropriate for all projects, they provide the opportunity to answer research questions that require analysis of both observable processes (video) and that involve sound-related or spoken (audio) features of behaviour. Through video recordings it is possible to examine talk, images, gestures, facial expressions and text. You can analyse issues such as body language, spatial distance between participants and consider other issues such as their posture (LeBaron *et al*, 2018). However, the advantages of video methods, which include their extensive possibilities for analysis, also comprise the main disadvantage. The challenge here is that with so many options and choices available to you, it is easy to become distracted away from the focal objectives and research questions that you have set out to answer. Table 7.2 sets out some of the choices you might make to ensure that you remain 'on track'.

Table 7.2 Video recording issues

Question	Options
Who should control your camera?	You (the researcher) or your research participants
Where should you locate the camera?	The camera location can be fixed or mobile
Where should you point the camera?	The direction of the camera can be fixed or you might choose to change its direction
How should you frame the shot?	Will you include many participants or 'zoom in' to focus on specific participants?
Should you use more than one cameras?	Alternative perspectives might offer different avenues for analysis
When should you turn the recording on and off?	Different times of the day might offer different perspectives on the issues
Should you stay with the camera or leave the room?	To what extent might your presence influence people's activities and behaviour?

(LeBaron *et al*, 2018)

Data from individuals

Interviews

Interview data are probably the most frequently used form of information in HR research projects and they can provide unique entry points when researching issues in organisations (Saunders and Townsend, 2016). However, their usefulness will depend on the choice of participants and the extent and depth of people's responses to the questions they are asked. Careful planning of the interview process, and thoughtful consideration of the sample of participants to be invited to take part in interviews, is necessary for a good quality research project. Qualitative data are obtained by in-depth, unstructured interviews and can also be generated from semi-structured interviews. Structured interviews generate quantitative data, and are considered in Chapter 9.

A key issue with interviewing, often overlooked by HR students, is to determine the type of interview that is most suitable to answer your research questions (Figure 7.3). Each different type of interview has implications for the approach you will take to questioning, recording and analysing data. There are also choices to make about the 'media' and 'method' of the interview. Most interviews are undertaken on a face-to-face basis. Increasingly, however, telephone interviews or electronic conversations/chat are utilised in HR research and some researchers also choose to follow up their data gathering with some form of electronic 'conversation' using e-mail with some or all of their respondents.

Figure 7.3 Types of research interview

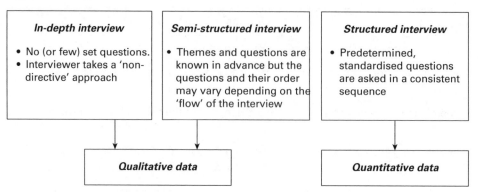

 Case Example 7.3

Researching into employability

Jessica was a full-time student who was struggling to find employment. Her qualifications were excellent but it seemed as if there were always too many graduates applying for graduate level positions in organisations. Jessica decided to make the issue of employability the focus of her research project. Jessica wanted to find out what characteristics employers describe as comprising graduate employability, and how this compared with what students understood by the term employability. She managed to persuade the careers service at her university to help her access some employers so that she could interview them. However, she also needed to gain access to some students.

Discussion questions

1 In what ways might data generated by semi-structured interviews enable Jessica to answer her research questions?

2 What problems might she encounter in collecting data in this way?

Feedback notes

Jessica envisaged that interviews would help her to explore and investigate underlying themes or issues related to the concept of employability. Semi-structured interviews offer the possibility of modifying 'lines of enquiry' in a way that a questionnaire or structured interview would not. Answers can be probed enabling interviewees to explain or build on what they have said. In this way data of a 'rich' quality can be gathered, that allows for people to provide information about their experiences, feelings and motives. Indeed, the responses of one interviewee might alert you to a line of enquiry that you had not previously thought of and so allow for some form of incremental development of thinking with potential benefit for your research outcomes. In addition, Jessica hoped that the students would find the interview opportunity helpful as a way of reflecting on their own preparations for job seeking and selection processes.

However, Jessica encountered a number of problems. Semi-structured interviews are time-consuming. Her tutor told her that any interview of less than half an hour would be unlikely to generate qualitative data of much value but pressures and deadlines at work made it unlikely that interviewees (graduate recruiters) would be available for more than an hour. The time intensive nature of interviewing meant that the number of participants had to be quite low and Jessica also started to worry about the extent to which she could generalise her conclusions given the highly contextualised nature of her interview data.

Another problem Jessica experienced was the issue of recording data. She conducted two pilot interviews, one with an employer and one with a student, and discovered that transcribing each of these resulted in about 20 pages of closely typed text for each interview. Committing to this for all of her interviews was a daunting prospect. However, Jessica was conscious that note-taking during the interview might distract both her and her interviewees and provide only a partial record of what was said.

Although Jessica was given access to people for face-to-face interviews there were one or two employers whose work roles were in a different area of the country. Therefore, she could not undertake all her interviews on a face-to-face basis. One option she considered was for telephone interviews and the other was the use of Skype. This raised some interesting issues. Conducting interviews in this way was easier to arrange across a wide geographical area. However, she was worried that it would constrain the interpersonal relationship between her and her interviewees, which might detract from the quality of the data. Jessica was concerned that Skype might limit the extent to which probing questions would be possible as non-verbal 'cues' are somewhat distorted in Skype-type conversations.

Another problem that Jessica faced was that it proved difficult to find times when she could interview students. When she was available they were not! To overcome this challenge Jessica decided to expand her range of qualitative data gathering by organising a focus group for her sample of students. This was also a worry, however, as she was concerned that not all the students who said they would come along would actually turn up. After discussion with her tutor and discussion with the research ethics advisor at her department she decided to offer a very small incentive for the students to participate (the promise of pizza at the focus group meeting).

Preparing for the interview

Key issues to take account of to maximise the usefulness of data gathered in unstructured or semi-structured forms of interviewing, and for focus groups are:

Interview design

Allocate time for preparation for all the data gathering you intend to carry out. Clarify what research objectives or questions your interview data will contribute towards answering and identify the key areas that you need to explore. These decisions will be influenced by your literature review, discussions with your tutor and, perhaps, from other activities such as reviewing organisational documents. A process for designing interview topic areas is shown in Figure 7.4. For each of the topics that you identify, write down a number of questions that you could ask. Be prepared to be flexible in the way you ask your questions. It is also important to be open to the possibility of new aspects or issues that may arise from the interviews. At this stage, therefore, you are clarifying what ground you need to cover. This means that, as the interviews progress, you can check the extent to which you are gathering the data that you need. At the planning stage it is important to make sure that you are not being overambitious with your range of questions. Although you may find that some people will be happy to talk for much more than the initial time they promise to give to you, your interview will be time-limited. A common mistake is to try to gather information on too many issues and then find that there is no time to explore things in a deeper way. Another error, frequently made, is to ask ambiguous or leading questions. Before you start your interviews you would be wise to ask your tutor or supervisor to review the questions that you plan to ask. This checking process is a requirement in many universities as it helps you to avoid mistakes that will limit the value of the data that you gather.

Figure 7.4   Factors in the design of a topic guide

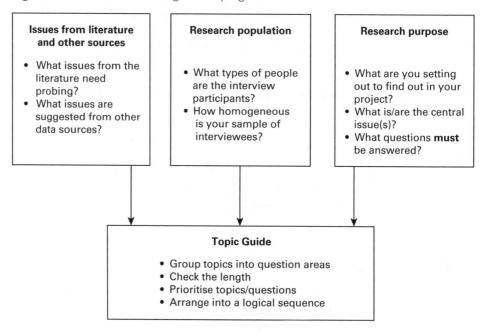

Preparation of the participants

You are likely to get more cooperation from your interviewee(s) if they feel fully briefed and confident of your competence as an interviewer and as a researcher. It may be appropriate, for example, to provide your interviewees with some guidance about the topics you would like them to speak about, in advance of the meeting. Many people, once briefed, may also be prepared to give you documents that are relevant to your research and this provides a useful basis for 'triangulation' (see Chapter 5). If your research is likely to involve you in asking questions about personally or organisationally sensitive issues, you will also need to think about how you will prepare the interviewee for the interview and how you will conduct it to establish and sustain a relationship of trust.

Preparation of yourself

As with all forms of interviewing, first impressions are important. In recruitment processes the candidate wants to make a favourable impression on the interviewer. In a research interview the situation is somewhat reversed. You need to make an appropriate impression if a rapport is to be developed to allow for a productive interview. This means thinking carefully about what you will wear and the language that you will use. Clothes that are too smart or imposing may inhibit responses from employees who dress differently. 'Dressing down' may be less appropriate when interviewing the HR director of a work placement organisation. Undertaking some prior research into the key issues for the organisation (key challenges or successes, for example) can be advantageous in two ways. First, by drawing on relevant examples during the interview your credibility may be enhanced. Second, your prior 'fact-finding' may also allow you to assess the accuracy of some of the information generated by the interview.

 Activity 7.1

Research interview skills

Think back to any interview skills training that you have participated in – either as a trainee or as the trainer. If you have never attended an interviewing skills course, think back to recruitment interviews that you have been involved in, either as the candidate or the interviewer.

1 Make a list of all the key skills necessary for effective interviewing.

2 To what extent are the skills needed for recruitment interviewing the same as those needed for undertaking effective qualitative interviews for research purposes?

Feedback notes

An activity such as this can generate many relevant points, all of which have relevance to conducting in-depth or semi-structured interviews. Key issues include:

- the interview environment;
- structuring the interview;
- opening the interview;
- using appropriate questions;
- listening actively;
- using silence;
- using appropriate language;
- observing body language;
- probing answers;
- moving from one question to the next;
- using summaries;
- closing the interview;
- keeping accurate records.

Skills for effective research interviews are very similar to those needed for other types of interviews. However, there are some differences. Most HR practitioners utilise a semi-structured approach to selection interviewing to allow comparisons to be more easily made between different candidates. With qualitative research interviews, however, the aim is to gather data that reflects the experience of unique individuals. As such, a less structured approach is used. This can be a challenge for a practitioner-researcher who is used to a more controlled form of interview with behaviourally structured questions that have been more or less predetermined.

The key skills and issues that underpin successful research interviewing are summarised below:

- **The environment.** It is important that all your research participants feel 'safe' so that they can have confidence that it is OK to share their thoughts and experiences with you. An unfamiliar or noisy environment is likely to inhibit the quality of discussion. 'Phones on silent' must be a rule for the interviewer although it is increasingly likely that participants will glance at their phone, during the interview. For this reason it is important to get across to the participants how helpful it will be if they can give you an agreed spell of time with no disturbances.

- **Structuring the interview.** Although the questions and format of responses will not be formally structured, it is important to have a framework for the interview. This will normally involve:
  - opening/introduction;
  - 'warm up' questions;
  - main body – exploring the main topics in a logical way;
  - 'cool off' questions;
  - conclusion/ending – thanking the interviewee; explaining the next steps in the research process, etc.

- **Questioning and listening.** Your job is to get participants to speak freely and openly. To achieve this, it is important that you listen more than you speak. It is also necessary that you express your questions in a clear, understandable and open way. People will only 'open up' if they feel that you are interested in what they are saying. Therefore, it is important to ensure that your behaviour and body language does not influence the opinions they offer. Active listening, involving verbal and non-verbal signs of your continued interest in the conversation, is necessary. Many research interviews are carried out to explore general issues about the experience and perspective of the interviewee. However, encouragement of examples and/or a focus on 'critical incidents' or situations that are relevant to your topic, may help to identify further information that is relevant to the research questions. This may involve identifying the important aspects of a situation or incident, as perceived by the interviewee, before going on to consider the effect of the situation as experienced by the respondent and others. Whatever the nature and purpose of the research interview, the most productive types of questions to ask are:

  - **open questions** where the interviewee is encouraged to describe or explain an experience;
  - **probing questions** such as 'tell me more about...' or 'what factors contributed to...?' 'how did you feel when...?' which enable interviewees to reflect on issues in more depth for responses to be further explored.

It is unlikely that specific or closed questions will be appropriate. Multiple questions, long questions, leading questions and also those involving jargon should be avoided.

- **Probes.** In addition to the use of specifically probing questions, successful research interviewers will also use other non-verbal methods of encouraging interviewees to talk more about a topic. Robson and McCartan (2016) indicate four useful techniques of probing in unstructured interviews:

  - allowing a period of silence;
  - offering an 'enquiring glance';
  - using verbal signals such as: 'mmhmm';
  - repeating back all or part of what the interviewee has just said.

- **Summaries.** As with other forms of interviewing, the use of summaries at appropriate times can fulfil a very useful function. Sometimes, once started, interviewees just cannot stop talking or repeating themselves. The use of a summary, to check understanding, and then 'build' on the contribution by asking a different, but related question, can allow some 'steering' of the interview. Where complex issues are being discussed it may also be appropriate to offer a summary to check understanding, or to allow the interviewee to clarify where there may be some misunderstanding.

- **Keeping accurate records.** A key question to consider about unstructured or semi-structured interviews is how you will make and keep a record of the data. This is something that must be explained in the methodology section of your report. Three options are available: to video record; to audio record; or to make manual notes during the interview.

– **Audio or video recording your information.** The advantages of audio or video recording are that you can concentrate on the process of questioning and listening rather than being distracted by the need to take notes. You can also be confident of the accuracy of the record and you can listen or watch more than once to the recording. However, the interviewee may feel inhibited by the recorder and your relationship with the interviewee may be affected. You cannot rule out the possibility of a technical 'hitch' and you must also ensure that the recording device has sufficient capacity and battery life so that it will not stop partway through the interview. In addition, the time necessary to transcribe the entire conversation is extensive. Secure audio transcription services are available on a commercial basis but these can be expensive if you have a lot of 'audio minutes'. If you decide to use an audio or video recorder you should explain why you are doing so and seek the respondents' permission, allowing them, if necessary, to turn off the device partway through the interview if they feel uncomfortable with it (see Chapter 4 for the ethical issues of recording and data storage).

– **Taking notes.** There are many different approaches to taking notes. Some people have a sheet with spaces between headings as well as a spare space for unforeseen ideas and responses to be recorded. Others generate something more like a mind map or a concept map as a basis for noting down key pieces of information that are generated during the interview. One advantage of making some notes, even if you are recording the conversation, is that it encourages you to remain focused on what is being said and not to 'drift'. Whatever method you use to take notes during an interview it is important to make further, more detailed, notes of the meeting as soon as possible after it has concluded. These post-interview notes will be based on the short notes made during the discussion itself, but provide you with the opportunity to note down your reflections about the environment, the body language of the interviewee and the main information that was provided to you, in as much detail as possible. These extended summary notes will form the basis for your analysis of the interview data (see Chapter 8). They also provide you with the opportunity to reflect on what you have learned. This process of reflection might well lead you to follow up unexpected insights gained from the interview into your subsequent data gathering activities.

Table 7.3 provides a summary of what to do and what not to do in research interviews.

Where face-to-face interviews are not possible it may be feasible to undertake a telephone interview or online video hosted interview using a platform such as WebEx, Skype or Zoom. These are particularly useful when it is impossible to travel in order to achieve a personal meeting. The options for data recording are the same as with face-to-face interviews. Such interviews require particular attention as connection or bandwidth difficulties can mean that interviews undertaken in these ways tend to be shorter and the information may be less 'deep'.

Table 7.3 Qualitative data gathering: what to do and what to avoid doing

Do	Avoid
Be gently assertive – you want to hear what the interviewee has to say in a sympathetic way but you also need to guide the discussion through your research topics/themes	**Do not ask more than one question at a time** – avoid multiple questions
Ask both sides of a question – eg if you ask what someone likes about something, also ask what they dislike	**Avoid being led too far from the point** – keep the objectives of the interview clearly in your mind; some diversions lead to areas of interest but these are very rare
Tackle difficult or sensitive areas with discretion – when sensitive issues are discussed, make sure you reassure the interviewees, as appropriate, of the confidential nature of the process and of the maintenance of their anonymity. Be prepared to refer the interviewees to support services that may be available if they find the issues they discuss with you to lead to emotional discomfort or distress	**Avoid giving your own opinion** – if you do this it is likely that you will influence many answers that the interviewee gives

Social media data

The use of social media (Twitter, Facebook, WhatsApp, LinkedIn, chat rooms, discussion boards, contributions to blogs and e-mail exchanges, etc) have become popular ways of accessing qualitative data, particularly where 'physical' access to a sample of respondents is very difficult. One advantage is that time-zone constraints can be minimised and a 'conversation' between people in different regions of the world is more possible.

 Activity 7.2

Research using social media discussion threads

Imagine that, as a result of your studies of employment relations and/or corporate social responsibility you have become interested in debates about the 'future of work'. In the initial stages of your project you are not sure which 'angle' to take relating to this rather broad topic. Visit https://www.cipd.co.uk/Community/discussion-forum/future_of_work_is_human/

and scroll down or search for discussion sources that might be interesting to pursue as a source of qualitative data for your project. Take a few minutes to scan their contents.

Discussion question

What do you see as the advantages and disadvantages of obtaining qualitative data from one or more of these discussion threads?

Feedback notes

A number of issues are raised by the use of discussions hosted online as part of a qualitative data gathering strategy. There are various means of doing this, for example, through discussion threads or through keyword or hashtag topic threads on social media platforms such as Facebook, YouTube, Google+, Twitter, Instagram, LinkedIn, Snapchat, Pinterest and so on. With internet-based research the issues of potential bias, and incorrect information, have been highlighted as the concepts of 'fake news' and 'post-truth' have become important. In addition, although discussion threads and social media posts can receive a high number of 'hits', the number of contributions to the discussion is much smaller. On the other hand, you might argue that the people who contribute are most interested in the topic and so their views are important to consider in your research. As discussed in Chapter 4 anonymity is not possible. Equally possible is that contributors use an assumed identity. However, as a supplement to other forms of data, perhaps as a way of informing the development of other data gathering instruments, these forms of data can be useful.

Diaries and blogs

Another way of exploring aspects of people's experience in a particular context is through the use of narratives and stories (Elliott, 2005). Some form of diary, journal or blog, written by different participants in events may well be worthwhile as a part of a data gathering strategy. These form something of a reflective record of an individual or a group's actions over a defined period of time. A detailed record might be kept for just a few days (or even hours) or it might be undertaken less intensively over a period of weeks or months. 'Entries' can be written electronically, using pen and paper or spoken into an audio or video recorder.

 Activity 7.3

Data from blogs

Visit https://www.cipd.co.uk/Community/blogs/b/ leading-in-learning and skim through the blog contributions and the comments associated with them. Imagine that your research is focused on new developments in learning and development and that you hope to identify key challenges and opportunities for learning and development specialists.

Discussion questions

1   What advantages might the analysis of the content of one or more blogs focusing on learning and development offer as a source of data for your research? What other benefits might the use of data from some form of diary provide within a research project?

2   What problems might be experienced with the use of diaries or blogs as a method of data gathering?

Feedback notes

The use of blogs and other forms of 'journal' can provide a different, and often useful, 'reflective' perspective on a situation or on issues relevant to your research and can be a helpful complement to other forms of data. This allows for some degree of 'triangulation' (see Chapter 5). In addition, the use of diaries, blogs or other forms of journal might provide information about events that it is not possible to observe, but which can provide for more 'immediacy' that would be possible through an interview.

Like all other methods of data gathering, of course, there are a number of issues that must be taken into account, particularly if you are asking someone to keep a diary or blog specifically for your project. Not all potential bloggers are able to communicate systematically in a written or an oral form and many people are not natural diarists; it is likely that they may 'give up' along the way or only turn to the blog in (untypical) moments of exasperation or exuberance. Therefore, it is important to keep in touch and to encourage them – to reinforce how important it is to understand their perceptions of the particular situation or context. Linked with this is the issue that blogging is time-consuming and people should not be pressured into maintaining the process. Secondly, where the journal process is 'intentional' it is important that those completing one are clear about what to record. It may be that you want them to note down any reflections, feelings and motivations in response to what is happening in their lives. However, it is more likely that it is appropriate to provide guidance about what should be recorded, stemming from the research questions that are being answered.

A third area of difficulty is the inhibition people may feel about recording what they 'really' think about things or how they 'really' spend their time at work. Data confidentiality is not possible on the internet. The final issue to bear in mind is that of representativeness. How can you be sure that the week or months during which your blogger was writing was a 'typical' period? Choice of timeframes for the period you choose to draw down data for analysis is important.

Focus groups

An enduringly popular way of gathering qualitative data in HR projects is through focus groups. Focus groups are a form of group interview where a process of dialogue and discussion between participants about a particular topic provides the data to help you answer your research questions.

 Activity 7.4

Obtaining data about employee benefits and discounts

Imagine that a large organisation has committed to a more inclusive system of employee benefits and discounts. You have been asked to research into employees' current level of understanding and preferences about benefits. Specifically, the organisation is concerned to redesign or 'wind down' benefits it currently offers that are least used and to identify new forms of benefit that meet the needs and interest of those of different age groups, taking into account those with no dependents as well as those with childcare or elder-care responsibilities. The organisation has agreed that focus groups would be an appropriate way of gathering these data.

Discussion questions

1   How many focus groups would you plan to hold and who should participate in them?

2   How would you decide what questions/issues to ask about?

3   What key skills would be required to facilitate the group(s) in an effective way?

4   How would you record the data from the focus groups?

Feedback notes

Focus groups provide an opportunity to find out about a range of attitudes and values to different topics (Barbour, 2018). You might feel that, if your aim is to familiarise yourself with a range of attitudes towards the system of benefits and discounts, then a small number of focus groups would be sufficient. However, if it is possible that people's opinions may depend, in part, on their age, their length of service in the organisation, their personal circumstances, their role or position within the organisation, it might be necessary to organise a larger number of groups, each with between 6 and 12 participants. One focus group will provide interesting data but would be insufficient as a 'sole method' to ensure data validity and confidence that 'saturation' of all the potential issues has been achieved.

It will also be necessary to make sure that each group consists of similar kinds of people, with enough in common that they will not feel inhibited about contributing their views but with enough differences that a range of perspectives may be represented. In this case it would be important to ensure that people with different roles and contexts are included. The inclusion of men and women from different age ranges and ethnicities would also ensure an inclusive approach to data collection.

To find out people's views it would be necessary to pose a sequence of questions that stimulate and encourage a flow of discussion. The questions would need to be fairly broad ranging, but also relevant to the particular research purpose. Although you are seeking to explore opinions and feelings, it is also important to remember that participants may have personal sensitivities and these must be handled carefully. You will also be seeking to obtain data that are specific and detailed, so it is important to encourage people to avoid talking only in generalisations and to explore why they may hold the opinions that they do.

To achieve this, you are likely to want to pose about six or seven questions, which move from the more general to the more specific. In a semi-structured interview, the flow of conversation may be quite flexible but the group nature of a focus group suggests that the order of your questions is maintained each time. As facilitator you might also expect to probe, steer, and, where necessary, enable and legitimise seemingly 'unpopular' viewpoints. The prevention of some individuals from over-dominating the opinions of the group is another key factor in an effective focus group process.

Recording data from focus groups also needs careful thought and preparation. The energy and concentration you will require for facilitating the group is likely to mean that you will be unable to take many notes. Some people ask a colleague to join the group in the role of note-taker. Others obtain permission to audio record the discussion although, if any member of the group objects, then you have a problem. Transcribing focus group recordings is also a time-consuming process requiring more time than a conventional interview transcription process. Another way to keep a record of the points that are made is to utilise flip charts, white boards, etc. The data contained on these can then act as a trigger for you to produce a fuller account of the discussion immediately after the focus group meeting has concluded.

In addition to 'face-to-face' focus groups it is also possible to organise 'virtual' focus groups, making use of online video-conferencing facilities. As a method of research within HR these have the advantage of being quite 'acceptable' for many organisational stakeholders, especially if they are used to holding meetings in this way. There are, however, disadvantages as well as advantages of the method and these are summarised in Table 7.4.

In order to maximise the effectiveness of the focus group approach to data gathering it is important to take some process issues into account (Barbour, 2018). These include:

- **Carefully work out the boundaries of the topic you wish to be discussed.** This must link closely with your research questions/objectives.
- **Think carefully about who should be included (sample selection).** Ensure that the sample will be appropriate to provide insights to a range of perspectives.
- **Facilitating focus groups requires a high level of interpersonal skills.** If you doubt your abilities here you could ask someone else to facilitate and you could be the note-taker.
- **Think ahead to how you will ultimately analyse the data.** Allow decisions about analysis to influence how you record the data from the focus groups.
- **Generate and pre-test/pilot the questions you propose to ask.** As part of this process you can plan how to keep the discussion focused without leading it in an obvious way.
- **Introduce the purpose of the focus group.** This should be clear at the beginning, which is also an opportunity to communicate appropriate 'ground rules' and process issues.

Table 7.4 Advantages and disadvantages of focus groups

Advantages	Disadvantages
They are cheaper than individual interviews (in terms of the time cost) and can generate large quantities of data	The large quantity of data may be difficult to summarise and to analyse
Interaction between researcher and participants allows for clarification, probing and follow-up questions	The facilitator may influence the participants too much and so affect the opinions they express
Data can be collected in the participants' 'own words' and take account of deeper meanings and interpretations	There may be undue influence of some participants over others, affecting the quality of the data
In some circumstances, more than one topic can be explored in each session	The small number of participants (relative to the size of the research population) leads to concerns about generalisability of the data
'Snowballing' of ideas can occur as participants respond to the contributions of others in the group	The 'group dynamics' of the session may lead the researcher to attribute more significance to the data than is actually warranted
Participants can feel empowered, especially in action-orientated organisational research	A 'polarisation effect' may occur where people's attitudes become more extreme as a result of group discussion

(Neuman, 2012; Saunders, Lewis and Thornhill, 2019)

- **Build a good rapport with the group.** It is important that people think that they can speak freely to each other and in front of you.
- **Ensure that everyone has an equal opportunity to contribute to the discussion.** It is important to make clear that all contributions are valued.
- **Clarify feedback arrangements.** Be clear about whether you propose to feedback the results of the focus groups to the participants and communicate this at the time.

Sample selection for qualitative research

A key issue that has been raised many times already in this and previous chapters is that of data quality. This is a particular issue with qualitative data as conventional measures of validity and reliability are not appropriate. Therefore, the recruitment and selection of participants (the sample selection process) must be considered in advance and explained and justified in your research report.

Sampling is the deliberate choice of a number of people to represent a greater population. In a very small organisation it may be possible to gather data from everyone but in most cases it is necessary to choose a sample of people from whom information will be obtained.

There are two main ways of determining an appropriate sample. Probability sampling involves determining a sample that is statistically representative of the research population as a whole and so should reflect the characteristics of the population. This means that, provided you ask exactly the same questions to everyone in the sample, you should be confident that you can generalise the conclusions that you derive from the data to the wider population. Research enquiries that utilise a quantitative approach are likely to adopt probability sampling and more information about this is contained in Chapter 9.

Most qualitative data gathering, however, operates from a basis of non-probability sampling, which is considered now.

 Case Example 7.4

Determining an appropriate sample

Researching into perceptions of the use of technology and social media while at work

Ahmad was an HR student who wished to investigate the issues of the use of technology and social media by employees during their work hours. He wanted to find out the perspectives of those within the HR function, as well as those who worked in different parts of the business, such as marketing, operations and finance. Ahmad's reading around the subject of technology and social media highlighted a range of ambiguities. He was aware that employees in some parts of the organisation used their own digital devices to perform some of their work when outside of the workplace, including occasions when they were on approved annual leave or vacation. However, he was also aware that excessive use of digital technology may be

associated with distraction of time and attention resulting from negative effects on work–life balance, 'cognitive load' and unsustainable impact on employee well-being and performance. He decided to undertake semi-structured interviews to explore some of these issues in depth in different parts of the organisation.

Discussion questions

1   How might you go about accessing interviewees if you were undertaking this project? In your answer decide whom you would include in your sample.

2   How many interviews might constitute a 'sufficient' sample size to explore the different perceptions of employees about the use of technology and social media at work?

Feedback notes

Ahmad chose two different approaches to gathering his data. He firstly determined the criteria of those whom he wished to interview: namely those who had been employed in the organisation for at least two years. Ahmad had a target of 15 interviews and his organisation gave him permission to advertise on the organisation's 'notice board' for potential participants to volunteer to be interviewed. However, in some parts of the organisation, a number of those who contacted him were then not able to commit to an interview within Ahmad's timeframe, often as a result of pressure of work. In other parts of the organisation he received responses from too many potential interviewees and so some further selection of participants was necessary so that he could complete his research by the due date. This led Ahmad to consider further 'inclusion criteria' to use to ensure the most appropriate interview participants were selected.

There are different ways of tackling non-probability sampling, and Ahmad's initial approach might be referred to as accidental sampling (where a speculative 'convenience' approach is taken to attracting potential participants). The various forms of non-probability sampling strategies are described more fully below.

Non-probability sampling

- **Accidental sampling.** This is where the sample is chosen for reasons of convenience or practicability. Many students implicitly operate an accidental sampling approach to any observation that they undertake as part of their data gathering process. The advantages are that it is convenient and that time and expense trying to undertake a more robust sample selection process are avoided. However, it is possible that the data may not be representative of the 'wider picture'.

- **Purposive sampling.** This involves choosing people whose experience and perspectives are deemed to be important to the investigation. Purposive sampling involves a careful specification of the 'inclusion' and 'exclusion criteria' that will be used in selecting those who take part in the research.
  - **Inclusion criteria.** These are criteria that describe key features of the target participants that will make them eligible to provide information relevant to the research questions.
  - **Exclusion criteria.** These are additional characteristics of the potential participants who, while they meet the inclusion criteria, make it unlikely that the information they provide will be relevant for the specific research questions.

There are different ways of choosing a purposive sample. First, you may identify key informants, people who have specialised and unique knowledge and experience of the issue you are trying to find out about. Many HR projects involve a key informant interview with the HR director, for example, or someone with particular knowledge and expertise in the area of the investigation. Second, it is possible to undertake a sliced sample whereby respondents are chosen because they occupy positions at different parts of the organisation. 'Slicing' is possible horizontally (a selection of middle managers from a range of different functions) and/or vertically (respondents from the top, middle and bottom of the hierarchy). Third, snowball sampling involves finding new people from which to gather data on the recommendation of those already included within the sample.

Each of these approaches has the advantage that you feel confident that the data gathered will reflect perspectives that are pertinent to the research being undertaken.

However, the people and situations from which you gather data may not be 'typical', something which is worth exploring during the data gathering process (by asking people how typical they feel they are) and when formulating your conclusions.

- **Quota sampling.** This involves choosing a sample that reflects as far as possible the diversity of the wider research population in the same proportions. Thus, if you know that the organisation you are researching has a proportion of 40:60 men to women, your sample would seek to ensure that you included four women for every six men. Similarly, if you know that the age distribution of 'under 30s', '30–45s' and '46–60s' is 40:40:20 then you would try to choose a sample that reflected this proportionately. The advantage of this approach is that you can indicate it is broadly representative. However, this does not mean that every member of the research population had an equal chance of being included in your study. Quota sampling can also be applied to observations (Neuman, 2012). For example, if you are observing interactions or other management processes, it may be important to be sure to include all the different times of the day. Where different locations are involved (for example, in production, administration, reception areas, etc) it may also be important to observe in a proportionately representative way, at different locations.

Sample size

In addition to deciding on the approach you will take to recruit and select your sample, it is also important to determine how big the sample size should be. With probability sampling there are statistical 'rules' about sample size, but with qualitative enquiries things are less clear and other criteria must be taken into account. The ideal sample size occurs when new 'cases' (either respondents or observations) cease to add new information or insights. This is sometimes referred to as data saturation and is a matter of judgement. It is also important to be able to justify the lower limit to the size of a sample. If the characteristics of the sample are fairly consistent, and the research question is rather a limited one, then a smaller-sized sample may be adequate. Where the research questions are broader and the sample is characterised by greater levels of variety then the sample would have to be larger.

For qualitative data, it is fair to say that the issue of sample size is one of the most difficult issues about which to be definitive. Research published in top-ranked journal articles demonstrates a range of approaches and sample sizes. Where research takes place in a single organisation and forms the principal basis from which conclusions will be drawn then it is likely that a lower sample size of 15 interviews, each lasting for more than 45 minutes, will be desirable although some studies include as many as 60 interviews (Saunders and Townsend, 2016). However, the decision about the most appropriate number of people or events to include cannot be predetermined. Instead, confidence in the sample size can only be achieved as a feature of the data analysis process. Only after some analysis has occurred are you able to estimate the necessary sample size and then to test this. The term 'saturation' refers to a situation where no additional insights or potential categories or characteristics are generated – at the point at which you see the same themes or issues over and over again, so you can become confident that saturation has been achieved (Nelson, 2017). However, merely spotting a lot of repetition in your analysis will not automatically determine that saturation has been achieved. It is possible, for example, that your analysis has not gone into sufficient depth and that there is more variety 'beneath the surface'. The aim, therefore, is to have a sufficient sample size to achieve sufficient depth of analysis; that is to say that your analysis may be characterised as 'rich' and 'thick'. To achieve this, it is important that you have a sample sufficient to provide a wide range of evidence to illustrate subtleties in the issues that your analysis identifies as well as potential connections and patterns that resonate with literature about your research. Put simply, would the data be sufficient to give confidence that it is trustworthy to a 'constructively sceptical' reader (Nelson, 2017)?

The approach you take to sample selection will make a substantial difference to the extent to which your research findings will be considered to be credible and persuasive. To ensure that your research is taken seriously it is important that you keep clear records of the numbers of participants, documents, or events that comprised your sample and your reasons for structuring the sample in this way. In your dissertation or research project report you will also need to describe and justify the process through which you determined the number of participants as well as any changes in this number (perhaps drop-outs or the identified need to recruit more participants). In addition, you will need to provide an account of the demographic information, for example cultural or employment contexts, that might influence the data that were collected and your analysis of this information (Levitt *et al*, 2018).

In summary, non-probability approaches to sample selection as a whole are appropriate for qualitative data collection. They have the advantage of flexibility and are often more organisationally acceptable. In addition, they can provide opportunities for collaboration within a problem-solving and action-orientated project. The data that they generate are rich and meaningful, providing scope for interpretation and judgement during the process of analysis. However, the disadvantages of them must be taken into account when you explain and justify your approach to data collection.

Making sense of the data

There are many differences between the processes necessary to analyse qualitative and quantitative data. The most substantial difference is that, when you are working with qualitative data, there is a close link between the processes of data gathering and initial analysis (Anderson, 2017). This link arises as the process of 'writing up' notes after any qualitative data gathering process inevitably involves you in reflecting on the data and considering how these might affect your understanding of the issues you are researching into. Braun and Clarke (2006) suggest that familiarisation is an important first step in qualitative analysis and this might involve asking the following questions so that your data can also 'feed in' to further data gathering on an incremental basis:

- How do your data compare with the other data you have already collected? Are there any apparent trends or possible patterns? What 'picture' or 'story' seems to be emerging?

- What concepts and research from the literature seem relevant to the data?
- What 'sense' were you able to make from the data gathering process you are reflecting on? Does the information 'ring true'?
- In what ways might your initial impressions, formed by this information, be 'checked out'?
- How much did you as researcher influence what was said? How significant was this influence? Should anything be discounted as a result? How might this affect your approach to your next data gathering activity?
- What unexpected information was gathered? How can its relevance be checked within the ongoing data gathering process?

CHECKLIST

- Qualitative data gathering forms a part of many organisationally focused HR research enquiries. It may involve activities such as observation and participation, one-to-one interviews or conversations, electronically posted information, individual accounts, blogs, diaries of activities and focus groups.

- With qualitative data the organisational context should be taken into account and data focused on particular themes and issues can be generated. Data relevant to 'real time' activity as well as past events can be obtained.

- Those involved in qualitative data gathering must try to limit bias on the part of the 'subjects' as well as the influence of their own 'position' by clarifying what information is to be obtained and how it will be recorded.

- Observation and/or participation in organisational processes provide an opportunity to obtain 'direct' data about features, perspectives and behaviours 'in practice'. A range of options for observation and participation of behaviours and processes in the workplace are possible, ranging from complete participation to complete observation.

- Particular care must be taken to consider issues of confidentiality and anonymity for participants in your study. The ethical implications of observation or the use of social media or other online data must be taken into account.

- Semi-structured interviews are a common way of gathering qualitative data. These require careful preparation and implementation. Key skills for research interviews include: asking open questions, active listening, using silence, using appropriate language, utilising non-verbal communication and steering the interview.

- There are advantages and disadvantages to gathering qualitative data through video or audio recording or through some form of note-taking. Permission to record activities and conversations must always be obtained.

- Where face-to-face interviews are not possible, data may also be obtained through e-mail conversations, blogs, messaging through social media and diary entries. These types of data allow people to reflect on their feelings and experiences but lack the face-to-face interaction that is possible in interviews, focus groups and forms of participant observation.

- Focus groups are a form of group interview where data are gathered through a facilitated process of dialogue and discussion about a particular topic. More than one focus group is necessary to have assurance of data validity and confidence of saturation. One focus group on its own is not sufficient to generate data that might be evaluated as transferable or dependable.

- Focus groups are often organisationally acceptable ways of gathering data as they are more time-effective than individual interviews and can involve and empower participants within a problem-solving or action-orientated process. However, they can also lead to a polarisation of opinions among participants, and the data generated may be hard to transcribe and to analyse.

- Non-probability sampling is appropriate for qualitative research. Approaches to non-probability sampling include: accidental sampling, quota sampling and purposive sampling. Purposive sampling can include the selection of key informants, 'sliced' samples and 'snowball' sampling techniques.

- The nature of the research questions and the homogeneity of the research population will influence decisions about minimum sample size. The upper limit of sample size is a matter of judgement and is reached when it appears new 'cases' are not generating any 'new' or unexpected insights.

- The process of initial data recording and analysis can lead to an incremental development of the research project.

TEST YOURSELF

1 What is purposive sampling?

   a Deciding about the people you want to include before you have worked out your research questions.

   b Ensuring that your research sample provides an equal chance for all members of the research population to be selected.

   c Choosing a sample of respondents who are most likely to provide relevant information.

   d Asking your friends to recommend others to form part of your sample.

2 Which of the following best describes a qualitative interview?

   a The researcher seeks rich, detailed answers.

   b 'Wandering' away from the topic is expected.

   c The questions are standardised.

   d The interview can be undertaken in 10 minutes.

3 Why is it important to prepare an interview guide or schedule before you undertake a semi-structured interview?

   a So that you can work out the statistical inferences from the answers.

   b To make it easy to analyse the data using a computer software program.

   c To increase the reliability of your research.

   d So that data from different interviewees will be relevant to your research questions.

4 What is a 'probing question'?

   a A question that asks indirectly about people's opinions or feelings.

   b A question that encourages the interviewee to say more in response to your original question.

   c A way of finding out sensitive or highly personal information.

   d A way of summarising what someone has said before moving on to the next topic.

5 Which of the following is a characteristic of a focus group?

   a It has two or three participants.

   b It enables you to study decision-making processes in a group situation.

   c It is a way to get people to clarify your research methodology for you.

   d It is a form of group interview involving a facilitated process of dialogue and discussion about a particular topic.

6 What is the role of the facilitator in a focus group?

   a To evaluate the performance of the group relative to the questions being answered.

   b To encourage discussion and keep the conversation 'on track'.

   c To sit apart from the group to observe the behaviour of different members.

   d To ask leading questions.

7 Which of the following is an advantage of focus groups?

   a The facilitator cannot control how the discussion proceeds.

   b They can produce a large volume of data that represents a range of different experiences and opinions.

   c They show how reality is socially constructed.

   d They can lead to a polarisation of opinions among participants.

8 Which of the following statements are correct in relation to using video recording as a form of research data?

   a Takes a great deal of time to do.

   b The data must be interpreted.

   c Should be accurate.

   d Is technically difficult to achieve.

9 Which TWO of the following can be treated as forms of qualitative data?

   a Google analytics.

   b Social media posts.

   c LinkedIn connection requests.

   d Web pages.

Review Questions

1   How likely is it that some form of semi-structured or in-depth interviews would be an acceptable form of data gathering within the organisation?

2   What opportunities may exist within the organisation(s) in which your research is to be based for the use of some form of participant observation? To what extent would such approaches to data gathering help to answer your research questions?

3   Who might be 'key informants' for your research project? What access arrangements would be necessary to incorporate them into your sample?

4   To what extent might qualitative data from social media platforms contribute to the achievement of your research objectives or questions?

5   What sample selection process is most appropriate for your project? How confident are you (and your tutor or supervisor) that your sample will be sufficient to provide data of good quality?

Questions for reflection

This final part of the chapter enables you to reflect about your professional development and develop your skills and knowledge. This will enable you to build your confidence and credibility, track your learning, see your progress, and demonstrate your achievements.

Strengths and weaknesses

1   How confident are you of your skills as an in-depth research interviewer, or facilitator of focus groups? How might you further develop your skills in these areas?

2   How clear are you about the purpose of the different types of data gathering you plan to undertake? How clearly developed are the themes to be explored? How clearly are these themes derived from your literature review, other data gathering activities, your research questions, etc?

3   How well developed are your skills as a note-taker? What system can you develop to ensure that any notes you take while engaged in qualitative data gathering are formulated accurately and in detail?

4   If you plan to video or audio-record some of your data, how equipped are you to subsequently transcribe the dialogue into a written form? What arrangements might you make for this?

Being a practitioner-researcher

5   What organisational and ethical issues need to be considered if you decide to undertake some form of participant observation? What might be the best way to take this forward?

6   How aware are you of your own personal bias? How might this affect what you expect your data to show? What steps can you take to limit the influence of your personal perspective on the data that are generated?

7   What steps will you take to maximise the confidentiality of the data you gather and the anonymity of your 'subjects'?

Useful Resources

There are some excellent web-based resources relating to qualitative data gathering and analyses and these include:

http://onlineqda.hud.ac.uk/ (archived at https://perma.cc/AAW5-93CX)

National Centre for Research Methods – https://www.ncrm.ac.uk/resources/online/?catsearchquery=qualitative%20data (archived at https://perma.cc/BB4H-FRVP)
Sage Research Methods Online – http://methods.sagepub.com/ (archived at https://perma.cc/D88C-JH2K)

 References

Anderson, V (2017) Criteria for Evaluating Qualitative Research, *Human Resource Development Quarterly*, DOI:10.1002/hrdq.21282 [Online] http://onlinelibrary.wiley.com/doi/10.1002/hrdq.21282/full (archived at https://perma.cc/TT75-76RT)

Barbour, R (2018) *Doing Focus Groups*, Sage, London

Bell, E, Bryman, A and Harley, B (2019) *Business Research Methods*, 5th edn, Oxford University Press, Oxford

Braun, V and Clarke, V (2006) Using thematic analysis in psychology, *Qualitative Research in Psychology*, **3** (2), pp 77–101

DeWalt, KM and DeWalt, BR (2010) *Participant Observation: A guide for field workers*, AltaMira Press, Plymouth

Easterby-Smith, M, Thorpe, R and Jackson, PR (2018) *Management and Business Research*, Sage, London

Elliott, J (2005) *Using Narrative in Social Research: Qualitative and quantitative approaches*, Sage, London

Iacono, VL, Symonds, P and Brown, DHK (2016) Skype as a Tool for Qualitative Research Interviews, *Sociological Research Online*, **12** (2), pp 12

LeBaron, C, Jarzabkowski, P, Pratt, MG and Fetzer, G (2018) An introduction to video methods in organizational research, *Organizational Research Methods*, **21** (2), pp 239–60, DOI: 10.1177/1094428117745649

Levitt, HM *et al* (2018) Journal article reporting standards for qualitative primary, qualitative meta-analytic, and mixed methods research in psychology: The APA Publications and Communications Board

task force report, *American Psychologist*, **73** (1), pp 26–46, DOI: 10.1037/amp0000151

Nelson, J (2017) Using conceptual depth criteria: Addressing the challenge of reaching saturation in qualitative research, *Qualitative Research*, **17** (5), pp 554–70, DOI: 10.1177/1468794116679873

Neuman, W (2012) *Basics of Social Research: Qualitative and quantitative approaches*, International edn, Pearson Education, Harlow

O'Reilly, M and Parker, N (2013) 'Unsatisfactory Saturation': a critical exploration of the notion of saturated sample sizes in qualitative research, *Qualitative Research*, **13** (2), pp 190–197

Riese, J (2018) What is 'access' in the context of qualitative research? *Qualitative Research*, 1–16, DOI: 10.1177/1468794118787713

Robson, C and McCartan, K (2016) *Real World Research: A resource for social scientists and practitioner-researchers*, Wiley, Oxford

Saunders, MNK, Lewis, P and Thornhill, A (2019) *Research Methods for Business Students*, 8th edn, Pearson, London

Saunders, M and Townsend, K (2016) Reporting and justifying the number of interview participants in organization and workplace research, *British Journal of Management*, **27**, pp 836–52, DOI: 10.1111/1467-8551.12182

Šumak, B, Heričko, M and Pušnik, M (2011) A meta-analysis of e-learning technology acceptance: The role of user types and e-learning technology types, *Computers in Human Behavior*, **27** (6), pp 2067–77, DOI: 10.1016/j.chb.2011.08.005

08
Analysing qualitative data

LEARNING OBJECTIVES

This chapter should help you to:

- prepare your data so that you can both describe and analyse your qualitative data in order to answer your research question;
- undertake a thematic analysis of your data;
- identify the main components of discourse analysis and evaluate its use to analyse qualitative data;
- find out more about computer assisted qualitative data analysis software in relation to your project objectives;
- evaluate the trustworthiness of your data gathering and analysis process;
- formulate alternative explanations arising from your data analysis and justify the conclusions that you draw.

- The analysis process
- Different analytical strategies for qualitative data
- Using software to analyse qualitative data
- Data display options and ideas
- Evaluating alternative explanations and formulating conclusions
- Writing up your findings
- Summary checklist
- Test yourself, review and reflect questions
- Useful resources

How to use this chapter

This chapter aims to help you find ways of analysing, rather than merely describing, qualitative data. Because the processes of qualitative data gathering, data description and data analysis are integrated it is best to read this chapter before you start your data gathering process. However, if you have already gathered a huge volume of data and are now wondering what to do in order to make sense of the information then this chapter is also for you. Increasingly researchers in the qualitative data analysis field are making use of software applications to enhance their analytical thinking and record keeping and a number of different options are available. This chapter includes a consideration of the NVivo software (as well as others) and provides an indication of how they can help you with your project. However, if your work is primarily mixed methods and qualitative data, while important, is not a crucial feature of your research design strategy, or if you feel that your business issue investigation does not require such a specialised software then this chapter will also illustrate how you can undertake an analysis using word processing or spreadsheet packages.

 Activity 8.1

Developing 'whistle-blowing' policy and procedures

'Gender-based harassment' is a term that refers to offensive behaviour related to the gender of a person who is subjected to a behaviour that is unwanted. Such behaviour is intended to, or has the effect of, violating the dignity of the person concerned and prompts circumstances that may be experienced as intimidating, hostile, degrading, humiliating or offensive. Under UK employment law those who are subject to such behaviour have some protection as a feature of their employer's health and safety provision. This requires a risk assessment and an occupational health and safety plan to be in place and this might include an assessment of the probability of an employee being subject to gender-based harassment, sexual harassment or violence at work. A plan with preventive measures should also be in place to indicate what actions are to be taken to prevent gender-based harassment, and how to react if such behaviour does occur in the workplace as well as how to prevent it happening again.

Imagine that you work in an organisation where there have been one or two gender-based harassment scandals in the recent past and the newly appointed CEO has made a commitment to shareholders and employees to introduce a stronger stance. The HR Director wants HR to take the lead in this area, both in terms of policy development and for implementing the new approach. A policy is required that can handle gender-based harassment where the perpetrator is of any gender, and the victim may be of the same or different gender. The CEO wishes the policy to cover instances of there being more than one perpetrator and one or more victims and whether the harassment is verbal, symbolic or physical. The policy also has to provide measures to maintain confidentiality or anonymity where this is important for the victim of such harassment. The HR Director recognises that this new approach will require training for employees and management team members at all levels in the organisation.

The HR Director knows that you are undertaking a qualification in HR and thinks this will be a great topic for your research report. She wants you to explore the gender-based harassment issues from the perspective of different types of workers who undertake work on behalf of the organisation (permanent employees; trainees on fixed term contracts; agency workers; interns and contractors) and find out what they know and understand about their rights and obligations with regard to people's dignity at work. The HR Director also wants you to come up with a draft policy and procedure to identify reporting and record-keeping systems relating to gender-based harassment and other communication issues that will need to be addressed if the new workplace culture is to be introduced.

In taking this project forward you have undertaken semi-structured audio-recorded interviews with a selection of workers with different contractual arrangements in the organisation, each lasting about an hour. You have also looked back into documents and information related to the previous incidents where the company failed to deal appropriately with gender-based harassment leading to very negative reputational damage for the organisation and a poor employment relations culture in some parts of the organisation. You now have a huge volume of data, stored on memory sticks, audio recording devices, and in notes that you made for yourself as you have undertaken this work over a number of weeks.

Discussion questions

1   What steps might you take to make sense of the data in order to achieve your research objectives? Identify what you will 'do' with the audio recordings, notes, screen shots, etc.

2   List four or five problems you might encounter when formulating credible conclusions on the basis of the data that you have.

Feedback notes

There are many activities that you might undertake to make sense of the data you have collected. The main challenge, at the start, is the large volume of the information you have accumulated. The first challenge of qualitative data analysis is one of information management. A way must be found to establish a sense of control and identification of what is 'in there'. Once that has been achieved then it is possible to identify and explore key themes or patterns that the data may suggest. Only then will it be possible to draw conclusions.

You may have identified a number of other problems with analysis of qualitative data. First, data that are analysed 'early on', when the researcher is relatively 'fresh' might receive more careful attention than information that is considered later in the process. Another concern might be that you are not sure when you can decide that you have 'enough' information to underpin any conclusions you formulate. Perhaps some of your interviewees have been cynical about the 'real' intentions of a gender-based harassment policy and have been reluctant to talk honestly and frankly about how they understand the balance between loyalty to the organisation and the importance of speaking out if inappropriate behaviour is occurring or is experienced. You might be concerned that a contractor or intern might be worried that they will not be re-employed or they risk getting a poor reference at the end of their internship if they speak openly. If you have heard a range of different experiences and opinions expressed by interviewees can you be sure that all of their accounts are equally 'reliable' – perhaps one or more interviewees are carrying a 'grudge' or grievance against their current manager?

A further challenge, although it can also be seen as an opportunity, is that there is no 'one right way' of going about the analysis of qualitative data. Whereas with quantitative data analysis (see Chapter 10) there are procedures and processes that provide some degree of confidence in the conclusions, there is no such consensus with the analysis of qualitative data. However, it is important that qualitative data analysis is undertaken with equivalent rigour so that those who take action based on your findings can feel that the work is credible and trustworthy. The purpose of this chapter is to address these issues.

The process of qualitative analysis

From data gathering to data analysis

The process of data analysis can be a difficult one for first-time researchers. Becoming confident and competent takes time. Just as gathering data takes longer than people expect, so the time available for analysis, particularly with a submission date looming, may be limited. However, analysis of data is fundamental to the quality of the outcomes of your research project. Data analysis involves more than describing what people said or what you saw. When you analyse data you are seeking to find and justify an understanding or interpretation that tentatively explains why things are as you have found them. Indeed, raw data without a process of sense-making being applied has very limited value.

Analysis is a process of thought. Through analysis you can understand the nature of what you are investigating, the relationships between different variables in the situation, and the likely outcomes of particular actions or interventions. Analysis involves making sense of data to answer your research questions by considering issues such as what? why? and how? If people are to trust in your findings, then you must treat the evidence fairly and ensure that you include all possible explanations from the data rather than discounting evidence that you (or your project sponsor) would prefer had not been included in the dataset.

To achieve this, you need a good understanding and evaluation of the information that you have. It is also important to reduce the dataset to manageable proportions so that you can abstract information, explore key themes and patterns that are evident from the data before developing and evaluating a range of alternative explanations from which you can formulate conclusions. This process is illustrated in Figure 8.1.

Figure 8.1 Doing qualitative data analysis

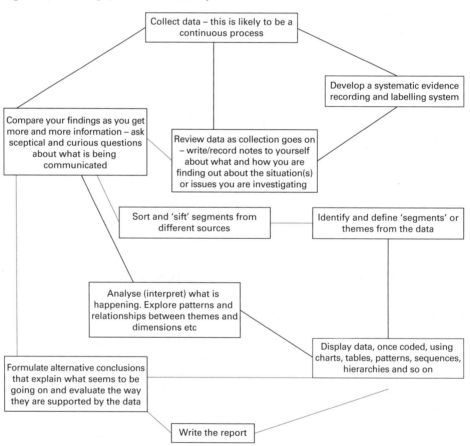

Case Example 8.1

Making sense of the HR function

Katy was an experienced practitioner who had joined her employing organisation with no formal HR qualifications or experience but had built her career in HR in the subsequent 10 years. During this time, she had undertaken foundation and intermediate level studies and had impressed her managers. Katy felt that opportunities for promotion were gradually becoming realistic. Her organisation agreed to sponsor her to study at advanced level, something that formed part of her CPD plan and objectives. In the months preceding Katy's choice of a project topic, she and her colleagues in the workplace received news that was both exciting and disturbing. As a part of a strategy in response to European political developments Katy's employing organisation had been subject to a merger/acquisition process with a large organisation that was owned and managed in Germany. As news filtered through to Katy's part of the newly merged organisation it became apparent that the HR functions in both organisations were to be merged into a broader

European HR function, based in Germany. As a result of her studies Katy was anxious; she was aware that assumptions about the role and contribution of the HR function might not be the same in both HR departments. Katy also learned that she might be tasked with project managing the merger process of the two HR departments but she felt unprepared for this task. Katy's tutor suggested that a good way to tackle this uncertainty was to focus her CIPD project on an investigation into the expectations about HR in the UK-based company and in the German organisation.

Discussion questions

1   What forms of data might Katy gather in order to take forward a project of this type?

2   Once she had identified forms of data, what sampling strategy should Katy adopt?

3   What challenges might Katy face when trying to make sense of the data?

Feedback notes

In considering these questions, you may have reflected that the field of HRM – what work is involved and how it 'fits in' with other features of the organisation – is understood and articulated in different ways and by different people. HRM is a term differently understood by people from different standpoints. Textbooks about HRM portray some 'pictures' or models of what HRM is 'for' (although this might vary in different country jurisdictions) but the words and meanings of senior managers in organisations, trades union representatives, local and national policymakers and employees with different levels of experience might indicate very different understandings. Therefore, a wealth of data might be available to Katy if she wished to pursue this line of inquiry.

Forms of data that you may have identified for a project such as this might include documentary sources from both organisations such as internal website materials,

HR policy statements and strategy documents, notes or minutes from HR function meetings or from organisational strategy documents where HR issues were included. In addition, you might have suggested that 'informal' data would be useful where they could be obtained. Analysis of 'all staff' e-mails and other materials used to communicate between the HR function and staff generally or between the Head of HR and all members of the HR function might also provide a useful perspective on the words and meanings associated by those involved in the different companies with the practice of HRM. Third, you might identify that interviews or focus groups could be another way of gathering data to answer questions concerning the current assumptions about the purpose and role of the HR function in the two different companies.

As discussed in Chapter 7, sampling issues with qualitative data are most often developed and justified on a purposive basis. Katy needed access to data from both organisations. Interviews featured in her data gathering process and her 'purposive' approach to sample selection included interview data from at least one person from each of the main 'sections' or specialisms of both HR functions in the two organisations. Key informant data were important to Katy – that is, the views of those who fulfilled senior HR positions in the two companies. The views of line managers and other 'stakeholder groups' were also important, such as worker representatives. In addition, Katy decided to analyse internal website information, which was available in both companies.

You may have come up with quite a number of challenges that Katy would face in a project of this type. First, the issue of language becomes important in any cross-cultural study of this type. In this case Katy was fortunate in that the language of the business was English in both cases and that website material and associated documents were published in both English and German. However, different interviewees had different levels of confidence in speaking English, something that Katy had to take into account when formulating her interview questions and when analysing the interview data. A second challenge for Katy was the sheer volume of data she gathered; her interview audio-recordings extended over 12 hours. She undertook a transcription of one interview of one-hour duration and, to her horror, discovered that this took up far more than one hour to do and resulted in a document of more than 20 sides (standard font and single line-spaced) text. In addition, she had downloaded further text-based data as well as images from the internal websites of both companies and found a variety of links to HR policies and strategies that were also relevant to her research questions. Therefore, selecting relevant materials and attributing priority was a challenge. Where should she pay most attention? How could she reduce her information to manageable proportions without losing the 'essence' of the data? The third challenge related to her own position in relation to the data she was gathering. As she got underway Katy soon came to realise that she may be bringing her own prior assumptions about 'the way things are' grounded in her 10 years with one of the two companies into her interpretation of the material she was gathering. This led her to wonder how she might be able to reassure those who had sponsored her project, as well as the tutors who would mark it, that a robust analysis procedure had been achieved. These issues are discussed further in the following sections.

The role of data analysis in qualitative research

Qualitative data analysis is very different from the analysis process for quantitative data. Most people who undertake quantitative data analysis are engaged in a linear sequence of tasks developed to make sense of the facts contained in the dataset. However, a key assumption of the interpretivist world view, within which most qualitative research is undertaken, is the intention to offer a credible interpretation of what is happening in different contexts or from different 'positions'. In addition, whereas quantitative data analysis is often a linear, standardised, staged set of procedures, qualitative data analysis is a continuous process, closely linked with ongoing data gathering. Since analysis is the search for explanation and understanding it is reasonable to begin the qualitative analysis process early on while data are still being collected. Therefore, evidence and concepts are 'blended' and assessed for plausibility on an ongoing basis; the analysis process is iterative rather than being a fully distinct 'last stage' of a project. There are many different and emerging traditions of qualitative analysis but in general terms there are four key steps, which are:

- to understand and assess the information you have collected;

- to reduce the information to manageable proportions – this is usually undertaken through a process of categorisation of the data;

- to explore key themes to identify the 'essence' of what is contained in a holistic sense in the data;

- to identify relationships between different themes and/or categories that provide a reasonable and credible explanation of the data you have gathered.

There is no one way of undertaking the initial process of understanding and assessing the qualitative data you have collected. You may decide to produce a summary of the information that has been gathered in note form. Alternatively, you may feel that a 'spider diagram' or some other visual form of representing features of the dataset is more helpful. However it is undertaken, the process of initial analysis involves asking 'what might be going on here, what categories/issues are evident in the data, what is the 'essence' of what these data are communicating (the themes) and what might be the dimensions or extent of the issues that are emerging from the initial assessment of the data?'

This process of asking genuinely curious questions leads to the next stage, which is the reduction of the data to manageable proportions. This enables you to make more credible judgements about what is there. This can be a daunting process as volumes of data that are generated by qualitative research are always large. As part of the data reduction process it is a good idea to undertake a process of writing 'memos' to yourself that summarise the thinking processes, and the evidence that you feel supports your ideas. This process of making memos is an important part of the analytical process and should occur close to the time that you undertake the initial data collection and also during the subsequent occasions when you are tackling the analysis of the dataset as a whole. Never discard these memos – you will be amazed at the good ideas you can forget as the process of trying to analyse data and undertake all your other work and life tasks get mixed up together. These 'memos to self' about what the dataset contains and your thoughts and ideas about it can also form vital additions to the analysis process and can comprise: your summaries of

Table 8.1 Template for qualitative data summary/memo

Data 'in focus': Date of the memo:	Reflections
Who/what was involved? Names/events Date Time Location	• Who or what else might be a useful source of similar data? • How might the date, time and location have influenced the data gathering process and the information obtained? • How might my presence have influenced what was said or done?
What issues were covered?	• What issues were omitted and why? • Were any 'unplanned' issues included? What prompted this?
What data of relevance to the research questions were obtained?	• What was surprising about the information?
What new concepts or issues might be relevant?	• What are the implications for subsequent data collection or subsequent data analysis?

what was said; what you did; your reflections and thoughts about the data. As you write up your analysis, however, remember to make a clear distinction in the notes or memos between your thoughts and what was actually said. A template that you might adapt for the production of a research memo is included as Table 8.1.

Having summarised the data and recorded your reflections you can then read carefully through your notes, or better still the dataset items themselves, to identify categories for the data. As you do this you will need to assign a code (or label) to each category, in the form of abbreviations or short words or phrases that you will recognise and remember. Having coded chunks of your data you are able to get a sense of the categories that are present, to make comparisons where appropriate, and to look for possible relationships or patterns within and between different categories. This process, which is cyclical and iterative, allows the evaluation of categories that will ultimately help you to formulate alternative explanations about what is going on. Figure 8.2 provides an indicative overview of the steps in the process of qualitative data analysis.

Although there are no standardised 'rules' for qualitative data analysis, Silverman (2015) provides five 'tips' for an effective process:

1 Start early – don't wait until all your interviews or observations have been completed.

2 Try out different approaches to analysing the data – find what 'works for you'.

3 Avoid thinking you have 'the answer' too soon – keep exploring and keep an open mind for as long as possible.

Figure 8.2 The qualitative data analysis process

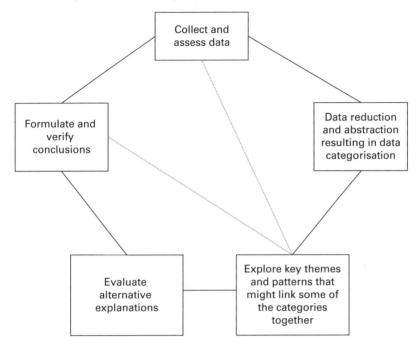

4 Don't get 'obsessed' with one or two productive (or 'telling') interviews or cases so that you neglect what other information you have. It is important to analyse **all** your data in a fair and thorough way.

5 Focus your early attention intensively on a small (and appropriate) part of your overall dataset. Allow yourself to look for sequences and 'nuances' within the data and then expand your focus onto the dataset as a whole.

Categorising and coding data

Coding is at the core of qualitative data analysis. A code is a label designed to 'catch the meaning' of part of your data. Coding is the process you use to label categories from within your dataset so that you can make comparisons and look for regularities and different characteristics of the situation you are investigating. A category is a grouping of behaviours, descriptions or particular events that have shared characteristics. Identifying categories is an important first step in analysis. However, it is also important to look out for 'themes' – the meaningful 'essence' that runs through the data and which may be present in more than one of your categories. Themes relate to what may be going on 'beneath the surface'. In this respect coding is an iterative and ongoing process. The initial codes that you devise are likely to result from a range of different features of your project, developed from your research aims and objectives; issues highlighted in the literature, or matters that reflect the question structure that you have used. However, as your research proceeds you might include new codes that result from your reflections about categories and themes that have emerged from the memos that you have produced, or notes you have generated as a result of reflecting about the data and how you might make sense of what is going on.

The process of coding involves 'marking up' and labelling your data so that you can easily locate material within the same category. Codes are labels that represent a 'unit of meaning'. The size of 'chunks' of data that you associate with codes may vary. It might be specific words that are coded, it might be a phrase, or it may be a paragraph of your notes. Often it is a combination of the three. It is also possible (and often highly desirable) that one 'chunk' of data may be categorised in more than one way and therefore assigned more than one code. There are four levels or types of codes:

Descriptive codes

These tend to be the first (and almost obvious) codes that you assign. In many ways they are your route to summarising what is in the text. Neuman (2012) refers to them as 'manifest' or 'obvious' codes. They reflect what is going on 'on the surface' and are the result of your first attempt at categorisation. Once you have established these categories (which might result from the amalgamation of some initial coding ideas that you have) you will be able to undertake some comparisons within the data. While you are reviewing the data you have categorised in this way you may notice that specific terms or phrases seem to recur within all or part of the data. These might suggest some analytical themes and you may choose to label for further consideration as you probe more deeply into the sense of the data. Once you have identified your categories and have labelled them appropriately it is important to assess whether some of them can be grouped together and whether some of them are also part of a 'hierarchy' where you can identify one main code and then a series of 'sub-codes' in what might look like a 'family tree'. Indeed, some qualitative researchers sometimes refer to 'parent' and 'child' codes and others refer to 'tree codes', with the image of a tree trunk, branches and twigs as the sense-making process.

Case (demographic) codes and attributes

In addition to the identification of initial categories emerging from the data you will also need to label the different 'cases' in your dataset – the individual participants, artefacts or organisations within your scope. Each unit 'source' of data will need its own label (so from a focus group comprising 10 people you would generate 10 case codes). You can also assign appropriate 'attributes' to each case; for example, the age range of each participant, the organisational function they are assigned to and so on. In this way you can group together data from respondents into sets depending on (say) the type of organisation they work for, their occupation, their gender and so on. You will be able to compare the extent to which these attributes might influence different experiences and interpretations that have been expressed in the dataset.

Thematic codes

As indicated already, these are generated as you go deeper into the analysis. They relate to what may be happening 'beneath the surface' and are your opportunity to identify and label topics, concepts or ideas within the data, which may help to explain relationships between some of the different categories you have identified. Neuman (2012) refers to these as latent codes and Silverman (2015) refers to them as interpretive codes. These codes require judgement and interpretation as you set about assessing the data for meaning as well as for description.

Axial codes

Sometimes called **relationship codes** or **pattern codes** these are a further useful level of analysis. Here you are looking for potential connections or relationships between themes or between or within categories and subcategories. You will not be able to identify and assign these until you have almost reached the end of your analytical process. Once you have generated some ideas about relationships that might support provisional explanations of the phenomena you are investigating it is important that you re-examine the dataset to locate examples of the association you have wondered about. When you find examples in the data then you assign a new (relationship) code to each occasion in the data when you find the evidence that supports your idea. This will enable you to offer a credible justification of the explanations you build to make sense of the data.

Once you have undertaken this process of coding and categorisation you are in a position to start to consider the potential answers to questions such as those in Table 8.2.

Table 8.2 Levels of analysis

Initial (First Level) Analysis	Deeper Level Understanding	Pattern/Relationship Level
What interpretations of the world/the issue/the topic is conveyed by the participants/data?	Why do they have that view? How did they come to that view?	What is the nature of the relationship between these phenomena? How might these relationships be depicted diagrammatically?
How do the participants identify or classify themselves and others in what they say or report?	Why do they have that view? How did they come to that view?	
Where are there any areas of tension or ambiguity?	What might explain these features of the data?	

Case Example 8.2

School for Health and Care Radicals

Extracts from CIPD (2015) The School for Health and Care Radicals: what impact has it had? Accessed from: https://www.cipd.co.uk/knowledge/strategy/development/health-care-radicals-report

The School for Health and Care Radicals (SHCR) is a massive open online course (MOOC)… Centred on five weekly online modules… its purpose is to develop effective change agents, ultimately contributing to fast, large-scale, sustainable improvement in health and social care, leading to better patient outcomes.

The review comprised two phases. Firstly, we conducted background research with participants from the 2014 school and the NHS IQ team involved in designing and running the school. This gave us an understanding of the intention, working and potential value of the school, from which we developed an impact model.

Secondly, we assessed the impact of the 2015 school. This was done through a before and after survey, a Facebook forum run during the school, and in-depth case study interviews with 15 participants.

Measuring the impact of the SHCR: in-depth case studies

The interviews were conducted in April and May 2015. The recruitment strategy involved an e-mail being sent to all SHCR participants by the NHS IQ to invite them to take part in the interviews. Twenty-five participants responded that they were willing to be interviewed.

From these, 15 interviewees were selected to include mainly NHS employees, two UK based non-NHS employees and two participants based outside the UK. Thus, we used an initial convenience sample, inviting participants to volunteer as interviewees, followed by a purposive sample to broadly reflect the international nature of SHCR participants…

Once informed consent had been obtained, the interviews were conducted and digitally recorded. The critical incident technique was used in the interviews to drill down into participants' stories of how they have developed as a consequence of being part of the school. The interview recordings were transcribed using a confidential service and the transcriptions thematically analysed by the research team using the qualitative data analysis software NVivo.

Discussion questions

1   What research methods were used in this research project?

2   What sample selection process was used for the qualitative data gathering?

3   What are the advantages and disadvantages of combining analysis of survey data, social media data and interview data in this research project?

4   What challenges might arise from the analysis of the qualitative data?

Feedback notes

This case example provides an example of a mixed methods research strategy where quantitative data (before and after) as well as qualitative data were gathered in order to evaluate the impact of the School for Health and Care Radicals' technology enhanced learning initiative. In this case the qualitative data comprised interview transcripts as well as data from a Facebook forum. Discussion questions posed at the time by SHCR facilitators with the Facebook group associated with the programme made it possible to explore additional features of people's experiences as they had experienced it at the time. This process underpinned the identification of new codes and categories.

Attention was also given in this case to the recruitment and selection of members of the sample group for qualitative data gathering. For the Facebook data all participants were included. For the interviews a 'convenience' approach was taken to **recruit** potential participants and then a second stage of **selection** of a sample from within this group (a purposive sample) was achieved.

This case example gives a clear sense that an orderly and systematic process was undertaken in planning for and implementing the research project; an important feature of any analysis if the conclusions that are drawn are to be persuasive.

A key challenge faced by qualitative researchers is the quantity of data that are likely to be generated. In this project the NVivo qualitative software was used to help manage this feature of the project. The advantages and disadvantages of using such software are discussed later in this chapter.

The analysis process

The issues arising from this case example highlight important questions that must be addressed by any qualitative analysis, which may be summarised as:

- What themes, trends or patterns are evident from groups of people or organisations?
- Are there similarities and differences between the different data groups?
- Are there interrelationships between different parts of the data?
- What interesting issues emerge?
- Do the findings suggest that additional data might usefully be collected?
- Are there deviations from the main patterns or trends that might be identified?

Although there is a range of different types of qualitative data and a range of different approaches to qualitative analysis, a commonly used approach is thematic analysis. Researchers undertake thematic analysis in different ways but there are some general principles for the process set out by Braun and Clarke (2006), which are briefly described and discussed in the next part of this section.

Thematic analysis

Table 8.3 sets out a summary of the thematic analysis approach recommended by Braun and Clarke (2006).

Table 8.3 Summary of the thematic analysis approach

Familiarising yourself with the data	Read (and reread) the data (for example, transcripts, documents, notes) and/or listen to recordings. Note down initial ideas.
Generate initial codes	Identify preliminary codes – features of the data that appear interesting and meaningful. These codes may be numerous and specific.
Search for themes	This is the start of the interpretation of the codes you have identified. Sort extracts and 'chunks' from the data according to overarching themes. Keep a note of your thought processes as you ponder possible relationships between codes, themes and subthemes.
Review the themes	Undertake a deeper review to question whether to combine, refine, separate, or discard initial themes. Data within themes should link together meaningfully but there should be clear and identifiable distinctions between themes.
Define and name the themes	This will require some ongoing analysis to further refine the themes you have identified and provide them with theme names and working definitions. At this point, one or more potential 'stories' or interpretations of the data should begin to emerge.
Draft the 'report'/analysis chapter or section	At this stage you transform your analysis into a written 'narrative' form. This account should go beyond a description of the themes. Use illustrative examples that relate to the themes, your research questions and the wider literature.

While the approach to thematic analysis set out by Braun and Clarke is popular in the HRM (and other) fields, other scholars have offered further advice (see for example, Robson and McCartan, 2016; Neuman, 2012, Silverman, 2015, and Yin, 2017). The main points that they highlight are:

- **Clarify the research questions and the data sources that are required to answer them.** Starting with organisational documents or pages of interview notes, diary entries or focus group discussions and wondering what they may be able to tell you can be a recipe for time-wasting. You will achieve a more effective analysis if you are clear about what questions you need to answer and the data that will be relevant.

- **Make use of an appropriate sampling strategy.** Sample selection for qualitative data was considered in Chapter 7. Analysis of qualitative data is always time-consuming. It is detailed work that is difficult to hurry. A justifiable sampling strategy will be necessary. You may, for example, decide

to study half of the company e-mail bulletins of the organisation, or 20 per
cent of the available appraisal forms. In selecting focus groups or interview
respondents it is important to be able to justify the criteria and methods of
selection (inclusion and exclusion criteria) that you adopt.

- **Decide on the initial categories for your analysis.** It is important to work out
how you will deal with, and make sense of, the information you propose
to analyse. The research questions should provide your principal focus. In
addition, categories should reflect the **subject matter** of the data.

Piloting

Before investing too much time in a full-scale analysis of a large volume of data, try
out your categories and your analytical process on a small selection of your data. Is
your approach to categorisation clear? Are there some things for which there do not
seem to be any appropriate categories? At this stage it is worth getting someone else
to help you with the pilot process. You might both look at the same data so that you
can assess the extent to which you have both coded in a similar way. This provides
you with a measure of the trustworthiness of the process (see Chapter 5) and will
help you to make revisions to enhance the credibility of your process before going
forward with the main analysis.

Proceed with the analysis

Identify categories to make sense of the data that might help you to find further
themes that you will label using codes and which can be incorporated in the analysis.
Activity 8.2 demonstrates how a coding procedure may be undertaken.

 Activity 8.2

Coding qualitative data

For this practice exercise you are invited to
access materials that are publicly available
online and to undertake some initial coding.
Edward Snowden is a high-profile character
who revealed the practices of the US National
Security Agency (NSA) in relation to privacy
issues in North America and beyond. Opinions
about the actions Edward Snowden took in
2012–13 remain strongly polarised.

　　You can access data from interviews of
different lengths undertaken at different times
and from different locations through simple
searches of internet news sites. Examples are:

http://www.spiegel.de/international/world/
　　interview-with-whistleblower-edward-
　　snowden-on-global-spying-a-910006.html

https://www.mic.com/articles/47355/edward-
　　snowden-interview-transcript-full-text-read-
　　the-guardian-s-entire-interview-with-the-
　　man-who-leaked-prism

http://www.theguardian.com/world/2014/
　　jul/18/-sp-edward-snowden-nsa-
　　whistleblower-interview-transcript

https://www.ft.com/content/9d8fd9cc-76eb-11e6-bf48-b372cdb1043a

Locate at least two transcripts. Read them carefully and identify possible:

- contextual issues pertinent to interpreting the data (location, date, background to the data source);
- potential descriptive categories;
- potential themes.

Feedback notes

One of the interesting things about qualitative data analysis is that two analysts may analyse data in different ways. This is because data analysis is affected by the personal assumptions and interests of the analyst – something that must be reduced as far as possible. Your assumptions will be influenced by your context and 'position' – if you expect a particular outcome you may also, unconsciously, 'see' things in a way that you feel is expected in a given situation. It is important, therefore, to be aware of the difference between 'is' and 'ought' and to undertake the analysis with as open a mind as possible. It is also very important to value (and code) data that does not 'fit' with what you expect.

Some of the contextual issues that you may have come up with might reflect: the length of time since Edward Snowden left the United States; the country in which the interview took place; the newspaper/journalist to whom the interview was granted.

Descriptive codes might include:

- Edward Snowden's role at the NSA;
- NSA surveillance capabilities;
- partners of the NSA.

Thematic codes that you may have identified might include:

- process of revelation;
- Edward Snowden's attitudes.

Having established these codes, you are in a position to review them and to return to the data and work through all items to 'mark up' the text where each code is evident. As you do this you may find that you identify new items that you missed the first time so your list of codes is likely to grow in a cumulative way and there will come a time when you may need to reorganise it, sort it, combine codes (to create broader categories) where appropriate and discard or extend codes for further analysis.

A possible coding outcome from this activity, produced by a DBA student using the NVivo software is shown in Figure 8.3.

Data coding and initial categorisation forms the first part of your qualitative data analysis process. It enables you: to reduce the information you have; to compare

Figure 8.3 Illustrative coding list

Nodes		
Name	**Sources**	**References**
Edward Snowden's role at the NSA	1	14
Authorisation	1	2
Experiences	1	8
Job description	1	2
Role	1	2
NSA surveillance capabilities	2	32
Criticism of Edward Snowden	1	7
Extent of surveillance	2	13
Laws	2	6
Objective	1	1
Technical	2	5
Partners of the NSA	2	38
Agencies	1	8
Authorities	2	6
Internet provider	2	7
Social Media	2	4
States	2	13
Process of revelation	2	21
Feelings and concerns	1	4
Master Plan	1	1
Hawaii	1	1
Hong Kong	1	1
Russia	1	4
Motivation and purpose	1	5
Preparation	2	4
Press & Media	2	2
Security	2	5

(Reproduced with kind permission of Ferhat Eryurt, DBA student)

the evidence from a number of different sources; to identify similarities; and to start the process of identifying themes and patterns. The process also means that you can generate ideas to help you find features of the data that may be particularly important. The quality of your coding activity is very important for the quality of your analysis. Sloppy coding will lead to a poor analysis. It may look sophisticated but it will actually have very little value. For this reason, particularly if you have had to code for long periods of time in order to meet a deadline, you should review the codes you have applied on a subsequent occasion, to make sure that you are allocating text to codes in a meaningful way.

Maintaining a set of memos or notes, often in the form of a researcher's diary, in which you can reflect about events and record thoughts and ideas that occur to you as you are working with data is also an important part of the qualitative data analysis process; successful students invest time in keeping a provisional running record of their analysis and interpretation processes and this gives them a basis to follow up on ideas and evaluate alternative explanations. Although the process of data analysis means that you will become very close with the data (something to be encouraged) it is also important to take care to limit the influence of your prior assumptions on the interpretations you generate. As you set about generating interpretations and explanations try to 'distance yourself' and to consider the issues from more than one perspective. It is especially important that you value (rather than ignore) data that do not fit with what you expect to find. At the early stages of coding, therefore, and at regular points thereafter, it is highly advisable to connect with your tutor and ask him or her to act as a 'critical friend' – looking for interpretations or features of the data that you may have overlooked or overemphasised.

Deduction or induction?

Data display can form the basis of both inductive and deductive approaches to analysis. The differences between inductive and deductive approaches to research are highlighted throughout this book (see Chapter 5 in particular). Many practitioners who are new to academic research assume that induction requires a qualitative approach and deduction requires a quantitative approach. However, a deductive approach to research is frequently plausible with qualitative data. Concepts from the literature review can guide the initial coding process and then some form of data display enables you to undertake a comparison of the evidence with what relevant theories, typologies or frameworks lead you to expect. Robson and McCartan (2016) and Bell, Bryman and Harley (2019) indicate that the use of a tentative hypothesis, even in qualitative research, can be useful in assessing the extent to which the data compare with what might be expected. Indeed, it would be possible for the analysis of qualitative data to be as useful in a theory modification process as might be expected with a deductive approach to research.

A 'pure' inductive approach to research is associated with 'grounded theory' (see Charmaz, 2014; Silverman, 2015). This is where data coding is undertaken in an emergent way through careful and close reading of your 'texts' and a process of 'memo-writing' (notes to self) about what categories are evident in the data. Once you have started this process you then keep gathering new data to add detail and depth to the properties of your emergent categories and to widen out the contexts/situations from which the data are drawn to examine whether the emergent concepts still seem to be appropriate. The process of continuous and purposive data gathering, which incrementally increases your sample size, is known as 'theoretical sampling'. You keep going until you find that new cases are not adding new conceptual insights – something referred to as 'theoretical saturation'. As you are undertaking this process it is important to engage with and continuously revise your data display as you undertake constant comparisons to modify or broaden your initial categories. Therefore, you will find yourself moving constantly between your data, the memos you are writing for yourself and the concepts/categories that you are developing.

It may be that your project involves both deduction and induction. You might start with concepts from the literature and then, as a result of the process of analysis, examine new areas and insights that are evident in the data.

Different analytical strategies

Although thematic analysis is a popular strategy in organisational and HRM research studies it is possible that an alternative analytical approach may be appropriate to answer your research question. The approach that you choose will depend on the purpose and objectives of your research and the types of data you have gathered. Some research questions can be answered through a thematic analysis. Other types of questions might be addressed through different analytical approaches that enable conclusions to be drawn from the rich and complex data that have been collected. In this section a very short introduction is given to content analysis and to narrative analysis. A slightly longer overview is then provided of discourse analysis, which you may find lends itself particularly well for some (but not all) of the qualitatively orientated research questions posed by researchers in the HR domain.

Content analysis

Content analysis is an analytical approach that systematically describes written, spoken or visual communication. Although it is included here as a qualitative analysis technique it is also possible to undertake a quantitative assessment of content and often researchers who set out to gather and analyse qualitative data, find themselves also working with numbers as well as meanings. In order to undertake a content analysis, you need textual data and/or visual images. The principles behind content analysis are to:

- determine the categories you wish to analyse (these might be drawn from the literature AND from the data themselves);
- establish some coding 'rules' (what 'counts' as being in this category and what would be 'out of bounds');
- carefully scrutinise your data to apply the codes;
- establish a data file where you gather together all the instances of each of your categories to assess their 'frequency' (how many of your sample group exhibit evidence of these codes?) and 'density' (how many times do these codes recur within the dataset: do some categories recur throughout the dataset?).

Interpreting data in this way is based on your assessment of how the data 'breaks down' although qualitative researchers would argue that although 'the numbers' are helpful in providing a description of the data a deeper' and 'richer' level of analysis is possible through an examination of what is being communicated in a more 'holistic' rather than 'reductionist' way.

Activity 8.3

Content analysis of pictorial data

HR professionals' mental models of middle managers: Implications for the HR business partner model

This paper examines the implicit assumptions (prototypes) HR professionals hold about middle managers and considers how these affect the HR Business Partner relationship. A social constructivist approach is adopted. The prototypes are elicited through an innovative pictorial analysis of participant produced drawings generated by 37 HR professionals representing six nationalities and 32 different organisations…

In seeking to explore and examine prototypical images of middle managers from the perspective of HR professionals this research utilised a projective technique involving the use of participant produced drawings. The aim was to make implicit images explicit and to illustrate 'essence' in relation to manager prototypes by gathering data from practising HR professionals. This approach has the benefit of being 'language independent' and also enables contextual information to be included…

The drawing exercise involved participants working in groups of three or four. Participants were invited to think on an individual basis about middle managers in general: their characteristics; what they do; what they do not do. Next, in groups, they were asked to share their thoughts and highlight areas of consensus and disagreement. Third, they were asked to 'make a drawing of a middle manager'. Twelve drawings, made on 'flip chart paper' were produced as a result of this activity [examples below]. There were two phases to the analysis.

First, an inventory of the main features in the drawings was made and the pictures were content-analysed…

The drawings [see Figure 8.4] were analysed by two independent coders. They had not been present when the pictures were constructed and had no prior involvement in the research process. This ensured that the influence of prior knowledge and assumptions was minimised. Following initial independent coding the coders met and discussed results until agreement was reached. The principal codes and frequencies are shown [see Table 8.4]. In addition to these codes, it was noticeable that many drawings contained words and phrases… [operational focus; behaviour; strategic focus; delivery pressure; targets].

The second phase of analysis involved the interpretive identification of themes and subcategories that emerged from the pictorial representations. Seven main themes emerged: [Middle Management Role; Pressures/Burdens; Relationships; Emotions; Self-Protection Strategies; Priorities/Direction; Capability/'Know-How'].

Discussion questions

Review the extracts from this unpublished paper, take a look at the illustrative drawings and study the table summarising the content of the images.

1   What challenges face research participants in any visual research methods process?

2   What challenges face researchers who wish to analyse visual sources?

Figure 8.4 Example drawings

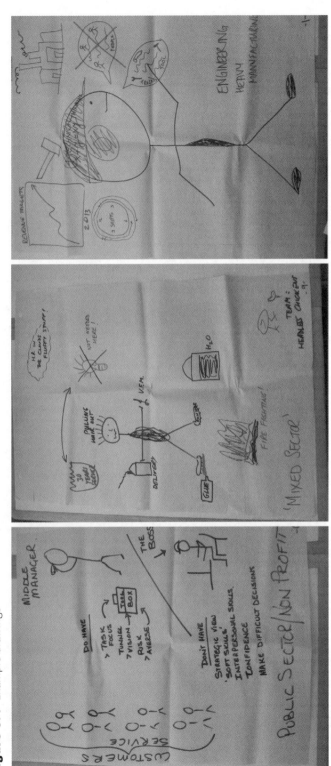

Table 8.4 Descriptive codes from Activity 8.3

Category	Description	Frequency (n=12)
Middle manager present in picture	Yes	11
	Indeterminate	1
Person versus metaphor	Generic person	8
	More than one person	1
	Collection of features	1
	Indeterminate	1
	Mouse	1
Gender	No gender	8
	Indeterminate	3
	Male	1
Subordinates	Yes	11
	No	1
Size of subordinates	Very small compared with MM	2
	Small compared with MM	7
	Same size as MM	2
Others present	No others	5
	Senior manager	3
	Customers	2
	Indeterminate	2
People development represented	Yes (positive)	3
	Yes (negative)	4
	Yes (indeterminate)	1
	No	4
Depiction of MM competence/ skills	Yes	7
	No	5
Depiction of constraints on MM	Yes	6
	No	6

(*continued*)

Table 8.4 (Continued)

Category	Description	Frequency (n=12)
MM role conflict depicted	Yes	8
	Indeterminate	2
	No	2
MM Technical/operational priority depicted	Yes	10
	No	2
HRM/D processes depicted	Yes (positive)	3
	Yes (negative)	5
	No	4

Feedback notes

One of the challenges that you may have identified is the unfamiliarity of this sort of approach for those involved in producing the artefacts. Asking for self-initiated drawings or other 'artistic or creative outputs' in the management, business or HRM field is quite uncommon and it can engender feelings of inadequacy among participants ('I just can't draw…') as well as feelings of hostility towards the request. In such circumstances participants require reassurance and encouragement to be imaginative and creative; to express feelings as well as thoughts; and to express their ideas without a concern that their representation may not be considered 'legitimate' by 'knowledgeable others'.

Further challenges emerge for the analysis process. One issue you might have identified is the extent to which the viewer's (analyst's) interpretation may be unique to them rather than something that multiple viewers might associate with a picture, photo image or other created artefact. Will two viewers draw the same conclusions from the same picture? In such circumstances many researchers encourage participants to orally explain the meanings contained in the image and they include this data into their analysis process to provide a check on the participants' intentions. Elliott and Robinson (2011) recommend a four-stage process: first, to record the first impressions (of the analyst); second, to ascertain stakeholder views of the artefacts and their meanings; third a 'visual semiotic approach' (see bullet points below); and finally, a reflexive account of the interpretations taken as a whole. The visual semiotics approach they refer to here involves taking account of:

- **Representational meaning** – what the 'viewer' analyst understands from the picture.
- **Modality** – the extent to which the picture appears 'realistic' or imaginary – for example, through use of caricature or cartoon image.
- **Composition** – how the different elements of the image are included in the overall construction or composition. What are the various size variances,

for example, and where on the page are different parts of the image incorporated?

- **Interactive meaning** – the extent to which the images evoke any relationship with the viewer; for example, do people in the picture look directly at the viewer or 'face away'? How 'close' in distance terms, is the viewer from the individual(s) depicted on an image?

Narrative analysis

Narrative analysis involves a process of analysing the meanings involved when people share or recount an experience or event. Sometimes there is a single 'story-teller' but often the recounting of a narrative involves a conversation between more than one person. Whatever the context of the narration, narrative analysis works on the basis that stories or narratives share common structural features that can help the analyst to draw conclusions not just from what the story is about but from how the story has been told.

  Activity 8.4

Narrative analysis

....

A narrative study of repeat expatriates and international itinerants

Extracts from: Global careerists' identity construction: A narrative study of repeat expatriates and international itinerants, Malin H Näsholm (2012) *International Journal of Managing Projects in Business*, **5** (4), pp 804–12. Reproduced with permission.

Through a narrative approach, 20 interviews with Swedish global careerists were analysed and comparison of two types of global careerists was made – repeat expatriates and international itinerants...

A narrative can be understood as an account of events and actions that are chronologically connected... but also as an entire life story, or narratively organised compositions from interviews; constructed stories from data. Narratives are seen as a way for individuals to understand their own and others' lives, and the narrative is reconstructed in interaction

with others as it is accepted, rejected or improved upon... In order to reach the subjective experiences of these individuals the participants were asked to tell their stories in in-depth interviews... the focus was on identity as reflected in the self-narratives as given during the interviews, in this case repeat expatriates and international itinerants...

In an approach similar to life story interviewing... all the interviews were started with the open question 'Could you tell me about yourself and your career?' The interviews continued with follow-up questions to encourage more detailed accounts. Interview guides covering relevant themes to be addressed had been prepared for the repeat expatriates and international itinerants, respectively...

To maintain the entire narratives over the course of their careers and the plot, how the events are connected, each narrative was structured... What could be considered complicating actions leading to or meaning a transition, new results or states of equilibrium that were reached, and how the participants evaluated their careers and what they learned from their experiences were identified. The different elements in the structured narratives, for the repeat expatriates and international itinerants separately, were then mapped out and compared to each other, with the emphasis on the plot and identity processes. Two aggregate narratives, of repeat expatriates and international itinerants, respectively, were then constructed to illustrate common patterns in their careers and identity construction.

Discussion questions

Read the extract about a narrative analysis research project and answer these questions:

1   What form of questioning is required for successful narrative forms of analysis?

2   What are the key questions an analyst will try to address when making sense of the data using narrative analysis?

Feedback notes

As shown in this short extract, narrative analysis is grounded in the assumption that people build an understanding of their own and others' lives through a process of 'narrating' – something that may be an iterative process involving others as stories tend to emerge and be shaped through the 'telling', which inevitably involves inter-action with others where narratives may be accepted, rejected or improved upon. Narrative analysis is ideally suited to research questions that incorporate issues of change over time, at the level of the individual, the group or the organisation and that are grounded in an acceptance that 'reality' is not fixed in time but is continu-ously constructed and reconstructed through social interaction.

If you were tempted to undertake a narrative analysis, therefore, it would be important to acknowledge that, in prompting the narrative through your open ques-tions, and in the process you enact to make sense of it, you (the researcher) and the research participants are both using narratives to make sense of these experiences. As suggested in the brief extract used for this activity, although the actual words used in a narrative are very important to understanding what may be going on, narrative analysis seeks to look 'beneath' the words that are spoken to understand the under-lying structure and meaning. The 'form' as well as the 'function' (the structure and the purpose) of the narrative are both important features of a narrative analysis.

Important questions to ask when examining the underlying narrative features of a dataset are:

- What kind of 'story' is being told?
- What is the 'position' and context of the 'storyteller' in relation to what they are narrating?
- How are other people, organisations, departments that are part of the story 'positioned' in relation to one another and in relation to your research participants (and what does this 'tell you')?

Discourse analysis

The work that HR professionals undertake in their organisations is mostly undertaken through words, expressed through policies, procedures, statements and dialogues with those who work on behalf of the organisation. Although informational functions are vitally important (such as record keeping and providing appropriate information for payroll) the 'added value' of HRM is achieved through impact on organisational culture – this cannot be achieved without communication and 'talk'. Some HR scholars (see, for example, Sambrook, 2006) suggest that the 'management' feature of the role of 'human resource management' professionals is only achieved through 'social' and discursive 'construction'. In short, how practitioners talk about HRM delineates how the purpose of HR is understood by managers and employees. This 'talk' also helps practitioners themselves to 'make sense' of their identity as a professional. Therefore, discourse analysis may be a useful approach to understand and probe more deeply into some of the work employment issues with which the HR function is involved. However, discourse analysis is not straightforward and requires deeper levels of critical thinking than taking 'talk' at face value. This part of the chapter aims to provide a 'user-friendly' introduction but if you wish to pursue discourse analysis then further reading and study will be required.

What is discourse analysis?

The term 'discourse' refers to 'communication of thought' undertaken in different ways. For example, words expressed through ways such as 'formal speech', are important but so are other written artefacts (text on websites, for example) and visual images. Discourse is a dynamic process – people are constantly constructing, reconstructing, defining and redefining their meaning and understanding of their situation through both 'talk' and 'text'.

What is the difference between discourse, content and narrative analysis?

Whereas content analysis focuses on '**what** is said' (the content) and narrative analysis focuses on '**how**' it is said (the process of narration), discourse analysis tries to go beneath the level of literal meaning and consider how communication affects people's 'mental models', their personal memories and their assumptions about the 'way the world is'. To access this deeper level discourse analysts scrutinise:

- the abstract structures (the 'rules' of sense-making) within (say) an HR news report;
- the implicit or explicit strategies of 'impression management' that might legitimise policies or, conversely, might lessen the credibility of those involved in the talk or the substance of what is said.

In order to get underneath the literal meaning, discourse analysis uses theory to 'frame' the process of sense-making by assessing the 'structure' 'form', 'organisation' 'order' and 'patterns' of what is being analysed. Cunliffe (2011) identifies two alternative 'pathways' of discourse analysis:

- Looking for multiple interpretations of 'communicative interactions' in local settings (sometimes referred to as the **'d' level** of discourse) (Gee, 2011). This involves identifying multiple and competing discourses and examining the way people construct (and reconstruct) their understanding of their day-to-day interactions.
- Looking for ways in which wider context, for example, cultural norms or power relationships, order and organise the ways in which people interact, interpret and communicate. This is sometimes referred to as the **'D' level** of discourse. From this perspective the 'authors' or 'speakers' of language as well as those who 'receive' their communications are not seen as 'free agents' or objective communicators. This form of analysis examines how those involved in the discourse are positioned within a pattern of activities and 'dominant discourses' that constrain choices about language, patterns of interaction and behaviour.

When is discourse analysis most useful?

Discourse analysis is not for the faint-hearted but the process has been used successfully by HR researchers, particularly those interested in the role and function of HR and HR professional identity (see, for example, Keegan and Francis, 2010; Lawless *et al*, 2011). Other interesting research questions, particularly those in the domain of the employment relationship, that might be addressed using discourse analysis include:

- In what ways are meanings transformed in situations of corporate change?
- How are issues of agency, responsibility and blame negotiated and communicated in situations of organisational crisis or conflict?
- How do organisational and informal communications affect the socialisation of new employees?
- How do trades unions contribute to meaning and understanding of (say) health, safety, security, organisational restructuring or redundancy issues?
- How are assumptions about members of minority groups communicated and perpetuated in organisations?
- How does organisational discourse shape the experiences and views of (say) part-time employees/interns/those on fixed-term contracts?
- How are mental health issues constructed and communicated in different forms of corporate communication?

How can discourse analysis be undertaken?

This section provides a 'way in' to some discourse analysis techniques, drawing primarily on the approach set out by Gee (2011). These are illustrated in Figure 8.5. If you decide that discourse analysis is the fundamental approach for your project

Figure 8.5 Discourse analysis process

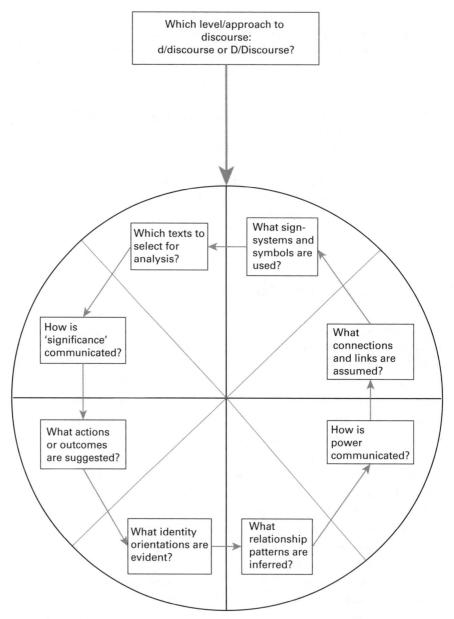

then more specialised sources of guidance, suggested at the end of the chapter, are recommended.

- **Step 1 – decide your focus.**
  - 'd' – focus on social interaction processes;
  - 'D' – focus your study on culture and social/employment relations;

- both 'd' and 'D' – focus your study on sense-making and identity development.

- **Step 2 – select your 'texts'.**

  - The term 'text' can be understood in many different ways and may include: transcripts of interviews or focus groups; scripts from corporate videos; advertisements or web pages; internal company documents.

- **Step 3 – identify how significance is communicated in these texts.**

  - Identify 'what' is communicated and 'the way' that it is communicated.

- **Step 4 – identify what actions the text encourages.**

  - Most communication fulfils certain action-orientated functions; it might *encourage* or *direct* you to do something (perform one or more tasks); it might *inform* you; *warn* you and so on. What is the intended outcome for the 'reader' and how is this achieved?

- **Step 5 – examine the identity orientation of the communication.**

  - Identify who is communicating and from what 'position', for example, as a tutor; as a learner; as a colleague; as a senior manager? What impact does this have on what and how the 'messages' are communicated?

- **Step 6 – look for discourse between people.**

  - **How** people and organisations communicate says a lot about the relationships they are building or sustaining. How formal are the messages? What tone is adopted? Are relationships depicted as (say) deferential, confrontational or collaborative? Is the language 'passive'? Do images 'engage' with the viewer or 'look away'?

- **Step 7 – identify how power is evident in the text.**

  - Whether or not you have decided to incorporate 'D' discourse into your analysis there may be evidence of power relationships in the texts that you analyse. Warnings that 'plagiarism will be punished', for example, serve to reinforce the hierarchical power of tutors. In a similar way discourse patterns might build 'solidarity' or 'bonding' or generate a sense of being an 'outsider' or being 'highly respected'. These may be interpreted as ways through which power relations are implicitly or explicitly communicated.

- **Step 8 – examine how the text makes connections between different phenomena.**

  - Consider how connections are established by communication and discourse.

- **Step 9 – Examine sign systems and views about knowledge and belief.**

  - Include symbols in the analysis as these often infer status or importance. What words, forms of grammar, jargon, pictures and other images might reinforce certain understandings of the situation you are interested in?

Activity 8.5

Discourse analysis: CIPD Annual Review

Visit the CIPD website and download a full copy of the Annual Review, which will be located at an address similar to: http://www.cipd.co.uk/cipd-hr-profession/about-us/annual-review/2014-15.aspx

This is a long document and time may be short. If so, select a small number of pages (about 6–10 pages). Using Steps 3–9 from the process for discourse analysis, undertake an initial examination of the text, including the graphics and the images. What key features of the text emerge as relevant for the analysis?

Feedback notes

Although the annual report is a different document each year there may be particular features you have highlighted as a result of your discourse analysis. For example, the photo images that are used: are there patterns relating to assumptions about race, gender, age? What repetition and patterning is evident? What is the stance adopted by those in the images? What might this infer? What relationship patterns are communicated from the style and structure of the text and images? Are biographies included? What do they communicate? Are there interview extracts? What is the effect of this in meaning-making and sense-making terms? What relationships with the membership base of the CIPD are evident in this source? What significance issues are highlighted by 'infographics'? The order of the contents is also interesting. You may wish to include the front and back covers within the scope of your analysis. Through an analysis of these and other features it should be possible to develop an explanation of the CIPD discourse in relation to both members of the professional body and to those who are not in membership.

Use of software for qualitative data analysis

An important characteristic of the discussion about qualitative analysis that has featured in the first half of this chapter is the volume and 'messiness' of information involved in any qualitative analysis. In addition, qualitative analysis is complex and iterative. It involves identifying categories, undertaking initial coding processes and then moving on through a process of generating reflective memos to identify themes and to undertake further coding and analysis associated with enquiring about patterns and relationships.

Qualitative data analysis involves dealing with high volumes of data, expressed as words and/or pictures generated from a range of sources as well as audio and video files. This is time-consuming and it is difficult to keep a track of different items of data. If qualitative data form any significant part of your project, then some form of database management system will be required; merely storing printed documents and audio recordings in a box file will not suffice. If you choose to analyse the data without any computer software, then multiple copies of the texts and images that form the dataset will be required. As you undertake your coding process you will then need to copy relevant chunks of data (associated with your codes), reference them to the original source document and then pass them into some form of filing system.

In order to move beyond the initial process of categorisation and start to look for patterns, groupings or themes then a process of 'laying out' the various relevant items (on a very large table or even on the floor) will be necessary. The main difficulty with this manual approach is the difficulty of 'keeping track' of all the different data. The transcript of a one-hour interview is likely to take up 20 pages of close-typed text and the volume of the data can lead to errors in the manipulation process, thus affecting the credibility and trustworthiness of the conclusions. If the quantity of qualitative data for your project is fairly limited and other forms of data (quantitative) are more important for the project as a whole, then this approach may be sufficient. Hahn (2008) and Lewins and Silver (2014) provide some useful advice about using proprietary software, such as Microsoft Access and Excel to help with the data management and coding process.

Opinions vary about the usefulness of more specialised Computer Aided Qualitative Data Analysis (CAQDAS) software packages (see, for example, Atherton and Elsmore, 2007; Lewins and Silver, 2014) although the users of qualitative analysis software packages are beginning to outnumber those who prefer not to use them. Study centres are increasingly investing in site licences for the most well-established software packages and free-to-download software is also available. Most software packages include: functions to assist with coding, searching and retrieving data, reporting, and generating images and models. A useful comparison of the different packages available is provided by the online qualitative data analysis learning resources site funded by UK Economic and Social Research Council (ESRC) National Centre for Research Methods (NCRM) at http://www. restore.ac.uk/lboro/research/software/caqdas_comparison.php. If you are considering using some form of qualitative data analysis software it is important to explore the functions that the software offers so that you can make best use of it as you make progress with the data collection. As a first step it is worth finding out if qualitative data analysis software is available to you from your university or study centre and then to find out how you can access training to use it. Most reputable software has a range of online video and interactive tutorials to explain at least the basics. If you have to purchase the software yourself then look for the 'education rate', which might provide you with a personal licence for limited time duration. Demonstration and trial copies are likely to be available but often for only a short trial period. Although qualitative data software packages have a range of impressive functions they will not code the data for you nor will they undertake the analysis for you. Analysis is a thinking process – your judgement and intellect is still required. Also, if you code things in a sloppy way, even if you use a qualitative data analysis package you will still generate a sloppy analysis – however sophisticated the software makes it look.

The main functions of one commonly used QACDAS software package (NVivo) is provided here and it is possible to find out more about the functions of all of the software packages through websites from the software houses.

Data management features

- **Data storage.** NVivo, like other CAQDAS software packages, provides one repository for all the source materials relating to your research. This includes all the 'raw data' (text, audio and video files, visual images, social media data and so on). In addition it provides you with the opportunity to maintain a reflective journal and write memos to yourself about your ideas and the progress you are making. In this way you can keep a record (an audit trail) of the incremental process of data gathering and interpretation. You can also store other documents associated with your research such as your research proposal, ethical approval form and important literature sources.

- **Coding facility.** Within NVivo, codes are referred to as 'nodes' and the software enables you to code (and then retrieve as appropriate) descriptive codes, case codes, analytical codes and relationship codes. NVivo provides the opportunity for you to work with emergent codes (called 'free nodes') as well as with a more structured or hierarchical system of codes (called 'tree nodes'). You can also assign attribute values to your participants' 'case nodes' (for example, age, gender, organisational size) in the form of numbers, dates or words. Once you have assigned these attributes you are able to view the data according to the attributes that you have chosen and so make comparisons between the codes and issues that emerge for the different groupings.

- **Data grouping functions.** Most qualitative data analysis software enables you to group together data in different ways according to different characteristics. In NVivo such groupings are referred to as 'sets' and, once you have established these, you can carry out a specific analysis within particular groups or compare issues across the groupings.

- **Social media data.** Some qualitative data analysis software enables you to import social media data in a tabular form so that it is possible to analyse user accounts and their related messages or postings, sort by hashtag to understand online discussions around particular topics, and examine location based issues based on the profiles of the participants.

Analysis features

As indicated earlier in this chapter, there are many different approaches to qualitative data analysis but, at some stage or another, you will find yourself needing to identify and explore possible relationships both within your categories and between different categories. To help with this most software packages have a number of different 'query' functions:

- **Search and query functions.** The NVivo software works like a web-based search engine, which creates an index to all the words in all your sources. Therefore, it is easy to carry out a range of different text searches to find data that meet your search criteria. As qualitative data analysis is an iterative and incremental process it also allows you to save your queries for future use so that you can rerun them when data have changed and you can also edit them to make a similar but different search. It is also possible to view the results as a preview or to save the results in the form of a new code (node) or group (set). Different forms of queries are available: text search (words; phrases; combinations of words or phrases); coding search (retrieve one code restricted in a particular way or retrieve a combination of codes); matrix coding (to gather responses with particular attributes); or compound searches where a text and coding combination is interrogated. If you are searching over a combination of codes you can use the 'boolean' operators (and; or; not) and also give proximity operators (near content; preceding content; surrounding content) in order to examine data that may be relevant.

- **Data display function.** Almost all CAQDAS packages have a variety of data display functions to help you to use figures and diagrams to help you identify and describe key features of your data. Two examples, generated by researchers using NVivo are provided as Figure 8.6. As the analysis process is near completion, to generate, depict and continuously revise models that help you to explain your interpretation and sense-making of the data you can save each tentative model as you proceed and so have a record of your developing ideas.

Access to specialised software can be problematic for practitioner-researchers. Although many universities have site licences for SPSS to enable quantitative data gathering, provision for qualitative data analysis is less widespread. Most software providers offer an 'educational' list price for a single-user licence, usually for a defined one-year period that may be more convenient and appropriate. Qualitative data analysis software takes time to learn to use. For projects where a limited amount of qualitative data has been gathered the required investment in both money and time may not be sufficient to justify specialised software. Where large quantities of data have been gathered, however, it is likely that a more thorough analysis will be possible.

The use of software programs for qualitative data analysis, while making it possible to manage greater volumes of data, does not take away the requirement to think in a logical, evaluative and systematic way as part of the analysis process. Software packages organise data but the initial conceptualisation and the interpretation process still remain the province of the person undertaking the research. If your research involves smaller quantities of qualitative data or the qualitative component of your mixed methods study is supplementary rather than central then it is perfectly feasible to undertake an analysis using word processing software or spreadsheet software.

Data display processes

Data display is another pillar of qualitative data analysis (Lee and Lings, 2008). Data display helps you to explore possible relationships within categories and between themes. Having undertaken an initial analysis of your data, figurative depiction can be used to **describe** how things link together and can also be used to **propose explanations** about what seems to be happening. You may choose to undertake 'within case' data display (this is most common for practitioner-researchers) but if your research spans more than one 'case' (and remember that a 'case' may be a department, an

Figure 8.6 Illustrations of data display using QACDAS

Nodes clustered by word similarity

individual, or an organisation) you can undertake cross-case data display. The objective is to find a way that can bring different categories of relevant data together. Experimentation with different forms of data display is a productive way forward.

Methods of data display

There are no hard-and-fast rules about how data must be grouped or assessed but the following sections briefly describe some alternative ways of displaying your data. Most people find that, through a process of trial and error, they can find the most appropriate ways to display their data to assist them with taking forward their interpretive work (Miles and Huberman, 2014).

Charts

One way of making sense of data, particularly in the early stages of analysis, is to use charts or grids where one dimension (eg the rows) represent one set of categories and the other dimension (eg the columns) represent the evidence from different sources. Charts can be thematic (where you give examples of data from each theme across all respondents or cases) or *by case* for each respondent across all themes. An example of the use of a chart is shown in Table 8.5. In this fictional example the chart is used to describe the outcomes where people from each different function have been asked similar questions but, following a coding process, it becomes apparent that there are the similarities and differences of response.

Another use of the chart can be to explore and display possible patterns that you find in your data.

Table 8.6 shows an example of a matrix that provides an overview of the relationship between different understandings of the purpose of talent management and functional location of interviewees in a qualitative study of Talent Management where SM = Senior Manager; LM = Line Manager and HR = HR practitioner.

Table 8.5 Fictional example of a data chart: What do different departments expect from the HR function?

Department	Theme: Welfare/ Employee Advocate	Theme: Strategic Partner	Theme: Administrative Functions
Operations	• Protect us against management excesses • Redundancy consultation	• HR planning support	• Pay and reward • Absence control • Rapid recruitment
Sales		• Performance related incentives	• Metrics for revenue targets • Short-term sales training
Finance		• Information for budgeting and forecasting	• Pay and reward • Record keeping

Table 8.6 Fictional data matrix: Purpose of talent management

	Culture Change	Strategic Change	Business Plan Implementation
Important	SM1 HR1/HR3	SM1 LM1/LM3 HR1/HR2/HR3	SM1
Moderate		SM3	SM3/LM3/HR2
Unimportant	SM2/SM3 LM1/LM2/LM3 HR2	SM2 LM2	SM2 LM1/LM2 HR1/HR3

The important thing with any data display is that you must be confident that the data you have gathered provide credible evidence for the cells you have identified. You should demonstrate this by the use of illustrative examples from your data. This requires a fair amount of 'data management' and there are different ways of doing this. For small projects it is possible to undertake it with pen and paper. A large surface, such as a white board, or a generous covering of the floor with coded extracts from the original data are quite common. Even for larger projects it is possible to compile matrices making use of database functions for common computer software packages (Hahn, 2008). Specialised qualitative data analysis software will also enable the production of any number of matrices to help you assess the extent to which there may be patterns or trends in your data.

Another popular way to represent data is to present issues in a hierarchy format, something that is particularly useful if you think your data supports the proposition of a taxonomy or classification system that might describe or explain a phenomenon. Figure 8.7 provides an example of data displayed as a hierarchy relating to factors affecting workplace conflict in an organisational setting.

Yet another way of displaying your data is to organise it in some form of order, for example, by timeframes, length of service, size of location, etc. An example of such a display is shown in Figure 8.8.

Display by modelling

Modelling provides another useful approach to considering the relationship between different categories of data. There are a number of different ways that data can be 'modelled'. A popular and fairly straightforward way is to 'draw' the layout of a work

Figure 8.7 Data display using a hierarchy

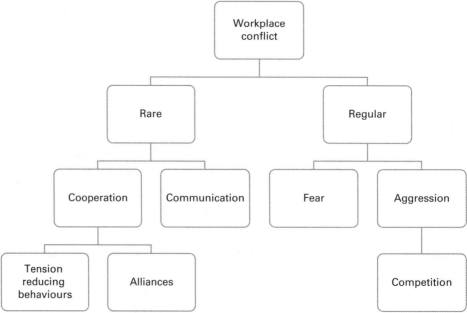

Figure 8.8 Illustrative example of a time ordered display relating to stages of stress management

Time				
Stress risk assessment				
	Stress management training			
		Medical referral	Treatment	
				Return to work/ Confidential support/EAP/ Workplace counselling

situation or a 'flow chart' of a number of processes, perhaps to extract and describe the different actions that led to particular outcomes that you have been investigating. While this can be a useful way of proceeding in an inductive way, it is also possible to use this approach in a more deductive way by devising an overall flow chart of what you expect a process to involve and then to compare this with the data you have collected. This approach also enables you to map any critical paths, decision points, and supporting evidence that emerge from the data. Once you have an initial flow chart, perhaps generated from data from a few of your sources, you can assess the extent to which it also represents what you learn from other sources within your sample.

Figure 8.9 and Figure 8.10 show two slightly different models, both of which relate to different research areas. Figure 8.9 displays concepts emerging from research into the career influences of executive level HR professionals. Figure 8.10 is an example of a network diagram suggesting causal influences on the success of apprenticeship schemes.

Figure 8.9 Influences on the career experiences of executive HR professionals

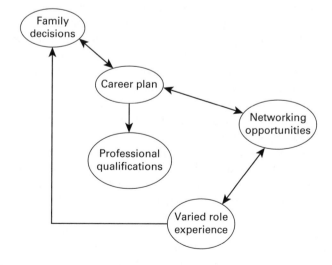

Figure 8.10 Network diagram for apprenticeship success

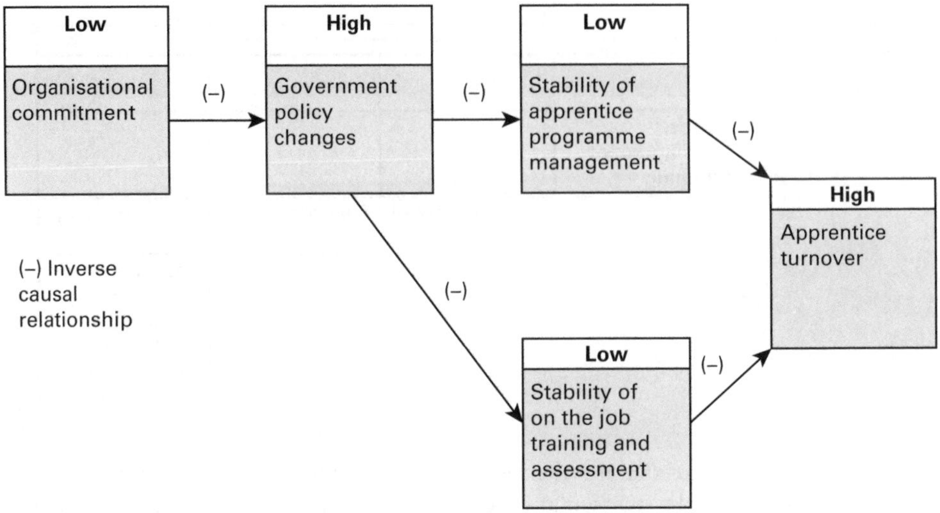

Discussion questions

1 What are the advantages of the data display and modelling processes?
2 What challenges do they present?

Feedback notes

The process of generating a model is a useful way of examining interrelated features of the phenomena or situation that you have examined in a qualitative way as it helps to represent patterns of experience, and the relationships between them. Often it is helpful to try out different forms of data display before arriving at a model that best 'suits' your findings. One of the challenges of qualitative data analysis is determining how to start and where to stop. A further concern is the issue of the extent to which, as you get engrossed in making sense of your data, there is a tendency to produce a lovely diagram or figure and then wonder (or your assessor may wonder) to what extent the data really do support your interpretation. Effective qualitative research requires you to include the evidence to support the model and also evaluate the weaknesses of your model as a vehicle for explaining what is going on, as well as its strengths. In many cases an iterative process is required of: data display; model formulation; re-examination of the data; revision of model, etc. As you engage in these forms of data presentation it is important to keep a note of your different drafts of data display and models as they evolve. Then, when you write up your analysis you will be able to explain how the model was amended and improved to take better account of all of your data. This will greatly enhance the credibility of your conclusions as well as the mark you get for your dissertation or research report.

Taken as a whole, therefore, qualitative data analysis involves testing ideas and hunches that you may develop as you think about and try to make sense of your data. It is important to look for emerging themes that may be scattered over different places in your dataset or which occur from data from different data gathering episodes. There is a strong likelihood that the process of analysing your data, using data display and modelling will involve you in subdividing and recoding some of your original categories and you may end up integrating one or more categories. This is time-consuming and, if you have left the analysis to the last minute, you will find it very frustrating. However, the quality of your final outcome will be much enhanced and, if you keep a clear record of what each of your categories mean (their definitions) you should be able to build in an incremental way as you continue with your data gathering and analysis processes.

Evaluating explanations and formulating conclusions

The iterative nature of qualitative data analysis also applies to the process of formulating explanations and conclusions on the basis of the evidence that you have gathered. The process of moving from data gathering to data reduction and then to analysis and the evaluation of provisional explanations is an iterative one without a clearly defined 'end point'. At some point, however, ideally when new 'cases' shed no new light on the topic of investigation (something referred to as data saturation), you should reach a point where alternative explanations have been evaluated and one or two interpretations seem most plausible.

The data analysis process, therefore, as illustrated in Figure 8.1, towards the beginning of this chapter, involves the generation of a range of possible explanations and/or propositions and the evaluation of these in the light of the evidence that has been gathered. The criteria by which alternatives might be evaluated (see Collis and Hussey, 2014; Neuman; 2012; Silverman, 2015) can include asking questions about:

- **Credibility.** To what extent are the different explanations supported by evidence from different sources (triangulation)? How explicit have you been about the theoretical stance of your interpretation? Has this 'promoted' some explanations and excluded others?

- **Transferability.** To what extent are the explanations context-specific? Could they be applied to another situation? How clear are you about the limits of transferability?

- **Dependability.** How well documented is the research process? Are there things that the people or organisations in the research may not have revealed? To what extent might you have overlooked or not reported some issues? Have commonplace occurrences been overlooked in the explanatory process? Has coding/categorisation been undertaken in a consistent way?

- **Meaning in context.** To what extent are your explanations feasible within their context? Has the process of analysis fragmented the evidence such that the analysis has become removed from the original context from which the data were gathered?

- **Recurrent patterning.** To what extent can the explanations be seen to relate to more than one particular timeframe? Is the sequencing within the explanations plausible?

Having evaluated the alternatives, conclusions about what is highly unlikely and what explanations are plausible can be drawn. The content and format of conclusions drawn from qualitative data are also characterised by diversity (Robson and McCartan, 2016). Different factors that can help with the formulation of conclusions based on the analysis of qualitative data are shown in Table 8.7.

Table 8.7 Factors in drawing conclusions from qualitative data

Factor	Example
Counting	less than half of the interviewees perceived...
Patterning	recurrent patterns in the analysis of the organisational documents were...
Clustering	responses from focus groups in location B reported particular difficulties with... whereas those closer to... suggested...
Factoring	key factors underpinning the perceived effectiveness of the appraisal scheme were...
Variables	the analysis suggests that the practice of... occurs when... but it is unlikely to take place when...
Causal networks	the following model indicates the relationships between the six different factors...
Relationship to theory	the incidences of... that the analysis has identified may best be understood within the... theory relating to...

(Robson and McCartan, 2016; Neuman, 2012; Yin, 2017)

Figure 8.11 Evaluating explanations and formulating conclusions

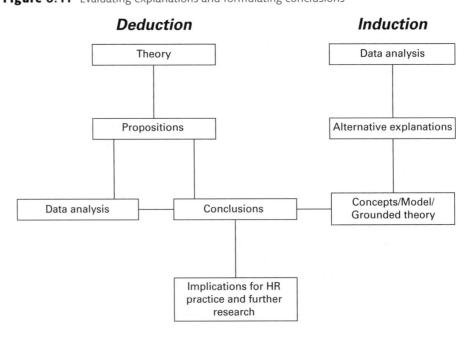

The nature of the conclusions that you draw will depend on the nature of your research questions as well as the broad (deductive or inductive) approach that you have adopted. The way that conclusions are drawn, however, is something of a point of convergence between these two different approaches.

If you have used a deductive approach and have compared your data with theory then you will need to consider the evidence and the extent to which it supports propositions or explanations from relevant theories. The conclusions of the analysis will then be able to indicate areas where the propositions are plausible (note – not 'confirmed') and areas where the explanations stemming from the propositions are unlikely. The implications of the analysis for further research as well as for HR practice can be considered as a result of this.

If you are adopting a more inductive approach you will also be able to draw conclusions and reflect on the implications of your analysis for further research and practice. The 'path' to this point, however, will involve gathering and analysing data without utilising prior theories or frameworks to explore 'what is going on'. The output of this iterative process (the conclusions) may be a model or an explanatory framework. Reflections about the implications for HR practice and further research to explore the conclusions will also be appropriate. In this way you are moving towards generalisations that are likely (but not certain).

Writing up your analysis

During the process of data analysis, you will find yourself immersed in the data and this can lead to problems when you write up your analysis for readers who are less familiar with the dataset. Therefore, when you write up your project it is important to be clear about:

1 **The process you used to manage the data and how you undertook the coding, categorisation and analysis.** This is usually included within the methodology section.

2 **The themes and categories that you identified from the data.** These need careful explanation and justification so that they 'make sense' to your readers. The most common way to do this is to offer an overall summary of the main features of the themes and then to illustrate them with a quotation or some other form of example. Therefore, it is important that you have a strategy for recording and referencing quotations accurately so that you are able to access them when you need to provide an illustration. It is also important that the quotations that you use must fairly represent the dataset – avoid the temptation to select the evidence to fit your preferred explanation.

3 **The justification for the conclusions that you reached.** Make clear for your reader all the different explanations that you have evaluated on the basis of the data and the reasoning behind your conclusion as being the most plausible.

CHECKLIST

- Qualitative data are concerned with language and meaning attached to different phenomena. Qualitative data are not 'standardised'. Qualitative data are characterised by 'volume' and 'messiness'.

- Analysis is the thought process that underpins understanding of the relationships between different elements in situations, and the likely outcomes of particular actions or interventions. It involves finding answers to your research questions using the data that you have gathered by exploring the relationships between different categories and themes.

- Qualitative data analysis is an integrated and iterative process. It informs data gathering and the formulation of conclusions. Data analysis involves data reduction and categorisation; grouping and display; and the evaluation of alternative explanations before conclusions are reached.

- Data coding is at the heart of qualitative data analysis. Coding involves labelling 'chunks' of data in relation to their meaning. Chunks of data may vary considerably in size, from individual words to a phrase or paragraph. One unit of data may be categorised in more than one way and therefore be assigned more than one code.

- Codes can relate to contextual information or they may be thematic. Categories and codes can emerge from the data; be developed from the aims, objectives and research questions of a study; be derived from concepts in the literature; or follow from the analysis of other sources of data.

- Different analytical techniques can be used for qualitative data analysis. Commonly used techniques are thematic analysis, content analysis and narrative analysis. Discourse analysis can be particularly useful to many of the qualitatively orientated research questions posed by HR researchers.

- Content analysis systematically examines the components of written, spoken or visual communication.

- Narrative analysis involves examining the meanings involved when people share or recount an experience or event. The focus of narrative analysis is on 'how' people narrate events as well as on 'what' their narrative contains.

- Discourse analysis involves examination of processes of meaning as they are constructed, reconstructed, defined and redefined through structures of 'talk', 'text' and visual imagery.

- It is important to analyse the data from a range of perspectives and to value data that do not 'fit' with what is expected.

- Qualitative data analysis may include some element of counting or quantification as well as the identification of patterns, clusters, factors, variables, causal relationships, and the development of a theory, model or framework.

- Maintaining a diary in which notes, ideas, reflections and procedures are recorded assists with the ongoing analysis process and can provide a basis for evaluating the degree of 'detachment' that you have achieved.

- A range of qualitative data analysis software products is available, which can enhance data manipulation processes for text-based, visual and audio forms of data. It is important to evaluate available software at an early stage in your research so that the software functions can be utilised throughout the research process.

- Qualitative data analysis can be undertaken utilising an inductive or deductive approach.

- Data display processes such as charts, time-sequence diagrams, hierarchies and models form an important component of the data analysis process.

- The evaluation of alternative explanations is an important part of qualitative data analysis and leads to the formulation of conclusions on the basis of likelihood and plausibility.

- It is important to clarify and justify the analysis process that has been undertaken. Information about the data recording, reduction and coding processes should be included within the methodology section. A description of the main themes that have been identified, illustrated from the data, and used to evaluate alternative explanations should be included in the section(s) devoted to data presentation and analysis.

TEST YOURSELF

1   When undertaking qualitative data analysis why should you start coding your data as soon as possible?

   a   Because you will get short of time when the deadline approaches.

   b   Because it is a fun thing to do.

   c   To ensure that you find the interpretation that your manager is hoping for.

   d   To sharpen your focus and identify areas to look out for in future data gathering processes.

2   The generation of charts, grids, hierarchies, matrices and so on are all forms of:

   a   Template analysis.

   b   Data display.

   c   Grounded theory.

   d   Analytical induction.

3   Keeping a chronological record of your ideas and reflections as your research project goes along, to help you develop your analysis is known as:

a Research summaries.

b Data transcripts.

c Research diary.

d Self-memos.

4 Which of the following would be suitable for content analysis?

a Interview transcripts.

b Newspaper articles.

c Website content.

d All of the above.

5 Which of the following describe narrative analysis?

a An enhanced form of interview technique.

b A form of analysis of organisational documents.

c An approach to examine how people sequence and represent people and events.

d A different name for thematic analysis.

6 Discourse analysis involves examining:

a The ways in which communication is undertaken to produce desired effects.

b Forms of communication both written and visual.

c The way discourses 'frame' people's understanding of their situation.

d All of the above.

7 The purpose of keeping a record of your codes in some form of 'coding manual' is to:

a Test your knowledge of statistics.

b Provide you with a reminder about what each of your codes represent.

c Formalise instructions about how to code the data.

d List everything that you have decided to omit from your research.

8 What does the acronym 'CAQDAS' stand for?

a Complicated analysis of qualitative data and statistics.

b Constant analysis, qualitative data and simplicity.

c Computer assisted qualitative data analysis software.

d Content analysis, qualitative data software.

9 Which of these could be considered to be advantages of CAQDAS packages?

a You can find concealed data.

b Report writing is straightforward.

c You can re-analyse data easily.

d No training is necessary.

10 Which of the following is not a type of node used in NVivo?

a Tree node.

b Case node.

c Free node.

d Shrub node.

❓ Review Questions

1 How successful have you been in organising the data that you have collected so far? What sort of filing system or structure might be applicable?

2 In what format are your data at present? Do they require transcription or summarising?

3 What software options may be available to you through your study centre for the analysis of your qualitative data?

4 What is your tutor's or supervisor's opinion about the quantity and quality of the data you have collected?

5 Does your supervisor or tutor have specific expertise in data analysis that would be helpful for you?

6 How clear are you about your research questions? What are the main themes that you are likely to explore when you analyse your data? What initial categories might you use for the analysis?

7 To what extent are you familiar (or have you experimented with) analysis techniques such as thematic analysis, content analysis, narrative analysis or discourse analysis?

Questions for reflection

This final part of the chapter enables you to reflect about your professional development and develop your skills and knowledge. This will enable you to build your confidence and credibility, track your learning, see your progress, and demonstrate your achievements.

Strengths and weaknesses

1 How skilled are you at producing useable summaries of data gathering 'events' that will remain meaningful in a number of weeks? Is there some way you could practise in advance?

2 How successful have your early attempts at coding data been? What have you learned from these early attempts and how might you apply what you have learned to subsequent coding activity?

3 To what extent will you need to utilise individual quotations as examples of the categories you identify? How will you ensure you can identify, store and retrieve them?

Being a practitioner-researcher

4 How might you utilise a 'research diary' throughout the duration of your project to inform your thinking?

5 What organisational factors might influence the way that you interpret your data? What strategies can you utilise to maintain a detachment from the data?

6 What explanations of the data might be 'organisationally preferred'? What alternative explanations might there be? What might enhance your ability to develop and evaluate a range of explanations as part of the analysis process?

7 What actions can you take to maximise the credibility and dependability of the data that you analyse? How can you ensure that the organisational and personal context in which the data have been generated is not lost as a result of the fragmentation involved in the data analysis process?

Useful Resources

There are some excellent resources focused on issues associated with qualitative data analysis that can be found at:

http://onlineqda.hud.ac.uk/ (archived at https://perma.cc/AAW5-93CX)

http://hsc.uwe.ac.uk/dataanalysis/qualIssues.asp (archived at https://perma.cc/Y7BG-CHLA)

http://www.learnhigher.ac.uk/analysethis (archived at https://perma.cc/4RT9-7M4K)

http://www.restore.ac.uk/resources/qualquanres.php (archived at https://perma.cc/B2UC-NN85)

Other useful web resources are:

YouTube channel to support NVivo users – https://www.youtube.com/user/QSRInternational/videos (archived at https://perma.cc/23AB-Y6VL)

http://www.sagepub.co.uk/richards/ (archived at https://perma.cc/ZH5G-37N3)

Internet addresses for software houses where further information about QACDAS packages are available are:

http://www.qsrinternational.com (archived at https://perma.cc/KN53-KW9P)

http://www.atlasti.com (archived at https://perma.cc/55D2-EQD9)

http://www.qualisresearch.com (archived at https://perma.cc/7GFD-TBGU)

Other useful sources of reading about analysing and reporting on qualitative data include:

Anderson, V (2017) Criteria for evaluating qualitative research, *Human Resource Development Quarterly*, **28**, pp 125–33, DOI:10.1002/hrdq.21282

Atherton, A and Elsmore, P (2007) A dialogue on the merits of using software for qualitative data analysis, *Qualitative Research in Organizations and Management: An International Journal*, **2** (1), pp 62–77

Bazely, P (2013) *Qualitative Data Analysis with Nvivo*, Sage, London

Dopson, S, Fitzgerald, L and Ferlie, E (2008) Understanding change and innovation in healthcare settings: Reconceptualising the active role of context, *Journal of Change Management*, **8** (3–4), pp 213–31

Elo, S and Kyngas, H (2008) The qualitative content analysis process, *Journal of Advanced Nursing*, **62** (1), pp 107–15

Keegan, A and Francis, H (2010) Practitioner talk: the changing textscape of HRM and emergence of HR business partnership, *The International Journal of Human Resource Management*, **21** (6), pp 873–93

Lawless, A, Sambrook, S, Garavan, T and Valentin, C (2011) A discourse approach to theorising HRD: Opening up a discursive space. *Journal of European Industrial Training*, **35** (3), pp 264–75

Levitt, HM, Bamberg, M, Creswell, JW, Frost, DM, Josselson, R and Suárez-Orozco, C (2018) Journal article reporting standards for qualitative primary, qualitative meta-analytic, and mixed methods research in psychology: The APA Publications and Communications Board task force report, *American Psychologist*, **73** (1), pp 26–46, DOI: 10.1037/amp0000151

Lewins, A and Silver, C (2009) Choosing a CAQDAS Package. NCRM Working Paper. University of Surrey, Guildford, UK. (Unpublished) [Online] http://eprints.ncrm.ac.uk/791/ (archived at https://perma.cc/CBP5-7LQU)

Richards, L (2009) *Handling Qualitative Data: A practical guide*, Sage, London

Sambrook, S (2006) Management Development in the NHS: nurses and managers, discourses and identities, *Journal of European Industrial Training*, **30** (1), pp 48–64

Saunders, MK and Tosey, P (2015) *Handbook of Research Methods on Human Resource Development*, Edward Elgar, Cheltenham

Symon, G and Cassell, C (eds) (2012) *Qualitative Organizational Research*, Sage, London

References

Bell, E, Bryman, A and Harley, B (2019) *Business Research Methods*, 5th edn, Oxford University Press, Oxford

Braun, V and Clarke, V (2006) Using thematic analysis in psychology, *Qualitative Research in Psychology*, **3** (2), pp 77–101, DOI: 10.1191/1478088706qp063oa

Charmaz, K (2014) *Constructing Grounded Theory: A practical guide through qualitative data analysis*, Sage, London

Collis, J and Hussey, R (2014) *Business Research: A practical guide for undergraduate and postgraduate students*, Palgrave, Basingstoke

Cunliffe, AL (2011) Crafting qualitative research: Morgan and Smircich 30 years on, *Organizational Research Methods*, **14** (4), pp 647–73

Elliott, C and Robinson, S (2011) MBA imaginaries: Projections of internationalization, *Management Learning*, **43** (2), pp 157–81

Gee, PG (2011) *How to do Discourse Analysis: A toolkit*, Routledge, Oxford

Hahn, C (2008) *Doing Qualitative Research Using Your Computer*, Sage, London

Lee, N and Lings, I (2008) *Doing Business Research: A guide to theory and practice*, Sage, London

Lewins, A and Silver, C (2014) *Using Software in Qualitative Research: A step-by-step guide*, Sage, Thousand Oaks, CA

Miles, MB and Huberman, AM (2014) *Qualitative Data Analysis: A methods source book*, Sage, London

Neuman, W (2012) *Basics of Social Research: Qualitative and quantitative approaches*, International edn, Pearson Education, Harlow

Robson, C and McCartan, K (2016) *Real World Research: A resource for social scientists and practitioner-researchers*, Wiley, Oxford

Silverman, D (2015) *Interpreting Qualitative Data*, Sage, London

Yin, RK (2017) *Case Study Research: Design and methods*, 6th edn, Sage Publications, Thousand Oaks, CA

09
Collecting and recording quantitative data

LEARNING OBJECTIVES

This chapter should help you to:

- consider how quantitative data can contribute to your research;
- discuss different sources of numerical data;
- design and evaluate an effective survey instrument;
- administer a survey to an appropriate sample of respondents;
- collect, organise and store quantitative data in an effective way;
- describe and present a summary of data you have collected.

CHAPTER OUTLINE

- How to use this chapter
- The uses of quantitative data in HR research
- Where does quantitative data come from?
- Undertaking your own survey

- The internet and quantitative data collection
- Administering surveys and evaluating responses
- Collecting, organising and presenting quantitative data
- Summary checklist
- Test yourself, review and reflect questions
- Useful resources

How to use this chapter

It would be almost impossible to investigate an HR problem or issue without the use of some numerical data. This chapter aims to give you some ideas about where to look for quantitative data, how to evaluate the extent to which numerical information will help you to address your research questions and how to collect quantitative data. The focus of the chapter is on gathering, presenting and describing data; Chapter 10 will help you to analyse and interpret your data in order to formulate meaningful conclusions. This chapter does not require you to become an expert in statistical techniques or specialised software programs.

 Activity 9.1

Making sense of the numbers

Visit the survey reports page of the CIPD website and examine either: a Labour Market Outlook survey (https://www.cipd.co.uk/knowledge/work/trends/labour-market-outlook); and other recent reports, such as the Reward Management Survey (https://www.cipd.co.uk/knowledge/strategy/reward/surveys) or the Megatrends: Flexible Working Report (https://www.cipd.co.uk/knowledge/work/trends/megatrends/flexible-working) that you will find there. For this activity you do not need to read the findings carefully – skim-read the report and answer the following questions.

Discussion questions

1   What information does the report provide? What does it **not** tell you?

2   What information would you need in order to evaluate the trustworthiness of the data on which the report is based?

Feedback notes

Depending on the report you have chosen you may feel either very interested by the information it contains or you may feel that it is not immediately relevant to your concerns in relation to your work and/or your research. These reports contain a lot of charts in various formats. Depending on your background and learning style you may find these helpful or you may find numerical and statistical data of this sort to be boring or somewhat alienating. Nonetheless, these reports contain useful information about general trends in employment, labour markets and the development of HR. The figures and charts that are provided offer a useful **description** of some trends relating to employment and HR. The figures and charts present in these reports normally do not **explain** the reasons for the trends although the context at the time the data were gathered is always discussed as part of the report. It is, however, **wrong** to say that only qualitative data would help explain the reasons for the trends. In fact, quantitative data can be addressed by means of **descriptive statistics or inferential statistics** – while descriptive statistics only display general trends, inferential statistics are used to try to explain differences between groups or to understand the relationships between the different variables that the reports address (more information on descriptive and inferential statistics will be provided in the next section). This means that inferential statistics have some explanatory value. However, inferential statistics are limited to the type and number of variables we have available on a survey. In other words, we can find appropriate explanations for the main trends, but we would have had to think about these explanations a priori (before the survey was conducted). Qualitative data would indeed be very valuable as it would allow us to discover other reasons and explanations that we may not have considered beforehand.

In order to evaluate the trustworthiness of the report you have chosen it is also necessary to know more about it. The CIPD 'outlook reports' are usually published fairly close to the data collection on which they are based so you might comment that one of the positive features of the report is its 'up to date' quality. Questions that might also occur to you might be: How were the questions put together? To what extent are the roles fulfilled by the survey respondents (all of whom were CIPD members) representative of all the employers in the United Kingdom? How confident can you be that the response rate to the survey (often around 15 per cent of CIPD members) reliably represents the views of all those involved in employing people in the United Kingdom? CIPD reports are highly scrutinised and comply with strict research criteria, but it is important to think about this type of question when reading quantitative reports.

These issues and others underpin this chapter. Quantitative data are likely to form part of any assessment of an HR issue or problem and it is important to be clear about their purpose and to use the data in an appropriate way. This chapter provides a framework through which to consider how best to use quantitative data in HR studies.

The uses of quantitative data in HR research

All research needs data. 'Quantitative data' is the term given to data that can be counted and quantified to shed light on features of organisational and employment situations. Such data deal in **variables** that can be counted, measured, described, compared and correlated. Quantitative data have an important part to play in answering research questions. Examples of quantitative data in HR research are:

- The number of employees who left an organisation in one given year – this could then be used to calculate turnover rates.

- Employee tenure, also addressed as the amount of time an individual has been working for an organisation.

- The employees' engagement can be measured by their quantitative responses on a Likert scale. A Likert scale would be rating the frequency in which an employee feels or acts in a certain way, for example. This is the approach used by the Utrecht Work Engagement Scale by Schaufeli and Bakker (2004), where this frequency is rated from 0 to 6. The aggregated interpretation of this numeric data would lead to an interpretation of the levels of engagement of an individual. In this particular case, we are attributing a numeric value to a more subjective construct.

Using quantitative data: descriptive statistics and inferential statistics

In HR research there are many types of quantitative data, from objective data about employee turnover and absenteeism, to data representing employees' attitudes and well-being. Nevertheless, all of these data are suitable to be analysed statistically.

There are two main types of statistical analyses: descriptive and inferential. **Descriptive statistics** show, summarise or **describe specific patterns** that might emerge from the data. These include measures of frequency, central tendency or dispersion (Field, 2017). Some examples are:

- **Frequency.** How many people over the age of 50? How many times were certain behaviours manifested?

- **Central tendency.** What is the average salary of employees?

- **Dispersion.** How wide is the difference between the lowest and highest rates of absence between different departments?

You can compare this information with data from other sources (maybe from other parts of the organisation) and you can describe trends (spend on training over a four-year period, etc). These procedures are common in most organisations and underpin decision-making and the evaluation of achievements. However, quantitative data can also be more fully analysed to explore potential relationships between different variables and to assess their significance. We can also establish relationships between variables in a sample that may be potentially generalised to the population from which the sample was retrieved. This happens when we use inferential statistics.

Inferential statistics allow us to use quantitative data to **explain** different phenomena. By using inferential statistics on a certain sample, we are able to make generalisations about the population from which the sample was drawn. This is why it is so important to make sure that the sample accurately represents the population. This means that the results obtained with inferential statistics are not completely certain as we can never be sure they apply to the whole population. However, we could claim that the results are valid by using a percentage of reliability, usually addressed as level of confidence. Inferential statistics often test hypotheses, about a population, which can be confirmed or rejected by the data in the sample. Some examples of uses of inferential statistics are:

- **Comparing the means of different groups.** For example, one can compare the mean job satisfaction levels of men and women.
- **Correlating variables.** For example, if you wanted to know how strong (or significant) is the relationship between employees' job satisfaction and their intention to stay in the organisation.

 Case Example 9.1

Sources of quantitative data

Yammeh was a part-time student who was a trades union member and had recently become a safety representative in his organisation, a large provider of transport services. For his dissertation he decided to research into the concerns of trades union safety representatives. However, Yammeh discovered that the Trades Union Congress (TUC) itself commissions a survey of safety reps every two years. In the most recently published survey report, the TUC indicated that stress, bullying and harassment, overwork, back strains, slips, trips and falls, and long hours of work were the most commonly cited issues of concern although there were regional variations in the data (https://www.tuc.org.uk/

sites/default/files/Safety%20Reps%20report%20 2018.pdf). To take his research forward Yammeh decided to find out about the health and safety concerns of employees in different parts of his own organisation across the country and then to compare the findings with the TUC's national survey.

Discussion questions

1   What information would Yammeh need in order to undertake the comparative research he wished to pursue?

2   What variables or issues might he want to identify and analyse?

Feedback notes

You have probably commented that, if Yammeh wanted to undertake his comparison, he would be wise to find out what survey questions were asked in the TUC survey and then to try to replicate these in his own research. As this survey is undertaken every two years it is reasonable to assume that the questionnaire itself asked the same questions as in previous years and it may be interesting to examine trends over time and also to assess relationships between variables.

Variables that you may have identified that Yammeh might be interested in include: hazards in the workplace, stress at work; occupational health provision; safety audits; counselling and well-being services. In addition, other variables that Yammeh might be interested in for his research might include demographic features such as: the age of his respondents; the nature of their work; their length of service as a safety rep; and their geographical location. Having obtained this sort of data it is then possible to 'interrogate it' in order to try to draw conclusions about health and safety issues and compare his organisation in the transport sector with the overall picture presented by the TUC survey.

Sources of quantitative data

Much of the quantitative data used in HR research comes from surveys of one sort or another. However, useful information can also be generated from structured observations, from content analysis of texts and from other artefacts. HR information systems are another rich source of quantitative information.

There are three main sources of survey data:

- **Published surveys.** These are undertaken for purposes other than your research. Skills and Employment Survey 2017 is an example of such a survey (see https://www.cardiff.ac.uk/research/explore/find-a-project/view/626669-skills-and-employment-survey-2017). Surveys such as these are useful sources of secondary data.

- **Unpublished surveys,** undertaken for purposes other than your research (regular employee engagement survey data from an organisation, for example). These are further examples of secondary data.

- **Surveys undertaken as a part of your specific research,** including postal or online surveys, telephone interviews and structured face-to-face interviews. These would be sources of primary data.

Most of this chapter considers issues relevant to undertaking a survey of your own but some information about published surveys is provided first.

Data from published surveys

Practitioners undertaking HR research projects, particularly those that are organisationally based, often make little or no use of published surveys although the data might offer useful points of context or comparison. The data from most surveys, in tabulated form (the so-called raw data), are available electronically, mostly through an internet link. Registration is often required but does not usually involve a cost. Useful data might include:

- **Census data.** Many countries collect data from nearly all of their population from time to time. In most countries completion is required and there is a wide range of questions.

- **Regular surveys.** Many regular surveys are likely to be of interest to those working in HR. These include surveys undertaken on behalf of the government, research organisations or professional institutes (such as the CIPD). Some examples are shown in Tables 9.1 and 9.2.

- **Ad hoc surveys.** These are often undertaken for particular purposes and are sponsored by those with a particular interest in the issues being examined. The CIPD website has links to a range of survey reports that can be found at: http://www.cipd.co.uk/onlineinfodocuments/surveys.htm.

Table 9.1 Examples of regular surveys

Name	Sample / Frequency	Sponsor	Description
Labour Force Survey	40,000 / quarterly	UK Office for National Statistics https://www.ons.gov.uk/surveys/informationforhouseholdsandindividuals/householdandindividualsurveys/labourforcesurvey	A quarterly sample survey of 40,000 households in Great Britain to provide information on the employment circumstances of the UK population. It is the largest household survey in the UK and provides the official measures of employment and unemployment. The LFS is carried out under a European Union Directive and uses internationally agreed concepts and definitions. It is the source of the internationally comparable (International Labour Organisation) measure known as 'ILO unemployment'.
National Employer Skills Survey	87,000 employers	UK Department for Education https://www.gov.uk/government/publications/employer-skills-survey-2017-uk-report	Data relating to employment from the perspective of employers about issues such as recruitment and retention, skills gaps, training and workforce development activity. Responsibility for this survey changes quite often as changes in local employment support arrangements have been made. Currently, it is managed by the UK Department for Education, but it was previously managed by the UK Commission for Employment and Skills.
Workplace Employee Relations Survey	2,680 managers, 1,002 employee reps, 21,981 employees. Undertaken initially as WIRS and later as WERS in 1980, 1984, 1990, 1998, 2004 and 2012.	ACAS, ESRC, UKCES, NIESR https://www.gov.uk/government/collections/workplace-employment-relations-study-wers	Survey collects information relating to employment relations in workplaces in the UK. Data on issues such as union recognition, negotiating structures, collective bargaining, procedures and agreements, pay systems, consultation and communication, workforce composition, performance measures etc.
Reward Management Survey	Reward specialists and people managers in about 570 organisations / annual	CIPD https://www.cipd.co.uk/knowledge/strategy/reward/surveys	An annual survey of UK reward management is based on responses received from organisations, across all industrial sectors. The main aim of the research is to provide readers with a benchmarking and information resource in respect of current and emerging practice in UK reward management.

Table 9.2 Examples of cross-national surveys

Name	Sample/ Frequency	Sponsor	Description
European Commission Public Opinion Analysis	Approximately 1,000 face-to-face interviews per country / Twice a year	European Commission http://ec.europa.eu/ commfrontoffice/ publicopinion/index. cfm	Data from both quantitative and qualitative surveys undertaken on behalf of the European Commission. Different types of data and analysis found in different reports: Standard Eurobarometer, Special Eurobarometer, Flash Eurobarometer and Qualitative Eurobarometer.
European Social Survey	Biennial survey monitoring attitude change in over 30 European countries	Economic and Social Research Council (UK) + other country funding bodies https://www. europeansocialsurvey. org/	Data from quantitative surveys from over 30 countries. Data available to registered users (free to register).
GLOBE (Global Leadership and Organisational Behaviour Effectiveness) Research Project	A multi-phase and multi-method project. Data from 24 countries / cultures and from 100 CEOs and over 5,000 executives	Collaborative project involving a network of 70 social scientists from different parts of the world. https://globeproject. com/	Quantitative and qualitative data from 24 countries. Data gathering instruments available with permission.
GEM (Global Entrepreneurship Monitor)	200,000+ interviews a year in 100+ economies	Collaborative project led by Global Entrepreneurship Research Association (200+ funding institutions) https://www. gemconsortium.org/	Quantitative data from over 100 countries. Datasets available to registered users (free to register).

Undertaking your own survey

Surveys are perhaps the most widely used method of gathering data in business and management and HR projects are no exception. As with any form of data gathering, surveys can contribute to the achievement of a range of different research objectives. A key issue, if you plan to use a survey, is to be clear about its purpose. Some surveys operate from within a **deductive** approach where the researcher aims to test the relationships between variables. A hypothesis is formulated and then the data are analysed to test the propositions derived from the hypothesis. (See Chapter 5 for a fuller discussion of the deductive and inductive approaches to research.) Gill and Johnson (2010), however, point out that some surveys fulfil a more exploratory and **inductive** purpose, by indicating patterns and frequencies that can contribute to theory building. Other surveys have a comparative purpose, seeking to describe data and consider similarities with data from other research populations. The surveys undertaken in many HR projects, particularly for the purposes of CIPD management research reports, tend to fulfil a descriptive purpose although those at Masters level should go further than data description and preferably undertake a more explanatory inferential statistical analysis.

Determining a sample

The issue of sample size and selection is crucial to the usefulness of any survey and the trustworthiness of the findings. As noted already in previous chapters sampling is the deliberate choice of a number of units of analysis to represent a greater population. A population can be described as the abstract idea of a large group of many cases from which a researcher draws a sample and to which results from a sample are generated (Neuman, 2014). Censuses are examples of studies that examine the whole population. However, it is generally very difficult to survey the entire population, owing to aspects such as budget and time constraints. Instead, researchers collect data from a subset of cases or elements – a *sample* – and use those observations to make inferences about the entire population (Figure 9.1 depicts this process).

Figure 9.1 A sample is used to make inferences about a population

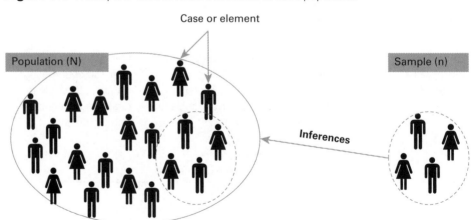

There are two main approaches to sampling. Non-probability sampling (discussed in Chapter 7) is most often used for qualitative data gathering. For quantitative data probability sampling is more appropriate. This involves determining a sample that is statistically representative of the population as a whole and so should reflect its characteristics such that you could be confident that your conclusions can be generalised to the wider population.

There are two key decisions with any survey. First, you must determine the size of the sample that you will select. Second, you will need to work out how you will select the respondents for your survey.

Sample size

A common question asked by student researchers is: 'how large must my sample be?' and there are no simple answers. Some books (see, for example, Saunders, Lewis and Thornhill, 2019) give calculations for desired sample size for cross-sectional research, which follow from a decision about how closely you want your sample to resemble the research population. However, these calculations are often not feasible if you are including quite a few variables in your study (see, for example, Lee and Lings, 2008). This means that you may be influenced as much by practicalities as by calculations (for more detailed information on sample selection, effect sizes and statistical power analysis, see Kraemer and Blasey, 2016). One practical issue to think about is the likely rate of return of your survey questionnaires and another issue to take account of is your plans for data analysis as some statistical tests require larger samples. It is also important to consider the costs associated with conducting a large survey. Another practicality to consider is the nature of your research question. Longitudinal studies are admittedly quite rare for many HR student projects, but increasingly used by PhD students in the HRM and organisational behaviour fields. If you are undertaking some form of longitudinal study, where data from the same individuals are collected at more than one moment in time, you may need to develop and justify your sampling strategy and ratio in a way different from the approach you might use for cross-sectional research. For example, it is likely that, as time passes, some of your original sample group may withdraw from your project and so you will need to build this risk into your initial sample selection process.

The following general principles (Neuman, 2014) are helpful:

- The smaller the population then the bigger the ratio of sample size to population size (sampling ratio) should be (see Figure 9.2). Thus:
  - for small populations (under 500), a ratio of about 30:100 (30 per cent) or 150 people is advisable;
  - for large populations (over 150,000), we can obtain equally good accuracy with a sampling ratio of 1 per cent or 1,500. In this case, the population of 150,000 is 30 times larger, but the sample is just 10 times larger.
- The higher your requirement for accuracy (and generalisability), the greater your sampling ratio should be.
- The higher the degree of diversity in the population, the higher the sampling ratio should be.
- The higher the number of different variables to be examined in the analysis of the data, the higher the sampling ratio should be.

Some of these factors are illustrated in Figure 9.2. Table 9.3 indicates the recommended sample sizes for different populations (associated with a reasonable degree of statistical accuracy) that Hart (2013) recommends.

Table 9.3 Recommended sample sizes for different populations

Population Size	Sample Size	Population Size	Sample Size
10	10	175	122
20	19	200	134
30	28	250	153
50	44	300	172
60	52	350	187
80	66	400	201
100	81	500	222
125	96	750	258
150	110	1000	286

Figure 9.2 Influences on sample size

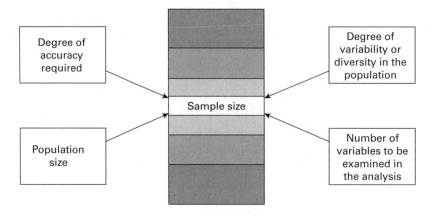

Case Example 9.2

Determining a sample size and method of sampling

Sarah was Operations Director for a medium-sized charity employing 350 people operating a large number of food banks to provide emergency help and support for people in the United Kingdom experiencing a crisis. The charity operated through local partners (for example, religious groups or community organisations) and the strategic objective of the charity was to increase its number of food banks to provide support to every town in the United Kingdom. As part of its social responsibility strategy the charity employed a large number of disadvantaged people in its warehouses and distribution centres and there were particular challenges with their training and development. In addition to responsibility for Operations, Sarah also had responsibility for Training and Development throughout the warehouse and distribution functions of the charity and for her research project she wanted to focus on achieving greater consistency and effectiveness of training in different warehouse locations. Like Sarah, all of the 'trainers' in the organisation had been given their training responsibilities without any prior background or training in HRM or HRD and, for her project, Sarah decided to evaluate the benefits that might be achieved if trainers in the organisation were encouraged (and sponsored) to study for some form of training qualification. She decided to issue two questionnaires: one questionnaire would investigate the trainers' perspective on this issue

and another questionnaire was to be completed by a sample of warehouse and distribution centre managers to assess the extent to which they would feel it would be beneficial and whether the cost (in both time and money) could be justified. She also decided to investigate the ways that other similar charities tackled this problem. Before she set about devising the questionnaires, however, she had to decide who to select to complete them and how many responses would constitute a representative sample.

Discussion questions

1 How might Sarah select potential survey respondents to ensure that her sample(s) would be representative?

2 What sampling ratio would you recommend for: a) the survey to trainers; and b) the survey to managers?

3 How might she get information from other charities and what approach to sampling would she need to think about?

Feedback notes

Decisions about the sampling ratio must take a number of factors into account. Although the organisation was quite small Sarah needed to know how many managers and how many trainers were employed as it is these groups that would form her 'survey populations'. She knew that there were 50 people involved in different training roles across the organisation and Sarah decided to sample all of them (a 100 per cent sample). There were just over 100 managers and she thought about approaching a 70 per cent sample. However, Sarah's supervisor discussed with her the likelihood that very few of these managers would bother to respond and Sarah anticipated that it might be hard to get a good response rate. Therefore, she decided to sample them all in the hope that she would get sufficient responses overall. This also meant that managers from smaller warehouses would have an equivalent chance of being invited to complete the survey. Having decided on the sample Sarah needed an accurate listing of all those whose role involved training and all those who were line managers and she obtained this information from the payroll listing. This list formed the 'sampling frame'. When she glanced through the list she realised that she would need to do some more work as she noticed the names of people whom she

Figure 9.3 The sample selection process

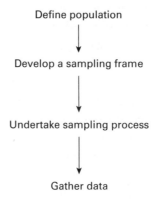

Define population

↓

Develop a sampling frame

↓

Undertake sampling process

↓

Gather data

knew to be on long-term sick leave. Sarah then had to decide whether these people should remain within the sampling frame.

Sarah faced a different set of sampling issues when considering getting data from other charities. Here there was very little chance that she could undertake a randomised probability sample; she would need to make a deliberate choice of which organisations to approach. This is known as a non-probability sample (which was discussed in Chapter 7). As this case illustration demonstrates, even the simplest situation involves decisions: there are no hard-and-fast 'rules' about sample size and selection; your judgement will be needed and you will need to justify your decisions in the methods chapter or section of your report. The process of sample selection is illustrated as Figure 9.3. When reading the research of others, it is worth critically evaluating their approach to sample selection and sample size, as well as being prepared to discuss the benefits but also the limitations of the approach that you have taken for any sample you select as part of your project.

Sample selection methods

Simple random sampling

This is the most basic type of probability sample, which should eliminate the possibility of undue bias within your group of respondents in terms of their general characteristics. This approach requires the development of an accurate sampling frame and then the use of a mathematically random procedure (usually the use of published random number tables) to select the elements (the respondents) from the sampling frame. Random number tables are published in many statistical textbooks and are also easily available on the internet (see, for example, http://www.randomnumbergenerator.com; http://www.graphpad.com/quickcalcs/randomN1.cfm; http://stattrek.com/Tables/Random.aspx). Begin the sampling process by giving each potential respondent (all the cases in the sampling frame) a number – the first is 0, the next is 1 and so on. It is important to have as many random numbers as there are cases (elements) in your frame. Go to the random number tables and choose a number at random. This is the first selection for your sample and you can read off more random numbers in a systematic and regular way (this can be along the rows of the sheet of numbers; every fifth number; etc) until you have chosen the number of respondents you require. This approach does not guarantee a perfect representation of the population, but it does mean that you will be close to it. In addition, it is possible (see Chapter 10) to calculate the level of confidence, or probability of the sample being inaccurate. However, having used a random approach it is very important that you actually deliver your survey to every respondent represented by the random numbers – hence the importance of an accurate sampling frame. Also remember that every non-respondent diminishes how representative your sample can be considered to be.

Systematic sampling

This approach also requires numbering of all the elements or cases in your sampling frame. However, instead of using a randomised approach you determine a set sampling interval or ratio. So, for a 10 per cent sampling ratio, you would choose one respondent randomly and then 'count down' one in every ten cases. While this might seem easier than the random number approach it is important to remember that you may not achieve a random sample if the sampling frame (for example, the listing from an HR information system) is itself organised in some form of pattern or cycle; perhaps by grade or by department or even alphabetically.

Stratified sampling

With this approach the sampling frame itself is divided into sub-populations (perhaps by department, or by grade, or by age group) and you then draw a random sample from each one. This approach may be particularly useful when one of the sub-populations is quite small and so could be missed by a simple random or stratified approach.

Cluster sampling

Here you identify sample clusters (units) from the overall population and then you draw a random or a systematic sample from within each of your clusters. This multi-stage approach is often cheaper and easier than a simple random approach when the population is very dispersed and difficult to access. However, each stage in the clustering and selection process introduces sampling errors and so limits the reliability of the data.

Survey choice or design

Surveys are a very popular method within HR research. Sometimes they are adopted because it is felt it will be easier and quicker than undertaking interviews. In reality, however, surveys are equally challenging. Survey instruments that are valid and reliable are difficult to construct. Poorly designed surveys, which have limited validity and reliability, mean that your data will be very difficult to analyse and the quality of your findings will be diminished. If you decide to pursue a cross-sectional survey within your research design you might be well-advised to find out what instruments have been used by other researchers in your area and to consider using a pre-validated instrument or scale (Table 9.4 provides examples of pre-validated scales frequently used in HRM and

Table 9.4 Examples of pre-validated scales used in HRM and organisational behaviour research

What is Being Measured?	How Many Items Does the Scale Have?	Reference (or Where Can I Find It?)
High Performance Work Systems (Assessed by Employees and Managers)	21	Takeuchi, R, Lepak, DP, Wang, H and Takeuchi, K (2007) An empirical examination of the mechanisms mediating between high-performance work systems and the performance of Japanese organisations, *Journal of Applied Psychology*, **92**, pp 1069–83
HR Attributions (Employee Attributions of the 'Why' of HR Practices)	25	Nishii, L, Lepak, DP and Schneider, B (2008) Employee attributions of the 'why' of HR practices: Their effects on employee attitudes and behaviors, and customer satisfaction, *Personnel Psychology*, **61**, pp 503–45
Perceived Organisational Support	36 (short version: 16)	Eisenberger, R, Huntington, R, Hutchison, S and Sowa, D (1986) Perceived organizational support, *Journal of Applied Psychology*, **71**, pp 500–507
Employee Commitment to the Organisation (Affective, Continuance, Normative)	19	Meyer, JP and Allen, NJ (1997) *Commitment in the Workplace: Theory, research, and application*, Sage, Thousand Oaks, CA
Psychological Contract	80 (employees and employers)	Rousseau, DM (2000) *Psychological Contract Inventory. Technical Report*, Carnegie Mellon University, Pittsburgh, PA
Quality of Working Life	23	Easton, S and Van Laar, DL (2012) User manual of the work-related quality of life scale (WRQoL), University of Portsmouth, Portsmouth, UK
Employee Engagement	17	Schaufeli, WB and Bakker, AB (2003) UWES – Utrecht Work Engagement Scale: test manual. Unpublished manuscript, Department of Psychology, Utrecht University [Online] www.schaufeli.com
Burnout	22	Maslach, C, Jackson, SE and Leiter, MP (1996) *Maslach Burnout Inventory*, 3rd edn, Consulting Psychologists Press, Palo Alto, CA

organisational behaviour research). However, if like many students, you and/or your organisation have decided that you should design your own survey instrument then it is important to keep in mind some important features of effective questionnaire design. There are two main 'golden rules' for survey design: the first is to **maintain clarity** and the second is to **keep the respondent's perspective in mind** (Neuman, 2014).

Survey strategy

Before launching into the design of the survey it is important to clarify key issues. First, what is the purpose of your survey? What are your research objectives or questions and what important variables do you need to examine? Do you intend to compare the data you gather with data from other surveys? If so, you must carefully identify the basis on which the data in the other survey(s) was gathered. What form of analysis will you hope to achieve? If you want to test the relationships between different variables then you must ensure that your questions allow you to do this. How will non-responses to some of your questions impact on the subsequent analysis?

Question structure

This part of the thinking and decision process involves considering a range of issues such as the question format and the method of response. Although paper-based surveys are used in HR projects they are increasingly being replaced by surveys distributed by e-mail or hosted on a web page. Do you want respondents to 'click' boxes, circle numbers or make some other form of response? Will respondents be asked to make one choice from a range of options? Will they make a choice somewhere between two dichotomous ends of a 'scale'? Is some form of ranking of alternatives going to be appropriate? These are crucial decisions, which will influence the success of your analysis process and the implications of these are outlined next (Robson and McCartan, 2016; Collis and Hussey, 2013; Gill and Johnson, 2010).

Open versus closed questions?

The issues around the use of open questions have been considered in chapters 7 and 8. Although surveys will mainly use different forms of closed questions to be analysed quantitatively, a few open questions are sometimes included. This enables people to clarify their answers, provide additional detail and show the logic, or thinking process, underpinning different choices. Subsequent analysis requires thought, however, and 'statistics' will not be possible, because this is a form of qualitative data. Closed questions, by contrast offer a range of advantages. They are easier and quicker for a respondent to 'tackle'; answers will be unambiguous and can be more easily compared. It is also possible to repeat the survey at another time or with another research population. However, there are also disadvantages with closed questions. It is possible that by providing a 'menu' of answers in your survey instrument you are suggesting things to people that they would not have otherwise thought of (but may now choose). Also, respondents with no knowledge or opinion may still opt to 'choose an answer' or become frustrated that the answer they would like to give is not provided as one of the choices. A further difficulty is that there is no check as to the level of understanding of the question by the respondent, and simplistic choices may be 'forced'. Respondents may also answer by chance in order to finish answering the questionnaire quickly, which clearly would lead to incorrect findings. In order to avoid some of the limitations of closed-answer questionnaires, and the potential risks of common method bias (that is, the bias resulting from collecting data using only one method – surveys, in this case), Podsakoff *et al* (2003) have advanced several procedural remedies for questionnaire design, as well as statistical techniques to help identify possible bias. These are too detailed for the purpose of this textbook, but if you decide to design new large surveys in organisational settings, we recommend reading Podsakoff *et al*'s (2003) paper.

Decisions about the form of questions in a survey are crucial as they impact on what you can do with the data once the surveys have been returned. The material that follows describes the main options. Through the use of a scenario of trying to find out about management training and development, the different approaches to formulating questions are shown below.

Nominal scale data

Sometimes called category scales, these relate to data that describe things and allow you to classify responses into different groupings. Questions that ask respondents whether they are male or female, or which department they work in allow you to count 'how many' there are. Data in categories like these have no 'arithmetic value' (you cannot calculate the average gender, for example) but they are very useful. If you were researching into management training and development you could compare the proportion of women who have attended a management training course in the last 12 months with the proportion of men, or you could compare the proportion of people from different ethnic groups who have attended a management training course. The inclusion of these 'biographical' or 'situational' variables within a survey, therefore, allows for a range of comparisons to be made. As you start devising your questionnaire think about the nominal categories you will need to include.

Ordinal scale data

This is an approach that involves inviting responses to reflect a degree of **ordering**. Different points on the 'scale' show greater or lesser amounts of the phenomena, relative to other points on it. A question in a survey asking about the level of satisfaction with the training someone had received might range from 1 = low level of satisfaction; 2 = fairly satisfied; 3 = satisfied; 4 = very satisfied. Another approach to ordinal scale data is to ask respondents to 'rank' a set of attributes from the most preferred to their least preferred. For example, ordering the importance of attributes (eg participative activities; clarity of communication by the trainer; learning environment; quality of hand-outs) that respondents feel contribute to their satisfaction with management training programmes. Again, however, other than counting the numbers of responses, and establishing the 'order', such responses will not enable you to undertake many calculations or perform statistical tests as there is no clear distance between the points on the scale. What is the distance between 'fairly satisfied' and 'satisfied', for example, and would every respondent understand the distance in the same way?

Interval scale data

Questions utilising interval scales are similar to ordinal scales but the distance between the points is known and the intervals represent equal quantities. Measures of IQ that are calculated from most intelligence tests, for example, work on the basis of '100' as the norm and other points indicating the distance of the score from the average. As such you cannot achieve an IQ of zero but the distance between two people with an IQ of 85 and 100 is known to be the same as the distance between two people with an IQ of 100 and 115. The **Likert scale** is a well-known example of an interval scale:

I felt more confident in my management ability after the training.

Strongly agree						Strongly disagree
7	6	5	4	3	2	1

This example shows that an interval scale does not have a 'zero'; you cannot go lower than '1'. For this reason, statisticians are uncomfortable with calculations (such as averaging) being performed. However, you are likely to find research that does utilise mathematical processes on interval scale data in HRM research. In fact, one recurring methodological question is whether parametric data analysis techniques (more about this in Chapter 10) are appropriate and/or acceptable for these Likert scale data. Likert scales of five or more points have often been considered a good approximation to ratio scale data (Harpe, 2015). When examining constructs such as burnout, job satisfaction and organisational commitment, researchers are normally evaluating the data at the group level, where each aggregate measure (perhaps the mean) is based on many individual responses (eg samples of 100, 500 or 1000 respondents). In these cases, the original Likert scale item begins to take on properties that resemble an interval scale at the aggregate level (Harpe, 2015). This is why most studies involving survey data in HRM, published in highly reputable journals, will be using complex (parametric) inferential statistics with data collected via Likert scales of five or more points (see the examples of the scales provided on Table 9.4).

Ratio scale data

These data represent the highest level of precision. A ratio scale does have a zero (for example, height, weight, time) and so it is possible to say that something lasts for twice as long or costs three times as much. However, the nature of research questions underpinning many HR surveys, particularly in organisational enquiries, tends to mean that ratio scale questions are quite rare.

Activity 9.2

Questionnaire design

Extracts from: CIPD (2009) Coaching at the sharp end: Developing and supporting the line manager as coach [Online] http://www.cipd.co.uk/hr-resources/practical-tools/developing-line-manager-coaching.aspx Reproduced with permission.

Questions about you

1 Are you:
- Male ☐
- Female ☐

2 Your age range:
- Under 25 ☐
- 25–34 ☐
- 35–44 ☐
- 45–54 ☐
- 55–64 ☐
- over 64 ☐

3 How many people directly report to you? ____

4 Which best reflects your level in the organisation hierarchy?
- First line manager ☐
- Middle manager ☐
- Top level/Board manager ☐

Questions about training and support

In an ideal world what would be helpful to help you improve the way you manage your people?

Please choose the appropriate response for each item:

5 In-house training course.

Very helpful	Helpful	Not very helpful	Not helpful
4	3	3	1
☐	☐	☐	☐

6 External training course.

Very helpful	Helpful	Not very helpful	Not helpful
4	3	2	1
☐	☐	☐	☐

7 Being given space to learn by trial and error.

Very helpful	Helpful	Not very helpful	Not helpful
4	3	2	1
☐	☐	☐	☐

8 Advice and guidance from a senior manager/mentor.

Very helpful	Helpful	Not very helpful	Not helpful
4	3	2	1
☐	☐	☐	☐

9 One-to-one coaching from my manager.

Very helpful	Helpful	Not very helpful	Not helpful
4	3	2	1
☐	☐	☐	☐

Questions about the people you manage

Please select the number that best describes your level of agreement regarding the people you manage.

Please choose the appropriate response for each item:

10 I admire their professional skills.

Strongly agree						Strongly disagree
1	2	3	4	5	6	7
☐	☐	☐	☐	☐	☐	☐

11 I respect their knowledge and competence on the job.

Strongly agree						Strongly disagree
1	2	3	4	5	6	7
☐	☐	☐	☐	☐	☐	☐

12 I work for them beyond what is specified in my job description.

Strongly agree						Strongly disagree
1	2	3	4	5	6	7
☐	☐	☐	☐	☐	☐	☐

13 I am willing to apply extra effort to further their interests.

Strongly agree						Strongly disagree
1	2	3	4	5	6	7
☐	☐	☐	☐	☐	☐	☐

14 I do not mind working hard for them.

Strongly agree						Strongly disagree
1	2	3	4	5	6	7
☐	☐	☐	☐	☐	☐	☐

15 I am impressed with their knowledge of the job.

Strongly agree						Strongly disagree
1	2	3	4	5	6	7
☐	☐	☐	☐	☐	☐	☐

Questions about you

Please choose the number that best describes your level of agreement to each statement.

Please choose the appropriate response for each item:

16 I can remain calm when facing difficulties in my job because I can rely on my abilities.

Completely true					Not at all true
1	2	3	4	5	6
☐	☐	☐	☐	☐	☐

17 When I am confronted with a problem in my job I can usually find several solutions.

Completely true					Not at all true
1	2	3	4	5	6
☐	☐	☐	☐	☐	☐

18 Whatever comes my way in my job I can usually handle it.

Completely true					Not at all true
1	2	3	4	5	6
☐	☐	☐	☐	☐	☐

19 My past experiences in my job have prepared me well for my occupational future.

Completely true					Not at all true
1	2	3	4	5	6
☐	☐	☐	☐	☐	☐

20 I meet the goals that I set for myself in my job.

Completely true					Not at all true
1	2	3	4	5	6
☐	☐	☐	☐	☐	☐

21 I feel prepared for most of the demands in my job.

Completely true					Not at all true
1	2	3	4	5	6
☐	☐	☐	☐	☐	☐

Discussion questions

1 Study the extracts from this questionnaire and identify which questions use nominal, ordinal, interval or ratio scale.

2 Critically evaluate the usefulness of the data that would be gathered from the questions shown in this extract from the survey.

Feedback notes

You should have identified that gender (question 1) and one's hierarchical position in the organisation (question 4) use a nominal scale that records characteristics of different respondents. Although it is not possible to perform 'statistics' on these types of questions they can be useful in assessing whether respondents in one category have responded in a greater or lesser way to subsequent questions. As such the variables in these categories are 'independent' and it may be possible to see if there is some form of relationship with other 'dependent' variables (such as remaining calm in my job). Question 3 provides for ratio data where people can put the exact number of people in their team. Questions 5–9 use an ordinal scale, as well as the age categories provided, where an order can be easily established. There is some degree of ordering but the 'distance' between each of the points within the order is not quantified and is not necessarily regular. Although these questions have the potential to yield interesting information, the extent to which data from this survey can be analysed, beyond descriptions of the frequency with which different categories were chosen, is somewhat limited. To establish interval scales would require a more obvious numbering scale visually representing equivalent distances between each point, something that occurs from question 10 onwards.

You may also have noticed that on some occasions a four-point scale is used, on other occasions a six-point scale appears and then sometimes a seven-point scale has been included. Different questions are also associated with scales of different length and so direct comparisons between the responses to these different items will not be meaningful.

This extract demonstrates how the question design process impacts upon the subsequent opportunities for analysis of the data. Careful planning is necessary with survey design. This involves clarifying what analysis will be required to answer the research questions or achieving the research objectives in order to ensure that the questions, and their scales, are appropriate and effective.

Survey design

The next stage in the survey process involves the design of the questionnaire itself. It is important to consider its length; structure; the order of the questions; the layout; and the method of administration (telephone, post, e-mail, online, etc). A summary of the main features of appropriate survey design are shown as Table 9.5.

Web-based surveys

Although many survey instruments are distributed and completed using a paper-based format you may prefer to use some form of electronic method of distributing your survey. You could attach your survey to an e-mail that is sent to potential respondents. The idea here is that the respondent opens the attachment and completes the survey before sending it back, often using the 'reply' command, to its originator. Here it is vital that those receiving the e-mail know what is expected and know how to send the completed survey (rather than the blank original attachment) back to the researcher. In addition, there are implications for anonymity as the e-mail carrying the completed questionnaire as an attachment can be traced to a named individual.

Table 9.5 Effective survey design

Initial request/ instructions	• Explain the purpose to all participants (a covering letter or e-mail is often used). Ensure that all requirements for informed consent are met. • Establish the timescale, processes for return, and confidentiality/ anonymity arrangements.
Layout	• Ensure the questionnaire looks neat and attractive and is a reasonable page length. • It must be easy to read with clear instructions. • Provide enough space and clear instructions for respondents to mark their answer. • Establish a logical order for the questions. • Use a numbering or sub-lettering system to show groupings of questions.
Questions	• Begin with 'warm-up' questions. • Keep the questions as simple as possible. • Check that all questions are relevant – ask 'need to know' rather than 'nice to know' questions. Be clear about what the objective of each question is in relation to your research questions. • Avoid jargon, specialist language, slang or abbreviations. • Phrase each question so that only one meaning is possible. • Ensure the language of your questions is not 'emotionally loaded'. • Check that there are no leading questions. • Edit out any 'double negatives' from the questions. • Utilise 'filter' questions where some questions may not be relevant for all respondents.
Final thanks/ return arrangements	• Thank respondents for taking the time to complete your survey. • Establish the return arrangements clearly. • Do not commit to more feedback after the research than you are sure you can provide.

(Collis and Hussey, 2013; Neuman, 2014; Robson and McCartan, 2016; Lee and Lings, 2008)

It is important that you are clear about the arrangement you will make to save completed questionnaires separately and delete evidence of the name of the sender.

An increasingly popular approach, which overcomes many of these disadvantages, is to design and use a web-based questionnaire. Here the survey is hosted on a web page that respondents access through a hyperlink. Anonymity is easier to manage and the survey software will also gather together the data from all the responses into some form of spreadsheet. The software underpinning web-based questionnaires is not difficult to use and a number of commercial organisations can provide it at a charge that varies with the number of questions to be asked; the time that the survey is to be 'live'; and the number of respondents that are anticipated (see, for example, http://www.surveymonkey.com; https://www.qualtrics.com/uk/).

The survey design principles outlined in Table 9.5 are equally applicable to surveys distributed electronically but Table 9.6 highlights some additional issues that should be considered if using a web-based survey design.

Survey piloting

Survey design is a complex process and it is easy to become so absorbed in it that potential errors are not picked up. However, if your survey has inappropriate features or questions, then the data that it generates will be of limited value. For all research

Table 9.6 Web-based survey design

General layout and features	• Begin the survey with a welcome screen that will motivate the respondent to proceed to the first page.
	• Discuss the conditions of anonymity and confidentiality, and present a box that respondents need to tick in order to start replying to the survey.
	• Only use colour as a visual cue to simplify the survey instrument – don't get too 'carried away'.
	• Provide clear instructions and consider a 'help button' for clarifications.
	• Avoid pop-ups – these distract and annoy respondents.
	• End the survey with a thank you note.
	• At the end you may also provide respondents with an e-mail address that respondents can use to provide feedback or comments, or to contact the institutional review board that approved the research.
	• You may also want to inform respondents about how to access the results of the survey.
Page/screen features	• Use hyperlinks if necessary to add help or additional information without adding to the apparent length of the survey.
	• Pre-program the survey to check for errors/validate responses (eg if input items do not add up to the required 100 per cent).
	• Pre-program a 'skip pattern': for example, a response of 'no' means to go to a later question.
	• Only have a few questions on each screen – too much scrolling can be a burden to respondents and they may quit your survey without completing it.
	• There is little agreement about the optimal length of a web-based survey, but in general a shorter questionnaire results in a higher response rate and a smaller number of respondents 'give up' in the middle.
	• Use a progress box, like the one presented on Figure 9.4.

(*continued*)

Table 9.6 (Continued)

Buttons/check boxes	• Remember that the 'radio button' size does not change even when the font size of the question changes.
	• Radio buttons are best used for 'select only one' options for mutually exclusive items.
	• Avoid 'default-filled' radio buttons as respondents may not answer the question but a response would automatically be recorded.
	• Too many 'check box' options for each question can be confusing. Consider using a simple matrix question instead (see Table 9.7 for an example).
	• Use 'check all that apply' as an instruction sparingly as respondents may themselves get 'carried away'.
Drop-down boxes	• Drop-down boxes require three clicks whereas other responses require only one – this means three times the opportunity for error!
	• Avoid the use of drop-down boxes where multiple selections are permitted (when only one option is possible, but there are many possible finite choices, like when asking about respondents' citizenship, drop-down boxes may be appropriate).
Text input options	• Make sure that the size of the box is appropriate for the information you require.
Confidentiality/ anonymity	• Consider a PIN to limit access to authorised users and inhibit anyone from completing the survey more than once.
	• Use password protected web survey software to ensure data security and avoid unlimited access.

(Cobanoglu *et al*, 2001; Couper, 2008; Ritter and Sue, 2007)

projects it is strongly advisable to pilot any survey, prior to its distribution, in order to answer the following questions (see Figure 9.5) (Robson and McCartan, 2016; Saunders, Lewis and Thornhill, 2019):

- Is the content of the questions appropriate for the research questions? Have any important variables been omitted? Will the questions that have been asked provide the information that is sought (validity)?
- How long does it take to complete the survey? How acceptable would the length of the survey be to the respondents? Are the instructions clear?
- Are all the questions clear and unambiguous?
- Are any questions likely to be too sensitive for the respondent group?
- How appropriate is the layout of the questionnaire?
- How easy was it for respondents to follow the instructions and submit their answers?

Table 9.7 Example of a simple matrix structure for web-based survey questions

Please select the number which best describes your level of agreement to these statements: Please choose the appropriate response for each item	1 Strongly agree	2	3	4	5	6	7 Strongly disagree
I feel a sense of loyalty to my organisation	O	O	O	O	O	O	O
I respect my manager	O	O	O	O	O	O	O
I am willing to work beyond what is specified in my job description	O	O	O	O	O	O	O
I am committed to my own personal development	O	O	O	O	O	O	O
I make suggestions for improvements in the way work is carried out in my department	O	O	O	O	O	O	O

Figure 9.4 Progress box

Progress

0%　　　　　　　　　　　　　　　　80%　100%

It will only be possible to answer all these questions if your pilot process incorporates a range of different people. It is a good idea to ask a 'subject expert' for his or her opinion of the strengths and weaknesses of your draft survey instrument first. Your project tutor, as a minimum, should have the opportunity to offer feedback. It is a requirement of many study centres that a tutor approve any data gathering instrument and this can form a useful stage in the survey design and piloting process. In addition, comments about the survey can be obtained from people who are similar to those in the respondent group. If your survey is web-enabled, you will also need to check that you know how to transfer the data to the software package you are going to use to analyse the data, and the piloting process is a useful way of checking this.

Case Example 9.3

Make or borrow?

Afrah was a student who was undertaking a course in the United Kingdom but wished to conduct comparative research for her dissertation involving some people working in a UK organisation and other people working in an organisation in her country of Kuwait. While undertaking a coursework assignment on knowledge management Afrah became intrigued by the concept of social capital: the extent to which relationships in an organisation underpin effective performance. The essence of social capital theory is that relationships are the key to success and Afrah was aware that work relationships in her country were more 'collectivist' than in the United Kingdom so she was keen to find out the extent to which differences in social capital would be found in the United Kingdom and Kuwait.

Afrah decided that a questionnaire approach would be most appropriate to examine social capital issues and she had to design a survey instrument to investigate the extent to which social capital in organisations is related to enhanced work performance by employees. The first challenge she faced was that there seemed to be very little consensus in the literature about the concept of social capital although there was general agreement that it involves networks and social relations between individuals and organisations, which promote trust, rapport and goodwill.

In the process of undertaking her literature review Afrah found that a set of questionnaire items relating to social capital in organisations had been developed and published (Ellinger *et al*, 2007) which measured individuals' perceptions of managerial behaviours that might represent 'organisational investments in social capital' and also came across some questionnaire items related with work-related performance (Babin and Boles, 1996).

Discussion questions

1   What advantages and disadvantages might there be for a research project that 'borrows' survey questions from another source?

2   What difficulties might you encounter in trying to obtain and use survey questions designed by another researcher or research institution?

3   What challenges would Afrah face when collecting questionnaire responses from two very different countries?

Feedback

Making use of survey questions that have already been developed and piloted by other researchers has many advantages but also some disadvantages. You may have identified the attraction of using 'proven' questions as a way of enhancing the level of reliability and validity of the survey instrument (assuming that your evaluation of the information about the survey instrument suggests that it does have a good level of validity). Validity and reliability are also the reasons why finding specific scales (like the ones presented in Table 9.4) would be recommendable. However, you might think that pre-existing questions might not be fully appropriate to the purposes of your research. In such situations you might choose to amend them, although this would mean that you could not be as sure of the 'statistical quality' of the amended items. You might also worry about issues of copyright permission and cost. Most published question-naire instruments are subject to copyright restrictions and it is necessary to obtain the permission of the publishers (for which there may be a cost or other conditions to be met). Research published in academic articles may well not carry the actual question-naire so it would be necessary to follow up on the contact details provided with the article and ask the author if you might have a copy and consider using some or all of their questions.

The third question raised here relates with the extent to which survey questions 'travel'. Cross-national research is becoming increasingly popular among HR students as interesting discussions occur about the extent to which traditional US or Western assumptions about people management issues apply in a straightforward way in other societies. The first issue to be faced is the need to translate questions from one language to another and many students have learned that translation is not as easy as it sounds; equivalent words may not be available in the 'second' language or they may be differ-ently understood (this issue is known as the problem of 'conceptual equivalence'). Therefore, a basic check of translation involves 'back translation'; you translate your questionnaire and then get an independent native speaker in the second language to translate it back into English and examine the similarity between the original and the back-translated version. For more information on issues and techniques of translation of standard measures for use in international research see Cha, Kim and Erlen (2007).

Administering surveys

The final set of decisions regarding the survey will relate to its distribution. Your objective is to ensure that the survey reaches all those in your sample in a timely way to maximise the chance that they will answer your questions and return the completed survey to you. The higher the level of non-response rate, the less reliable will be your findings. The main options for survey distribution are:

- postal, self-administered, questionnaire;
- delivered and collected, self-administered, questionnaire;
- structured telephone interview;
- structured face-to-face interview;
- e-mail questionnaire;
- web-based survey.

Table 9.8 indicates the key issues to be taken into account with each of these, as well as the advantages and disadvantages of each of them.

Collecting, organising and presenting quantitative data

Quantitative data has no value in its raw state; data need to be organised, analysed and presented. Data collection can be an anxious time. After expending effort to devise and pilot the best quality survey instrument that you are able to, once you

Table 9.8 Administering and delivering surveys

Method of Distribution	Key Issues	Advantages	Disadvantages
Postal, self-administered	• Pre-survey contact will enhance response rate • Covering letter • Reply-paid envelope • Follow up after one or two weeks to enhance response rate	• Cheap • Respondents possible across a wide geographical area within one country • Respondents can complete when convenient to them • Anonymity is possible • No interviewer bias	• Low response rate • Late returns • Conditions for completion are not controlled • Clarification of questions is not possible • Incomplete responses are more likely
Delivery and collection questionnaire	• Pre-survey contact and permissions on the basis of informed consent are necessary • Personal explanation of purpose of survey • Respondents can seal their completed survey and place it themselves in a collection box	• Good response rate is possible • Respondents slightly more involved • Anonymity is 'visible' • Clarification of a question is possible • Controlled conditions for survey completion	• Sample restricted to those that can attend at the given time and place • 'Reluctant' respondents may make more extreme responses • Organisational authorisation may be difficult to achieve
Telephone interview	• Initial contact with respondent may mean calling back at a more convenient time • Clear explanation of the purpose of the study is required • Decisions about how many calls to each respondent required	• Survey can be completed in a shorter timeframe • Geographical limitations can be overcome but time zone issues must be taken into account • Clarification of questions is possible	• Low response rate • Some interviewer bias may occur • No scope for recording non-verbal information
Face-to-face interviews	• Competence of interviewer is important • Pre-survey contact necessary • Possible areas for probes must be clearly specified	• Good response rates • More probing of issues is possible	• Possibility of interviewer bias • Expense (time intensive) • Geographical constraints of reaching respondents

(continued)

Table 9.8 (Continued)

Method of Distribution	Key Issues	Advantages	Disadvantages
E-mail survey	• E-mail addresses of sample are required • Pre-survey contact enhances response rate • Covering message required • Attachments may not work if in a different software version • Arrangements for anonymity required • Follow-up message to enhance response rate	• Speed of transmission • No geographical or time zone limits • No interviewer bias • Respondents can complete at a time suitable for them	• Respondent concerns about anonymity • Different software can affect display of images and the format of questionnaire • Poor response rate • Lost data (particularly attachments) • Potential for respondents to edit the questionnaire
Web-based surveys	• Establish a website with online questionnaire • Explain purpose and provide instructions for completion (replaces covering letter) • Hyperlinks need to be operational	• Questionnaire cannot be altered • Possible to monitor 'hit rate' on the site over the period in which the survey is 'live' • No interviewer bias • More (but not full) control over image and format of questionnaire	• Unclear sample unless respondents are e-mailed the link to the website • Those without access to the technology cannot be included • Security needs to be built into the web system to stop one person making multiple responses

(Neuman, 2014; Saunders, Lewis and Thornhill, 2019)

send it to your planned respondents you lose control of the process; once it leaves you it is impossible to know whether and how people will respond to your questions. However, once the data begin to arrive back with you it is an exciting time – at last you can start to make sense of the information to answer your research questions.

As with all stages of any research project, a systematic approach is necessary. The first challenge that you may face is one of volume. A first-time researcher, faced with

Figure 9.5 Stages in survey design and distribution

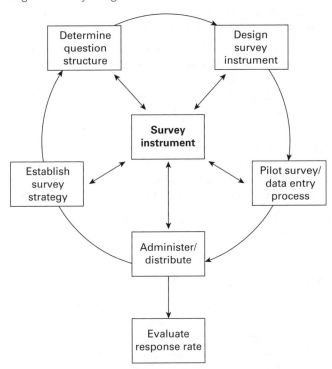

100 returned questionnaires and an impending deadline, can feel very daunted about the prospect of manipulating the data in order to answer their research questions. You will need to describe the frequency of responses for different variables within your survey and for this a spreadsheet package (most HR students use Excel) may be sufficient. Most students undertaking a CIPD business investigation or report (but not those working at Masters level) will find that this will suffice. However, if you wish to analyse the data at a deeper level (see Chapter 10) then the use of statistical software like SPSS (Statistical Package for Social Sciences), Stata or Matlab will be preferable. In this book, we will provide most examples from SPSS as it is relatively easy to use and is appropriate to address the statistical demands of research projects in HRM. Such statistical software should be available for student access at your study centre. Your project tutor or supervisor will be able to clarify this for you.

Record keeping

In order to evaluate the information provided from your survey it is important that you keep a record of non-responses. This should include:

- Number of non-located responses – the number of respondents in your sampling frame who could not be found (for example, a postal questionnaire which was 'returned to sender' or an e-mail survey that 'bounced back').

- Number of non-contact responses – the number of respondents who were perpetually out (in a telephone survey) or were away during the time of the survey (postal, e-mail or interview).

- Number of ineligible responses – those respondents who, as a result of any errors in your sampling frame, fall outside your sampling criteria (joined the organisation too recently, work in a non-sampled department, etc).

- Number of 'refusals' – those who were reached but would not participate in the survey. This will allow you to calculate the response rate to your survey, which would be particularly relevant when you send the link to a web-based questionnaire to all employees in one organisation. It will allow you to say whether you had a response rate of 32 per cent, 55 per cent, 71 per cent and so on.

- The number of incomplete responses – those who got partway through your survey but did not complete it fully. You need to decide at a later stage whether you keep surveys with missing data in your sample or whether you remove them from the sample. All of these processes need to be recorded.

For small-scale surveys (a sample size of fewer than 200) a simple 'tally sheet' will probably be sufficient.

Establishing a coding structure

This stage is where you work out how you will organise the software to record the different responses. Most software packages are organised in the same initial format as a simple spreadsheet, whereby the variables within your questionnaire are recorded in columns, and each respondent's responses are contained within a row (see the rows in Figure 9.7). For each reply option on your survey instrument there must be a discrete code. This will take a numerical form. The first item to code is the identity of the questionnaire response (not the individual). This is your 'audit trail' and ensures that you can identify each questionnaire in the future and, if necessary, return to check the data it contains. This is illustrated in Figure 9.6 and Table 9.9.

Data entry

Although rather laborious, once the coding structure is established the process of data entry is relatively quick. With web-based surveys the software will automatically provide the responses in a spreadsheet form although you may find that you need to re-label the columns and cells. Manual data entry is also not difficult although it can be boring and it is important to stay alert to ensure an accurate process.

It is a good idea to establish the coding structure for your questionnaire before you pilot it as the very activity of coding can highlight potential problems. You can also pilot the data entry process with the responses from your pilot study, to establish any potential problems. There are a variety of methods of data entry. The most common for many student projects is for a manual process but software packages will allow for structured interview data to be entered on a direct basis from a personal computer and some organisations have facilities for optical mark reading of questionnaire responses.

Figure 9.6 Illustrative survey questions

1. Are you male or female?

☐ Male   ☐ Female

2. What is your age?

☐ Under 26   ☐ 26–35   ☐ 36–45   ☐ 46–55   ☐ 56 or more
  years   years   years   years   years

3. How long have you worked for your organisation?

☐ Less than 1   ☐ 1–5   ☐ 6–10   ☐ More than
  year   years   years   10 years

Please tick the most appropriate box to answer these questions:

	A lot	Somewhat	Only a little	Not at all
4. To what extent do you trust your immediate line manager to look after your best interests?	☐	☐	☐	☐
5. To what extent do you trust your senior management to look after your best interests?	☐	☐	☐	☐
6. In general, would you say you trust your company or organisation?	☐	☐	☐	☐

	Yes – definitely	Yes – probably	No – probably not	Not at all
7. Do you feel you are fairly paid for the work you do?	☐	☐	☐	☐
8. Overall, do you feel you are rewarded fairly compared with other people doing similar jobs to you?	☐	☐	☐	☐

Clean the dataset

When your data have been entered it is important to evaluate the accuracy of the process. It is extremely rare that no errors will have occurred and it is important to identify them and correct them at the start of the data presentation and analysis process. First, you should carry out a visual check of the data to look for 'impossible' codes. A coding of '6' when there are only four attributes, for example, is an indicator that the responses for that questionnaire need to be checked again. Second, it is worthwhile choosing a random sample of questionnaires and checking the entries for them. If there are too many errors in your sample, then the whole dataset should be checked again. Table 9.10 provides an example of common data entry errors.

Present the data

Having entered and cleaned the data, the final stage in this part of the process is to describe and summarise the information using tables and/or charts. Both tables and charts (most often a judicious combination of the two) will provide you with

Table 9.9 Illustrative coding structure

Column	Variable Name	Codes
A	Questionnaire ID	Questionnaire ID (start at 001)
B	Q1 – Gender	1 = Male 2 = Female 9 = non-response
C	Q2 – Age	1 = under 26 years 2 = 26–35 years 3 = 36–45 years 4 = 46–55 years 5 = 56 or more years 9 = non-response
D	Q3 – Length of service	1 = less than 1 year 2 = 1–5 years 3 = 6–10 years 4 = more than 10 years 9 = non-response
E	Q4 – Immediate manager trust	3 = a lot 2 = somewhat 1 = only a little 0 = not at all 9 = non-response
F	Q5 – Senior management trust	3 = a lot 2 = somewhat 1 = only a little 0 = not at all 9 = non-response
G	Q6 – Organisational trust	3 = a lot 2 = somewhat 1 = only a little 0 = not at all 9 = non-response
H	Q7 – Job pay fairness	3 = yes – definitely 2 = yes – probably 1 = no – probably not 0 = not at all 9 = non-response
I	Q8 – Comparative pay fairness	3 = yes – definitely 2 = yes – probably 1 = no – probably not 0 = not at all 9 = non-response

Table 9.10 Illustrative data entry errors

ID	Q1	Q2	Q3	Q4	Q5	Q6	Q7	Q8
1	1	2	4	2	3	3	2	2
2	1	3	3	2	3	2	2	1
3	2	5	3	2	3	3	2	2
4	2	4	3	0	1	2	1	1
5	1	4	2	3	2	1	2	2
6	9	4	1	0	1	0	1	2
7	1	3	2	2	3	2	2	3
8	1	2	2	2	3	2	2	3
9	2	1	(11)	2	2	1	1	2
10	2	9	4	1	1	2	1	2
11	1	2	3	1	2	3	2	1
12	2	2	3	1	2	2	2	1
13	1	2	2	1	2	3	2	1
14	2	2	2	1	3	2	3	(11)
15	(22)	5	2	1	1	2	2	2
16	1	4	2	0	0	0	(11)	1
(178)	1	4	1	9	9	0	2	2
18	1	1	9	1	2	1	2	2
19	1	(33)	2	2	3	3	2	2
20	1	1	3	2	3	2	2	3
21	2	1	3	2	2	3	2	1
22	2	2	2	2	1	2	2	2
23	(21)	5	2	3	2	1	1	2
24	2	3	2	3	2	2	2	2
25	1	4	1	3	2	3	2	2
26	1	2	2	2	3	2	3	2
27	1	9	2	2	2	2	2	1
28	9	1	2	2	1	2	2	2
29	2	2	2	9	2	1	1	2
30	1	1	3	2	1	2	2	2

some insight about possible associations between different variables. This process of **descriptive analysis**, therefore, transforms raw data into a form that makes it possible to understand and interpret them. Although charts look attractive it is important not to 'over-do it' with charts and diagrams. Use them sparingly to add value to the analysis and understanding process. The first stage of this is to describe the frequency of all the different attributes within the survey. If you plan to use SPSS for your data analysis, then you will find the data presentation tools are easy and effective to use. To help those who decide to stick with Excel the examples given below describe some of the actions you can take. These are written with the needs of absolute novices in mind: if you are nervous about numbers and nervous about Excel then read on. If you are confident and competent in these areas, then jump ahead to the next section of the chapter.

Data presentation using Excel

Organise your worksheet

Once you have 'cleaned your dataset' you will want to make it easier to use:

1 Label the columns by positioning the cursor in the column heading you wish to label. What you type in will be shown in the ribbon above the worksheet.

2 Select the column you wish to work with and use the find and replace tool at the top right of the screen to re-label variables expressed as numbers with an appropriate label (see Figure 9.7).

3 Label your worksheet by positioning the cursor over the tab at the bottom of the sheet and 'right clicking'. Then choose 'rename' and type in the label you would like to use.

4 Excel can seem frustrating if you have a lot of data or a lot of variables as you can lose sight of the labels for your columns and rows. To overcome this, use the 'freeze panes' command to make the column and row headings stay in view when you are scrolling down and across your dataset (see Figure 9.8). You will find this on the 'view' tab on the menu options at the top of your screen. Before you use the command, make sure you position your cursor underneath the top row and next to the first column of your data.

5 You can amend the row height (your data will seem less squashed!) by highlighting the data and then using the format button (part of 'cells' on the 'home' tab).

6 A quick and easy way to adjust the column width for your columns is to position your cursor at the top of the column you wish to alter (at its right hand limit) and double click. This will bring the column to fit the widest entry in that column (so don't bother with this until you have finished all your other labelling!).

Figure 9.7 Labelling columns

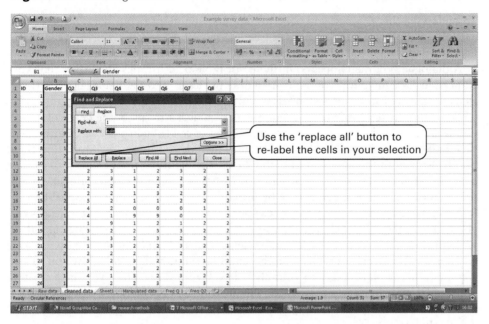

Figure 9.8 Freeze panes

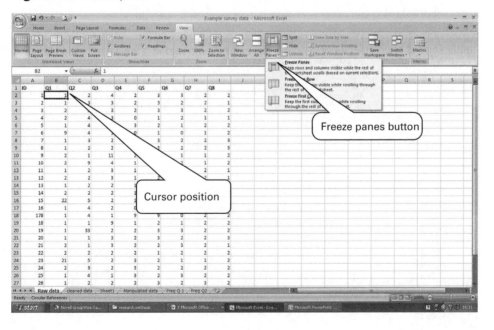

Present your data using tables and charts

To undertake this process, you need to 'flip' and summarise your data. For this you need to use the 'pivot table' command (see Figure 9.9). To generate a pivot table, highlight the data range you wish to include and use the 'insert' tab to find 'pivot table'.

A dialogue box then appears. In the pivot table field list, tick the boxes that you want to include in your pivot table. Also drag the items into the 'values box'. As long as your data are formed of text labels it will count the items for you (see Figure 9.10).

You can now tell Excel to calculate the percentages for you in the next column if you wish. Do this by using the '=' command in the cell to indicate a calculation and then highlight the first cell value you wish to include (b3 in this example) and then use the '/' symbol (divide by) and highlight the cell with the total count (b6) in this example. If you press return you will probably get a long decimal number, so tell Excel you want this as a percentage by using the 'number box' on the top ribbon.

Excel is quite good at charts too, once your data is nicely tabulated. To create a chart, you highlight the row labels and the associated columns you wish to include and then go to the insert tabs and choose from the range of charts available (see Figure 9.11).

There is also a very useful tool on the 'chart layout tab' that will allow you to ask Excel to add the percentages to your chart (see Figure 9.12). Once you have created your tables and charts it is easy to copy them and paste them into a Word file.

The most common forms of charts that may be useful to present a summary of your data include:

- pie charts, where percentage data is represented as a series of categories that are compared within a circle, which represents 100 per cent of all cases (see Figure 9.13);

Figure 9.9 Pivot table command in Excel

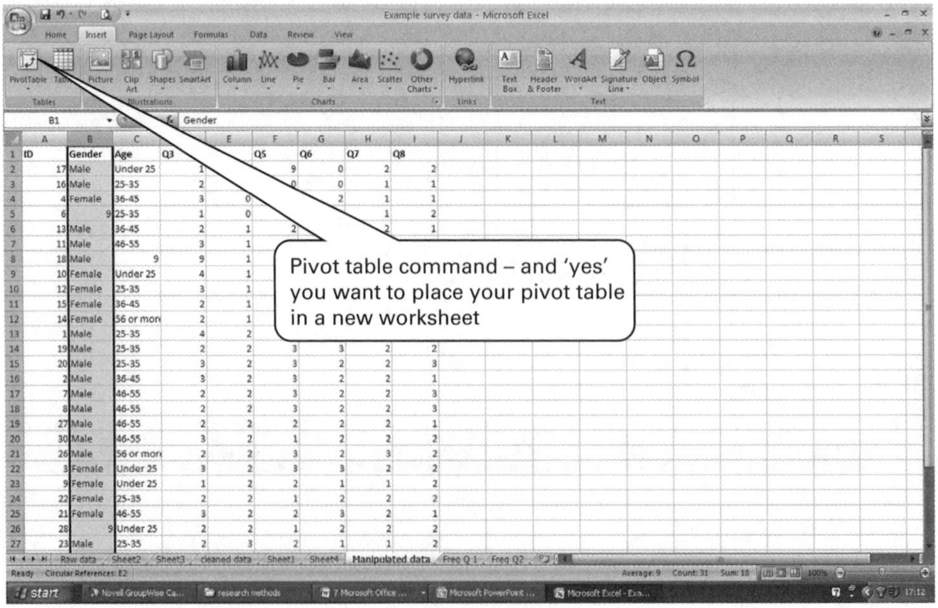

Figure 9.10 Selecting fields for your pivot table

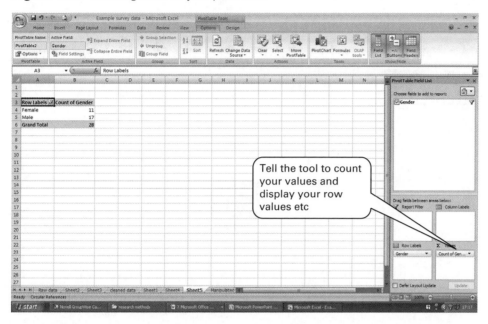

Figure 9.11 The charts options in Excel

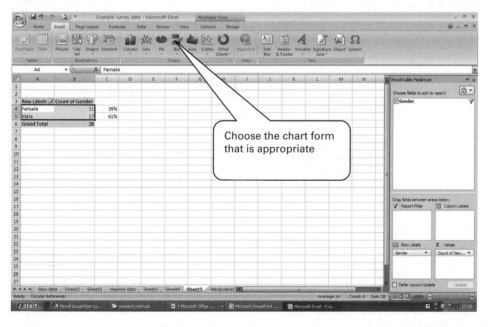

- bar charts, where the length or height of the bars (depending on whether they are presented on the horizontal or vertical axis) represents an appropriate number or percentage (see Figure 9.14).

Figure 9.12   Making use of the chart layout tab

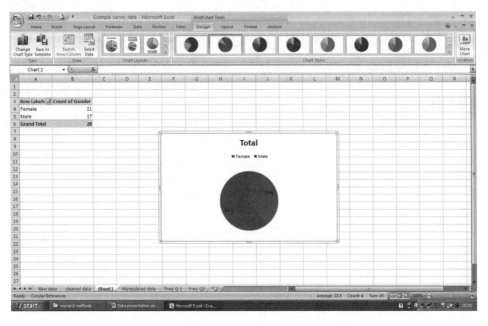

Figure 9.13   Example pie chart

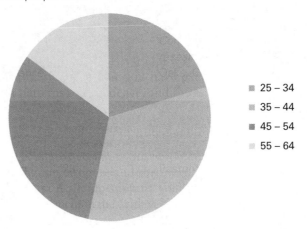

25 – 34
35 – 44
45 – 54
55 – 64

These methods of presentation are particularly appropriate for presenting nominal scale (category) data. Other forms of graph can demonstrate the relationship between two variables. A **line graph** can represent the relationship of one variable with time (the trend in pay rates for different types of staff is often represented in this way, for example). For interval scale data, **a histogram** is also an appropriate way of representing the data you have collected (see Figure 9.15).

Figure 9.14 Example bar chart

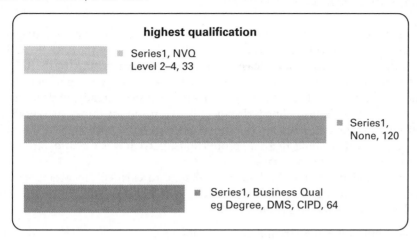

Figure 9.15 Example of a histogram

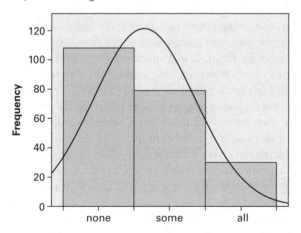

While a histogram looks similar to a bar chart, the regularity of the intervals means that the distribution of cases within the organisation can also be evaluated graphically and, where the intervals are the same, can be compared with the distribution in another sample group.

For most HR Management Research Reports, the use of summary tables and charts, rather than histograms, is likely to form the main approach to presenting data. It is important not to get too 'carried away' with the charting potential of software packages. For students undertaking a Masters qualification a fuller consideration of the data is likely to be required. There are occasions where charts can advance understanding and comparison, but used too frequently, with little more than a decorative purpose, they diminish rather than advance the persuasiveness of your research report.

First level data analysis

Describing the frequencies of different questionnaire responses is helpful in enabling you (and those who will assess your project) to make sense of the data. In addition, it is helpful to establish some measures by which you can compare the responses to different variables in a more concise way. The way that you approach this will depend on the type of data you have gathered. As noted already, with **nominal or ordinal data**, there is no defined 'distance' between the attributes of the variable. Therefore, inferential statistical operations are not viable although 'counting' the frequencies and describing these as **proportions, percentages or ratios** are possible and provide a means for comparison.

For **ratio and interval scale data** it is possible to calculate **measures of central tendency** (mean, mode and median) to assist comparisons between different variables. There are three forms of these:

- the **mode** is the most frequently occurring value;
- the **median** is the middle point of the range;
- the **mean** is the average value (calculated by adding all the values together and then dividing by the number of cases).

These can all be useful measures to help you make sense of the data that you have gathered. For example, you may have asked your respondents to indicate how many people directly report to them. A calculation of the mean may indicate that the 'average' number of direct reports is 38. This seems a very high figure and it may reflect a few respondents (referred to as 'outliers') who have indicated that they have over 200 direct reports. The median (middle point of the range) and mode (most frequently occurring response) are more likely to be helpful here. In such a situation you may find that the median is 8 direct reports and the mode (most frequently cited number) is 6 and this gives you a better 'overall picture' of the responses to your question.

If you are using Excel to store your data, you may be pleased to read that you do not have to create pivot tables to work out measures of central tendency – you can use the function command for this (see Figure 9.16). You can find this just above your dataset. You may, for example, wish to compare the mode (the most frequently occurring variable) for responses to a number of questions. To do this you take one question at a time: position the cursor at a suitable place (below the relevant column?), choose the function command and then choose 'mode' from the menu you are offered. Then highlight the range of values you wish to be included before pressing the OK or return button to see the value displayed where you left your cursor.

Another worthwhile characteristic to explore for single variables may be the spread or dispersion of the variables. This is interesting in its own right but also crucial to know about if you propose to do any data analysis along the lines outlined in Chapter 10. The calculation of an average length of service of 5.3 years for those who left an organisation during 2018 may mask the fact that one or two leavers had very long lengths of service and many others left with only a few months of employment with the organisation.

One way of calculating the dispersion of the data is by using the **range**, which is the distance between the lowest value and the highest. This is the simplest measure

Figure 9.16 Using the function command in Excel for simple procedures

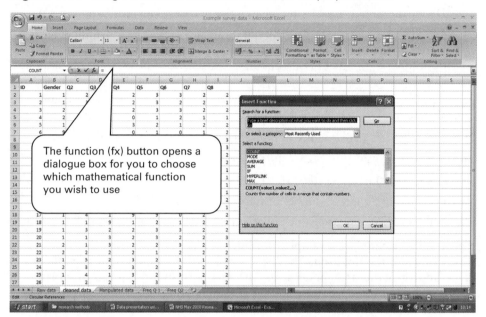

of 'spread' but it can be misleading (if only one person had 38 years of service and the rest had less than one year). A more informative way of assessing dispersion is to identify the point at which 25 per cent of the respondents (the distribution) have that 'score' or less and the point at which 75 per cent of the sample have that score or less. These are referred to as the 25th and 75th **percentiles**. The 50th percentile is the median (the middle point of the range). It would also be possible to divide your sample up into 10 percentile 'chunks', called deciles. A calculation of the 25th and 75th percentile, therefore, (or the 10th and 90th) may be more informative about the dispersion of the values than a simple calculation of the range. The most popular measure of dispersion that is derived from a calculation of percentiles within any sample is **standard deviation**. This is a measure of the average distance between all the values and the mean. The smaller the standard deviation, the more similar are the values within the distribution. Standard deviation is complex to calculate manually (see Figure 9.17) but is a common function of software and calculator programs and so can be undertaken easily enough. It is, however, not an appropriate function when applied to nominal scale data and should not really be used (although you may well see it used) with ordinal scale data.

Steps in calculating the standard deviation

1 Calculate the mean (sum of the cases, divided by the number of cases).
2 Subtract the mean from each score.
3 Square the resulting difference for each score.

4 Sum up the squared differences to get the sum of squares.

5 Divide the sum of squares by the number of cases. The result you get is the **variance**.

6 Compute the square root of the variance. This will give you the standard deviation.

Example

Employees' generic performance appraisal results (from 1 to 5 points):

Mean: 3+2+4+4+5+5+2+5+5+4 = 39/10 = 3.9

Sum of Squares: 0.81+3.61+0.01+0.01+1.21+1.21+3.61+1.21+1.21+0.01 = 12.9

Variance: Sum of Squares/Number of Cases = 12.9/10 = 1.29

Standard Deviation: Square Root of Variance = $\sqrt{1.29}$ = 1.14 points in PA results.

Figure 9.18 provides an example of a line graph that represents the distribution of responses to the question. The highest point of the graph represents the mean value and then the area underneath the line corresponds to the proportion of responses with a standard deviation more than (and less than) the central point. If your data approximate to an even 'bell curve' then it is likely that your responses fall within what is termed a 'normal distribution' (see Figure 9.18). This is worth knowing about if you plan to undertake any of the analysis processes outlined in Chapter 10.

   Assuming that you have some interval or ratio scale data, therefore, it is possible to calculate measures of central tendency and measures of dispersion as part of the analysis of your data and these calculations provide a useful start with making sense of your data. However, it is much more interesting to assess the relationship

Figure 9.17 Calculating the standard deviation

Participants	Performance Appraisal (PA) Results	PA Results – Mean	Squared (PA Results – Mean)
1	3	3 – 3.9 = –0.9	0.81
2	2	2 – 3.9 = –1.9	3.61
3	4	4 – 3.9 = 0.1	0.01
4	4	4 – 3.9 = 0.1	0.01
5	5	5 – 3.9 = 0.1	1.21
6	5	5 – 3.9 = 0.1	1.21
7	2	2 – 3.9 = –1.9	3.61
8	5	5 – 3.9 = 1.1	1.21
9	5	5 – 3.9 = 1.1	1.21
10	4	4 – 3.9 = 0.1	0.01

(Neuman 2014)

Figure 9.18 Example of a normal curve of distribution

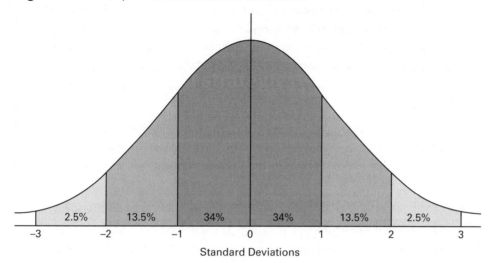

between different variables. This and other statistical tools that can be used are outlined in the next chapter.

CHECKLIST

- Quantitative data involves the measurement of variables that can be counted, described and compared.

- Quantitative data can be used as part of an inductive or deductive approach to research.

- In addition to surveys undertaken for a particular research purpose, quantitative data can be obtained from secondary sources, such as published surveys, which may be undertaken on a regular or an ad hoc basis.

- Effective sampling techniques are important if the data that are obtained are to be representative of the population being studied.

- The planning process for any survey must take into account the purpose of the research, the research questions, the advantages and disadvantages of different types of questions and the format in which responses are sought. Pre-validated scales are desirable for comparative purposes, but may not be applicable in all contexts. Response scales and structure will affect the forms of analysis that will be possible.

- A range of issues is relevant to the questionnaire design process. These include: the initial contact/request/instructions to respondents; the layout of the survey; the language of the questions; and the arrangements for return.

- Piloting the survey and the process of recording and organising the data (data entry) will enhance the quality of the questionnaire and the usefulness of the data it generates.

- Surveys can be undertaken in a range of ways. The main options are: postal, self-administered; delivered and collected; structured telephone interviews; structured face-to-face interviews; e-mail questionnaires; and web-based surveys.

- A coding structure, established in advance, enables data to be electronically organised and summarised.

- Following the initial data entry process it is important to 'clean' the data of any data-inputting errors.

- Data can be presented in the form of summary tables and charts. These include pie charts, bar charts, line graphs and histograms. Use charts sparingly to add value to the analysis and understanding process.

- Analytical processes for single variables include the consideration of frequencies, proportions, percentages and ratios. For some types of data, it is also possible to calculate measures of central tendency, such as the mean, median and mode, as well as the dispersion (range or standard deviation).

TEST YOURSELF

1 Quantitative data is the term used to describe:

   a All the data you include in your research report.

   b Charts and tables.

   c Statistical tests.

   d Data in the form of numbers and measures.

2 Which one of the following is the principal quantitative method of data capture in HR?

   a Focus groups.

   b Surveys.

   c Participant observation.

   d Discourse analysis.

3 Which one of the following scales is commonly used to measure opinions in a questionnaire?

   a Ranking scale.

   b Nominal questions.

   c Likert rating scale.

   d Open question.

4 Which of the following is NOT part of the sampling process?

   a Determining the sample frame.

   b Defining the research population.

   c Clarifying the research question.

   d Selecting an appropriate sampling technique.

5 A sampling frame is:

   a The different stages involved in survey design.

   b A list of all the people in the research population from whom the sample will be drawn.

   c A set of random numbers.

   d The structure of the questionnaire.

6 Which of the following is a type of probability sample?

   a Systematic random sample.

   b Snowball sample.

   c Convenience sample.

   d Purposive sample.

7 Which of the following is NOT a measure of central tendency?

   a Mode

   b Middle

   c Mean

   d Median

8 Which of the following is not a type of graph?

   a Box

   b Pie

   c Bar

   d Scatter

9 Name a software package for analysing quantitative data.

   a Atlas TI

   b Microsoft Word

   c SPSS

   d Microsoft Access

10 Which is the most comprehensive measure of dispersion?

   a Range

   b Standard deviation

   c Percentiles

   d Mean

 Review Questions

1 How clear are you about your research questions? How important will quantitative data be in answering them? Will this involve describing frequencies or undertaking a deeper level of analysis?

2 What depth of data analysis is required within the assessment criteria of your study centre for the qualification you are working towards?

Questions for reflection

This final part of the chapter enables you to reflect about your professional development and develop your skills and knowledge. This will enable you to build your confidence and credibility, track your learning, see your progress, and demonstrate your achievements.

Taking stock

1   What sources of quantitative data may already be available that might be relevant to your research questions? How can you go about accessing and evaluating them?

2   Who might you approach for help with the piloting of your questionnaire, and how might you make use of their feedback?

3   What software for data entry and analysis is available to you? What might you do to enhance your competence and confidence with using it?

Strengths and weaknesses

4   What experience do you have of survey design? What personal development areas are you aware of and how might you meet them?

5   How well do you understand the advantages and limitations of different sampling techniques in relation to your project? What information or support might help you to develop your understanding and apply an appropriate sampling process for your enquiry?

6   How well do you understand the implications of different question structures for subsequent analysis of the data? Who can help you with this decision-making process?

7   How confident are you about the level of your numerical/statistical competence? What development activities would help enhance this?

Being a practitioner-researcher

8   Is there anyone in the organisation (often there is someone marketing or planning) who would be able to offer advice and guidance on the survey design, administration and analysis processes? How might you find out about them?

9   How might you go about developing a sampling frame of good quality from which to select a sample? Who may be able to offer support with this process?

10 What organisational factors may influence decisions about sample size and selection? In what way might that affect the quality of the data that you obtain?

11 What 'permissions' do you need to undertake a survey within the organisation? Who might be able to influence these decisions? What actions can you take to influence the response rate for your survey?

12 What level of feedback from the data is required by the organisation? How will this impact the way you collect, organise and present the data?

Useful Resources

http://www.surveymonkey.com/ (archived at https://perma.cc/85DA-U6DP) – online survey provider – prices vary depending on the number of questions and the time the survey will be 'live'. There is also a charge to retrieve your data.

https://www.qualtrics.com/uk/ (archived at https://perma.cc/NVX9-2EVW) – online survey provider – prices vary depending on usage.

https://www.ons.gov.uk/ (archived at https://perma.cc/Z4HV-BLKX) – Office for National Statistics datasets and information on data sources from the UK.

https://www.gov.uk/government/collections/workplace-employment-relations-study-wers (archived at https://perma.cc/T2MR-DMZL) – information about the Workplace Employment Relations Study.

https://www.cipd.co.uk/knowledge (archived at https://perma.cc/5NUA-F7CS) – survey reports, factsheets, podcasts and guides, published by the CIPD.

Cha, E-S, Kim, KH and Erlen, JA (2007) Translation of scales in cross-cultural research: Issues and techniques, *Journal of Advanced Nursing: Research Methodology*, **58** (4), pp 386–95

Dillman, DA (1999) *Mail and Internet Surveys: The tailored design method*, John Wiley and Sons, New York

Kraemer, HC and Blasey, CM (2016) *How Many Subjects? Statistical power analysis in research*, Sage, Thousand Oaks, CA

Trades Union Congress (2010) Focus on health and safety: Trade union trends survey – TUC biennial survey of safety reps 2010 [Online] http://www.tuc.org.uk/extras/safetyrepssurvey2010.pdf (archived at https://perma.cc/KT2F-8736)

References

Babin, BJ and Boles, JS (1996) The effects of perceived co-worker involvement and supervisor support on service provider role stress, performance and job satisfaction, *Journal of Retailing*, **72** (1), pp 57–75

CIPD (2009) Coaching at the sharp end: Developing and supporting the line manager as coach [Online] http://www.cipd.co.uk/hr-resources/practical-tools/developing-line-manager-coaching.aspx (archived at https://perma.cc/4X34-ZA3P)

Cobanoglu, C, Warde, B and Moreo, P (2001) A comparison of mail, fax, and webbased survey methods, *International Journal of Market Research*, **43** (4), pp 441–52

Collis, J and Hussey, R (2013) *Business Research: A practical guide for undergraduate and postgraduate students*, McMillan International, Basingstoke

Couper, MP (2008) *Designing Effective Web Surveys*, Cambridge University Press, Cambridge

Ellinger, AE, Elmadağ, AB and Ellinger, AD (2007) An examination of organizations' frontline service employee development practices, *Human Resource Development Quarterly*, **18** (3), pp 293–314

Field, A (2017) *Discovering Statistics Using IBM SPSS Statistics*, Sage, London

Gill, J and Johnson, P (2010) *Research Methods for Managers*, Sage, London

Harpe, SE (2015) How to analyse Likert and other rating scale data, *Currents in Pharmacy Teaching and Learning*, **7**, pp 836–50

Hart, C (2013) *Doing Your Masters Dissertation*, Sage, London

Lee, N and Lings, L (2008) *Doing Business Research: A guide to theory and practice*, Sage, London

Neuman, W (2014) *Social Research Methods: Qualitative and quantitative approaches*, 7th edn, Pearson Education Limited, Harlow

(*continued*)

(Continued)

Podsakoff, PM, MacKenzie, SB, Lee, J-Y and
    Podsakoff, NP (2003) Common method biases
    in behavioral research: A critical review of the
    literature and recommended remedies, *Journal of
    Applied Psychology*, **88** (5), pp 879–903
Ritter, LA and Sue, VM (2007) The survey questionnaire,
    New Directions for Evaluation, **115**, pp 37–45
Robson, C and McCartan, K (2016) *Real World
    Research*, Wiley, Oxford

Saunders, MNK, Lewis, P and Thornhill, A (2019)
    Research Methods for Business Students, 8th edn,
    Pearson, London
Schaufeli, W and Bakker, A (2004) UWES Utrecht
    Work Engagement Scale Preliminary Manual,
    Occupational Health Psychology Unit Utrecht
    University, Utrecht

10
Analysing quantitative data

LEARNING OBJECTIVES
....

This chapter should help you to:

- make sense of basic terminology used in quantitative data analysis;

- undertake an initial analysis of your data;

- discuss the reliability of the data you have gathered;

- identify appropriate statistical tests to interpret your data and to either confirm or refute your hypotheses;

- draw appropriate conclusions based on your data.

How to use this chapter

This chapter has been written to help those who need to analyse and interpret rather than 'just' describe numerical data. Brett Davies (2014) notes that the world is divided into two kinds of people: the first (quite small) type of people comprises those who are statisticians. The second type comprises the rest of us. If you are a statistician, then you can work through this chapter very quickly and progress to more specialised statistical texts and discussions. If you are one of 'the rest of us' and you occasionally come close to a panic attack when statistical terms are used and multiple regression analyses or reliability coefficients are presented, then this chapter is for you. It sets out to explain 'in English' the main issues to consider if you wish to interpret data and formulate meaningful conclusions on the basis of your analysis.

If you intend to undertake statistical analysis you will need to develop some famil-iarity with appropriate software. Excel will be required as a minimum and you will be able to get further faster with IBS SPSS Statistics (more commonly addressed simply as SPSS). Most study-centre libraries have copies of SPSS that can be downloaded and installed for discrete periods of time onto your own computer and there will be networked versions within the university or college itself. If you are a part-time student it is worth asking if your employer already has a licence. If you are undertaking a Masters level dissertation (or aiming higher) then you should certainly arrange access to a copy. Some other similar types of software are Matlab, Stata or R – these are equally robust statistical tools, but in this chapter we will be using examples from SPSS since it is the most frequently used tool in HRM and organisational behaviour research.

 Case Example 10.1

Help – I have collected data – what should I do next?

Afrah was a student who was undertaking comparative research for her dissertation involving some people working in a UK organisation and other people working in an organisation in her country of Kuwait. Afrah was undertaking comparative research to investigate the extent to which social capital in organisations is related to enhanced work performance by employees (see Case Example 9.3). She spent some time devising a good quality survey instrument to explore people's experience of social capital and work performance. In particular, Afrah was interested to examine the extent to which social capital and performance were differently experienced in Kuwait and in the United Kingdom.

Afrah overcame a number of setbacks with collecting her data and was left with very little time to undertake the data analysis. Afrah had decided to use SPSS for her data analysis and set about entering her data onto the software. However, once she had completed the data entry, Afrah realised that she did not know 'where to start' with analysing and presenting her data. She found the way to generate some attractive looking frequency tables to provide an overall description of her data along the lines explained in Chapter 9. After that, however, the software offered numerous statistical tools, none of which she understood and she realised that she needed help fast if she was to interpret the data at a deeper level.

Questions for discussion

1 Why was it necessary for Afrah to explore the data more fully?

2 What questions did Afrah need to address in order to decide how to move forward with her data analysis?

3 Where might Afrah go for help?

Feedback notes

As noted in Chapter 9, descriptive statistics are very useful and they provided Afrah with a helpful summary of the main features of the data she had collected (see examples of presentations of descriptive data in Figures 9.13, 9.14 and 9.15). It was possible to see 'at a glance' the frequency with which different variables were reported by those who responded to her survey. This enabled Afrah to get a sense of the trends involved. However, although the descriptive summary 'painted a picture' in numerical terms it was not possible for her to assess the extent to which her results were purely due to coincidence or chance. Neither did the descriptive approach enable her to explore potential relationships between different variables, particularly the extent to which different groups (people in Kuwait and in the United Kingdom) responded to her survey questions.

In order to move forward with her data analysis Afrah needed to remind herself of her specific research questions and the assumptions she made, which take the form of hypotheses. With this in mind she could then begin to identify which statistical tools would be relevant to test her hypotheses. Afrah consulted one or two 'how-to' books on statistical analysis using SPSS in order to take her project forward. For many students (and other researchers) these form an invaluable basis for survival during the data analysis process. It is also a good idea to consult any friends, colleagues or tutors who have an interest and expertise in quantitative data analysis as they can help you to work out the best way to interpret your results.

 Activity 10.1

Fear of heights, spiders or statistics?

Think back to times when you have had to undertake a numerical analysis (maybe as part of your course or possibly when you were at school).

- Identify what worries you had when you started out.
- What helped you to 'get by'?
- What positive experiences did you associate with completing the numerical tasks?

Feedback notes

In response to these questions many people might confess to having 'bad memories' of maths from school. Maths, and other numerically based subjects, are often remembered as times where people recall frequently getting answers 'wrong' in classroom or homework situations. This can lead to a long-term aversion to numerical work so that it is avoided rather than practised. In addition, students often say that it is easy to forget the numerical 'terms' and/or 'formulae' and the process of revising these again in order to undertake some form of analysis is time-consuming and often does not seem to be worth the effort. As a result, many researchers, particularly those who either work in HR or who aspire to work in HR lack confidence in their numerical abilities. However, solving a numerical 'puzzle' or using numerical data to shed new light on a problem or issue can be very satisfying (in the same sense that completing a Sudoku puzzle might be gratifying) and most people have a greater numerical aptitude than they think. Numerical reasoning is very similar in structure to musical reasoning – it is not something that is only for 'clever types'. Furthermore, HR analytics is becoming an increasingly relevant area as it can bring information that may be crucial in helping businesses make informed decisions in terms of talent management, engagement, succession planning, as well as health and well-being. While HR analytics may not form part of your role, now or in the future, it is important that HR generalists know how to interpret results in order to develop HR policies accordingly. For these reasons, we try to address quantitative data analysis in a way that can be understandable and applied by those who so far have not had much contact with statistics.

Quantitative data analysis in 'plain English'

One of the problems that can beset HR researchers who try to 'read up' about statistics is the specialised language that is often used. However, don't be put off by the technical terminology. As Rugg and Petre (2007:168) point out **statistics** are really nothing more complicated than 'describing things with numbers and assessing the odds'. Indeed, the meanings behind many statistical terms are quite straightforward. Also, you do not have to be an expert in all aspects of statistics. Some features may not be relevant to your work and you should not feel 'forced' to use them. Before a consideration of which statistical tests are most likely to be appropriate to your research project, therefore, some 'plain English' definitions and observations about some of these terms are offered here (Rugg and Petre, 2007; Rugg, 2007; Brett Davies, 2014; Bell, Bryman and Harley, 2019):

- **Variable.** This is an important term and you will find yourself using it. It refers, simply, to something that is likely to vary. In HR research, for example, this may be an attribute of a person, a team or an organisation (eg age, level of commitment, individual-level performance, team-level performance, organisational size, organisational sector, and so on).
- **Independent variable.** This is the **cause** of something or some things that vary. For example, 'high levels of absence from work' (the independent variable) may lead to 'low productivity levels'.

- **Dependent variable.** This is the thing that varies because it is **affected** by the cause. For example, 'low productivity levels' (the dependent variable) may be affected by 'high levels of absence from work'.

When characterising variables as independent or dependent, we are basically assuming directionality in a relationship. In other words, we are assuming that the independent variable is an antecedent and that the dependent variable is an outcome. This idea of causality could actually only be tested with a longitudinal design (where the antecedent occurs before the outcome). This would mean that you would need to collect data at two (or more) moments in time, so that you could see this time lag between your independent variable and your dependent variable. However, it is actually very hard to collect longitudinal data for your research project. You would actually be lucky to get an organisation to run a survey at one moment in time (cross-sectional design) and it would be extremely unusual for organisations to allow you to run two surveys in separate moments. Although you cannot really claim that one variable causes the other, you *can* still point at their **directionality** based on your theoretical assumptions when collecting cross-sectional data (only one moment in time). This means that although you cannot really say that the independent variable causes the dependent variable, you can point at the direction of the relationship, saying that the independent variable is (negatively or positively) related to the dependent variable. In the example provided above, we would say that high levels of absence from work are negatively related to productivity levels.

Hypothesis

A hypothesis is an assumption or an 'informed guess' a researcher makes about the relationship between two or more variables. Once you have a hypothesis you can then analyse your data to test whether the data suggest that there is (or is not) a relationship and you can assess the significance (see below) of the association between the variables. Quantitative data analysis is strongly based on hypothesis testing. An example of a hypothesis was already provided above: 'high levels of absence from work are negatively related to productivity levels'. In opposition to any hypothesis, which assumes a positive or negative relationship between variables, we would have the so-called *null hypothesis* ('There is no relationship between high levels of absence from work and productivity levels.'). The null hypothesis actually means that when you test the likelihood that your results occurred by chance (which is certainly worth doing) you make an assumption that there is NO relationship between the variables (that is the null hypothesis). Then you run an appropriate significance test

Figure 10.1 Directionality in variables

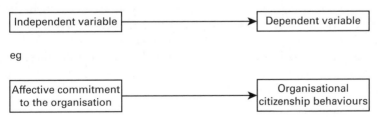

(using software) to see whether you can disprove your null hypothesis (and therefore show that there IS a significant relationship). In testing hypotheses, we are basically aiming to conclude whether our hypothesis (called the alternative hypothesis) has been supported by the data and the null hypothesis has been rejected.

Probability

This is important to quantitative data analysis. Probability refers to the extent to which your findings can be explained (or not) as the result of random chance. Probability is important: if you can show, for example, that there is only a one in a thousand chance of your findings being the result of coincidence then you can feel confident in them. Probability is often referred to as 'p' and the values are usually stated as decimal figures. The p-value is a number from 0 to 1. The closer the p-value is to 0, the more confident you can be that if you were to repeat the experiment or study, you would get the same results. In HR research, a p-value lower than 0.05 indicates strong evidence against the null hypothesis, so you can reject the null hypotheses and address the relationship between your variables as significant (see the meaning of significance below). The main figures to take notice of are:

- $p = 0.05$ means 1 chance in 20 of a result occurring through chance;
- $p = 0.01$ means 1 chance in 100 of a result occurring through chance;
- $p = 0.001$ means 1 chance in 1,000 of a result occurring through chance.

Significance

This is a useful term when you discuss your findings. Significance is a verbal signpost about how confident you can be that your results (generated by a randomly selected sample) are generalisable to the wider research population. Expressions of significance stem from measures of probability (see above). When evaluating your findings, you may want to use the following accepted expressions:

- **significant** means one chance in twenty or beyond that this happened by chance (where $p = 0.05$ or less).
- **highly significant** means one chance in a hundred or beyond that this happened by chance (where $p = 0.01$ or less).
- **very highly significant** means one chance in a thousand or beyond that this happened by chance (where $p = 0.001$ or less).

One-tailed hypothesis and two-tailed hypothesis

These are also confusing and frustrating terms if you are not a 'hypothesis type'. However, you will come across them in research that you read and also in the statistical tools that you use. A 'one-tailed hypothesis' is where you think (hypothesise) that there is an association between two variables **in a specific direction**. In HR research, for example, you may want to test whether stress levels lead to absence from work. Therefore, you might write your hypothesis in note form as:

stress → absence from work

You have one 'point' on your arrow and so this represents a 'one tailed hypothesis'.

For other relationships it may be unrealistic to assess the direction of the association. For example, you may want to test the association between 'manager self-confidence' and 'manager training undertaken'. Here it may be possible that training for managers improves their levels of self-confidence but it is equally possible that those managers who are already self-confident may seek out more training and development opportunities. Therefore, this hypothesis is expressed in note form as:

manager self-confidence ↔ manager training

Because the direction of the association could be either way there are two 'points' to the arrow and so you have a 'two-tailed hypothesis'. This may seem trivial but it affects the assessment you can make about significance, which is why the statistics software always refers to it. Usually probability values (*p*-values) are calculated by the software for a two-tailed hypothesis. If you have a one-tailed hypothesis you would need to divide the probability value by two. If you become advanced with statistics, there are also further tests that you can run for one-tailed and two-tailed hypotheses.

Parametric and non-parametric data

This is another term that is a source of irritation for non-statisticians. However, it is no more than a way of categorising different kinds of data. Parametric is the term used to describe data that meet certain criteria. If your data are parametric then there are specific statistical tests that are appropriate to use. If your data are 'non-parametric' then you simply use different statistical tools. To decide if your data are 'parametric' you must answer the following questions:

1 Are your data normally distributed or not? (See Chapter 9 for normal distribution.)

2 If you have gathered data from separate groupings and you wish to assess the differences between the groups (for example, in different companies, in different parts of the organisation or in different countries) are the sample sizes similar?

3 Have you asked all of the participants in your research the same questions? If you have asked different questions to different groups, then you are unlikely to meet the criteria for parametric data.

4 Are your data generated from ratio scale or interval scale measures? (See Chapter 9 to revise what these measures look like.)

If (hand on heart) you can answer 'yes' to all of these questions, then your data are suitable for statistical tests designed for parametric data. If you answered 'no' to one or more of these questions then you should use statistical tools designed for non-parametric data. This is not something that should unduly worry you. Non-parametric tests work differently but they still work. The different tests for parametric and non-parametric tests are shown in Table 10.12.

An 'analysis route map'

The question of where and how to start with data analysis can be a worry to HR students who are unfamiliar with the quantitative data analysis language. Figure 10.2 indicates the main steps you can take and the issues you should address as you set out on your 'journey' through the quantitative analysis process. The tests that are referred to in this figure are explained later in this chapter.

 Activity 10.2

Planning the analysis

Table 9.3 in Chapter 9 provides several examples of pre-validated scales in HRM and organisational behaviour research. Imagine that you have conducted a survey in one organisation trying to understand the main antecedents of employee engagement. The survey is composed of the 17 items of the Utrecht Work Engagement Scale (UWES) (Schaufeli and Bakker, 2003), as well as 16 items (short version) of the Perceived Organisational Support Scale by Eisenberger, Huntington, Hutchison and Sowa (1986). At the beginning of the survey, there were also some general demographic questions, such as 'gender',

'age', 'education', 'how long they had worked for the organisation', and 'whether they held a managerial role or not'.

1 What research questions might you formulate for your project?

2 Based on your research questions, what are the relationships you can expect between variables? Identify two or three hypotheses.

3 Making use of Figure 10.2 identify which types of statistical test would be most appropriate for you to test these hypotheses.

Feedback notes

There is a range of research questions that you might formulate. You might wish to examine whether those who are perceiving more support from their organisation will feel more engaged or not. You may also wish to investigate whether demographic factors (such as 'gender', 'age', 'education', 'how long they had worked for the organisation', and 'whether they held a managerial role or not') are important variables affecting employees' perceptions of organisational support, as well as their engagement. To answer these questions, you could formulate different hypotheses based on theory and previous empirical findings. Some examples of these hypotheses are:

H1. Employees in managerial roles perceive more organisational support than employees in non-managerial roles. In order to test this first hypothesis, we could go to Figure 10.2, more specifically to step 3. Hypothesis 1 is basically asking us to compare two groups (managers and non-managers) regarding their levels of

Figure 10.2 Steps and options for quantitative data analysis

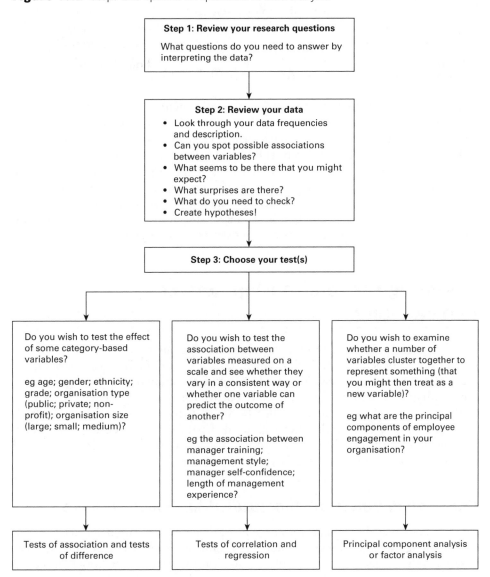

perceived organisational support. This means that over here we would be using tests of difference. In particular, if we want to compare two groups, which means that we would be using either a Mann-Whitney U test (if data are non-parametric) or a t-test (if data are parametric) – see Table 10.12 below.

H2. Higher levels of perceived organisational support are positively related to higher levels of employee engagement. This second hypothesis is actually asking us whether there is any type of association between two variables (see Figure 10.2): perceived organisational support and employee engagement. In particular, this hypothesis points at some directionality where the perceived organisational support is assumed to be an antecedent of employee engagement. If no particular directionality were anticipated, we would be looking at a correlation, either Spearman (for non-parametric data) or Pearson (for parametric data). However, as in this case we assume directionality, we would be using either a non-parametric regression or a linear regression analysis (parametric) to test this hypothesis.

H3. Employee engagement has different sub-dimensions. This final hypothesis would relate to previous conceptualisations of employee engagement. Previous research has demonstrated that engagement, when measured by the UWES scale (Schaufeli and Bakker, 2003), can be subdivided in three dimensions or factors: dedication, vigour and absorption. A factor means that a group of items seem to be largely associated with each other, thus measuring a specific sub-dimension in the concept of engagement. When conducting a survey, it is frequent to conduct some analyses to see how the items in a scale aggregate. According to Figure 10.2, we would be using a principal components analysis or a factor analysis here.

Assessing the relationship between two variables

Bivariate analysis is the term used to refer to an examination of the extent of any relationship between two variables. When dealing with more than two variables, it is called multivariate analysis. Where there is **no association or relationship** between the variables they are referred to as being **independent**.

If you are nervous of statistics, then bivariate analysis is a good place to start. It is not difficult to undertake, although it takes patience if you decide to include a number of different variables in the process. You can move forward in a number of ways depending on the type of data you have collected.

Cross-tabulation (sometimes called contingency tables)

You can construct these tables for any type of data and they are particularly useful for analysing nominal (category) data. Cross-tabulation involves assessing how the cases in each category of one variable are distributed into each category of a second variable. These require patience to construct manually but are easily produced using statistical packages. An example is shown as Table 10.1.

Table 10.1 shows an example of a cross-tabulation where raw data have been turned into percentages to reflect the proportion of each subgroup that are represented in each of the cells of the cross-tabulation table. (If you are using SPSS you have to tell it to do this – if you don't it will present the 'raw data' only).

What are the steps I need to take to build a cross-tabulation in SPSS?

Analyze → Descriptive Statistics → Crosstabs → Place the variables on the Rows or Columns → OK

Table 10.1 Example of cross-tabulation: age and highest qualification (*n* = 1709)

			Age					
			Less than 25	25–34	35–44	45–54	Older than 54	Total
Highest qualification	O-level/ GCSE	Count	1	20	48	24	9	102
		% within Age	1.2%	2.7%	8.2%	10.3%	13.2%	6.0%
	A-level	Count	4	49	53	44	12	162
		% within Age	4.7%	6.6%	9.1%	18.8%	17.6%	9.5%
	HNC	Count	0	7	16	19	4	46
		% within Age	0.0%	0.9%	2.7%	8.1%	5.9%	2.7%
	HND	Count	1	25	34	14	5	79
		% within Age	1.2%	3.4%	5.8%	6.0%	7.4%	4.6%
	Degree	Count	76	478	262	71	26	913
		% within Age	89.4%	64.9%	44.8%	30.3%	38.2%	53.4%
	Postgraduate degree	Count	1	117	63	15	3	199
		% within Age	1.2%	15.9%	10.8%	6.4%	4.4%	11.6%
	Professional qualification	Count	0	29	87	39	7	162
		% within Age	0.0%	3.9%	14.9%	16.7%	10.3%	9.5%
	Other	Count	2	12	22	8	2	46
		% within Age	2.4%	1.6%	3.8%	3.4%	2.9%	2.7%
Total		Count	85	737	585	234	68	1709
		% within Age	100.0%	100.0%	100.0%	100.0%	100.0%	100.0%

In this example there were more than 1,500 respondents to a large-scale questionnaire. The proportions represented by the percentage figures, therefore, make it possible to consider the relationships between the variables (in this case the distribution of educational qualifications across the different age groups). To 'read' the table you look for the direction (if there is one) that the percentages indicate. Where there is no relationship in a table the percentages will look roughly equal. Although percentages provide a useful mechanism for comparison, remember that where the numbers in the overall group are small (fewer than 50) it is probably more realistic to use numbers rather than percentages. If you would like to determine whether there is a significant difference between the expected frequencies and the observed frequencies in one or more categories, you can run the chi-square test. A chi-square test can be used to attempt rejection of the null hypothesis that the data are independent.

Probability and significance

Cross-tabulations are visually accessible ways of interpreting data. The drawback is that they do not tell you about the likelihood that these results might have arisen through chance or coincidence and this is an important feature of any discussion about the importance of your findings. Therefore, it is necessary to test the significance of the association between the variables. The most usual test to run is known as the 'chi-square test' ('chi' is pronounced 'kuy' – rhymes with sky). You may see the chi-square test represented as χ^2 in some articles. Karl Pearson proposed the chi-square test early in the last century and so (in SPSS at least) it still bears his name. It is widely used in research projects in the field of business and management generally as it can be used to evaluate whether there is an association between the rows and columns in a cross-tabulation (contingency) table. The chi-square test works by calculating what you might **expect** the counts for each of the cells in your table to be if there was no association between the variables and what the **actual** count is. It then compares 'expected' with 'actual' (rather like a budgeting process) and from this comparison it calculates the extent of any deviation from the null hypothesis (the assumption that there is no relationship whatsoever). The test is only reliable where there is an expected count of at least five in each cell. If your initial tests of association indicate that there might be a relationship between two or more variables you may also wish to establish the strength of any 'co-variation' and you can examine this further using a test of correlation.

If you are using the SPSS software, you can ask for the chi-square value to be calculated at the same time as the cross-tabulation is produced (see below).

How do I conduct a chi-square test in SPSS?

> Analyze → Descriptive Statistics → Crosstabs → Place the variables on the Rows or Columns → Press 'Statistics' and choose Chi-square → Continue → OK

The chi-square calculation for the example cross-tabulation (Table 10.1) is shown below as Table 10.2.

On the face of it the results of the chi-square test relating to the association between 'age' and educational qualifications taken from Table 10.2 indicates that there is a non-coincidental relationship between these two variables. The larger the chi-square value the stronger the likelihood of an association between the variables. However, it is also important to look at the column headed 'Asymp. sig (2-sided)' as this indicates the probability that these results might have occurred as a result of chance or coincidence. Table 10.2 shows that the probability figure is very low (in statistics the use of '0.000' connotes a value of less than a one in a thousand) so the chance that this relationship occurred as a result of chance is coincidental; you can trust that the results would be replicable on other similar occasions. In different words, you have found a significant association between age and educational qualifications.

Tests of correlation

Tests of correlation are useful tools to measure the strength and the direction of association between different variables. They enable you to see whether two or more

Table 10.2 Chi-square example

Chi-Square Tests			
	Value	df	Asymp. Sig. (2-sided)
Pearson Chi-Square	286.468[a]	28	.000
Likelihood Ratio	296.271	28	.000
Linear-by-Linear Association	30.706	1	.000
N of Valid Cases	1709		

a. 7 cells (17.5%) have expected count less than 5. The minimum expected count is 1.83.

of them vary in a systematic way. For example, you might want to see whether the extent to which an organisation makes use of classroom training is related to the extent to which they also invest in e-learning, coaching and in the professional development of their employees. You can draw one of three alternative conclusions from tests of correlation. A **positive correlation** occurs when the variables (for example, spend on training courses and spend on coaching) both increase together or decrease together. A **negative correlation** occurs when one variable gets bigger as the other gets smaller. A non-existent correlation occurs when the size of one variable is unrelated to the size of the other.

The two most frequently used tests of correlation are the Spearman correlation test (used for non-parametric data) and the Pearson correlation test (used for parametric data). You may see the Spearman test referred to as Spearman's rho (or r_s) and the Pearson test uses the symbol 'r'. Both tests calculate a 'correlation coefficient' ranging between -1 (perfect negative correlation) to 0 (no association) to **+1** (perfect positive correlation).

Where there is a probability that there was a less than one in a thousand chance that the results were due to chance ($p = 0.000$) then a correlation of 0.2 to 0.4 can be described as a good level of association; correlations of 0.4 to 0.6 can be described as strong and 'ratings' of 0.6 and above can be described as very strong in a business and management context (Collis and Hussey, 2014).

Remember that a correlation test tells you whether variables are associated – it does not mean that one variable causes the other.

How to conduct a Spearman or a Pearson test using SPSS?

Analyze → Correlate → Bivariate → Choose the test you require (Spearman for non parametric data or Pearson for parametric data) → For most projects you will want to accept the 'two-tailed test of significance' and you will also want to ensure that the 'flag significant correlations' box is ticked.

Activity 10.3

Take a look at Table 10.3, which provides a copy of the Pearson correlation test to assess the association (or lack of it) between different items contained in a survey.

1 How easy is it to make sense of these findings?

2 Which items seem to be most frequently correlated with other items?

3 What do the 'sig. (2-tailed)' figures represent?

Feedback notes

The first reaction of many of us to a correlation table like this is of confusion and panic. There seems to be no limit to the volume of numbers before our eyes and also the various 'stars' attached to some of the cells and not to others seem baffling. However, once you have got over the initial shock of the volume of data, correlation tables are relatively easy to interpret. The first thing to note is that all the data is provided 'in duplicate'. If you look along the labels for the rows you will see the variables listed and these also form the headings for the columns. This means that you only need to look at half of the data; the other half are repeat values. Which half you choose to look at is up to you. In Table 10.3 the 'line' dividing the duplicate sets of data is shaded grey and it covers the cells in the table where each question is (perfectly) correlated with itself – this is because the question is the same. When looking at these tables, therefore, you may find it helpful to draw a line through the bottom or the top 'triangle' so that you only focus your effort on one set of figures.

The next step with interpreting the correlation table is to scan across the cells either above or below the 'diagonal middle line' (shaded grey in Table 10.3). You will see that some cells have (**) next to them; some have (*) next to them and some have no symbols whatsoever. The notes at the bottom of the table are based on the ever-favourite null hypothesis, which makes the assumption that there is NO association between any of the variables. The correlation test then examines the data to see where there is a deviation from the null hypothesis. In this table the notes explain that for items flagged by the software as (*) there is one chance in twenty (or five in a hundred) that the association that is recorded has occurred through coincidence. Where the item is flagged with (**) there is a one in a hundred (or beyond) chance that the association results from coincidence and so these correlations may be more significant. Data analysis is about choices and judgement and so you next must decide if you wish to treat the cells with (*) as worthy of your attention. To provide a 'clearer view' some people will choose to highlight only the cells they wish to continue viewing on this basis and/or delete the cells on a copy of the table where there is no significant correlation.

As you assess the data you might be interested to see where the highest correlations occur and also the direction of the correlations. The negative correlations have a minus sign in front of the correlation coefficient value. You might mark the

Table 10.3 An example of a correlation table

		1. Gender	2. Age	3. Direct reports	4. Level	5. Qualifications	6. Tenure	7. Coaching	8. Relationships	9. Self-Confidence
1.Gender (Male =1; Female =0)	Correlation Coefficient	1.000	-.179**	-.194**	-.048	-.070	-.080	.124**	.047	.045
	Sig. (2-tailed)	.	.000	.000	.274	.110	.068	.005	.283	.300
	N	521	521	521	521	521	521	521	521	521
2.Age	Correlation Coefficient	.179**	1.000	.050	.146**	.056	.298**	-.026	.028	.007
	Sig. (2-tailed)	.000	.	.257	.001	.204	.000	.550	.522	.866
	N	521	521	521	521	521	521	521	521	521
3.Direct reports	Correlation Coefficient	.194**	.050	1.000	.147**	.063	.152**	.139**	.050	.073
	Sig. (2-tailed)	.000	.257	.	.001	.153	.001	.001	.259	.094
	N	521	521	521	521	521	521	521	521	521
4.Seniority	Correlation Coefficient	-.048	.146**	.147**	1.000	.290**	.114**	.044	.018	.021
	Sig. (2-tailed)	.274	.001	.001	.	.000	.009	.322	.676	.625
	N	521	521	521	521	521	521	521	521	521

Note: * = $p < .05$; ** = $p < .01$

(continued)

Table 10.3 (Continued)

		1. Gender	2. Age	3. Direct reports	4. Level	5. Qualifications	6. Tenure	7. Coaching	8. Relationships	9. Self-Confidence
5.Qualifications	Correlation Coefficient	-.070	.056	-.063	.290**	1.000	.029	.056	.029	.080
	Sig. (2-tailed)	.110	.204	.153	.000	.	.515	.202	.506	.067
	N	521	521	521	521	521	521	521	521	521
6.Tenure in this position	Correlation Coefficient	.080	.298**	.152**	.114**	.029	1.000	.086	.024	.106*
	Sig. (2-tailed)	.068	.000	.001	.009	.515	.	.051	.586	.015
	N	521	521	521	521	521	521	521	521	521
7.Coaching	Correlation Coefficient	.124**	.026	.139**	.044	.056	.086	1.000	.373**	.412**
	Sig. (2-tailed)	.005	.550	.001	.322	.202	.051	.	.000	.000
	N	521	521	521	521	521	521	521	521	521
8.Relation-ships	Correlation Coefficient	.047	.028	.050	.018	.029	.024	.373**	1.000	.354**
	Sig. (2-tailed)	.283	.522	.259	.676	.506	.586	.000	.	.000
	N	521	521	521	521	521	521	521	521	521
9.Self-confidence	Correlation Coefficient	.045	.007	.073	.021	.080	.106*	.412**	.354**	1.000
	Sig. (2-tailed)	.300	.866	.094	.625	.067	.015	.000	.000	.
	N	521	521	521	521	521	521	521	521	521

Note: *= $p<.05$; **= $p<.01$

'positives' in one colour and the 'negatives' in another. This should make it easier to make sense of the correlation test results.

Another feature of the correlation table is that the 'sig. 2-tailed' figure is also shown. The significance figures might suggest different levels of probability of the result occurring through chance for different correlations and you should reflect on this in your interpretation. If the correlation test indicates only correlations where the 'best' results were flagged (*) then you should reflect on the significance shown in the cells of the table to ensure you take account of the different levels of probability that they indicate.

Tests of correlation are not as frightening as they may first seem and they can provide a very useful interpretation of the data that you have collected. The example provided here is fairly complex and contains a large number of variables. It may be that your research will require assessments of correlations that involve fewer variables and so will generate simpler looking tables.

A consistent theme of this chapter has been that quantitative data analysis is a process of asking questions about the data and then choosing appropriate tests to use in order to answer those questions. Often, answering one question may lead you to 'wondering' about the answer to another question. In some cases, this may lead to another statistical test. In Table 10.3, for example, it seems that 'coaching' is positively associated with 'relationships' and 'self-confidence' although smaller positive correlations are also evident relating to 'gender' (in this case being male) and 'direct reports'. Having noticed this, you may begin to wonder which out of 'gender', 'direct reports', 'relationships' and 'self-confidence' are stronger predictors of managerial coaching. In order to answer this question, you would need a regression analysis.

Regression

To undertake a regression analysis your data must be generated through ratio, ordinal or interval scales. Nominal data can be used but only where it is 'dichotomous' – that is, there are only two possible responses (eg manager versus non-manager). Regression analyses often do not include only the test of the expected hypothesis, where one independent variable is going to be related to a dependent variable. Most studies use the so-called multiple regression, where you test simultaneously to what extent a number of independent variables is related to your dependent variable.

Multiple regression analysis requires a large sample. The number of cases in your sample of participants must substantially exceed the number of predictor variables you intend to include in your analysis. The minimum is that you have five times as many participants as predictor variables. A more acceptable ratio is 10:1, but some people argue that the ratio should be as high as 40:1. If you have a small sample, therefore, it is not appropriate to undertake a regression analysis.

How to conduct a multiple regression analysis in SPSS?

Analyze → Regression → Linear

In the linear regression dialogue box that then appears you select the dependent (outcome) variable and the variables that you think may be predictors (known in

SPSS as independent variables). You will also need to choose the 'method' (if in doubt choose the 'enter' method, but the 'stepwise' method is also frequently used). You should also click on the 'statistics' box in the right-hand corner of the dialogue box and make sure that 'model fit'; 'descriptives' and 'estimates' are ticked. If you are not using the Enter method you should also select 'R squared change'. Now click on 'continue' and then on 'OK'.

Why would you be testing the effect of so many independent variables on your dependent variable? Normally your main hypothesis advances a theoretically sound expected relationship between one independent variable and a dependent variable. In the example provided earlier, H2 predicted that 'higher levels of perceived organisational support are positively related to higher levels of employee engagement'. So why not just test the relationship between perceived organisational support and employee engagement? Well, in order to make sure that this relationship is indeed strong, we need to test whether there are other variables that could be alternative explanations for high levels of engagement. These would be the so-called **control variables**, which are basically added to the model (or to the regression equation) in order to make sure that we are acknowledging and testing potential alternative explanations for high engagement levels. These control variables are normally added first in the list of independent variables on SPSS when testing a multiple regression analysis. It would actually be desirable in this case to select the 'stepwise' method, where you would add your control variables in step 1, and your main independent variable(s) in step 2. Following the same example, you could probably add 'gender', 'age', 'education', 'how long they had worked for the organisation', and 'whether they held a managerial role or not' on a first step as control variables, and 'perceived organisational support' (your main independent variable) in step 2, having 'employee engagement' as the dependent variable.

With a regression analysis you will find that when you ask for a test you get lots of information. If you undertake a regression analysis on SPSS, you will find that the output file it generates provides you with six tables. Don't be put off – you will soon learn what to look out for. The first table describes the data in general terms. The second table (there is an example shown as Table 10.4) shows the correlations between different pairs of variables within the analysis using an example of an assessment of whether gross salary is predicted by employee gender, length of service in current job and/or length of time in employment. Here it is important to reassure yourself that there are not strong correlations between the predictor variables and the dependent variable. Notice here how the significance (p) values are for a one-tailed hypothesis as your hunch is that there is a one-way relationship between gross salary (the dependent or 'outcome' variable) and the independent (predictor) variables: gender, length of time in current job, and length of time in employment.

Table 10.5 is important as the **Adjusted R Square** value tells you the extent to which the model of prediction you are using accounts for variance in the outcome variable. In Table 10.5 you will see that 38.5 per cent of variance is accounted for by these variables. Therefore, it is likely that other factors are also important in determining gross salary. Nonetheless, the 'model' used here represents almost 40 per cent of what is going on.

The important part of Table 10.6 (ANOVA) is the significance column as it indicates the probability that any regression relationship occurred through coincidence. The '**Sig**' figure in Table 10.6 indicates there is a less than one in a thousand chance that the results of this regression occurred through chance; this is good news!

Table 10.4 Example of correlations table within a regression analysis output

		Correlations			
		Gross salary (£)	Gender	How long in current job	How long in employment
Pearson Correlation	Gross salary (£)	1.000	.225	.156	.596
	Gender	.225	1.000	.080	.140
	How long in current job	.156	.080	1.000	.418
	How long in medical sales industry	.596	.140	.418	1.000
Sig. (1-tailed)	Gross salary (£)	.	.000	.000	.000
	Gender	.000	.	.001	.000
	How long in current job	.000	.001	.	.000
	How long in medical sales industry	.000	.000	.000	.
N	Gross salary (£)	1534	1534	1534	1534
	Gender	1534	1534	1534	1534
	How long in current job	1534	1534	1534	1534
	How long in medical sales industry	1534	1534	1534	1534

Finally, you arrive at Table 10.7, which has the regression data. Here it is important to look at the **Standardised Coefficients (Beta)** numbers, which give a measure of the contribution of each variable to the regression model you are testing. A large value indicates that a unit change in this predictor variable has a large effect on the outcome variable. In Table 10.7 you will see that length of time in employment has a much higher value than the others. In addition, the 't' and Sig (p) values give an indication of the impact of each predictor variable – a big absolute t-value and small p-value suggests that a predictor variable is having a large impact on the outcome variable. Here again we see from Table 10.7 that length of time in employment has the largest predictive value although smaller contributions are also made by the other two variables.

Table 10.5 Example of model summary table

		Model Summary		
Model	R	R Square	Adjusted R Square	Std. Error of the Estimate
1	.622[a]	.387	.385	7186.686

a. Predictors: (Constant), How long in medical sales industry, Gender, How long in current job

Table 10.6 Example ANOVA table

	ANOVA[a]					
Model		Sum of Squares	df	Mean Square	F	Sig.
1	Regression	49814950757.485	3	16604983585.828	321.500	.000[b]
	Residual	79022137184.887	1530	51648455.676		
	Total	128837087942.371	1533			

a. Dependent Variable: Gross salary (£)
b. Predictors: (Constant), How long in medical sales industry, Gender, How long in current job

Table 10.7 Example of coefficients table from a regression analysis

	Coefficients[a]					
		Unstandardised Coefficients		Standardised Coefficients		
Model		B	Std. Error	Beta	t	Sig.
1	(Constant)	8158.784	930.050		8.772	.000
	Gender	2706.586	371.111	.148	7.293	.000
	How long in current job	−752.446	142.263	−.117	−5.289	.000
	How long in employment	4945.609	175.939	.624	28.110	.000

a. Dependent Variable: Gross salary (£)

Tests of difference

Tests of association are very useful approaches to use to interpret your data in order to test your hypotheses. However, they are a clumsy way of assessing whether there are differences in responses to some of your questions made by members of different groups within the sample. Afrah, from Case Example 10.1, for example, wanted to know whether people from two different countries responded differently to questions about social capital. There are two main tests that will enable you to form a judgement about differences between groups. If your data are parametric then the most appropriate tool is the t-test. If your data are non-parametric (which is often the case in HR Masters level projects) then the Mann-Whitney test is appropriate.

There are different types of t-tests based on the characteristics of your sample. If you have groups, or sub-samples, that are independent (cases within one group have no relation with cases in the other group), then you should run an independent sample t-test. For example, if Afrah wants to compare the people from two different countries, these are independent samples. In contrast, you can also have Paired Samples t-tests, which occur when there is a link between the two groups; for example, when analysing couples in heterosexual settings, you would have two groups, one of females and one of males, and these will be associated. Paired Samples t-tests are also frequently used when you have longitudinal data and you want to compare answers from the same individuals at time 1 and at time 2. The number of cases will always be the same for the two groups (eg if you have 35 heterosexual couples, you will have 35 women paired with 35 men; in a longitudinal setting, if you have 72 responses at time 1, and 65 at time 2, you have to remove the seven respondents with missing data at time 2 from the t-test analysis).

For non-parametric data, we can compare two related (paired groups) with the Wilcoxon signed-rank test.

How to conduct an independent samples t-test on SPSS

Analyze → Compare Means → Independent Samples T Test → The grouping variable will be a dichotomous variable that determines the two groups (eg 1 = Managerial; 0 = Non-managerial) → The test variables are the dimensions in which you want to compare the two groups (eg levels of engagement) → OK

How to conduct a Paired Samples t-test on SPSS

Analyze → Compare Means → Paired Samples T Test → On Pair 1, add the same variable for two related groups (eg engagement in time 1; engagement in time 2) → OK

How to conduct a Mann-Whitney test (Independent Samples) on SPSS

Analyze → Non-Parametric Tests → Independent Samples → Compare distributions across groups (you can also compare medians) → Run → In 'Groups', you will place a dichotomous variable that determines the two groups (eg 1 = Managerial; 0 = Non-managerial) → Add your independent variables in the 'Test Fields' → Run

How to conduct a Wilcoxon signed-rank test (Related Samples) on SPSS

Analyze → Non-Parametric Tests → Related Samples → Automatically compare observed data to hypothesized → Run → Select test fields → Run

Table 10.8 provides an example of the results from the Mann-Whitney test (independent samples). The Mann-Whitney test outcome shown here enables an interpretation

Table 10.8 Example of Mann-Whitney U output

Ranks				
	Choice	**N**	**Mean Rank**	**Sum of Ranks**
Developing people	UK	222	278.85	61904.00
	Kuwait	284	233.69	66367.00
	Total	506		
Giving feedback	UK	222	285.91	63471.50
	Kuwait	284	228.17	64799.50
	Total	506		
Goal setting	UK	222	276.58	61400.00
	Kuwait	284	235.46	66871.00
	Total	506		
Asking for opinions	UK	222	254.12	56415.00
	Kuwait	284	253.01	71856.00
	Total	506		
Communicating plans	UK	222	264.69	58762.00
	Kuwait	284	244.75	69509.00
	Total	506		

Test Statistics(a)					
	Developing people	**Giving feedback**	**Goal setting**	**Asking for opinions**	**Communicating plans**
Mann-Whitney U	25897.000	24329.500	26401.000	31386.000	29039.000
Wilcoxon W	66367.000	64799.500	66871.000	71856.000	69509.000
Z	−3.741	−4.894	−3.455	−.093	−1.679
Asymp. Sig. (2-tailed)	.000	.000	.001	.926	.093

a Grouping Variable: Country

of the extent to which there was a difference between the responses of two groups of managers from different countries to questions associated with management behaviours included in a survey used in some comparative research.

Yet again, if you use SPSS you will find that when you ask for a test you get lots of information and need to work out what to look out for. The first table produced here, for example, shows 'the workings' and the second table gives the outcome. Here it is possible to see the Mann-Whitney U test statistic and the ever important 'Asymp. Sig. (2-tailed)'. As with all other tests there is a null hypothesis that there is no difference between the groups. The significance measure indicates whether the test result can be seen as reliable. Here you may notice that the test suggests that there is a highly significant difference between the groups for three of the questionnaire items (Goal setting, giving feedback and developing people) which have high Mann-Whitney scores (look at the 'Z') and a probability of only one in a thousand or beyond that these results occurred through chance). However, the test also enables us to see that responses to the questions relating to communicating plans and asking for opinions show a probability figure that suggests that the results may have occurred by coincidence.

Examining features requiring 'multiple indicators'

A key challenge for researchers in HR is that most of the interesting things that we want to examine cannot be directly observed and measured. For example, although variables like people's age, length of service, gross pay and so on are interesting, you may feel far more curious about less directly measurable issues such as: organisational culture, engagement, leadership style, etc. These latter variables are referred to as 'latent constructs'. If you want to measure them, you are unlikely to get a very reliable or valid result if you ask one question (for example: do you have an empowering management style?). If you ask very 'obvious' questions, then it is highly likely that people will tell you what they think you want to hear or their responses may be 'skewed' by what they believe to be the 'right answer'. In such cases you will need to make use of multiple indicators that, taken in combination, will help you to measure what you are interested in. However, deciding which indicators within a 'batch' of questions really are indicative of the variable you are interested in and which are less effective as indicators takes some working out and for this a technique called factor analysis can be very useful.

Factor analysis

Factor analysis is useful in two main ways. First, it can assess whether responses to some of your questions indicate that there are patterns or 'clusters' of responses that might indicate a coherent construct (such as 'empowerment' or 'assertiveness'). Second, it can assess whether the responses to the questions you have asked suggest the presence of 'key variables'. Factor analysis and principal component analysis tests form part of two related 'families' of statistical procedures. The underlying maths is quite complicated (fear not – this is not covered here!) and the principles underpinning them are different in places, but the reasoning behind factor analysis and principal component analysis is fairly simple. They involve assessing how strongly each of your variables is correlated with each of the other variables and so identifying:

- groups of variables that all correlate fairly strongly with each other;
- the extent to which one or more variables account for all of the variation in the dataset.

Therefore, factor analysis is useful as a way of assessing the validity of questionnaire items (taken together) as it provides a mechanism to determine whether the questions in your survey actually do relate in a coherent way to the concept that you are trying to measure.

 Activity 10.4

Survey design and factor analysis

Imagine that you have decided to conduct research into 'levels of anxiety in HR students about statistics'. You have to devise a questionnaire that will try to capture the different features of this occurrence. You organise your questionnaire with the 'biographical' questions first and then a series of 10 statements against which survey respondents can give their measure of 'agreement/disagreement' on a scale of 1 to 5. Try to generate 10 questionnaire statements that you might include in your survey to examine 'anxiety about statistics'.

Feedback notes

Writing survey questions 'out of the blue' is a difficult task. It is often desirable to use pre-validated scales (see Table 9.4 for some examples). If you were writing survey questions 'for real' you might decide to interview some people first to get an idea of the things that might comprise overall 'anxiety about statistics' and then use your interview data as a basis for designing your survey questions. Having done this, it would be a good idea to try your ideas out on your supervisor or some other experts and get them to tell you which of your questions they think 'make sense' and which should be changed or eliminated. Some of the items that you may have come up with might be along the lines of:

	Strongly disagree 1	2	3	4	Strongly agree 5
I cannot understand the basis of calculations in statistics.	O	O	O	O	O
I do not feel confident in using software such as Excel.	O	O	O	O	O
Words mean more to me than numbers.	O	O	O	O	O
I would rather read quotations than look at tables of figures.	O	O	O	O	O
I am afraid that I will make miscalculations.	O	O	O	O	O
Statistical packages such as SPSS are a worry to me and I do not wish to use them.	O	O	O	O	O

Once you have got a set of items you think might represent 'anxiety about statistics' you will need to try them out by devising a survey and collecting some responses. You could send out your survey to as many HR students as possible (let's be optimistic and pretend you have got 300 responses). Factor analysis can then indicate for you whether all of your questions cluster in a coherent way and also whether there might be subcategories (for example: anxiety about computers; preference for words over numbers) in the data you have collected. Using SPSS and other statistical software packages it is possible to identify clusters and their effect on the variance within the overall responses.

How to undertake a factor analysis with SPSS

> Analyze → Data Reduction → Factor → Extraction (there are many options, but for the example below you would choose Principal Components) → In the 'extraction' dialogue box, make sure that you tick the 'scree plot' option → In the 'rotation' dialogue box' ask for the 'varimax' method → OK

The output from this process is quite extensive and if you can find a friendly statistics advisor (your tutor or someone recommended by him or her?) the advisor will be able to help you to use and interpret the outputs appropriately.

Tables 10.9 and 10.10 provide an example of some of the outputs of a principal component analysis in SPSS. After outputs with 'the workings' the output contains a table that indicates the proportion of **variance** that is accounted for by the 'factors' or groups of items that the software has identified. Opinions vary between disciplines (such as engineering, medicine, business and management) about what proportion of variance is significant and worth 'taking note of'. For HRM projects a contribution

Table 10.9 Example of principal component analysis output

		Total Variance Explained				
		Initial Eigenvalues			Rotation Sums of Squared Loadings	
Component	Total	% of Variance	Cumulative %	Total	% of Variance	Cumulative %
1	3.136	34.842	34.842	2.721	30.231	30.231
2	1.228	13.642	48.484	1.643	18.254	48.484
3	.929	10.325	58.810			
4	.781	8.678	67.488			
5	.707	7.854	75.342			
6	.669	7.433	82.774			
7	.581	6.452	89.227			
8	.497	5.523	94.750			
9	.473	5.250	100.000			

Extraction Method: Principal Component Analysis.

to variance of over 40 per cent can be seen as interesting given the complexity of the phenomena that are being researched. Table 10.9, which reproduces a factor analysis output, indicates that two 'components' (clusters) accounted for just over 49 per cent of the variance within the responses. You will see the term 'eigenvalue' used in this chart. This should not worry you; it refers to the total test variance that is accounted for by a particular factor (where the eigenvalue is less than 1 then there is no contribution to variance).

The effect of the clustering can be visually displayed by SPSS in the form of a 'scree plot', reproduced here as Figure 10.3. Making sense of scree plots can be rather baffling for 'non-scree plotters' but the trick is to look at the gradients between the points. The plot provides a graphic representation of the eigenvalue for each of the factors. Where there is almost no gradient and the curve is 'flat' this indicates that there are no 'worthwhile' clusters. The scree plot shown for these items, for example, indicates one quite powerful cluster (where there is a sharp 'fall' between coordinates on the graph). This reflects the 'descent' from a quite high eigenvalue for factor one and then a further (but much smaller) difference between the second and third eigenvalues shown in the table. This is a visual suggestion that there are two clusters; one being much more significant than the other in explaining variance within the responses as a whole.

The 'rotated component matrix' for the data is shown next as Table 10.10. This is much easier to read than an additional output (not reproduced here) of an 'unrotated component matrix'. The column headings for the rotated component matrix

Figure 10.3 Example of a scree plot

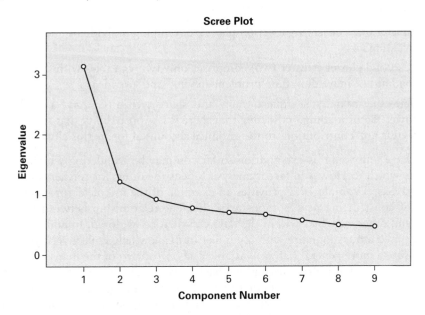

Table 10.10 Example of a rotated component matrix

	Component	
	1	2
Observing	**.772**	−.002
Action plans	**.768**	.089
Developing individuals	**.694**	.086
Feedback	**.654**	.247
Training	**.634**	.338
Problem-solving	−.077	**.803**
Use ideas	.093	**.628**
Share decisions	.389	.470
Questioning	.239	.437

Extraction Method: Principal Component Analysis.
Rotation Method: Varimax with Kaiser Normalization.
Rotation converged in 3 iterations.

indicate again that two clusters have been identified and the contents of the columns represent the 'factor loadings' of the questionnaire items within the two 'components' (or clusters). Most researchers would not take much account of anything with a factor loading below 0.6, and using this criterion you can identify which questionnaire items are associated with each cluster. The data in Table 10.10, for example, indicate a cluster of responses within component one, all of which have factor loadings above 0.6 as follows:

- **Cluster one:** 'observing'; 'action plans'; 'developing individuals'; 'feedback'; 'training'.

- A second cluster (**cluster two**) comprises only two variables with factor loadings of more than 0.6: 'problem-solving' and 'use ideas'.

- The other two items – 'questioning' and 'share decisions' – have a much lower factor loading, indicating that there is less probability that they make a significant 'contribution' to the variance accounted for by this cluster.

If you have followed this explanation so far you may be wondering whether all the effort is worth it. However, factor analysis 'opens the door' for further useful analysis and Case Example 10.2 provides an example of the use of factor analysis as a basis for constructing new 'composite' scales. The relationship between these new scales and other variables within the data can then be explored. In addition, if you have devised a questionnaire with a number of items which, collectively, you intend to measure a more general (latent) variable and one or two of the items do not cluster effectively then this provides a useful basis to consider removing these items from your analysis as the test suggests that they may not be 'fit for purpose'. With this in mind, if you have decided to devise your own survey instrument you may decide to include factor analysis is a useful part of any piloting process to help you assess the validity of your questionnaire items.

 Case Example 10.2

Factor analysis as a basis for further analysis

Extracts from Hashim, J (2010) Human resource management practices on organisational commitment: The Islamic perspective, Personnel Review, **39** (6), pp 785–99. © Emerald Group Publishing Limited all rights reserved.

Religious influences on human resource practices are important but are rarely highlighted in literature. The specifications of right and wrong, reward and punishment, work and spirituality, as well as relation to others and God address human resource issues directly and indirectly (Ali *et al*, 2000). In most countries, the influence of religion on human resource management (HRM) is formally incorporated in the rules and regulations governing employee-management relations, some more explicitly than others. These rules and regulations can be related to the employees' individual rights; such as equal employment opportunities, job security, and wage levels. They can also be related to the employees' collective rights; such as unionisation and participative decision-making...

This paper aims to examine the management of human resources from the Islamic perspective and its effects on organisational commitment among selected employees in Islamic organisations in Malaysia... The influence of Islam and its teachings on HRM, which are prevalent in certain countries, could be of interest to people and organisations that wish to do business with them, such as multinational organisations...

The study employed a self-developed questionnaire... Data were collected from eight Islamic organisations in Malaysia... well-known as Islamic organisations among the Malaysians. Six of the organisations are in the Islamic banking and financial business, and the other two are in Islamic services business.

The total respondents were 121 Muslim employees, who varied in positions and were purposively selected to represent each of the eight organisations. To ensure the respondents understood and were familiar with their organisations' HRM practices, the respondents selected were required to have worked for the organisation for at least three years and they must have performed some of the HRM functions (selection, performance appraisal or training) themselves ie they were supervisors.

Based on the interpretation of... related verses mentioned in Al-Qur'an and Hadith, a specially constructed questionnaire was developed in order to gather the data. The instrument consisted of 54 items seeking information about the organisations' background and HRM practices among these selected organisations. Specifically, there were four questions enquiring of the organisation background, the name of the organisation, the number of employees employed, and the type of organisation's ownership. There were ten items each enquiring about the recruitment, selection,

performance appraisal, training and development, and compensation practices. For each of these functions, the respondents were asked to indicate the extent to which each of the activities in the questionnaire were being practised in their organisations by using the seven-point Likert scales (1 = never, 2 = very rarely, 3 = rarely, 4 = occasionally, 5 = frequently, 6 = very frequently, 7 = all the time).

Organisational commitment was measured by a 12-item short version of the Organisational Commitment questionnaire developed by Mowday et al (1979). Before the actual data collection was conducted, a pilot test was conducted for the instrument...

Reliability test was conducted for 50 items for internal consistency purposes. The reliability coefficient for all 50 items was 0.951. Next, another reliability test was conducted for the ten items in each of the five HRM functions [recruitment, selection, performance appraisal, training and development, and compensation]. If they were reliable, then factor analysis would be conducted for each of these five functions. If the factor analysis produced more than two factors, then the most reliable factor between them would be selected for subsequent analysis in measuring the HRM practices.

For recruitment there were ten items asking how the organisations recruit new employees. The reliability coefficient for recruitment was 0.787. Factor analysis was then performed for all these ten items. The analysis produced one factor and it was reliable thus the factor was selected. Next, the same process was repeated for selection practices. The reliability coefficient for ten items in selection practices was 0.919. The factor analysis produced one factor and since it was reliable, all the ten items were used for the next analysis. For performance appraisal, the factor analysis produced three factors, and Factor 1 was chosen because it has the most loaded items and it was most reliable compared to Factor 2 and Factor 3. Factor 1 consisted of seven items. A reliability analysis was done on these seven items and it showed reliability coefficient value of 0.890. Meanwhile, factor analysis conducted for training and development function produced two factors, and Factor 1 was selected because it was more reliable than Factor 2. Its reliability coefficient was 0.891. For the compensation function, the factor analysis produced three factors. Factor 2 which comprised of four items was selected because it was the most reliable factor among the three factors with coefficient value of 0.855. For the organisational commitment variable, a confirmatory factor analysis was done and it produced one factor.

Discussion questions

1   In what ways has factor analysis been used in this extract?

2   What are the strengths and weaknesses of the approach described in this extract?

Feedback notes

Factor analysis has been used here to identify coherent clusters of questionnaire items that can be said to comprise different features of Islamic HRM. As a result of this analysis the researchers are able to 'discard' questionnaire items that do not coherently correlate together. This means that new scales, derived from the original responses, can be created for: recruitment, selection, performance appraisal, training and development, compensation, and organisational commitment.

Instead of trying to deal with 66 different individual variables, therefore, it is possible to create six composite variables to represent these multidimensional constructs. This then allows for a test of association between the new variables and, in this case, a composite measure of organisational commitment.

In evaluating the strengths and weaknesses of the research described in this extract you might have observed that the sample size was small. In addition, while developing a measure of Islamic HRM using data from Islamic organisations is an interesting exercise, it would be very interesting to now examine whether respondents from non-Islamic organisations would respond in similar or different ways to the questions. You may have noticed the frequent reference in this extract to 'reliability coefficients'. These refer to the Cronbach alpha (symbolised as 'α') test. You will find that this is frequently used in the analysis of quantitative data. It has been used as a measure of internal consistency (and hence reliability) of questionnaire responses since the 1950s. The calculation on which it is based will result in an output that varies from zero to 1 and higher values of alpha (values of 0.7 or higher) give greater confidence in the quality of a questionnaire and the extent to which a set of items measure a single construct. The reliability coefficients shown in this paper, therefore, give some confidence (although the sample size is still a concern) of the reliability of the instrument as a whole and the six scales that were created following the factor analysis.

Analysing data to test hypotheses and answer research questions

If you have persevered this far with the chapter you may now be feeling that the possibilities for analysis are endless and that you may never be in a position to formulate any conclusions as you will be spending all your hours on generating tests and trying to 'read' the results. Indeed, it is very easy to get fixated by all the tests that the statistical analysis packages can undertake and to feel the need to 'try them all'. This would be a mistake. Statistical packages are a **tool** and it is important to use your own judgement about the most appropriate way to use the tool. Analysis is fundamentally a thinking process and even the most expensive and up-to-date packages will not do the thinking for you.

The starting point for your analysis must be your research questions which help you create hypotheses. They form the basis for your interpretation of the data and they are also what those who mark your project will expect to be the focus of your conclusions. Having reviewed your research questions and your hypotheses, it is also important to then look over the type of data that you have collected. There are two important issues here. First, what measurement scales did you use? Did your questionnaire instrument generate:

- nominal or category data;
- ordinal data;
- interval scales;
- ratio scales?

If you are planning to analyse nominal or ordinal data, then you will need to make use of non-parametric tests. Second, is your data normally distributed? If the spread of the data across the extremes does not reflect a normal curve of distribution (with a 'hump' in the middle) then again you should use non-parametric tests.

If you are clear about your research questions and you are clear about the types of data you have collected then you are well placed to identify the most appropriate analysis tools to use and Table 10.11 provides an indication of the main options for parametric and non-parametric data (Collis and Hussey, 2014; Brett Davies, 2014).

Another useful depiction of analysis options and choices is also provided on Table 10.12.

As you proceed with the analysis process it is likely that you will want to explore the relationships between different variables using different tests (as appropriate and depending on your research questions). It is also likely that you will need to 'pick up' and 'put down' the analysis process over a number of different occasions. Therefore,

Table 10.11 Analysis options and choices

Test Purpose	Non-parametric Data Option	Parametric Data Option	Types of Data	Notes
Test of Association	Cross-tabulation	Cross-tabulation	All types. Especially useful with nominal (category) data	Need to report the significance of the association
Test of Association	Scattergram	Scattergram	Interval or ratio scale data only	Need to report the strength of the association as well as the significance
Assessment of Significance of Association	Chi-square (χ^2)	n/a	All types	
Test of Difference (Two Groups)	Mann-Whitney test (U)	t-test (t)	Never for nominal data	Report probability of chance (p) result as well as the test 'result'
Test of Difference (Multiple Groups)	Kruskal-Wallis test	ANOVA	Never for nominal data	Report probability of chance (p) result as well as the test 'result'
Test of Correlation (Without Directionality)	Spearman's rho (r_s)	Pearson's correlation (r)	Never for nominal data	Report probability of chance (p) result as well as the test 'result'
Test of Correlation (With Directionality)	Non-parametric regression	Linear regression	Never for nominal data	Report probability of chance (p) result as well as the test 'result'
Principal Component/ Factor Analysis	Factor/ principal component analysis	Factor/ principal component analysis	Never for nominal data	Report Chronbach's alpha (α) correlation coefficient as well as the test result

Table 10.12 Analysis options and types of variables

Comparing Means:				
	Dependent Variable:	**Independent Variable:**	**Parametric Test:**	**Non-parametric Test:**
Two Independent Groups	Interval or ratio scale	Nominal (dichotomous) scale	Independent samples t-test	Mann-Whitney U test
Two Related (Paired) Samples	Interval or ratio scale	Nominal (dichotomous) scale (eg time 1, time 2)	Paired Samples t-test	Wilcoxon signed-rank test
Three or More Independent Groups	Interval or ratio scale	Nominal (more than two categories)	One-way ANOVA	Kruskal-Wallis test
Three or More Related (Paired) Groups (eg Time 1, Time 2, Time 3)	Interval or ratio scale	Nominal (more than two **related** categories)	Repeated measures ANOVA	Friedman test

Relating Variables:				
	Dependent Variable:	**Independent Variable:**	**Parametric Test:**	**Non-parametric Test:**
No Directionality Assumed	Nominal/ Categorical	Nominal/ Categorical		Chi-square test
	One of the two would be Nominal/Categorical		Point-biserial correlation	Spearman rank order correlation
	Interval or ratio scale	Interval or ratio scale	Pearson correlation	Spearman correlation
Directionality Assumed	Nominal/ Categorical	Interval or ratio scale	Logistic regression	Non-parametric logistic regression
	Interval or ratio scale	Interval or ratio scale	Regression*	Non-parametric regression

NB: There are multiple forms of regression based on the type of expected relationship between two or more variables. For example, if you expect that the relationships between your main variables are not going to be linear, you may wish to calculate some form of nonlinear regression. There is no scope in this book to explore all different forms of regression in detail, but we encourage you to look deeper into this, especially in case you expect a nonlinear relationship between your main variables.

the following tips are offered to ensure that your time, on each occasion, is used to best effect and that you are able to formulate credible conclusions:

- Back up your work frequently (every 20 minutes is not excessive with data analysis).

- Work as neatly as you can. Keep a record of what tests you have done and what still needs to be done. Label all your outputs in a logical way so that you can find them again later. Repeating tests because you have 'lost' the output is a luxury that a student with a deadline cannot afford.

- Double-check your numbers and outputs. Results that look too good to be true usually are too good to be true.

- Check that the scoring you used on your scales all works in the 'same direction'. You might see what you think is a negative correlation but this may turn out to be a scale that went 'against the flow' for some reason.

- Double-check that you are using appropriate tests for appropriate types of data.

- If you are using SPSS, then remember that you can copy your outputs into a Word file. This is important because it means that there is no danger that you will make a mistake in typing data into your report document. Also you can edit the headings and tidy up the data for presentation within the research report or dissertation itself.

- Remember that the larger the sample the more likely it is that a relationship will appear to be significant. With a smaller sample you might assert a reasonable level of significance of $p = 0.01$ or even $p = 0.05$ but with a larger sample you would need to look for significance of $p = 0.001$.

- Don't be tempted to 'over-do it' with charts and diagrams. Use these sparingly where they add value to the analysis and understanding process. Remember that your tutor will not award marks for attractive charts – your tutor will reward meaningful charts – quality will outweigh quantity.

Multilevel analysis

This section of the chapter has been summarising and providing guidance on how to conduct the most important statistical analysis when focusing on data collected at the same level of analysis, often the individual level. In particular, we have been focusing on how variables like gender or age influence other variables at the individual level, such as perceived organisational support or engagement. However, it is important to acknowledge that our data may actually be multilevel.

Multilevel data occurs where responses are grouped (or 'nested') within one or a series of higher-level unit(s) of response. Some examples would be students being grouped into schools or employees being grouped into teams or (and) organisations. In the first example, schools would be the higher level and students would be the lower level of analysis. In the second example, we may actually have three levels, where organisations would be the higher level, teams would be a middle level and employees would be the lower level. Other datasets that can be analysed via multilevel modelling include longitudinal/time-series data. Observations over time would be nested within higher-level groups. For example, we could have diary studies of the same person registering data over time or perhaps studies registering organisational changes over time.

The treatment of multilevel or hierarchical data for purposes of statistical analysis has specific practical, technical and conceptual issues that *standard regression techniques are unable to adequately resolve* (Hox, Moerbeek and van de Schoot, 2018; Snijders and Bosker, 2011):

Problem 1: Modelling the cluster effect

With multilevel (or 'clustered') data, it is usual to find that respondents within the same 'cluster' or 'higher-level unit' will be more alike than respondents from different clusters. For example, children from the same school are more likely to get similar test scores than children from different schools. Therefore, the school a child attends will tell us something about the test score he or she is likely to get. Similarly, *relationships between variables* will often be more alike among respondents within the same higher-level unit than for those in different higher-level units. For example, in some schools the parents' education may predict performance; in others less so. Different relationships between variables can be found when we control for the clustering of a dataset by higher-level units. If we do not control for this and treat the data as a single lump we are ignoring this, which generates the so-called Simpson's Paradox. A Simpson's Paradox occurs when a trend appears in different groups of data but disappears or reverses when these groups are combined. If we treat the whole data as a lump, not acknowledging its possible multilevel nature, this can lead to a mis-specified model and incorrect conclusions.

Problem 2 – Sample size inflation

Where we have multilevel data, we often wish to predict responses at a lower level from variables that are naturally of a higher level (or see if higher-level characteristics moderate relationships at the lower level). For example, does school size predict a student's performance? Another example would be employees nested within teams: is the effect of gender on an employee's stress moderated by the team gender balance (percentage of males/females)? When performing the analysis, higher-level variables have to be replicated for each respondent within a cluster. Testing such a model with a method that pretends we only have one level of data and does not acknowledge this replication (eg standard multiple regression), consequently (falsely) inflates the sample size for these observations of higher-level variables. This leads to underestimating the variability of higher-level predictor variables and to underestimated standard errors for these variables, which results in Type I Errors: finding significant effects when they don't really exist!

At this stage you might be thinking: perhaps we can avoid the problems with multilevel by aggregating the entire dataset to the higher level (eg one row per school), right? Wrong! This assumption is flawed because: 1) variables may not make theoretical or statistical sense at a higher level; 2) there is a lack of agreement and/or group mean reliability may invalidate aggregated scores; and 3) we are not predicting what we want to predict (ie a student's actual test score). Ignoring the multilevel structure and using standard multiple regression or aggregating to create a single level are both clearly unsuitable.

So how should we analyse multilevel data?

We can do this by using **multilevel models**, also called hierarchical linear models. In its most simple form, a multilevel model partitions and analyses the variance of our dependent variable by the hierarchy of our data.

Multilevel analysis is a complex technique and we are not going to explain it here, but if you believe that your data are nested and you have a sufficient sample size at the upper level (see Maas and Hox, 2005), then it might be important to focus on some of the multilevel analysis books we recommend at the end of this chapter. You can run multilevel analyses using SPSS. Other relevant software is: HLM, Stata, SAS, MPlus and R.

Structural equation modelling

The previous sections addressed some of the most commonly used statistical tests in HR research and we provided some guidance and examples from SPSS. One other popular tool for data analysis in HR research is structural equation modelling (SEM). When you read recent quantitative papers in HR and organisational behaviour, you are likely to find some visual representation of the main variables in the study, usually in relatively complex models that simultaneously address relationships between many variables. Usually what is depicted is a series of regressions occurring simultaneously, where there can be many independent and dependent variables at the same time, and variables that are simultaneously outcomes and antecedents of other variables.

According to Ullman and Bentler (2013), SEM is also referred to as causal modelling, causal analysis, simultaneous equation modelling, analysis of covariance structures, path analysis, or confirmatory factor analysis (these last two are actually special types of tests in SEM).

SEM is an extension of the General Linear Model that enables you to fit more than one regression equation simultaneously. Its purpose is to study complex relationships among variables, where some or all variables can be unobserved, or latent (Byrne, 2016). It takes an approach of testing an a priori specified causal model-theory, which means that you basically need to have a sound hypothesised model (a set of hypotheses working together to explain one phenomenon) that is strongly based in theory. In SEM, we can also test competing models – SEM analytics show which ones fit, where there are redundancies, and can help pinpoint what particular model aspects are in conflict with the data.

SEM cannot be run using SPSS; you would need to have add-on software to SPSS called AMOS. Other commonly used SEM software are LISREL, MPlus, R at Stata. Modern SEM software is easy to use, but it is important that you know the reasoning behind the estimations you are running.

SEM is increasingly popular because it has several advantages when compared to multiple regression (Byrne, 2016; Kline, 2015; Wang and Wang, 2012):

- Multiple dependent variables are possible, which is something you cannot have in multiple regressions.

- Variables can be both a predictor and an outcome at the same time – usually these variables are called mediators.

- It allows for a complex set of interrelationships to be easily specified and tested.

- Testing alternative theories/models to identify the best one – you can compare different alternative plausible models.

- SEM has the ability to handle latent variables (unobserved), calculate and partial out their measurement error from the test of relationships. This is a major advantage compared to linear regression, because in order to test a variable like 'affective organisational commitment', you would need to compute the mean of the items used to measure it, before you can include it as a variable in the regression equation.

- SEM allows us to partition the variance – into model/trait variance, error variance, residual (unexplained variance) – for a better diagnostics and understanding of our data.

- SEM software often allows for a graphical modelling interface, which can be more user-friendly, even for non-statisticians.

- SEM can handle latent growth models, reciprocal causality models, autoregressive latent growth models, latent multilevel models, Bayesian models, Monte Carlo simulation models, nonlinear models, mediation models, multiple groups and invariance tests across the groups, etc. These are all very complicated names that you are very unlikely to use for your research project, but they are useful in more complex research designs.

- SEM can handle all kinds of variables simultaneously – binary, categorical to continuous.

When creating an SEM model, it helps if you are good at drawing, because you will normally be able to draw the model you want to test and it can be complicated to think about how to use space in the drawing window. Regardless of your spatial organisation skills, there are several conventions in using SEM diagrams (Ullman and Bentler, 2013):

1 Observed variables, also called indicators, or manifest variables, are represented by squares or rectangles.

2 Unobserved variables, also called constructs, latent variables or factors, are represented by circles or ovals in path diagrams.

3 Relationships between variables are indicated by arrows. A line with a regular arrow represents a hypothesised direct relationship from an independent variable (exogenous) to a dependent variable (endogenous). A two-headed arrow indicates a covariance between the two variables with no implied direction of effect (Figure 10.4).

In Figure 10.5, you will find the screenshot of a model we drew on AMOS testing the relationships from two independent variables (burnout – a latent variable with three indicators – and age – represented as an indicator or observable variable) to employee engagement. Employee engagement is presented as a second order latent variable, which means that it is composed by two other factors or dimensions within

Figure 10.4 Conventions in using SEM diagrams

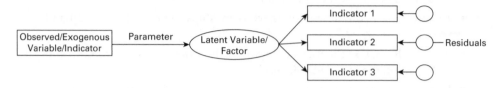

engagement: dedication and vigour, created based on three indicators (or question-naire items) each. Engagement is actually composed of another factor, absorption (Schaufeli and Bakker, 2003), but it was removed from this example for ease of presentation. In this example, we are basically testing two hypotheses: 1) Burnout is negatively related to engagement; and 2) Age is positively related to engagement. At the same time, we are testing a whole factorial structure of our latent variables. Figure 10.6 presents the screenshot of the AMOS output where we are able to find whether these two hypotheses were supported.

The AMOS output presented in Figure 10.6 may not be the easiest to read at first. You will have two tables: one with your regression weights and another with your standardised regression weights. The standardised regression weights are normally the values you would present in your results section, but you can only see their significance by looking at the P column on the first table, with the unstandardised regression weights. The first column on both tables presents the relationships that are being tested in the model. In order to test our two hypotheses, we focus on the first and second rows of the table: eng → burnout and eng → age. Over there, and looking at the P (p-value) column, we can see that there is a significant negative relationship between burnout and engagement (p <.001), which supports our first hypothesis. However, our second hypothesis was not supported by the data, since age was not significantly related to engagement (p = .081).

One key element in SEM is the model fit, which basically allows us to determine whether our hypothesised model is a good fit to the data, also allowing us to compare it to other alternative plausible models. This model comparison is often done at an initial stage, where we test the factorial structure of our data, by comparing a series of the so-called measurement models (where we are not assuming directionality on the relationships between variables – only covariates are placed between our variables). It is after you have reached a satisfactory measurement model that you then test regression paths like the ones you can see in Figure 10.5. Assessing model fit is a complex matter that we will not address in detail. However, if you feel that you should be using SEM in your analysis, we encourage you to carefully read the textbooks on SEM we recommend at the end of this chapter.

Figure 10.5 Example of an SEM model on AMOS – Do burnout and age impact employee engagement?

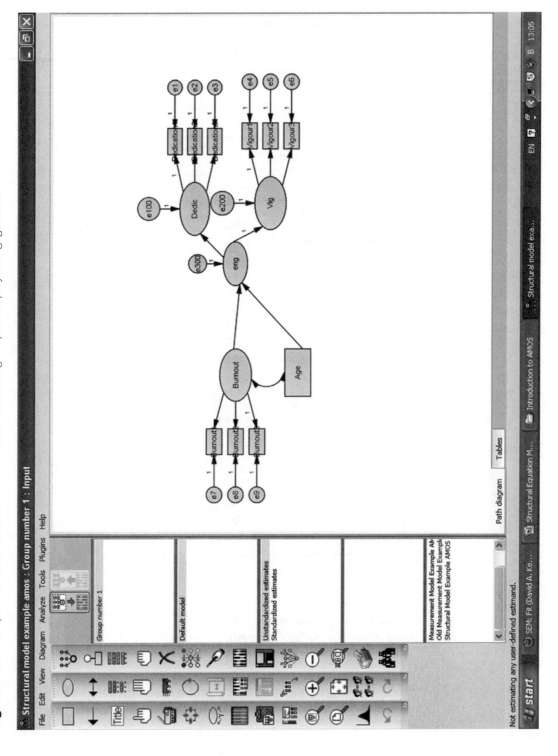

Figure 10.6 AMOS output with estimates

Estimates (Group number 1 – Default model)

Scalar Estimates (Group number 1 – Default model)

Maximum Likelihood Estimates

Regression Weights: (Group number 1 – Default model)

			Estimate	S.E.	C.R.	P	Label
eng	<---	Burnout	–.373	.049	–7.564	***	par_8
eng	<---	Age	.014	.008	1.743	.081	par_9
Dedic	<---	eng	1.019	.095	10.677	***	par_7
Vig	<---	eng	1.000				
Dedication1	<---	Dedic	1.000				par_1
Dedication2	<---	Dedic	1.337	.076	17.526	***	par_1
Dedication3	<---	Dedic	1.371	.086	15.857	***	par_2
Vigour1	<---	Vig	1.000				
Vigour2	<---	Vig	1.282	.070	18.249	***	par_3
Vigour3	<---	Vig	.765	.065	11.711	***	par_4
Burnout3	<---	Burnout	1.000				
Burnout2	<---	Burnout	.882	.063	14.058	***	par_5
Burnout1	<---	Burnout	1.152	.074	15.502	***	par_6

Standardised Regression Weights: (Group number 1 - Default model)

			Estimate
eng	<---	Burnout	–.511
eng	<---	Age	.091
Dedic	<---	eng	.969
Vig	<---	eng	.940
Dedication1	<---	Dedic	.750
Dedication2	<---	Dedic	.890
Dedication3	<---	Dedic	.804
Vigour1	<---	Vig	.774
Vigour2	<---	Vig	.904
Vigour3	<---	Vig	.598
Burnout3	<---	Burnout	.767
Burnout2	<---	Burnout	.741
Burnout1	<---	Burnout	.872

CHECKLIST

- Statistics can be defined as: 'describing things with numbers and assessing the odds' (Rugg and Petre, 2007:168).

- IBM SPSS is the most commonly used software package to help with quantitative data analysis in student research projects in HRM and most other Business and Management disciplines.

- It is important to use your own judgement about the most appropriate way to use statistical packages and which tests to undertake. Analysis is fundamentally a thinking process and even the most expensive and up-to-date packages will not do the thinking for you.

- Before you choose your statistical tests you should review your research questions or objectives and review the types of data that you have gathered and the extent to which they are normally distributed.

- Cross-tabulation allows for an assessment of the relationship between any two variables. It is particularly useful for nominal (category) data.

- A scattergram involves plotting a graph where each axis represents the value of one variable. This method of data analysis is never appropriate for nominal (category) data and is most appropriate for interval or ratio scale data.

- The chi-square test (χ^2) is a useful way of evaluating the probability that results in tests of association occurred through chance.

- The Mann-Whitney U test and the t-test are useful tools with which to assess different patterns of responses within sample groups.

- Tests of correlation measure the strength and direction of association between different variables. The two most frequently used tests are the Spearman's correlation test (for non-parametric data) and the Pearson's correlation test (for parametric data). Both tests calculate a correlation coefficient that ranges between -1 (a perfect negative correlation) and $+1$ (a perfect positive correlation).

- Regression analysis enables you to examine the extent to which different variables may 'predict' the strength of a dependent variable but this procedure requires a minimum sample size to be reliable.

- Factor analysis can assess whether there are 'key variables' in the data or whether some variables can be grouped or clustered together to form a coherent (multidimensional) composite variable.

- The Cronbach alpha ('α') test provides a measure of internal consistency (and hence reliability) of questionnaire responses. Higher values of alpha (values of 0.7 or higher) give greater confidence in the quality of a group of questionnaire items to measure a single one-dimensional latent construct.

- Charts and diagrams can be a powerful way of presenting parts of your analysis but use them sparingly, and only when they are directly relevant to your research objectives or questions.

- Multilevel analysis can also be useful when dealing with nested data, for example, several employees nested into a certain team or department in the organisation.

- Structural equation modelling (SEM) is a frequently used tool in HR research and it has several advantages when compared to multiple regression, mainly because it allows for multiple dependent variables and makes a more accurate treatment of latent (unobserved) variables, such as organisational commitment, engagement, psychological contract fulfilment, etc.

TEST YOURSELF

1   The terms 'parametric' and 'non-parametric' refer to:

   a. Two main groups of data types that are linked to different groups of statistical tests.

   b. Measures of statistical significance.

   c. Alternative forms of data display.

   d. Forms of questionnaire response scale.

2   Tests of probability that a test result occurred by chance is known as:

   a. Multiple regression analysis.

   b. Chi-square test.

   c. Significance testing.

   d. Chronbach alpha.

3   A reliability coefficient is a measure of:

   a. The difference between two variables.

   b. The strength of the relationship between two different variables.

   c. The extent to which the responses to a group of variables are internally consistent.

   d. Whether the data are measuring what you think they are measuring.

4   What information can a cross-tabulation provide?

   a. It shows the results for all of your questionnaire items.

   b. It lists different measures of significance.

   c. It summarises the frequencies of different variables so that they can be compared.

   d. It compares the different results from a regression analysis.

5   A perfect positive correlation between two variables in a test of correlation would give a result of:

   a. −0.123

   b. +1

   c. 0

   d. −1

6   A commonly used 'test of difference' for parametric data is known as:

   a. Mann-Whitney test

   b. Chronbach alpha

   c. Factor analysis

   d   t-test

7   Factor analysis can be used to:

   a. Assess whether some variables can be grouped or clustered together to form a coherent composite variable.

   b. Work out the extent to which two variables are co-related.

   c. Identify the extent to which different variables can 'predict' the strength of an independent variable.

   d. Divide results by a multiplier.

8   Structural equation modelling (SEM) has advantages compared to multiple regression because:

   a. It allows you to test several relationships between variables at the same time.

   b. Variables can be both a predictor and an outcome at the same time.

   c. It allows us to partition the variance into model/trait variance, error variance, residual (unexplained variance).

   d. All of the above.

Review Questions

Questions for reflection

These questions are designed to enable you to identify key areas for development with your project that you should discuss with your project tutor, supervisor or advisor if possible. The responses to them can also form part of a Continuing Professional Development log or portfolio. This is required by CIPD for those who wish to upgrade their membership status.

Taking stock

1   What quantitative data analysis software is available to you through work or your study centre? Do you have (or can you obtain) a personal copy?

2   What books or manuals might you obtain to help you through the data analysis process?

3   How clear are you about your research questions and the implications of them for choosing appropriate quantitative data analysis tests?

4   How realistic do your outputs look? Might some of them really be 'too good to be true' meaning that you need to carefully check the appropriateness of the test and the way it has been undertaken?

Strengths and weaknesses

5   What are your strengths and weaknesses with numerical reasoning? Where might you look for help with statistics (family member; work colleague; fellow student; colleague; tutor; friend)?

6   What are the strengths and limitations of the data you have collected? What are the implications of the sample size and response rate for your analysis? What seem to be the main features of the data you have collected?

7   What steps can you take to build your confidence on the statistics software you have decided to use?

Being a practitioner-researcher

8   What help is available at your place of work with running statistical tests and making sense of the findings?

9   What are the data security and ethical issues with storing your data in paper or electronic form? What password protection do you need to use to ensure that no unauthorised access occurs?

 Useful Resources

Recommended books related to SPSS

Field, A (2018) *Discovering Statistics Using IBM SPSS Statistics*, Sage, London

Pallant, J (2016) *SPSS Survival Manual*, McGraw Hill Education, Maidenhead

Useful books related to structural equation modelling

Byrne, BM (2016) *Structural Equation Modeling with AMOS: Basic Concepts, Applications, and Programming (Multivariate Applications Series)*, 3rd edn, Routledge, New York

Kline, RB (2015) *Principles and Practice of Structural Equation Modelling*, 4th edn, The Guilford Press, New York

Wang, J and Wang, X (2012) *Structural Equation Modelling: Applications using MPlus*, John Wiley and Sons, Chichester

References

Bell, E, Bryman, A and Harley, B (2019) *Business Research Methods*, 5th edn, Oxford University Press, Oxford

Brett Davies, M (2014) *Doing a Successful Research Project: Using qualitative or quantitative methods*, Palgrave Macmillan, Basingstoke

Byrne, BM (2016) *Structural Equation Modeling with AMOS: Basic concepts, applications, and programming (Multivariate Applications Series)*, 3rd edn, Routledge, New York

Collis, J and Hussey, R (2014) *Business Research: A practical guide for undergraduate and postgraduate students*, Palgrave, Basingstoke

Eisenberger, R, Huntington, R, Hutchison, S and Sowa, D (1986) Perceived organizational support, *Journal of Applied Psychology*, **71**, pp 500–507

Hox, JJ, Moerbeek, M and van de Schoot, R (2018) *Multilevel Analysis: Techniques and applications (Quantitative Methodology Series)*, 3rd edn, Routledge, New York

Kline, RB (2015) *Principles and Practice of Structural Equation Modelling,* 4th edn, The Guilford Press, New York

Maas, CJM and Hox, JJ (2005) Sufficient sample sizes for multilevel modelling, *Methodology*, **1** (3), pp 86–92

Rugg, G (2007) *Using Statistics: A gentle introduction*, Open University Press, Maidenhead

Rugg, G and Petre, M (2007) *A Gentle Guide to Research Methods*, Open University Press, Maidenhead

Schaufeli, WB and Bakker, AB (2003) UWES – Utrecht Work Engagement Scale: test manual, Unpublished manuscript, Department of Psychology, Utrecht University

Snijders, TAB and Bosker, RJ (2011) *Multilevel Analysis: An introduction to basic and advanced multilevel modeling*, Sage, London

Ullman, JB and Bentler, PM (2013) Structural equation modelling, in *Handbook of Psychology*, ed IB Weiner, 2nd edn, John Wiley & Sons, New Jersey

Wang, J and Wang, X (2012) *Structural Equation Modelling: Applications using MPlus*, John Wiley and Sons, Chichester

11
Writing up your project and making recommendations

LEARNING OBJECTIVES

This chapter should help you to:

- clarify what is required by different audiences with whom you will communicate about your research;
- draft a research report or dissertation;
- revise, redraft and proofread your work to maximise its credibility and accuracy.

CHAPTER OUTLINE

- How to use this chapter
- Why, what, when and for whom to write
- Structuring and organising your writing
- Writing your conclusions, recommendations, the abstract and the personal development sections

- Style and expression
- Reviewing, revising and submitting your work
- Summary checklist
- Test yourself, review and reflect questions
- Useful resources

How to use this chapter

When you reach this chapter you will rightly feel that you are on the 'home run'. Many of the previous chapters of the book contain suggestions about how to write up specific sections of your final report. However, the conclusions, recommendations and personal reflections sections do not feature in these chapters. Therefore, an additional section has been added to this chapter to provide you with a starting framework for thinking about how to write these important chapters or sections in an effective way.

The focus of this chapter is on helping you to communicate the results of your research in a credible way. Academic 'audiences' for your work have different priorities to those in work organisations and this chapter should help you to clarify the expectations of both sets of stakeholders. Although we would like to think that you will read this chapter before you start the writing process we recognise that most of those who are now staring at this page will be acutely aware of the need to write fast to meet a rapidly approaching deadline. All the activities in this chapter, therefore, are focused on helping you to develop the skills you need to write effectively and submit on time. The guidance will also help you to 'sell' the experience that you have gained through the research process and the output of your report, to support your employability and career development.

 Case Example 11.1

Finding the right style

Lucas has spent the last 10 years working for the same local government body. When he joined in 2009 he worked as a marketing assistant and he enjoyed that role for four years until the department was reorganised. In 2013, Lucas was transferred to the HR team where he took the role of payroll assistant. While working as part of the wider HR team, he developed a real interest in people management and was subsequently promoted to HR Officer. After being in the role for two years, Lucas's manager agreed to provide financial assistance for him to undertake his Advanced CIPD qualification at a local university.

Lucas has enjoyed his course so far and has gained some excellent marks in the modules that are assessed by examination or presentation; however, he has found the long written assignments more challenging. Lucas has done enough to pass all of his modules but is conscious that he needs to get a good mark on his management report if he is to receive an overall 'merit' for his studies.

Lucas's planned research topic was training transfer and so his investigation was directly relevant to an organisational project he is currently working on. However, tutor feedback on his assignments had stressed that his work was not characterised by sufficient 'depth'; that his reading was too focused on 'reporting' what he had read and that his style was 'prescriptive and descriptive'. Tutors also said that Lucas

made too much use of bullet points and was not sufficiently evaluative and analytical. Lucas became increasingly anxious about the extent to which he would be able to deliver a much longer dissertation document to meet the 'academic' requirements of his tutors. He had always taken a very thorough approach to his studies but was baffled about the distinction between terms that tutors used such as description, prescription, analysis and evaluation.

Discussion questions

1   What advice would you give to Lucas to help him feel more confident of developing an appropriate writing and thinking style?

2   Make a list of verbs that would help Lucas to write in a more analytical style.

Feedback notes

This case example highlights a number of challenges that many students encounter when undertaking academic writing. In this case, Lucas is experienced as a practitioner and has an excellent HR vocabulary but it is the style of writing that is less familiar. Like Lucas many people are baffled and confused by tutor comments (which may be brief and lack much detail) on the text of assignments saying things like 'too descriptive' or 'lacks critical evaluation'. Perhaps the best advice you might offer Lucas is to try to 'stand back' from what he reads about his topics and make a 'rounded assessment' of strengths and weaknesses. Lucas might be well advised to think about the issues from more than one perspective. The perspective of an HR practitioner came easily to him, but what about the perspective of those affected by the transfer of training he is reading about or the perspective of senior managers, line managers or the L&D team.

While bullet points may be useful to summarise key points and to show that Lucas 'knows about' things, they are less helpful in convincing an academic reader that he understands the things he has listed as they don't demonstrate his own analysis and the 'value' he is adding through his arguments. Lucas might also be well advised to try comparing different themes and issues that crop up in the literature rather than listing them one at a time.

You might suggest that Lucas focuses on verbs such as 'to argue', 'to assert', 'to refute', 'to compare', 'to challenge'. You could also refer back to Chapter 2, which outlines useful verbs for research objectives to see if any of them would be suitable.

This chapter explores ways in which the writing process can be managed effectively and can become a rewarding part of the overall research process.

Why, what, when and for whom to write?

Why and when to write?

Like many HR practitioners you may feel that 'academic writing' seems dry and uninteresting and that the seemingly endless references that are cited within the text are distracting rather than helpful. Writing a lengthy project report or dissertation in an academic style can seem daunting. Some students find the writing process makes them feel clumsy and inarticulate. Some find they have plenty of ideas in their head but that translating these into a written format is nearly impossible. However, for other people, the opportunity to create a piece of writing can be a rewarding opportunity for reflection and 'sense-making'.

Whether you hate or love writing, there are a number of very good reasons for doing it. First, once the writing process is finished you can submit your work and reclaim a significant part of your life: you can do some of the things you have been promising yourself you will do 'after the course'. Second, writing about your research helps you to reflect on and communicate what you have found out. Third, provided that you meet all the assessment criteria for your course you can be awarded credit for your achievements: you can qualify!

These are powerful motivators, but writing is 'a good thing' for other reasons too. Saunders and Lewis (2018) point out that by engaging in the writing process you are forced to clarify your thinking and they remind us that the actual process of writing develops and cements your learning. It is difficult to commit ideas onto paper but the more times you try the clearer your thinking becomes. Within this process some ideas will be discarded, others may be reformulated but, as time goes by, what you are trying to explain will become clearer to you and to those with whom you need to communicate.

Writing and reflection go hand in hand. Therefore, writing is a learning process and the way to learn to write is by writing (Neuman, 2012). The more you write **at all stages of the project**, the more you will reflect on what you are doing and the more guidance you will be able to receive from your tutor or supervisor. The message, therefore, is write often and write throughout the project process. If you have not done this and now have to face up to writing 'from scratch' don't fret too much – many others have been in your position and they have survived.

Who is the audience for your research and what are they looking for?

As you write your dissertation the most important and urgent stakeholder to focus on is your university or study centre as they will assess your work and determine whether it meets the criteria for a pass.

Activity 11.1

Knowing your readers

Draw up two short checklists. One list relates to your tutors; the other relates to any organisation sponsor(s) or client(s) who may want a report about your research. For each checklist identify:

- why the reader needs to read about your research;

- their professional background and how this may influence what they expect to see in your report;

- their attitude towards the research process;

- what they really need to know about;

- the differences in requirements for the format and presentation of your work.

Feedback notes

The two lists that you have compiled may well have some similarities but it is likely that there will also be some differences. Your tutors will read your report because they have to mark it and confirm that it meets the requirements of the centre as well as CIPD. Assessors are interested in your level of knowledge and understanding, as well as your ability to apply a consistent and appropriate research methodology to investigate a defined HR issue, problem or opportunity. They are looking for analysis, critical evaluation, different perspectives and synthesis of information from different sources. They will be particularly interested in the implications of what you have found for their understanding of HR more generally. Organisational sponsors and/or clients will be interested in the findings of your research and the recommendations that you are making. They may also wish to check that you have respected the ethical permissions that were provided for the study.

The academic report – clarifying institutional requirements

It is very important to remind yourself about the details of what your particular study centre is expecting. In particular, find out about:

- **Length.** What is the minimum and maximum word count?
- **Structure.** What sections must be included?
- **Style.** What conventions are expected with regard to 'first or third person', what 'tense' to use (present or past) and so on.
- **Format.** What line spacing? What margins? How should the title page be laid out? What font size and typeface?
- **Referencing.** Which method is required? The most commonly used are Harvard and APA but your institution may have developed its own style.
- **Appendix.** What are the basic requirements for what should be provided? Are there any restrictions?

- **Requirement for a reflective learning statement.** In what format should this be provided? Is specific supporting evidence required for this section?
- **Assessment criteria.** You will have been given a copy of the criteria by which your work will be assessed. Find this again now – take a good look at the requirements and then refer to them frequently while you are writing up. Pay specific attention to the percentages allocated to different sections/chapters as this provides useful guidance on how you should manage the respective word counts.

Research report or dissertation?

At the end of the research project some courses require the submission of a **business or management research report**. At undergraduate (intermediate) level this may be part of the 'Using Information in Human Resources' module, or at postgraduate (advanced) level the module 'Investigating a Business Issue from a Human Resources Perspective'. Other courses (at undergraduate and leading to a Masters level qualification) may require a dissertation. These different forms, and the different word lengths that you may be given, can generate anxiety so here below are some comparisons. First, the difference in expectations between **undergraduate and postgraduate level** work is expressed in Table 11.1. Here the difference is essentially one of 'depth'. Postgraduate level researchers are expected to probe more deeply and work at a higher level of uncertainty, achieving outcomes at a more 'professional' level than are undergraduate students. There is also an expectation that postgraduate students offer some 'originality' through their work.

Table 11.1   Comparison of expectations for research reports at undergraduate and postgraduate levels

	Undergraduate Level Expectations	Postgraduate Level Expectations
Knowledge and Understanding	Systematic understanding and coherent and detailed knowledge of the subject area. Work is underpinned by studies at the forefront of the subject.	Systematic understanding and knowledge of the area including theoretical and research-based knowledge at the forefront of the topic. A critical awareness of current issues and insights.
Analysis	Use of established techniques of analysis in the subject area.	Comprehensive understanding of the techniques of analysis in the subject area. Originality in the application of knowledge and an understanding of the research process.

(*continued*)

Table 11.1 (Continued)

	Undergraduate Level Expectations	Postgraduate Level Expectations
Conceptual Understanding	Ability to develop and sustain arguments and analysis relevant to the topic area, including recent studies. Ability to describe research and scholarship in the field.	Critical evaluation of advanced scholarship in the area. Evaluation of methodologies of scholarship in the field.
Thinking Skills	Application of thinking skills and appreciation of levels of uncertainty and ambiguity with awareness of the provisional nature of knowledge.	Ability to deal with complex issues, demonstrate originality and make sound judgements in the absence of complete data.
Learning Skills	Ability to manage own learning and make appropriate use of academic sources.	Demonstration of self-direction, autonomy and originality to advance knowledge and understanding and develop new skill.

(Adapted from QAA, 2014)

The difference between a business research report and a dissertation

Some general marking criteria of a dissertation (adapted from Fisher and Buglear, 2010; Brown, 2006; Fox *et al*, 2007) are shown here and this is followed by CIPD guidance about the marking criteria for a business research report at advanced level.

GENERAL ASSESSMENT CRITERIA FOR A MASTERS LEVEL DISSERTATION

- Research objectives. Clear and relevant objectives, derived from an identification and definition of a valid and practicable project.

- Research design. The research design and methodological approach and issues of access and cooperation are appropriate and justified in order to generate sufficient quality and quantity of data. An evaluation of issues of research ethics and the reliability and validity of the data, taking the methodological approach into account is undertaken.

- Literature review. Relevant literature drawn from a range of appropriate sources is analysed and critically reviewed. The literature review provides a structure and focus for the dissertation. Concepts are defined and structured and an appropriate analytical framework is developed to give a theoretical grounding and focus in the dissertation.

- Data collection and analysis. Primary and/or secondary data that are relevant to the research objectives are gathered and presented. Data are analysed in a thorough and critical way, using (where appropriate) the analytical or conceptual framework derived from the literature review.

- Conclusions. These are clearly expressed, supported by the evidence and derived logically from the analysis. Where recommendations are also appropriate they are practical, imaginative and relevant.

- Presentation. Clear written expression utilising a style and use of language and referencing that is credible and appropriate for academic purposes.

- Integration of academic knowledge. The research process demonstrates originality or use of initiative, and there is evidence of a 'learning process' for the researcher.

If you are undertaking an advanced level CIPD qualification then the learning outcomes for 'Investigating a business issue from an HR perspective' (CIPD, 2018) are that you:

1 Identify and justify a business issue that is of strategic relevance to the organisation.

2 Critically analyse and discuss existing literature, contemporary HR policy and practice relevant to the chosen issue.

3 Compare and contrast the relative merits of different research methods and their relevance to different situations.

4 Undertake a systematic analysis of quantitative and/or qualitative information and present the results in a clear and consistent format.

5 Draw realistic and appropriate conclusions and make recommendations based on costed options.

6 Develop and present a persuasive business report.

7 Write a reflective account of what has been learned during the project and how this can be applied in the future.

If you compare the general assessment criteria for dissertations with the learning outcomes outlined above, you will see that there are more similarities than differences. **Both** sets of criteria emphasise the importance of clearly expressed and relevant research aims and objectives, a review of relevant literature, the use of appropriate methods to collect data, and the analysis of that data in an integrated and appropriate way. Although individual study centres operate slightly different assessment criteria, these components would be expected in any postgraduate level project report. A CIPD advanced level **management research report** tends to be shorter (7,000 words is the norm) and there is greater emphasis on the use of the analysis of primary data to generate business focused, practical, costed, timely and realistic recommendations.

If you are undertaking Masters level research, therefore, you will be expected to focus more on the:

- analytical focus, scope and contribution of the literature review;
- evaluation of different research design and methodological issues and the skill with which methods of data collection are undertaken;
- analysis of the data – particularly its thoroughness, the questioning nature of the approach you use and the analytical links with the literature review;
- reasoning process behind the formulation of your conclusions, and the links between the conclusions and your analysis of the literature and the primary data.

Structuring and organising your writing

Getting started

 Activity 11.2

Barriers to writing

Think back to other pieces of writing you have undertaken as part or your studies.

- Identify what hindered, inhibited or made the writing process difficult.

- What feedback have you previously received on your writing style? Did you understand the comments?
- What factors were important to you for getting the writing done?

Feedback notes

Everyone (even your tutor) feels daunted when faced with writing a long document. The more anxious you become, the more you may be tempted to put off the moment of getting started. People often worry that they do not have enough information or they delay starting as they feel the word limit is too long (or too short). In addition, interruptions to writing, pressure of other work, and an inability to concentrate are common concerns, all of which can contribute to 'writers block'. You are likely to have received feedback on your writing style within earlier assignments; however, you may have overlooked it and focused on the assessment-specific comments. It

Figure 11.1   Factors that can delay progress with writing

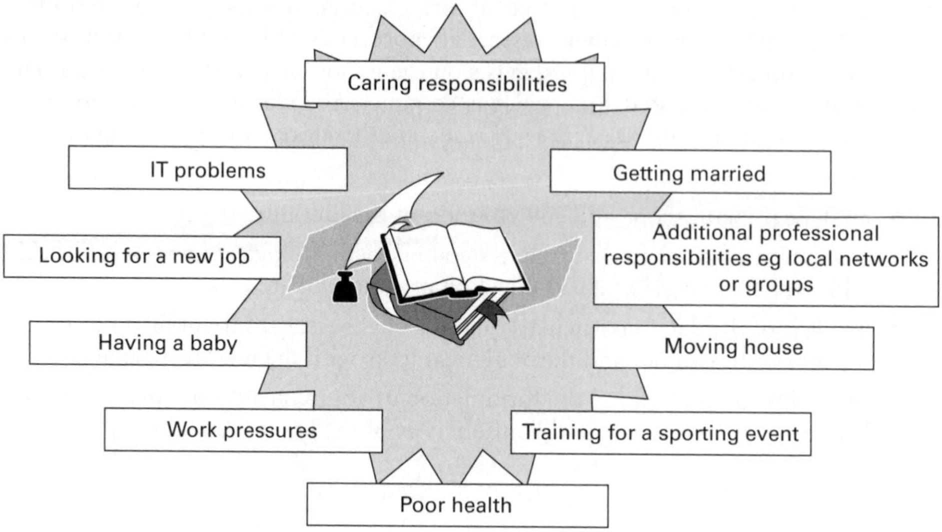

is useful to review the feedback again to see if there are any transferable issues, for example: writing in shorter sentences; joining paragraphs together more neatly; or the way that you integrate references within your work. Other delaying factors, that may well have affected you at some stage in your studies, might include those expressed in Figure 11.1.

The factors illustrated in Figure 11.1 as well as the concerns you may have listed in response to Activity 11.2 can be difficult to cope with and, when it comes to the writing process it is important to try to deal with the things that are partly within your control so that you are better able to manage in spite of those that are outside of your control.

A key issue for any writer is to overcome any tendency to procrastination and to work through writer's block. Some suggestions for this are provided in Table 11.2. No one will find all of these 'tips' appropriate so it is important to take what works for you and use it in your own way.

Safety first

If you can develop an approach that enables you to plan each section within the overall report, and utilise personal strategies so that you maintain a habit of writing, then you should be able to achieve your objective of finishing and submitting your report on time. However, there are other technical obstacles that may seem trivial but can afflict any one at any time and cause misery. Most tutors have had occasion to commiserate with a student whose computer has crashed less than a week before the submission date and who has no backup copy of the work, or whose printer has failed for no apparent reason. Writing is hard work and these technical problems are dispiriting and, in extreme cases, can cause total despair. Given the availability of a range of storage and backup solutions now available at little or no cost, these issues should be avoidable. The following suggestions (written from the heart) are, therefore, offered:

Table 11.2   Making yourself write

Planning to Write	• Divide up the word limit and set sub-limits for each of the chapters or sections. • Set yourself a writing timetable and deadlines. • Draft out the structure for the section or chapter you are about to write. • Break down main parts of the section or chapter into smaller parts – it is much less daunting to produce 200 words than 2,000. • Set up a word processing template for each chapter: set the correct font and point size; line spacing; margins; style for headings and subheadings. This can save you about a week at the end of the writing process. • Use outlines, structures and plans to keep you focused.
When to Write	• Begin early – the closer you get to the deadline the more the pressure mounts up. If you write something now there will be time to improve on it. • Create time ('prime time') for writing – put off other jobs so that you are not exhausted when you begin writing. • Write regularly and develop a pattern or rhythm of work on the report. Try never to miss a writing session. • If the going is getting tough, try writing at a different time of the day or time of the week. • Write up a section as soon as possible. • Reward yourself for little achievements – try to look forward to what you are about to achieve.
Develop Your Own Individual Writing 'Habits'	• Engage in your own personal writing rituals that might help you to get going (music in the background; sharpen your pencils; cup of tea, etc). • Begin wherever it is easiest – start in the middle if that is what it takes! • Don't expect perfection – you are drafting something – you can improve on it later. • Reduce interruptions – do what it takes to work for a defined period without distractions. Turn off your mobile phone for defined writing periods. Do not check your e-mails until you reach a predetermined 'break time'. • Find a regular place for your writing (particularly if you are using a laptop). Familiarity with the surroundings means they won't distract you. Don't waste time getting everything out and putting it away again if you can avoid it. • If you need to, start by speaking your ideas aloud. You might also consider using voice recognition software if you find it easier to speak than to type or write. • Take a short break if you get 'stuck' and then come back to it after a walk/cup of tea, etc but don't leave it for too long. Try not to stop midway. If you can struggle through to the end of a 'troublesome section' you can revisit it another day, when you are fresh, and you will find that you can improve it then. • Where possible, stop writing at a point from which it is easy to resume work again the next time.

(continued)

Table 11.2 (Continued)

Monitoring Your Progress	• Set yourself a target for writing a given number of words each week or month. • Reward yourself when you achieve significant 'word targets'. • Allow someone else to oversee your writing progress (partner, child, colleague, fellow student?). Get someone else to read what you have written. This is hard but well worth it as they can comment on how understandable your material is and suggest some easy ways of making your work much better. • Ask your supervisor/tutor to read your drafts so that you can identify any writing 'issues' early on and deal with them. • Plan to finish – look forward to the day when you submit the project report or dissertation and can then forget about it if you want to.

(Blaxter *et al* 2012; Robson and McCartan, 2016; Neuman, 2012; Jankowicz, 2005; Hart, 2013)

- Save your work every 1,000 words or every hour, whichever is the soonest.
- At the end of each session (or more frequently), back up your work to at least one other device or cloud, ensuring that documents are appropriately secured.
- Never trust your writing solely to a networked system or cloud – always back it up so you can access your work.
- Once each section is drafted save it with a version number (one is never enough!) and print off a hard copy as your ultimate backup. This may be expensive although print options to print two pages on one sheet and to print 'double sided' will make some savings to your print bill. A hard copy is an insurance policy against more than one crisis occurring at the same time.
- Don't keep your backup (for example, on a flash drive) in the same case as the laptop you are using. If one is stolen then the other will disappear too.
- If you are required to submit an online copy of your work, ensure that you are clear about exactly where, in what format and by which deadline this must be completed. Saving your work in the incorrect place could lead to it not being marked using the full spectrum of marks available.
- Have in mind two alternative printers you can use when the time comes to print the final version. Ensure that you have a backup copy of your work in a format that both printers can work from.
- If you have to physically submit a copy of your work, ensure that you leave sufficient time to get to the hand-in location; having a backup plan of public transport is advisable.

Planning your writing

Students tend to adopt one of two approaches for their writing. Some plan the contents of each section to a greater or lesser extent and then work through their plan, amending it as necessary as they proceed. Although this is the approach recommended by almost every tutor, anecdotal evidence suggests that only a minority of students follow this advice. Many students, it appears, have a rough (often implicit) idea of where they will go in their writing and start writing just 'hoping for the best'.

The 'hoping for the best' approach is not for the faint-hearted. As noted in Table 11.2, breaking down what must be written into smaller parts makes writing less daunting. It also promotes structure and coherence. Writing that is undertaken without much of a plan usually has to be significantly revised and restructured two or three times until coherence gradually emerges. Work that has been planned is still likely to need revision, but the process is less extreme and quicker to achieve.

There are a number of ways to plan your writing and it is likely you use them in other aspects of your work and life outside study. These techniques can be used in isolation or in different combinations to facilitate the planning process. You can choose whether to use pen and paper, Word/Excel, or one of the many electronic applications available:

- **Brainstorming.** Use this technique (you could work with a colleague) to generate a list of all the possible ideas or items you need to include in the section you are concerned with. Then set about taking out the ideas that are not relevant, editing out repetitions and putting the remaining ideas into a logical order.

- **Mind mapping.** Construct a mind map that represents different ideas or themes and how they branch out from one another. Use the 'shape' of the map to identify the main sections and the more detailed points to include within them.

- **Concept mapping.** This is a more structured form of 'mapping'. Start with your main topic at the top of a large piece of paper. Use sticky notes to write down all the associated concepts and issues that are relevant and then arrange them on the paper. Draw lines (in pencil) to indicate the links between them AND the nature of the relationship between the concepts or issues (eg 'Stems from', 'leads to' or 'requires' etc). You will find you move your sticky notes around on the page and edit your lines quite a lot before you are 'happy'. However, the end result will be a hierarchically arranged, graphic representation of the relationships between concepts and this will provide you with the basis to structure what you write and you are more likely to achieve the analytical approach that your tutors are looking for.

- **Linear planning.** Jot down the main themes you feel are relevant for the section you are planning. Under each one write down points that 'drop out' from it. Put the main themes into some kind of order (it might be chronological; by category; or by significance to the issue being researched).

- **Sticky notes.** Write headings for all the different points you need to make onto different sticky notes. Then, on the basis of each heading, break it down into sub-points (rather like task analysis if you are engaged in project planning). The sub-points also go onto sticky notes and you can organise and display your notes visually on the wall in front of your computer. This means that you can visually check your progress by removing sticky notes from the wall or flip chart as you have covered them in your writing.

Regardless of how you structure your initial thoughts, it is good practice to keep hold of all of our notes and rough drafts in case you want to go back to ideas at a later date. A second rough document that contains deleted writing, quotes and sections could be revisited towards the end of your project so try not to delete any of your work permanently.

Structuring your report

Your study centre will have given you guidance about the structure of the report although most will allow for some variation where it is appropriate to the nature of the topic and the research approach that has been utilised. In brief, your report or dissertation needs to tell the reader why, how and when you carried out your research; what you found; what it means and how it compares with other research and practice in your field.

The main areas that will be incorporated within most project reports and dissertations are:

- **Title page.** Title of the report; your name; date of submission; any other information required by your study centre.

- **Summary or abstract.** A very short overview that indicates the issue being researched, the research questions, the approach taken to the investigation, the main findings and the conclusions. The next section in this chapter provides some more thoughts about writing a good abstract or summary. Some centres may also require an executive summary.

- **Contents page.**

- **Introduction.** An introduction to the topic and its significance for the organisation and/or HR practice more widely as well as an explanation of the research objectives, aims, terms of reference, or the principal research question to be examined. In this chapter it can be helpful to introduce your case study organisation and give some brief contextual information that will bring it to life for the reader. If you are required to make organisational recommendations, make sure that you include the need to make recommendations as one of your report's objectives. There should also be a brief overview of the logic of the forthcoming sections or chapters.

- **Literature review.** This is where you set your research in its wider context and indicate how your research builds on what is already known. Make sure you show how the review of the literature has informed your research questions as well as the research approach you have adopted. By the time the reader has finished reading your literature review they should be clear about: the way that your issue or topic is defined (by others as well as by you); the important concepts; the strengths and weaknesses of previous studies and how your research can add to knowledge and/or practice in this area. You should ensure that the chapter is presented in a logical order and refer to the advice offered in Chapter 3 on how to achieve this.

- **Research methodology.** An explanation of how you investigated your topics as well as a description of procedures you carried out to gather, record and analyse data. In addition, discuss the ethical issues you took into account; any logistical problems that you encountered as well as an evaluation of the strengths and weaknesses of your approach. By the time the reader reaches the end of this chapter they should be clear about: what data you collected and what data you did **not** collect (and why); what methods, tools and sampling procedures you used and what data analysis procedures you undertook. Chapter 5 provides more detail on how to write the methodology.

- **Findings/results.** This chapter sets out the results of your data gathering activities. The way this is presented will depend on the research approach you adopted. This section is where you **describe** what you found (the facts) rather than your interpretation of your findings. Tables rather than graphs are more appropriate in this section. Save the graphs and figures for the analysis chapter. Remember, if you have a low number of respondents (fewer than 50 responses) then use 'whole numbers' rather than percentages to describe the frequencies. Chapters 7 and 9 indicate different ways of presenting qualitative and quantitative data.

- **Analysis.** For some research approaches the analysis of the data may be integrated within the findings chapter/section. For others it is possible (and preferable) to differentiate between the presentation of data and the data analysis. Lee and Lings (2008) point out that in general terms your research will lead to one of three outcomes, illustrated in Figure 11.2.

Each of these 'outcome positions' requires discussion and interpretation and, in addition, the analysis chapter provides you with the opportunity to answer the 'so what' questions by interpreting your data in the light of the research objectives and questions. Your actual 'outcome position' is less important than how you explore and evaluate the project that you have carried out; the marker is looking for evidence of you managing and following through a research process, regardless of the final findings and recommendations. Chapters 8 and 10 indicate different approaches to writing about your analysis of qualitative and quantitative data.

- **Conclusions.** This part of the report should provide a summary of the main features of your analysis and the implications for both the study of HR and for practice. Make sure your conclusions are clearly drawn from the **evidence** rather than from your opinions. Highlight any areas where further research would be beneficial. The next section in this chapter offers more suggestions about how to tackle the conclusions.

Figure 11.2 Research outcomes spectrum

You found what you expected to find	Some of what you found was expected but there were also anomalies or fresh insights	What you found was not what you expected to find

- **Recommendations** (where appropriate). Where these are required (for example, for CIPD research reports) they should be action orientated, indicating costs, timescales, accountabilities and contingencies. Whereas your conclusions are orientated to the past (they relate to what you found out) the recommendations are future orientated and indicate your views about what should happen now. The next section in this chapter offers more suggestions about how to tackle the recommendations.

- **Personal reflection** – if you are undertaking a CIPD qualification then there is an expectation that you will write a reflective account of what you have learned during the project and how you can apply your learning in the future. The next section in this chapter offers more suggestions about how to tackle the personal reflection element of your report.

- **References.** If you do not reference your work appropriately you may be penalised for plagiarism, which is a serious form of cheating. It is wise to ask your tutor for feedback about your referencing technique and obtain any necessary guidance in order to ensure your work provides evidence of good academic practice. Remember to retain copies of resources you have used alongside your notes and annotations in case you are asked to share your working papers.

- **Appendices.** These will include copies of your research instruments (questionnaires, interview schedules, etc) and other material that is relevant to the understanding of the main report. Research reports should 'make sense' without having to refer to the appendices. Avoid using the appendices as a way around the word limit.

Writing the conclusions, recommendations, abstract and personal reflection

Most of the other sections of the report or dissertation have been given a chapter in their own right with information and ideas about what to include and how to structure each chapter. However, the abstract or summary, conclusions, recommendations and personal reflection have not had their 'own' chapters and so I have produced an additional section for this latest edition of the book, which focuses on these important chapters or sections of your report.

The abstract is the first element of your report or dissertation that will be seen by any of your readers and it is important that this provides a 'solid start'. In some cases this is used to identify appropriate markers for your work. Although it is the first part of the report most people find they have to wait until they have completed all the sections of their report (including their conclusions) before they are able to write the abstract. Following this logic, you will find some ideas about how to write the abstract after the material relating to formulating the conclusions and recommendations.

The conclusions section

By the time you get to write your conclusions chapter or section you are likely to be very close to the submission date and you will probably have been working 'flat out' on your report for the previous few weeks. Like many others, you may be tired and feel fed up by the time you get to the conclusions chapter, wondering what else to write that would not be a repetition of what you have covered already. As a result, you may be tempted to 'write anything' to fill two or three pages so that you can finish the project and move on with your life.

This is a temptation to be resisted as, in many study centres, the conclusions carry a lot of marks; underperformance here can be costly in terms of your grade! However, do not despair. The conclusions chapter should not require more work or research, just one last effort of serious thinking. This is the point where things need to come together. In the conclusions chapter or section you discuss your own findings in the light of the literature and the context of the wider frameworks of HR in which you are working. It is also the point where you need to reassure your reader that the research questions you set out to address really did 'drive' the research design and your interpretation of the data. If, on reflection, you find that your conclusions seem to be addressing rather different questions or issues it might be worth redrafting some of the material in the introduction chapter.

To help you develop your conclusions in a meaningful way try following this 'template' for the chapter structure:

1   Introduction to the conclusions chapter:

   a   Remind your readers about the aim and the research objectives or questions you have addressed in your research. This is one place where a copy and paste, word for word, of your research aim and objectives from the introduction would be acceptable.

   b   Indicate that this chapter will discuss the significance of the research findings and evaluate the implications for both the study of HR and for practice.

2   Research design:

   a   Summarise the way you designed your research (and your reasoning) and provide a short reflection on the strengths and limitations of your research process.

   b   Indicate the extent to which your findings may be generalisable for HR practice generally and/or across different types of organisations and contexts. This is contingent on your research approach and whether generalisation was one of the aims or expectations.

   c   Highlight areas where your project findings indicate a need for further research. Remember that all knowledge is 'provisional'; you will get credit for identifying what your research has shown but also what needs further examination.

3   Taking one objective/question at a time:

   a   What were your main findings and how do they relate with the literature/ theories?

   b   What was surprising in what you found and how does the literature help you to understand what may be happening? What issues came up that the literature does not fully reflect?

4 What are the implications of what you have found for the study of HR?

5 What are the implications of what you have found for HR practice and practitioners?

6 Taking your research as a whole what is the 'big thing' that emerges from the project findings? Highlight the 'added value' of your project – end strongly and confidently!

The recommendations section

The requirements for Masters level dissertations at your institution may or may not require you to formulate an implementation plan or some recommendations at the end of your report. However, a set of feasible and costed recommendations is expected in CIPD management research reports and is one of the overall learning outcomes of the associated module. Many students feel unsure about how to go forward with these, particularly in relation to the costings element. Again, provided that you are prepared to do some thinking, you should be able to achieve a good mark for this section. You will get more marks if you include an implementation plan showing timescales and accountabilities. A discussion about possible barriers/ points of resistance and how these might be overcome will earn you even more marks, alongside appreciation of potential impact.

A useful way to think about your recommendations is to set them out in a tabular form, rather like the template shown as Table 11.3.

Table 11.3   Template for recommendations

Action	Priority	Timescale	Accountability	Resource Implications	Potential Impact of the Action(s)
Indicate in this column the actions you propose	High?	Immediate (within four weeks)?	Indicate clearly who should be responsible for making sure this is implemented	If you can estimate a direct cost then do so (work in round numbers)	Make it clear what the potential benefits could be
Make sure they follow from your data/evidence rather than from your assumptions	Medium?	Short term (within three months?)	HR (who specifically?)	Your resource estimate may relate to time needed rather than to financial estimates	You could identify the key stakeholders
	Low?	Medium term (3–6 months?)	Line managers?		

Starting out with a table can provide a helpful basis for you to think through what actions you recommend that follow from the conclusions that you have drawn from your research. It is important to convince your readers that your recommendations are based on the data and the analysis. The value of the report will be extremely limited if people feel that you could have made your recommendations without undertaking the project in the first place. You may be tempted to 'make do' with just a table for this section of your report but if you can supplement this table with some additional text setting out what alternative 'ways forward' you considered and why the ones you have put forward seem most appropriate your recommendations will seem more persuasive. You can do even better with a brief discussion of the potential points of resistance to your recommendations and some ideas about how these might be overcome or what 'fall back' plans are possible.

The abstract or summary

This part of the report may well not 'count' in the overall word count but its function is to be a 'taster' of what is contained in the full report and it is important to communicate the 'essence' of your report in an effective way. Check out how many words or pages you are 'allowed' for the abstract or summary by your study centre. Some indicate no more than one page, others 250 words, etc. A common mistake in writing the abstract or summary is to reproduce a few parts of the introduction but this part of the document should contain a more general overview of what you have researched: your research questions, your methods of inquiry and your main findings and conclusions. It is daunting to condense all this into one page. The template below (adapted from Biggam, 2018) might help you to plan what to include:

- This research examines...
- The study is important because...
- Data for this study were gathered in the following ways(s)...
- The findings suggest that...
- The main conclusions from the study are...
- (If appropriate) the main recommendations arising from this report are...

If you wish to visualise what a completed abstract looks like, go back to some of the key journal articles that you used to develop your review of the literature. Abstracts from Emerald journals follow a clear format that aligns with the above suggested format.

The personal reflection section

If you are undertaking a CIPD accredited programme then this section is likely to be a requirement but the ability to undertake reflective and reflexive thinking is an important characteristic of HR professionals. Therefore, even if this section is not required for your dissertation it would be useful for you to include some form of personal reflection in your continuing professional development processes. The personal reflection section is the place to write about what you, as a person, have learned: what challenges did you face and how did you overcome them? What would you do differently in the future as a result?

This is likely to be a short section within the overall word count of your report but it will carry marks and it would be a shame if you missed out on them. Some suggested areas for you to reflect on and write about are:

- What was your level of skills, knowledge, attitudes, etc relating to research at the beginning of the project?
- How did you feel at the start of the project? What has changed?
- How did you use your learning from previous modules? How successful were you?
- What problems did you encounter and how did you overcome them?
- What strengths have you been able to build on and what development areas have you become more aware of?
- How will you set out to apply the skills, knowledge and attitudes you have developed over the duration of the project in your work role or future career?
- What feedback have you received during the process? How did you feel about this feedback?
- What are your priorities for your further development? Specific actions here are useful in positioning your commitment to your continuous personal and professional development.

Style and expression issues

Working out a structure for your report will help you clarify **what** to write. It is also important to develop an appropriate style (**how** to write) to enable successful communication with your academic readers.

 Activity 11.3

Writing for different purposes

Think back to all the texts, tweets, Facebook postings, e-mails, and (occasional) letters that you have received during the last week at home and at work. Try to classify them as to:

- their purpose (why they were sent to you);
- the different styles used by the authors to communicate with you and achieve their purpose.

Feedback notes

Predicting the contents of someone's e-mail inbox and social media alerts is impossible but it is likely that your mail has included:

- **Junk.** These general communications (paper-based, texts, electronic mail, internet 'pop-ups'; unwanted postings) were not written for you personally but encourage a rapid response. They use a style that suggests you 'must' or 'should' respond in some way, or that you would be foolish (or churlish) not to respond. Although expressed in quite emotive terms, these are not memorable and you may have forgotten about them already.

- **Letters, cards, e-mails, postings from family and friends.** These may be to thank you for something, to wish you luck, to send birthday greetings, to send you news/updates; to suggest a social gathering, etc. As well as giving some information these usually express feelings and are often written in a semi-humorous or 'chatty' style.

- **Bank statements, insurance documents, payment reminders, pay slips, etc.** These are not at all 'chatty' and their purpose is to provide you with information on which you may want or need to take action. Their style is impersonal and official and people rarely read all the information (the small print) that they provide.

- **Everyday communications.** These provide snippets of information or suggestions and questions. They are partial and often only understandable to the people involved in the communication. They rely on participants being able to 'read between the lines'.

Activity 11.3 indicates in a very simplistic way how the purpose of different forms of writing influence the style that is appropriate for it. The purpose of your research report is to provide a formal record of your research process as well as your findings. This enables others to evaluate what you have done and to learn from your research. Most often, the appropriate style to achieve this purpose will be succinct and will express some 'distance' from the subject matter. Research reports are not the place for language that moralises, is humorous or is 'chatty'. The purpose of the report is to inform rather than to entertain. Try to avoid the temptation to advance one position while ignoring other points of view as this is likely to reduce your mark on the grounds of being not sufficiently analytical. However, it is also important to produce a report that is more interesting than the small print on a broadband bill or direct debit statement. While adopting a formal style, therefore, it is also important to maintain the interest of the reader and to organise what you write to communicate the logic of the document.

The report as a whole will have a 'storyline' something like the one illustrated in Figure 11.3. Each of the main sections of the report will also require a framework through which the purpose of the section can be explained, fulfilled and the progression to the next section is indicated. A framework through which this might be achieved is shown as Figure 11.4.

The framework indicated in Figure 11.4 shows that it is advisable to subdivide each of the main chapters or sections, using subheadings and to have an introduction and a conclusion to each of the sections. This provides some form of 'signposting' to enable your reader to follow the logic of your report. Other stylistic 'hints and tips' are included below (Robson and McCartan, 2016; Saunders and Lewis, 2018; Blaxter *et al*, 2012, Collis and Hussey, 2009; McMillan and Weyer, 2011).

Figure 11.3 Developing a project report 'storyline'

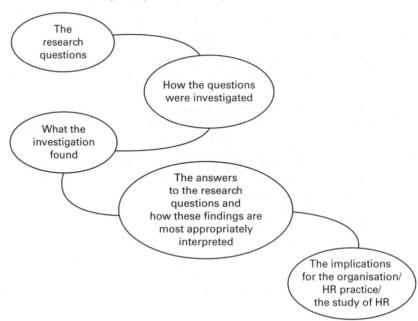

- **Write clearly and simply.** Many students assume that academic language should be more complex and sophisticated than 'normal' writing. In fact, clear communication is enhanced by the use of simple sentences. Where you have drafted a long sentence, check to see if you could rewrite it as two shorter ones.

- **Avoid using too many direct quotations.** You will get credit for your own thinking and your ability to express what is already known in your own words. Using other people's expressions too often makes the report look 'second hand'. Use quotations sparingly and to support a point rather than to 'prove' a point.

- **Avoid using jargon, slang and abbreviations.** Written communication is different from the spoken form. Abbreviations such as 'don't' should be written as 'do not'. Avoid informal language such as 'the flip side of this is…' Use words that are precise rather than overgeneralised and objective rather than emotive. Where you have to use technical terms, include a glossary.

- **Use a new paragraph for each new idea.** Ideas cannot normally be expressed in one sentence. If you find you are using a new paragraph every one or two sentences check that you are explaining your ideas fully or see whether two paragraphs really relate to the same idea and could be combined.

- **Avoid repetition.** Make sure that you have not repeated yourself in two different sections. Look particularly carefully at the introduction to see if some expressions occur again in the same form in the literature review or in the conclusions. Where this is the case, redraft one of the passages.

Figure 11.4   Outline framework for each section/chapter

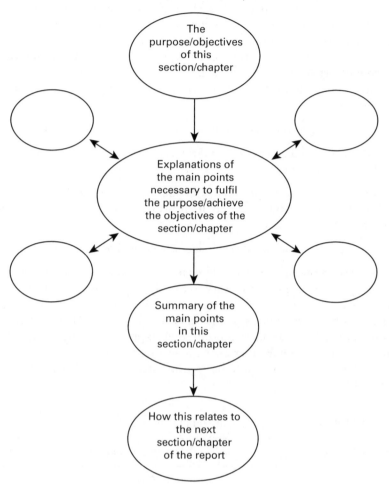

- **Be consistent (and appropriate) with the 'person' and tense.** Different study centres have different expectations about the 'person' with which you write. Most formal academic communication is written from the 'third person' as in the example below:

  The process undertaken for the research was as follows. First, a literature review was undertaken and key themes were identified. A questionnaire was then devised to...

Some research projects, particularly those adopting a more action orientated and qualitative approach, can be appropriately written in the first person, provided that this is acceptable at your study centre. An example of this is shown below:

  At the beginning of the research process I reviewed the literature about... In order to explore the key issues about... I then organised a focus group consisting of...

Some study centres permit the use of the third person in some sections or chapters of the report, and the first person in others. Having decided what 'person' to write from, however, it is important to maintain a consistent approach to it within each section or chapter. The reflective learning piece at the end of your work should be written in the first person as you are reflecting on your own experience. The same consistency is required with regard to the 'tense' with which you write. The normal convention is to use the present tense when you are referring to work that is published as in the examples below:

> Jones (2018) highlights four key aspects of… and these are briefly described now…

> XYZ Ltd is a large employer situated in the north of England. The firm produces… for high street retail outlets.

Where you are referring to primary data that you gathered for your study and the process by which you gathered it, however, the past tense may be more appropriate:

> Questionnaires were issued to 78 people and 62 completed returns were received.

- **Avoid discriminatory language.** In order to maintain an objective stance within your writing it is necessary to avoid using language that can be interpreted as offensive or discriminatory. Check your writing and eliminate them. Writing should be as 'gender neutral' as possible. Thus, 'her manager said that he…' can be more appropriately expressed as, 'the manager indicated that…' Some other expressions that can occur within writing about HR, and which need to be appropriately expressed, are indicated in Table 11.4.

Table 11.4   HR language – avoiding discriminatory language

Try to avoid	Alternative expression
businessman	business manager
committee chairman	the person who chairs the committee or committee Chair
manpower	staffing
manpower planning	HR planning
manning levels	staffing levels
spokesman	representative
the average man	the average person
one man (operation)	run by one person
tradesman	tradesperson

Reviewing, revising and submitting your work

Evaluating what you have written

Achieving perfection in one draft is not likely to occur, which is why time for multiple drafts should be built into your timeline and project plan. Once you have a draft report or dissertation it will be necessary to revise and edit it. This will help you to clarify your thinking and communicate more effectively. You will need to 'clean up' or 'tighten up' your writing as well as undertake more significant revisions such as inserting some new sections, deleting some material and moving material around within the structure. Key questions to be addressed, when evaluating your early drafts are (Saunders and Lewis, 2018; Brown, 2006; McMillan and Weyer, 2011):

- How clear and appropriate is the structure of the report as a whole and the structure of each section or chapter?
- Is the context of your work clear? Have you introduced your case study organisation(s) and been clear about sources of information?
- Are the research objectives or questions expressed clearly and consistently throughout the report? Have you achieved them?
- Is the meaning clear? What passages seem obscure or 'clumsy'? Are all your terms clearly defined?
- Are there occasions where you have inadvertently used biased, emotional or imprecise language?
- To what extent does the literature review inform the methodology and the data analysis?
- Is it clear how you came up with questions that you posed to your participants?
- To what extent does your literature review describe what others have written, analyse the issues **and** advance a line of argument?
- Where are the missing references? If you can't find them, you will need to source alternatives or rewrite the sentences.
- Have your presented **and** analysed your data in a way that readers can follow and is meaningful?
- How close to the word limit are you (too long or too short)? There can be implications for your mark if the word limit is not respected.
- How **logical** and well explained are the points made in each chapter? Do they follow-on in a sensible way from each other?
- How **trustworthy** or reliable is the evidence that you have presented in your chapters? Have you demonstrated your criteria for including your sources?

Honest answers to these questions should help you to prioritise your work as you set about revising what you have written. Your tutor may also be able to provide a useful evaluation (but not at the last minute). Family and friends, although not 'technically' knowledgeable, may also be able to spot the areas that need more careful explanation.

Losing or finding more words

At the beginning of the project process you may have thought you would never have enough words to write to meet the required word length of your dissertation or research report. At this stage, however, you may be facing the opposite problem and experiencing difficulty staying within the word limit. The prospect of losing words can seem very painful, especially if you struggled to write some of them in the first place. For a minority of students, the problem is the reverse; you may discover that your report is 'thin' or that some sections of it are not as long as your tutor expects. Some ideas about how to tackle these opposite areas of difficulty are provided in Table 11.5.

Table 11.5   Losing or adding more words

Making More Into Less	Making Less Into More
Check each subsection in each section. Which one(s) are not central to your argument and analysis? Lose the 'nice to have' but make sure you retain the 'need to have' subsections.	Add new sections. Identify which section(s) might benefit from a fuller explanation or discussion and ensure that paragraphs link together.
Shorten lengthy descriptive passages by using tables, charts or diagrams.	Do you have a lot of appendices and not enough text? Consider working material from one or two of the appendices into the text (but don't engage in 'padding').
Take a good look at the quotations you have used. Do they repeat ideas you have already explained? Do you really need them? Could you express the ideas they articulate in a more concise way?	Look for more references or quotations on the subjects or issues you are writing about. Try to find some contradictory viewpoints that you could analyse.
See if you can summarise the ideas in two or more sentences, or even in a whole paragraph into one (shortish) sentence.	Are you making too many assumptions? Build up sentences into paragraphs by developing your argument or making your line of thinking more explicit.
Engage in 'word weeding' (a form of literary gardening). Remove unnecessary, qualifying or repetitive words from sentences.	Go further in your evaluation of different aspects of your methodology and how appropriate it was. (This section is often not discussed in enough length – particularly in management or business research reports.) Ensure that your recommendations are sufficiently detailed.

(Blaxter *et al*, 2012)

Describing and analysing

In writing your report it is important to minimise description of the work of others and undertake more analysis. Description involves summarising what other people have written or said, more or less in the terms of the original author. **Analysis,** however, is a search for **explanation and understanding.** If you are concerned that some parts of your work are too descriptive (or your tutor has indicated this to you) try the following steps. Steps 1–3 should help you make your writing more critically evaluative. Steps 4–7 should help you make your writing more analytical.

Being critical

1 For each theory, framework, concept, research procedure or method that you describe, write beside it the words *'prove it'*.

2 On a sticky note try to note down possible objections to each 'prove it' point where the opposite or a different situation might apply.

3 Redraft your work into a more critical and evaluative style by using this thinking process to highlight the limitations as well as the strengths of the ideas you are describing.

Being analytical

4 Read through your work again and after each idea that you have evaluated write the words *'so what'*?

5 Redraft your work again, attempting to answer the 'so what' questions in the light of your research objectives or questions.

6 Read your work again. You may find that some of the answers to some of the 'so what' questions are the same. If so, this means you are starting to identify some analytical themes. This is a very good sign.

7 Have a go at reorganising your work so that you tackle one theme at a time. This will involve considering more than one author's work at a time. There may also be implications for the order with which you consider the data in your findings section. If this is the case, give yourself a reward, as it means you have probably started to think and write in a more analytical way.

Final checks

The process of drafting and revising your report can be both frustrating and rewarding. As the submission date approaches there are some important final checks to make prior to printing the final version. The aim at this stage is to arrive at a form of presentation that is as near to perfection as can be achieved. Look carefully at the text to ensure that spelling errors have been eradicated and that the punctuation and grammar are correct. This is something that cannot be hurried. It is also necessary to check the formatting. Have all the section numbers, table numbers and labels for the appendices been consistently applied? Are all the font sizes consistent? Are there any 'glitches' in the page layout? Are there still any missing references? Is the list of references at the back in the right order and formatted in a consistent manner?

The first few pages of the report are crucial. Check the title page – does it have all the necessary information? Are all the pages numbered and are the page numbers on the contents page still accurate? Have you listed the appendices on the contents page? Is the abstract or summary still appropriate or does it require revision in the light of redrafting you have recently undertaken? Are the research objectives and questions explained clearly in the introduction? Do you need to include a copy of a completed ethical review process?

Once you are satisfied you can print your work. Before making any subsequent copies, make a final visual check to ensure that the printer has not inserted the odd blank page or the numbering system has not been disrupted by a section break. Then make sufficient copies and securely bind them ready for their journey to your study centre.

CHECKLIST

- The process of writing about your research underpins the learning process. It enables you to reflect on what you have found, clarify your thinking and communicate more effectively about your research.

- Readers in different contexts have different expectations of what they read. **Academic readers** expect a formal and objective style of writing and a demonstration of your knowledge and understanding of your subject area. They will want to assess how you have applied and evaluated an appropriate research methodology for your enquiry. **Managers and other organisational sponsors** expect a more persuasive and accessible written style and a report that focuses on recommendations and implementation that can contribute to the resolution of HR problems, issues or opportunities.

- All research reports or dissertations, whatever level or type of qualification they are associated with, should clearly express the research aims and objectives; review relevant literature; report the use of appropriate methods of data collection and analyse data in an integrated and objective way. Business research reports have more emphasis on the generation of practical, costed, timely and realistic recommendations. Masters-level dissertations have more emphasis on: the analytical focus, scope and contribution of the literature review; the evaluation of different research design and methodological issues; the analysis of data; and the reasoning process linking conclusions with analysis of the literature and other data.

- To overcome factors that inhibit the writing process it is important to develop 'writing habits', to write regularly, to plan your writing, to reward yourself when you achieve your writing targets and to ensure that everything you write is regularly 'backed up'.

- Planning can reduce the stress of writing. Useful techniques that can enhance the planning process are: brainstorming; mind mapping; concept mapping; linear planning.

- It is important that readers of any report can follow its 'logic' through the structure, style and expression. Effective writing is expressed clearly and simply with appropriate paragraphing and a consistent system of headings and subheadings. Jargon, slang, abbreviations, informal, emotive and discriminatory language are not appropriate.

- Involving others in evaluating your draft report, or sections of it, will enable you to prioritise the revisions that are required to ensure that it meets the assessment criteria by which it will be judged.

TEST YOURSELF

1 Your abstract would not usually include:

　　a Key findings.

　　b List of references.

　　c Methodology.

　　d Conclusions.

2 Which chapter is most likely to provide an overview of the case study organisation(s)?

　　a Introduction.

　　b Literature review.

　　c Methodology.

　　d Findings.

3 When are direct quotes most useful for your work?

　　a To prove that you have read something.

　　b To meet the requirement for the minimum number of references.

　　c To demonstrate a key point.

　　d To meet the overall word count.

4 Which of the following do not usually feature in the findings chapter?

　　a Recommendations for HR professionals.

　　b Overview of research sample.

　　c Limitations of findings.

　　d Direct quotes from participants.

5 Each chapter/section should include:

　　a Introduction and summary.

　　b A separate list of references.

　　c An overview of the case study organisation(s).

　　d Charts and graphs.

6 The justification for your sampling strategy should be outlined in:

　　a Introduction.

　　b Literature review.

c Methodology.

d Conclusions.

7 Which of the following would not usually be provided as appendices?

    a Sample interview transcripts.

    b Your interview or survey questions.

    c Your research objectives.

    d Ethics approval form.

8 When data are presented in the findings it is important to:

a Include information about sample and response sizes.

b Conceal data that do not 'fit' what you hope to show.

c Leave out information about the response scales.

d Make use of quotations from only one or two responses to the 'open questions' you included.

 Review Questions

Questions for reflection

These questions are designed to enable you to identify key areas for development with your project that you should discuss with your project tutor if possible. The responses to them can also form part of a continuing professional development log or portfolio. This is required by CIPD for those who wish to upgrade their membership status, and full information and useful resources can be viewed on the CIPD website (https://www.cipd.co.uk/learn/cpd/cycle).

Taking stock

1 What written reports about your research are required by your study centre, employer, or other sponsor or client? How clear are you about the required length, format and content required by these different readers? Are any additional outputs required? For example, a presentation or podcast.

2 How much time do you have before the submission date for your research report?

Who can help you to evaluate your draft sections? How can you share learning with peers in your class? Does your centre have any formal requirements for peer feedback?

3 In addition to getting feedback on your content, what arrangements will you make to have your work proofread? What are the time implications of this? Be sure to check if your centre has any regulations around the use of proofreaders?

4 Where do you learn and work best? Where will you physically undertake your writing? What steps do you need to take to have the 'space' to write without distractions?

5 Do you need to make your manager (and other stakeholders) aware of your forthcoming deadline? Do you need to request any specific support?

6 Do you have any training needs relevant to the submission process? For example, if your work needs to be submitted through anti-plagiarism software, do you know how to do this?

7 What arrangements will be necessary to ensure your work can be printed, copied and bound when the time comes?

Strengths and weaknesses

8 What improvement areas have been highlighted in previous assignment feedback and how might you develop the skills that you need?

9 Consider your strengths as a writer. What steps can you take to ensure that you tackle the 'difficult' sections in a timely and effective way?

Being a practitioner-researcher

10 What writing conventions or styles are you most comfortable with? How compatible are they with the expectations for academic writing? Create a personal checklist of key things you know you will need to avoid when writing up your project.

11 What opportunities to disseminate your research findings might there be within your organisation? What constraints are there on dissemination? Are some details from your research particularly sensitive – how will you establish the limits to what you can communicate?

12 If you agreed that your research participants would receive a summary of your overall work, what will this look like? To what extent is it useful to share your specific recommendations?

13 In what ways might your organisation or department benefit from wider dissemination of your research? Are there other companies within your wider organisation, or within the supply chain or network, that might benefit from hearing about what you have learned? Which internal gatekeepers would you need to discuss these plans with?

14 Which individuals or groups may not wish to be identified through any dissemination process? What steps could you take to ensure that appropriate anonymity and confidentiality are maintained and that you work within the constraints of the informed consent arrangements that you made with those who participated in your research?

 Useful Resources

It is very difficult to read about writing. The best way to learn to write is to critically evaluate the writing of others, get going with your own writing and then seek feedback about it. Therefore, the process of reviewing the literature will help you to learn to write. It is also worth reading projects submitted by past students at your study centre to identify the ways in which other students have communicated in an objective and reasonable way. To make sure that you are able to learn from the more effective writers make sure you only review the work of those who achieve a mark equivalent to a 'merit' or higher.

You can find information about voice recognition software from: http://www.bbc.co.uk/accessibility/guides/voice_recognition/ (archived at https://perma.cc/AN9F-CN2C)

The market leader for 'paid for' software seems to be: **Dragon (Nuance)** https://www.nuance.com/en-gb/

dragon/dragon-for-pc.html (archived at https://perma.cc/B6YF-P54Y)

Other useful resources

CIPD (2018) Advanced level specification [Online] https://www.cipd.co.uk/Images/cipd-advanced-specification-human-resources_tcm18-18946.pdf (archived at https://perma.cc/GA7A-D82Q)

Marsen, S (2013) *Professional Writing*, 3rd edn, Palgrave Macmillan, London

Quality Assurance Agency (QAA) (2014) *UK Quality Code for Higher Education: The frameworks for higher education qualifications of UK degree-awarding bodies* [Online] https://www.qaa.ac.uk/docs/qaa/quality-code/qualifications-frameworks.pdf (archived at https://perma.cc/386A-38K4)

 References

Biggam, J (2018) *Succeeding with Your Master's Dissertation*, 4th edn, Open University Press, Maidenhead

Blaxter, L, Hughes, C and Tight, M (2012) *How to Research,* 4th edn, Open University Press, Maidenhead

Brown, RB (2006) *Doing Your Dissertation in Business and Management: The reality of researching and writing*, Sage, London

CIPD (2018) Advanced level specification. Available at https://www.cipd.co.uk/Images/cipd-advanced-specification-human-resources_tcm18-18946.pdf

Collis, J and Hussey, R (2014) *Business Research: A practical guide for undergraduate and postgraduate students*, Palgrave, Basingstoke

Fisher, C and Buglear, J (2010) *Researching and Writing a Dissertation: An essential guide for business students*, Pearson Education, Harlow

Fox, M, Martin, P and Green, G (2007) *Doing Practitioner Research*, Sage, London

Hart, C (2013) *Doing Your Masters Dissertation*, Sage, London

Jankowicz, AD (2005) *Business Research Projects for Students*, Thomson Learning, London

Lee, N and Lings, L (2008) *Doing Business Research: A guide to theory and practice*, Sage, London

McMillan, K and Weyer, J (2011) *How to Write Dissertations and Project Reports*, 2nd edn, Pearson Education, Harlow

Neuman, W (2012) *Basics of Social Research: Qualitative and quantitative approaches*, 3rd edn, Pearson Education, Harlow

Robson, A and McCartan, K (2016) *Real World Research*, 4th edn, John Wiley & Sons Ltd, Chichester

Saunders, M and Lewis, P (2018) *Doing Research in Business and Management: An essential guide to planning your project*, 2nd edn, Pearson, London

12

Making an impact: the relationship between research and practice

LEARNING OBJECTIVES

This chapter should help you to:

- consider how to 'bridge the gap' between research and evidence-based HR practice;
- plan how to achieve impact in practice from your research;
- take courage and 'go public' with your work in order to share your learning;
- communicate your research to non-academic audiences in an impactful and credible way.

CHAPTER OUTLINE

- How to use this chapter
- Evidence-based HR
- Communicating for engagement and impact

- Bridging the practice–scholarship gap
- Becoming an impactful practitioner-researcher
- Summary checklist
- Final review and reflection questions
- Useful resources

How to use this chapter

The previous chapters of the book have focused on the achievement of an academic research report or dissertation. The focus of this chapter is on achieving practical and applied impact from your research. Once you have submitted your research report or dissertation, you may feel as though you never want to hear or write another word about your topic. However, activities to ensure that your research can inform organisational decisions and processes and to share your learning are important. The first activity in this chapter focuses on impactful research and the importance of 'aiming high' as a practitioner-researcher.

 Activity 12.1

Fads and fashions in HR?

1   Take a few minutes to compile a list of popular HR trends in recent years. Here are a few to get you started. You can probably add a further four or five HR or management 'fashions' to the list.

   – The manager as coach

   – Employee engagement

   – Talent management

   – HR analytics

2   Write down some criteria that would help to distinguish between an HR 'fad' and an enduring innovation in the practice of HR.

3   Consider at least three of the HR trends you have identified and/or the developments listed here.

   – To what extent might they be considered to be an 'HR fad'?

   – To what extent have these trends had a lasting impact on organisational policy and practice?

Feedback notes

In undertaking this activity you may have reflected that it can be difficult to identify which HR initiatives and innovations are merely fashions and fads and which provide the basis for a robust contribution to effective HR practice. However, the distinction is important. In spite of the new jargon often associated with a new HR practice, the ideas behind HR fads and fashions frequently represent 'received wisdom' and are appealing to senior decision-makers. They are often attractive at first sight and many consume vast amounts of HR resource, both money and time. However, their medium or long-term impact may be limited or even negative. If the HR function promotes new initiatives without a careful evaluation then managers and employees can be forgiven for losing faith and trust in their HR colleagues (Gubbins *et al*, 2018). Therefore, it is important to find out whether the evidence they rely on is representative and trustworthy.

Generally speaking, fashions and fads tend to have these characteristics in common (Miller, Hartwick and Le Breton-Miller, 2004):

- the motivation for adopting them is influenced by their 'novelty value';
- they are based on simple (or over-simple) ideas;
- they rely on 'buzz words' to inform their 'newness';
- their appeal is in part a result of the reputation of 'hero-figures', high-profile HR practitioners or CEOs who endorse them;
- they offer a simple recipe that promises universally positive results;
- although they claim to be what 'cutting edge' employers are doing, in fact only a few organisations have implemented them.

A key benefit of undertaking a research project as part of an HR qualification-bearing course is to develop the ability to evaluate the research that others have undertaken. This is an important skill as HR credibility relies on robust decision-making and the use of valid evidence as a basis for evaluating its initiatives. For example, if employee retention is a problem for your organisation and you have met an HR practitioner who assures you that investing in an employee engagement initiative will improve retention, what is the evidence? Merely your colleague saying 'it worked wonders for us' is insufficient evidence on which to base substantial HR policy change. Credible practice-relevant research and an analysis of available data is one way by which you can navigate your way through the many HR fads and fashions that are on offer and help the HR function improve the quality of its decision-making.

The premise of this chapter, and the book as a whole, is that effective and trustworthy HR practice requires a commitment to decision-making informed by good quality, evidence-based information. Initiatives based on shoddy evidence and impoverished thinking should be challenged. In particular, this requires acknowledgement that what works in one organisational context may not work in another context. In addition, it is possible that results claimed from an initiative in one organisation may, in fact, be attributed to factors other than the initiative itself. Therefore, although introducing a new procedure or initiative may lead to some short-term gains for the organisation, the change may also result in unintended consequences that may have negative effects.

HR practitioners face a difficult challenge when they decide whether or not to pursue a new trend in the HR field. Reading, or hearing about case studies where success has been claimed is tempting but the 'halo effect' is not something that only applies to recruitment and selection or performance appraisal processes. This leads to an important question – what evidence should HR practitioners trust?

Evidence-based HR

 Activity 12.2

This activity provides an opportunity to consider which information and evidence is trustworthy. What criteria should be applied to judge the truth or the reliability of information and opinions, even if no absolute 'proof' is available? The activity requires that you tackle three questions, either on your own or as part of a group.

1 What is fake news?

2 How real is fake news?

3 In what ways is fake news 'fake' and in what ways is it 'real'?

Feedback notes

Fake news is a type of journalism or communication that consists of misinformation or hoaxes spread via news or online social media. Fake news is concerning because people may act on what they **believe** to be true and this may be different from what is actually true. In response to this question you may have noted that although fake news may be based on partial, poor, unreliable or even misinformation, it can assume a 'reality'. In politics this can lead people to act on what they believe rather than on what they know. In organisational contexts it is also possible that people at all levels in the organisation may act on what they think might be true rather than on any specific credible evidence. Even when there is some evidence it may be partial and in such cases acting on poor quality information is unlikely to lead to sustainable improvement. A further danger is that – as in politics and society more widely – acting in this way can lead employees, customers, suppliers and community organisations or members to lose trust in the organisation and its leaders.

This activity – while set in very general terms – prompts us to ask important questions for the HR function. First, what evidence and information is worth having as a basis for HR decisions? Second, how can HR practitioners distinguish between trustworthy and untrustworthy evidence?

One answer to these questions, increasingly articulated in recent years, is to highlight the value of robust evidence-based and data-driven HR information as the basis for decision-making. Those who advocate this evidence-based approach to HR highlight the importance of thoughtful evaluation and diligence in HR practice. Trust in the HR function can never be taken for granted but is more likely to be gained where evidence-based decisions are made that increase the probability of beneficial outcomes for individuals and their employing organisations.

Principles of evidence-based HR

Evidence-based HR involves making decisions through the careful, systematic and sensible use of the best available evidence. Evidence-based HR acknowledges

Figure 12.1   Forms of evidence to inform HR decision-making

that evidence from one source is insufficient for a robust decision-making process. Therefore, evidence-based HR involves finding evidence that sheds light on issues of cause and effect in relation to the variables in the phenomenon that requires a decision. Different forms of evidence might inform a decision and these are illustrated in Figure 12.1.

Figure 12.1 indicates the four main forms of evidence that might comprise components of evidence-based HR decision-making. As an HR student you will be aware of the extensive volume of published studies relating to many features of HR practice. Careful selection and evaluation of these sources provides the basis to establish available evidence and identify the extent to which the findings are trustworthy and relevant to the particular decision issue. Identifying multiple sources of research data also enables you to pull together the evidence to more fully estimate potential outcomes that might be expected as a feature of the decision-making process (Barends, Rousseau and Briner, 2014).

In addition, it may be necessary to add further data and information about the variables involved from within the organisation. Figure 12.1 also refers to experiential evidence. This includes situated practice-led knowledge – the professional experience and judgement of practitioners. Finally, information about the concerns and principles of those people (stakeholders) who will be affected by the decision may be important to consider. Figure 12.1 illustrates that evidence-based HR is not about making HR practitioners behave and think like academics and nor is it about turning HR academics into practitioners. Instead, evidence-based HR encourages practice-relevant knowledge, understanding, explanation and application. However, to be effective, it requires that practitioners are prepared to look for evidence before they make policy or change-related decisions. It also challenges academics to ensure that their research studies are communicated in a way that will be accessible to busy practitioners with organisational deadlines to meet. Evidence-based HR also values findings from organisationally based research projects such as yours!

As the term evidence-based HR has been increasingly used, especially by academics, it has become subject to different interpretations or schools of thought. For some people (see, for example, Gubbins *et al*, 2018), evidence-based practice assumes a hierarchy of evidence where the most 'scientific', valid and reliable studies are valued more highly than other forms of information. If you are familiar with the debates considered in earlier chapters of this book you will know that this world view is contested and that other HR practitioners and scholars place equivalent value on knowledge generated in other ways. Maxwell (2019), for example, argues that advocates of evidence-based practice underestimate the extent to which policies and programmes are applied in practice. Maxwell highlights the importance of taking into account the different ways in which people interpret and respond to policies and the different ways in which policies and initiatives may or may not achieve their results. These issues are critical as features of the ways in which policies actually achieve their goals and for the avoidance of unintended or damaging consequences (Maxwell, 2019).

However, taken as a whole, the aspiration towards evidence-based practice commits the HR profession to valuing research processes and to making use of the best evidence available as a basis for trustworthy HR decision-making. Single studies, and individual case study stories are a poor basis for making generalised assumptions. As you will know from your work in the literature review, examining the wider body of evidence is necessary as the basis for examining what makes for effective HR policy and practice.

Generating impact from HR research

Impactful research involves deriving real-world benefits from systematic HR investigative projects. Regrettably most HR research work, especially studies that have been undertaken by students, remain a well-kept secret, known only to the researcher and a few other close friends or colleagues. In spite of the acknowledged benefits of knowledge management and the importance of evidence-based HR, many HR professionals are reluctant to share their own research findings. However, a lot of work will have gone into your project and it is a shame if your work were not to achieve the impact that it deserves. There are many personal benefits to be achieved through maximising the impact of your research. These include:

- **personal recognition**, both professionally and within your current or future work organisation, to increase your profile and (possibly) your career prospects;
- **recognition for organisations that participated in/or supported your research;**
- opportunity for **further clarification** of your thinking by considering how your work has been applied in practice and how the outcomes of this might stimulate further development of your ideas.

Opportunities for impact

Many students assume that issues of impact only arise once a research project has been completed. However, as scholars and practitioners have become more experienced in impactful research, they have recognised that 'pathways to impact' open up throughout the research process.

 Case Example 12.1

Pathways to impact

Jagriti worked in the health and social care sector. It is a legal requirement for care providers in England to have appropriately qualified, experienced and competent managers in place. Jagriti was studying part-time for an HR qualification while fulfilling the role of area manager for a medium-sized care home provider. She also had responsibility for the training and development of care home managers in her area. Care home managers have responsibility for upholding care service standards and the regulatory body in the United Kingdom emphasises the importance of 'strong leadership', 'good leaders' and 'good managers' in the care sector. From her work in the sector Jagriti was well aware of the intensity and unpredictability of care home managers' day-to-day jobs and the challenges they face providing services in a highly regulated context while also coping with limited resources. She was also aware that most managers 'worked their way up' to their current roles from non-management work in the care sector. There was no infrastructure

for management training and development in Jagriti's company. She decided to focus her research project on the training and development needs of managers of adult residential care facilities. Jagriti was committed to the idea that her work should make a difference and have impact, not just in her own company, but also in relation to training and development for care home managers more widely in the United Kingdom.

Discussion questions

1   Residents of the care homes and their families were likely to benefit from the outcomes of Jagriti's study but which other groups of people might benefit from Jagriti's project? Identify at least two further groups of potential beneficiaries and then note down how each group might benefit from her research.

2   How might Jagriti involve potential beneficiaries in her research project?

Feedback notes

In tackling this question you may have identified a number of individuals and groups who could potentially benefit from this project. An obvious group of beneficiaries are the care home managers within Jagriti's organisation as well as care home managers working in other settings. The owners of care homes who, in the United Kingdom at least, have a legal responsibility to provide appropriate training to ensure the competence of the managers are a further group of potential beneficiaries. You may also have identified that others in the HR profession (for example, management training and development consultants) could benefit from this research if they wished to utilise Jagriti's findings in any training services that they might provide in the care sector or in other similar contexts. Knowing about the study could be useful for many groups of people in relation to policy-making and revision. For other groups the study had direct application to their practice.

Jagriti's supervisor encouraged her to involve potential beneficiaries in her research at an early stage rather than waiting until after her project had been completed. In responding to the second question for this case example you might have identified that one way to get people involved is to ask care home owners beyond her own organisation to give permission for her to gather data from their care homes. Another way that Jagriti managed to get people interested and engaged was by telling them about the project – through conference presentations whenever she got the chance, through short articles in care sector magazines and newsletters and through appropriate use of her social media channels.

A key issue that Jagriti's case illustrates is that impactful research is achieved primarily through stakeholder engagement. Impact can be designed into a project right from the start. Planning an impact strategy into the project design and implementation process is worth considering. Impact can be generated through many different mechanisms that include: asking potential beneficiaries to provide advice before a study; requesting access to data to help with the study; and asking stakeholders for feedback on initial findings as well as subsequent conclusions.

To summarise, it takes a brave person to 'go public' about a study while it is still in the planning process but you are likely to have more impact if you can make your engagement activities integral to the project rather than 'bolt-on' at the end. It is also important that you are realistic about what you can achieve in the timeframe that you have and whether your sponsoring organisation, if you have one, will give permission for you to engage 'outsiders' in the research process. The following points are useful as part of a thinking process about a plan for impactful research:

- Find out what potential beneficiaries want to get out of the project – give them a reason to be involved – who are the potential stakeholders in your project and how might they be engaged from the early stages?

- Prioritise two-way engagement of potential beneficiaries. Avoid merely 'telling' people about your research. Find out what they can contribute.

- A sense of shared ownership or a co-designed project will ensure your project has relevance and encourage more stakeholders to put your research findings into practice.

- What actions can you take to build impact and engagement at the beginning, the middle and after the end of your project?

- Work out in advance some strategies for disseminating progress updates throughout the project. This might enhance your impact and also help to maintain your own motivation to complete the project.

- Identify any channels of influence you have that you might involve in your project such as professional association contacts, organisational stakeholders and other potential beneficiaries.

Communicating for engagement and impact

This part of the chapter focuses on ideas that can help you to communicate about your research to build impact in a credible way.

 Activity 12.3

How do you and your colleagues learn about HRM?

This activity requires you to brainstorm the different ways you have come to learn about different features of HR throughout your career. If you are a part-time student with some experience as an HR practitioner then reflect on both the practical and taught 'avenues' to the knowledge that you have. If you are a full-time student who is undertaking a course in order to develop a career in HR then reflect on what and how you learned in any work placement or internship as well as on your course. There may also have been important learning 'moments' in your life as a part-time or full-time worker or life experiences that your friends and family have shared with you from which you have learned important 'lessons'.

Feedback notes

It is very likely that this activity has stimulated you to think back to a time before you commenced your current course. You may have reflected that, before you embarked on your current course, you gained very little knowledge about HRM from a scholarly book, lecture or journal article. Most people learn facts, obtain information and develop skills through experience or from accessing websites and social media. Informal forms of information sharing through practitioner conferences, CIPD or other professional association branch events, seminars or workshops are also popular forms of professional development. Practitioner-focused books, reports from government or specialist organisations are all preferred by most practitioners to academic articles with pages of citations and references.

This diversity of routes to knowledge is not surprising given the diversity of backgrounds of most HR practitioners and their different learning styles and preferences. There are many different, overlapping 'ways of knowing' about HRM. This has implications for you if you wish to engage members of the practitioner community in your research process. Non-academic stakeholders may be interested in what your research can do for them but they will be less excited than your academic tutors about your extensive knowledge of the literature. They will also be potentially indifferent to the detailed features of your methodological approach. Practitioner and management-level readers are interested in the 'so what' points.

Activity 12.4

Staying up to date

This activity requires you to undertake some 'simple' research.

1   Compile a list of the way you and your colleagues keep up to date with developments in their fields. Ask your boss, your colleagues, people who are younger or older than you.

2   Take a look at the list you have generated. What ideas does this give you for how to 'get the message out' to engage people in your research?

3   From your list choose three opportunities that might be appropriate for you to consider.

4   What challenges would they present to you?

Feedback notes

In response to this activity you may have identified a number of ways of keeping up to date. Within organisations there is a range of organised information dissemination processes such as: centralised updates and alerts; 'brown bag' events that include short presentations by people who need to share information with other interested people on a face-to-face basis; knowledge sharing events through team briefings; and data repository facilities where people's experiences are recorded so that others can benefit from them. Some organisations or multidisciplinary groups organise 'sandpit' events where specialists from a wide range of disciplines, organisations or functions get together to share issues and challenges around a particular issue or problem and then generate ideas to try to solve the problem.

Other ways of keeping up to date involve social media and social networking sites. News update and alerting systems have become a key feature in many professional updating strategies. Although they are not listed as official learning platforms, many people use social media sites such as YouTube, Facebook, WhatsApp, WeChat, QZone, Instagram, Twitter and Google+ to keep informed about professional trends. Other enduring ways of information sharing include: attending specialist conferences or workshops; attending professional association meetings or webinars to hear presentations about practice innovations; and chatting with other practitioners about the work that they are engaged with.

Having compiled an extensive list of potential ways to share what you have learned through your research project you might now identify three to five methods that you feel would be appropriate for you and work out how you might use them and what challenges these would present. Before you take forward any dissemination opportunities, however, you must ensure that you will not be contravening any ethical assurances you gave to your research participants (individuals and organisations). Organisational concerns about confidentiality and anonymity must be taken into account. If you indicated that information you gathered would only be used for your academic study purposes then you must seek the permission of your research participants for any further dissemination. It would, of course, be better to have included your intention to undertake anonymised dissemination in the informed consent processes you enact prior to commencing any 'fieldwork' data collection.

Once you are ready to begin disseminating information about your project, the first challenge you may experience relates to the need to write (and speak) more succinctly. Having spent a number of months learning to communicate in what seemed like excessive detail to meet the assessment criteria of your study centre, you now have to reverse the process. The following steps can help you with this (Day, 2008):

1   **Clarify the purpose, scope and value of what you did.** It is important to be clear about your research problem and its context so that you can articulate it to those who will read your work or hear what you have to say. Useful questions to ask yourself include:

   – What did I investigate, and why?

   – How far did I decide to look, and why?

   – What related issues did I not examine, and why?

   – What constraints impacted on my work, and why?

In any dissemination that you undertake you should communicate what you have found out and what this means for your readers/audience. Day (2008) suggests that a good way of preparing to communicate about your research is to write down an answer for yourself, in no more than 20 words, to the question: 'What do I want to say and why should anyone care?' This is challenging and will probably take at least five attempts (and even then you may still not achieve the 20-word target). Having done it, however, you will find you have a useful focus to help you prepare and target dissemination actions concerning your research.

2   **Summarising your work.** Once you have clarified the purpose, scope and value of your research you can go on to express the following aspects of your work, in no more than one paragraph each:

   – **Findings.** What did you (or are you) find(ing) out? In what ways do your findings matter?

   – **Literature.** What does it say and how did it affect your research?

   – **Methodology.** What did you do and how did it affect the findings?

   – **Analysis.** How did the techniques you used to analyse the data affect your findings?

   – **Implications.** What are the implications of what you found for potential answers to your research problem? How far are you prepared to go, and why?

Writing these paragraphs enables you to establish what you have to communicate and, from this point, you can develop presentations, or write papers or articles to meet the expectations of the audience/readership. Some will be longer and fuller than others, but you have a basis on which to build.

Communicating with impact

Activity 12.4 highlights the importance, when you are sharing news about your research for non-academic audiences, of making your work accessible to non-specialists.

Remember that the language of academics can seem dense, opaque and impenetrable to a practitioner audience. If you aim to help shape HR policy or practice for the better then it is important to summarise your findings and draw out, where appropriate, the practice-based implications and key issues. Engaging potential beneficiaries and communicating about your research is to understand the perspective of your intended audience(s) and communicate in a language that they understand. It is also important to plan these activities and communicate any interim outcomes that your audience might take forward and use in their sector. This will help you to maintain engagement and obtain feedback to help you as you take your project forward.

Organisational reports

If you are undertaking a work-based project then there may be many potential opportunities for you to share your work. You may be required to submit some form of report at regular intervals to the manager who has sponsored your project. In such circumstances, remember that most managers will not have the time to work their way through the detail of your full dissertation or even a full draft chapter of your final report. Before you begin writing such an internal document, therefore, find out what your organisational 'audience' expects from you in terms of document format and length. Although you will be able to draw extensively on the material you prepared for your dissertation or research report, there are likely to be a number of differences in what you produce:

- **Less detailed content suitable for a 'manager in a hurry'.** You will need to write in a more accessible style, with less use of 'academic speak'. Focus on the broad issues rather than the detail.
- **Well thought-through action points.** This is likely to be a key issue for the organisational sponsors of your research. Make sure your suggestions are clearly derived from the data and expressed in direct and practical terms. Consider presenting recommendations as a set of options. Be clear about accountabilities, costs, timescales, priorities and contingencies.
- **Write persuasively.** Indicate the benefits of implementing the action points that you are putting forward.

Making presentations

You may find many opportunities to talk about your research on an informal basis, but the occasions where you will 'present' your research more formally are likely to be as presentations to different groups of staff within the organisation, or through a presentation made at a conference, workshop or a local CIPD branch meeting. You might also consider making your research more widely available through your social media networks.

Commercial conferences

These are advertised quite widely, take place in comfortable venues and delegates pay to hear from experts about good practice and research relating to particular topics. The format tends to involve a range of expert speakers making a 40–50 minute presentation, with short question and answer sessions following each of them. The emphasis is on the practical implications of the topic being presented and delegates are interested in what it means for them and their organisations. Conference organisers usually 'source' their speakers through a fairly extensive system of networking and 'colleague referral'. If they approach you they will be fairly explicit about what is expected in terms of the length of the presentation and any supporting material they require, as well as any fee they may be prepared to pay.

It is likely that your presentation will be supplemented with some additional information. Copies of the PowerPoint or Prezi slides you have prepared will be expected. While restricting your supplementary information to 'visuals' may suffice for internal presentations within your own organisation, for any other external presentation, this may be something of a lost opportunity. Provision of more detailed information, for which there will not be time during the presentation, will enable you to disseminate your work more fully. Robson (2016) suggests a 'pamphlet form' using an uncluttered layout and use of photographs, tables and diagrams. Don't forget to make sure your name and contact details are on this pamphlet so that interested people can follow up with you at a later date.

Academic conferences

Other conferences are more **academic** in focus. These are usually less 'glossy' and delegates are likely to be academics undertaking research in similar areas. Here an organiser will make a 'call for papers' 9–12 months before the intended date of the conference. This 'call' may be published in relevant journal publications, through internet databases and via university networks. Potential speakers submit a paper to the conference organisers, who will then decide whether to accept the contribution. If you are interested in this sort of opportunity it would be a good idea to ask your dissertation supervisor to suggest appropriate conference opportunities. See, for example, conference information at: http://www.ufhrd.co.uk/wordpress/ and https://www.emccconference.org/ and https://www.cipd.co.uk/learn/events-networks/applied-research-conference. The audience at these conferences will be interested in the academic as well as practical context of the research, the methodology and the way in which data were analysed. If your paper is accepted, it is likely that the organisers will suggest you submit a fuller version to them, which will be made available for all the participants at the conference. You will also make a presentation about your paper (usually about 20 minutes in length). Often these presentations are to smaller numbers of people (up to 50). There will be scope for questions at the time of your presentation and it is possible that those who were interested in what you have to say will contact you later for a further discussion of your work. Although these presentations may be rather daunting, they are a useful way of clarifying your thinking, and for making contact with people who are also interested in similar areas. The feedback that you receive as a result of the process is also very valuable if you are thinking about going further and publishing your findings in a written form.

The content of presentations for different types of conferences varies considerably although the overall structure of the different presentations may be similar and is likely to involve:

1 Objectives of the presentation.

2 Research purpose/problem/context.

3 Methods of enquiry.

4 Findings (what did you expect to find and what did you actually find?).

5 Implications – for practice and for further research.

6 Final summary – main interest of the findings for you and for the HR profession more widely. Aim for three 'summary sentences':

- sentence 1 – the purpose;
- sentence 2 – the main points and methodology;
- sentence 3 – the main conclusions.

Poster presentations

A less stressful contribution to make at an academic conference is to present a poster about your research. This is where you design and print a large poster (usually A1 in size) that summarises what you have done and any plans for further research or implementation. You do not have to make a spoken presentation but you need to be present at the conference so that those who see your poster and have similar interests can make contact with you to offer suggestions and feedback and discuss ideas for the future. If you decide to produce a poster about your research remember that posters are a visual presentation of information about your research – not a simple reproduction of your written work. This is your chance to be creative with design so that your poster is attention catching and understandable to the 'reader' without the need for verbal comment.

Table 12.1 Hints and tips for poster preparation

Information	Make sure your project title and your name are prominent and eye-catching. Make your poster title the 'punch line' so that it will be seen during the first 11 seconds of the time a person spends looking at your poster.
Narrative	Tell a story. Provide a clear flow of information from the introduction to the conclusion.
Focus on your major points	A common fault is to try to cover too much – people are not likely to read everything on your poster, so get to the point. Keep the word count low.
Visuals	Use graphs, tables, diagrams and images where appropriate. Use boxes to isolate and emphasise specific points.
White space	Use all the space but do not cram – white space is important. Take out all unnecessary text or visual distractions, including borders between related data and text. This will help the 'reader' to assimilate your ideas easily.
Colour	Use colour sparingly for emphasis and differentiation. Have a white or muted colour background and avoid colour combinations that clash or cause problems for people with colour-blindness.

(continued)

Table 12.1 (Continued)

Layout	Use layout to make the flow of information clear; avoid using too many arrows. Communicate information in a **spatial sequence.** People (in the West) tend to look at things from top to bottom and from left to right. Put the most important message in the centre top position followed by the top left, top right, bottom left, and finish in the bottom right corner.
Labels	Label diagrams/drawings and provide references to them in the text where necessary.
Font	Choose a clear font: Arial, Verdana, Georgia, Calibri. Title text: at least 48-point text; and body text: at least 24-point text. The use of multiple fonts in a poster can distract from the message.

Although specialised software is available you can use Microsoft Word or PowerPoint to create your poster. There are plenty of video tutorials on platforms such as YouTube to give tips on how to 'scale up' to poster size.

Writing articles and papers

You might be tempted to share your findings through internal, local or professional publications or contributions to social media sites. Your organisational supervisor/ mentor will be a good source of advice about potential avenues for dissemination. If you wish to pursue academic means of dissemination, then you may aim to publish your work in an academic journal. Here your academic supervisor would be able to provide you with some guidance.

Other ideas for communicating about your research include:

News releases

These might be for a local intranet site, or directed at the editors of local press and social media outlets. Editors are always in a hurry and need to find the easiest ways possible to present topical news stories. A news release should be shorter than one side of A4 (or its electronic equivalent) and written in a lively style with a 'catchy' heading. You should also provide a contact number for editorial enquiries. If your release is used it is likely that the journalist who authors the item will use some of your text on a word-for-word basis (hence the need to write in a topical and accessible way). However, you should be prepared to read something that is not wholly familiar to you as journalists may also add their own 'spin'. It is very important to check the PR policy of any of the organisations involved with your research and gain any necessary 'permissions' before sending out any news releases. It is also important to render anonymous any organisations or participants in your research if there is even the slightest chance that they are not comfortable with media coverage. (See Chapter 3 on research and professional ethics.)

Professional journals

Most professional and industry sector associations produce journal publications in print and/or online, which might provide an opportunity for you to disseminate your research findings. The word limit for a feature article is likely to be 2,000 words at most and an accessible writing style is expected. If you are considering offering a contribution then it is worth contacting the editor with a short (500 words maximum) summary of your contribution, explaining how your paper would be of interest to readers. Useful headings for such a summary would be:

1 Target readership.
2 Aims of the intended contribution.
3 Implications of your findings.
4 Treatment (style, etc).
5 Your contact details.

Use your covering message to make clear your name and the working title of your paper, providing a brief paragraph describing the contents and explaining why you chose this outlet.

Often an editor will not respond for many weeks or months, if at all. If the editor does wish to go ahead then the deadline is likely to be fairly prompt. However, once agreement in principle is achieved, the writing of the article can be achieved quite quickly and may be structured in a similar way to a presentation.

Peer-reviewed journals

These are the most demanding articles to write. If you think you would like to submit your work to a peer-reviewed journal (such as *Human Resource Management Journal, European Journal of Training and Development, Human Resource Development International, Journal of Management Development, Journal of Workplace Learning,* etc) you should first find and read the guidance for authors that is provided in each copy of the journal and on the journal's website. It is also a good idea to review some recently published papers in the journal you might target to ensure that you would feel 'comfortable' with the style and approach that the editor would expect. If you wish to proceed (and your supervisor is supportive) you would write your paper and submit an electronic copy to the journal, usually through a journal submission platform. If the editor believes the paper may be publishable, then it will be sent, without the details of the author(s), to a number of subject expert reviewers who will be invited to critically evaluate the article and to advise the editor whether it might be appropriate for the journal as well as how or where the paper could be improved. This is a lengthy process, rarely taking less than three months. It is very rare for an article to be accepted without revisions and the process of further enhancing the paper means that many articles are not accepted for publication for at least a year from the date of their original submission. This process is quite daunting but can be very rewarding when your paper finally appears. Some 'first time' researchers choose to publish in a non-refereed section of an academic journal first. Others, who wish to achieve a peer-reviewed paper find it helpful to 'team up' with a more experienced academic writer, often their supervisor or someone recommended by him or her.

Bridging the practice–scholarship gap

This part of the chapter identifies how you might build on the skills of systematic research you have developed through your course to develop your role and contribution to organisational change and effectiveness. Hopefully you might be encouraged to reflect on ways in which you can make use of your research skills in new contexts and situations to the benefit of both organisational performance and developing wider knowledge and understanding of HRM.

 Activity 12.5

The different worlds of research and practice

Human Resource Development Quarterly is a journal you may have come across as part of your professional studies. It is a scholarly journal that addresses HRD research issues. This journal is published primarily for academic readers but, like other journals in HRM and HRD, it aims to ensure that the research it publishes is relevant and applicable in practice. Make use of your electronic library access to find *Human Resource Development Quarterly* (2018) Volume 29, Issue 2,

pages 99–105. Read this paper and answer these questions:

1   Identify what the authors believe to be the main benefits of HR scholars having knowledge and experience of HR practitioner roles.

2   To what extent do you agree with their claim that HR practice experience should influence the formulation of research programmes?

Feedback notes

This paper summarises a number of reasons why it is important that scholars have a full understanding of the perspective of practitioners. They point out that this can enable a direct link to be achieved between HR research and HR interventions in practice. Second, they suggest that experience of being an HR practitioner can provide scholars with better opportunities to work with management teams to identify important problems that require more research and to do something about them in an evidence-based way. Third, they point out that the purpose of HR scholarship – to enhance practice at the level of individuals, teams and organisations, is fully aligned with the challenges faced by most practitioners. Fourth, they argue that executive education programmes can be enriched by research-informed studies that have been undertaken in practice-based contexts. Finally, they argue that a closer 'walk' between scholars and practitioners provides some protection from the 'faddish' approaches to HR that were discussed earlier in this chapter.

However, in response to the second question in this activity you might have reflected that many managers choose not to engage with academic 'theory' and 'research' as, however hard both parties try, the studies seem remote from the 'real world' and irrelevant to the day-to-day, business focused, priorities. You may have pointed out that HR practitioners have to undertake work that is inherently challenging and, at the same time, to cope with significant limits to their power and influence. Therefore, although practitioners may be 'information hungry', they may rarely choose to look to academic research outputs to inform their practice.

As Brown and Latham (2018) suggest, academics and business practitioners, it seems, 'walk different paths'. One path focuses more on generalised (and sometimes slow-moving) theories and concepts. The other focuses on business imperatives and is results-orientated. However, the argument underpinning this book is that business-relevant and good quality HR practitioner research provides an opportunity for a 'bridge' between robust research and excellence in HR practice. Indeed, such a bridge might overcome the dangers of exclusive reliance by practitioners on 'experience', which can lead to a situation of 'superstitious learning' where past experiences are replicated without any evaluation of issues such as cause, context or important factors, and which can lead to operational inefficiencies and strategic failures. Your own experience or your reading of business pages in newspapers or news websites might provide you with examples where this has occurred; perhaps where a new chief executive or director has joined an organisation and tried to replicate the system that was successful in his or her previous company, only to find that the approach is not as transferable as was assumed and a crisis occurs. Such a scenario can also occur at a national level where national policy relating to HR or human capital is formulated in one country to 'copy' the HR practices that have been developed in other continents, only to find that there are unexpected (and often very significant) factors that make these approaches much less successful.

Accessible HR research can transform HR practice and excellent HR practice innovations have much to offer for 'theory development'. In an area like HRM and HRD a productive relationship between research, policy and practice is highly desirable but remains stubbornly problematic for three main reasons.

Time pressures, demands, reward systems and priorities

An important reason for the gap between academic and practice communities is the different time pressures, demands, reward systems and priorities of the two communities. This leads them to make different judgements about the 'value' of different types of HR knowledge and to formulate different views about information quality and relevance. For academics, institutional and government cultures and policies mean that they have to prioritise conceptual work that has the potential to make a lasting 'contribution to knowledge'. As a result research projects tend to go on for a long time and focus on 'depth' and analysis. In addition there is a potential 'time delay' of up to five years between an original research process and its publication in a scholarly journal. Research of this type is highly unlikely to be appealing to many HR practitioners.

At the same time, management initiatives rarely occur as a rational process of logical planning, control, communication and coordination. In reality, managerial work is fragmented and characterised by the need to deal with many different issues at the same time (Trullen *et al*, 2016; George and Hayden, 2018). For HR practitioners the priority is to achieve multiple results in a short timeframe and to provide a rapid response to changing management priorities. As a result practitioners find themselves launching new initiatives and organisational processes that require rapid evaluation and, in such circumstances, 'practice' runs ahead of 'theory'. Developments in talent management, human capital management and HR analytics are all examples of where this has occurred in recent years. Managers under pressure, therefore, are always likely to prefer accessible research that is 'strikingly packaged' and well publicised although there is a danger here as this can lead to oversimplified and naive forms of knowledge which, over time, have limited value.

'Mystification' of research

Second, a factor that inhibits the impact of HR research is the perceived 'mystery' and jargon of the research process itself. It is not just international students who may find the language of research methods and of academics to be inaccessible; this is a common complaint of time-starved HR practitioners in demanding organisational roles. Equally, the 'business-speak' language used in many organisations can also seem mystifying to those 'on the outside' who do not understand the 'jargon'. As you will have discovered as you undertook your course, members of the academic community are encouraged to spend most of their time publishing 'high quality' research in a small number of academic journals using language that is conceptual and 'dry'. However, practitioners, particularly once they have completed their course, hardly ever access these journals and prefer other forms of accessible information. As indicated in Chapter 1, higher status is given by governments and research-orientated higher education institutions to research that is focused on describing, explaining and predicting phenomena (sometimes referred to as 'Mode 1' research). This tradition has, over time, become progressively embedded within the academic community as an indicator of 'worth' and 'quality' and so academics give less time to the complementary (Mode 2) form of research, which focuses on designing solutions to 'applied' problems with more immediate practitioner relevance. The preference for 'pure' or Mode 1 approaches to research means that, even when highly relevant HRM knowledge is generated by researchers, these findings are rarely if ever communicated in a way that busy managers can access.

Dissemination and communication of research findings and outcomes is a key issue for any 'bridging' between the research and practice communities. It is not just academics who do not share their work with practitioners. Most practice-orientated student research reports or dissertations, once completed, are put somewhere safe and never read or discussed again. If research outcomes are to be applied and developed in practice, therefore, it is important that HR practitioner-researchers are willing and able to articulate the development of their understanding and learning so that those not directly involved in an investigation or piece of research can take something from it.

Separation of HR research from HR policy and HR practice

A third factor that inhibits the impact of HR research in practice may be a 'separation of roles' within the HR community. Large-scale research, for example, tends to be undertaken in university departments by those who specialise in it. Policy decisions, that may or may not be informed by such large-scale research, are made by a different group of people, such as those working in government departments or those in strategic decision-making roles in large organisations. The communication and implementation of those policy decisions is the responsibility of yet another group of HR practitioners and managers. The effect of the lack of 'ownership' is to diminish the impact of HR research. This separation of roles stems from an assumption by policy-makers and many academics of an 'objectivist' and linear process involved in research. (Objectivist assumptions about research are discussed in Chapter 1.) This assumes that knowledge is generated by academics as 'research outcomes' that are then disseminated to be adopted, adapted or applied by practitioners (Nutley, Walter and Davies, 2007). While this is a convenient 'common sense' understanding of research (which underpins the argument for evidence-based HR featured in Activity 12.2 and in Figure 12.1) there remain few examples of its successful use in practice. Both research and practice occur in dynamic multilevel contexts involving multiple stakeholders and are characterised by messy and often fragmented processes (Renkema, Meijerink and Bondarouk, 2017).

The argument of this book is that the relationship between research and practice is best understood as a process that is complex and multifaceted. Both academics and practitioners 'frame' and understand knowledge of HR in the light of their tacit knowledge and pre-existing experience. The research–practice gap is not a problem that can be easily resolved but a more productive and synergistic relationship between practice-aware academic researchers and research-aware HR practitioners is feasible (Tkachenko, Hahn and Peterson, 2017). However, this requires both communities to engage in a process of interaction, which accepts that knowledge of HR is 'provisional' and likely to be developed through 'messy' and socially interactive processes. In such circumstances both academic and organisational cultures could play a mediating role to narrow the 'cultural gap' and promote greater collaboration and coproduction of relevant and robust knowledge and understanding of the HR field. Good quality HR research, and excellence in HR practice, both involve systematically investigating people management and development issues to increase knowledge and underpin effective action. Therefore, HR research is inextricably involved with the 'real world' and is devalued if it ignores the need of practitioners to solve problems, to evaluate innovative practices and to develop and implement new forms of HR intervention. HR research has the potential to help organisations change and, at the same time, to generate knowledge (Aguinis *et al*, 2015) if a pluralist and engaged approach to scholarship is taken instead of assuming a binary opposition between scholars and practitioners. This approach to practitioner research and to researcher-practitioners recognises relationships between the research topic and methods, and between researchers and practitioners as participants in the research process. Such actionable knowledge generation can be undertaken by organisations of all sizes and sectors. It requires a systematic and rigorous approach to defining a research issue, problem or opportunity and also to gather and analyse data of good quality. These forms of practitioner-researcher partnerships have been used in a range of management development, organisation development, HRM and HRD settings (see, for example, Brown and Latham, 2018). However, it is difficult for academic researchers to 'let go' of traditional research assumptions and so actionable knowledge generated by practitioner-researcher projects are often overlooked by 'mainstream' academic traditions and very few systematic evaluations of the approach have been published.

Becoming an impactful practitioner-researcher

There are a number of benefits that could be achieved if a closer relationship between HR practice and research were achieved. From a practitioner perspective, research enables practitioners to:

- recognise tensions in good practice, and challenge attitudes and assumptions about 'the only way' to understand things;
- identify alternative options and courses of action;
- understand the issues involved in different practices in order to understand and improve them;
- enable fast, reflective action;
- deliver new knowledge and understanding.

Theory and research will not provide any practitioner with one 'prescription' for success. However, engaging with research processes and findings can help to generate a set of alternatives that can form part of the response when a strategic, policy level or practical issue arises. This requires that HR practitioners remain 'in-touch' with research and evidence about the topics they are interested in so that the alternatives they consider represent up-to-date knowledge. Aspirations of finding 'one right way' or one 'quick fix' lead to disappointment over the medium and long term. However, engaging with, and participating in, research can raise awareness of important concepts and provide insight, knowledge and understanding about important issues. On occasions, learning about (or discovering for ourselves) new research insights results in changed attitudes and might lead to much-needed changes in practice or policy.

Equally, a practice-led research agenda has a lot to offer for the academic community. 'Experimentation' through the implementation of new practices can stimulate new concepts and understanding Research agendas and theory can be refined by practice, and new and relevant areas for research can emerge. Although this pluralist approach towards research-engaged practice and practice-engaged scholarship is not the easiest of options for both sets of stakeholders, it provides a more robust approach to cope in times of economic challenge as well as growth. Being an effective practitioner-researcher does not require simultaneous fulfilment of two separate roles nor 'waiting-around' for academic researchers to disseminate the outcomes of their research studies. Instead the aim is to develop an approach to work that is neither typical practitioner nor typical researcher. Instead of seeing practitioners as merely 'consumers' of relevant knowledge generated by academics, the practitioner-research role means that HR professionals can become part of, and add value to, the process of generating practice-led knowledge and theory development. In this way research and practice together can provide a valuable 'ingredient' in HR decision-making processes in organisations.

This more engaged approach to applied research in the HR and wider business and management field is increasingly recognised and encouraged by those in government and policy positions. Procedures to assess research quality at UK national level, undertaken every few years, for example, now involve an assessment of the effect of research outside of academia. Researchers are increasingly encouraged to engage a variety of potential beneficiaries of their research in the research process itself, to engage as appropriate in research projects that span across different disciplinary boundaries, and to include a focus on ensuring a careful process of evaluation and measurement of the impact of their study in terms of the effect on, or change or influence on organisation(s), the economy, quality of life, public policy or services and so on (Research Excellence Framework [REF] 2021, 2019).

If research and practice are to become more closely linked in this way then there are implications for both practitioners and researchers. First, it is important to value the activity of systematic research within the role of HR practitioners at all levels and within all types of employing organisation. 'Applied' research within organisations is a valuable activity and, when done well, the activity deserves affirmation by both practitioners and academics (Robson and McCartan, 2016). Second, it is important to see the 'research' process as a part of the 'HR toolkit' of effective practitioners. Good quality HR research and theory can be just as relevant to operational as to strategic issues. The research process itself can become 'demystified' as HR professionals engage more with 'research' and HR researchers engage more with 'practice'. This 'demystification' process will be enhanced if research outcomes are communicated to suit the timescales and priorities of practitioners and by using language that is straightforward and engaging. At the same time, it is important that HR practitioners assert themselves to influence the research agenda of universities and research institutes so that a balance between the rigour of an excellent research process and the relevance of the issue or topic that is being researched can be achieved.

This book celebrates and encourages the contribution of research undertaken by 'practitioner-researchers' where 'local theory' (Titchen, 2015), which is relevant to particular organisations, can be developed, evaluated and revised as appropriate. These forms of research are as valuable as specialised and highly theoretical projects undertaken by groups of researchers in universities and research centres. Where practitioner-researchers, and those who work with them, have been involved in gathering and analysing data relevant to organisational problems or issues there is more chance of effective implementation of the solutions that their work suggests. As practitioner-researchers reflect on and learn from the research processes they engage with there is also more chance that the benefits will be realised to the benefit of the individuals involved and the organisation(s) in which the research took place.

The premise of this book is that systematic research is a valuable process and, since the publication of the first edition in 2004, there has been a step-change in acceptance by many scholars of the need for evidence-based practice but also for practice-informed research. This book seeks to raise the profile of research that explores the dimensions of HR issues and problems from the perspective of both practitioners and researchers. If practitioner-researcher projects, which are advocated in this book, become more integrated within professional practice then it is likely that a mixed-methods approach, involving a justified use of both quantitative and qualitative data will become a feature of HR research (Bell, Bryman and Harley, 2019).

Finally, it is important to explore the characteristics, or competences, that might underpin an effective 'practitioner-researcher'. The advantages and disadvantages of this role are considered in Chapter 1. Having explored the different features of the research process in the main body of this book it is worth a consideration of the qualities of an effective practitioner-researcher, which may also be worth reflecting in any personal development chapter or section your study centre suggests that you include in your submitted work (Costley and Pizzolato, 2018; Nutley *et al*, 2007):

- **Being critical and committed.** Implicit preconceptions about issues and situations are inevitable if you are part of, or close to, the organisation being researched. The effective practitioner-researcher will, therefore, be able to critically evaluate and question 'received wisdom' at the same time as maintaining and communicating a commitment to the development of the organisation. In this way they will encourage challenge and 'paradigm shifts'.

- **Encourage research enthusiasts but be realistic about limits.** Organisational realities may make it difficult for some research to be undertaken or taken seriously. It is important, therefore, to 'aim high' but, at the same time, to be prepared and able to work within the limits of organisational realities.

- **Collaborate effectively with other stakeholders in the research process.** As a part of the organisation, practitioner-researchers have access to a range of contacts and sources of information. At the same time it is important to contribute an authentic perspective into the research process and into relationships with other people involved in an inquiry-based project.

- **Take ownership of research through being proactive, reflective and, where appropriate, reflexive.** A feature of commitment to actionable knowledge is encouragement of reflection on the wider context of the problem or issue that is being researched, both within the organisation and with regard to practice and developments outside of the organisation. In addition, it is important that practitioner-researchers acknowledge a process of mutual and interactive 'shaping' between the research, the researchers and others involved in the project that is often referred to as reflexivity.

- **Recognise the benefits of diversity of disciplinary expertise and different assessment criteria.** Practitioners and researchers who focus exclusively on one method or form of 'measurement' are unlikely to realise the situated nature of the phenomenon they wish to research. A benefit of a research-practice synergy is an acknowledgement of the value of different methodologies in order to have impact through novel procedures or products. Effective practitioner research is also alert to unintended consequences of interventions.

- **Building trust with research participants through a commitment to ethical research and practice.** Practitioner-research involves engagement with organisational problems where the solution is uncertain and where a variety of stakeholders are involved. Trust is vital in research collaborations in such contexts. Practitioner-researchers may already have a reputation as an HR professional in their organisation, but trust in their research-related or enabling role is also required, particularly as the research process may lead to recommendations for change that will impact, directly or indirectly, on research participants. As discussed in Chapter 4, positionality, personal ethics and values are key factors in implementing the outcomes of the research. Practitioner-research makes even higher ethical demands if trust is to be maintained.

Achieving good quality, practitioner-relevant research also requires members of the academic community to reassess their assumptions. Practitioner involvement in research will not occur unless academics who are responsible for research projects are prepared to integrate practitioner involvement into their systems and practices. Key to this is an acknowledgement of the value of practice-led as well as conceptual knowledge, 'translation' of research findings into practitioner-accessible language and encouragement of those able to make links between organisations or practitioners to facilitate examination of issues in a scholarly and systematic way.

Achieving impactful HR research and practice also requires action from institutional leaders. Practitioners working alone will not achieve a closer integration between the 'established domains' of academic research organisations, employers, professional body or sector-wide institutions. Potential advances in the synergy from research and practice can be achieved through:

- **institutional interaction** to embed research through meaningful research-practice partnerships and two-way flows of information;
- **influence channels** facilitated by professional associations such as CIPD to foster research champions who can gradually change the mindset and actions of practitioners and researchers;
- **alignment of research with sustainable organisational performance** to generate a 'user-pull' focus and encourage evidence-based practice as part of professional development and organisational development;
- **incentives and reinforcement** where the use of current research is affirmed and recognised through both extrinsic and intrinsic reward processes.

CHECKLIST
....

- The role of many HR practitioners is fragmented and characterised by the need to deal with many issues at the same time. As a result they may not access and evaluate the findings of many HR research projects. However, evidence-based HR practice can improve the quality of decision-making, through demonstrating valid evidence for its initiatives and so enhance the credibility of the HR function. This involves making use of the best evidence available as a basis for trustworthy HR decision-making. Different forms of evidence include: research evidence; organisational evidence; experiential evidence; and stakeholder evidence.

- Impactful HR research involves deriving real-world benefits from systematically undertaken HR investigative projects. Research will have more impact if stakeholder engagement is designed in to the project from its planning to its evaluation rather than left until the end. Research is likely to be more impactful if potential beneficiaries of the research are identified and engaged from the beginning of the project. Impactful research requires two-way engagement to develop a sense of shared ownership or a co-designed project. Impactful research also requires stakeholders to be involved at the beginning, middle and end of the project.

- There are many ways to communicate research findings and research progress. These include: internal reports; presentations and updates undertaken within one or more organisations; and more 'public' means of communication through social media opportunities or through face-to-face networks and professional publications.

- Communicating your research insights to non-academic audiences requires that you produce less detailed content, use accessible language and focus on broad issues rather than the detail. Non-academic audiences are interested in hearing your recommendations for action and expect you to write persuasively and indicate the benefits of your findings for organisational performance.

- There are mutual benefits to be gained by researchers and HR practitioners working more closely together. Practitioner-researcher relationships can achieve a stronger link between HR research and HR interventions in practice. It means that important problems that need research can be tackled and HR decisions can be made in an evidence-based way. It also provides some insurance against 'faddish' approaches to HR that may lead to damaging and unforeseen consequences.

- Practitioner-researcher collaborations are likely to lead to greater acceptance of mixed methods approach, involving a justified use of both quantitative and qualitative data.

- Effective practitioner-researchers are curious, critical and committed to systematic enquiry and evaluation of evidence as a basis for decision-making. They are proactive in their approach to research collaboration and are reflective and reflexive. They recognise the value of multidisciplinary expertise and variety in measurement and assessment criteria. They focus on building and maintaining the trust of all those who are involved in, or may be affected by, research projects and have a visible ethical commitment.

 Review Questions

Questions for reflection

As indicated in Chapter 11, research reports that are part of a CIPD professionally accredited qualification route are expected to provide some reflection about how the research process has contributed to your personal and professional development. This chapter urges you to go further. Having reflected on what you have learned through this demanding process it urges you to consider how, as a result of the capabilities of effective research and scholarship you are developing, it would be possible to bring together the often separate worlds of academic researchers and HR practitioners to ensure a greater synergy between the two fields.

Taking stock

1   To what extent do you routinely use your critical judgement to assess the reliability and validity of evidence, including that based on your previous experience?

2   How often do you systematically and routinely gather high-quality data about the issues your organisation faces? To what extent do you critically assess the quality of these data?

3   What opportunities might there be to engage potential stakeholders or beneficiaries with your project? What opportunities are there for you to disseminate the progress or interim findings from your project?

4   What skills will you need in order to share what you have learned more widely?

5   What features of your research benefited from your involvement with other stakeholders? What have you learned that you might not otherwise have been able to learn?

6   In what ways did your position (as an 'outsider', 'insider', 'colleague', 'manager' and so on) affect trust between you and others? If you were to have the opportunity to 'start over again' with your research project, what might you do differently with regard to stakeholder relationships?

Future options

7   What skills and qualities, relevant to being a practitioner-researcher, would you like to further develop in the future? How might you go about developing in these areas?

 Useful Resources

Civil Service (2014) Rapid evidence assessment toolkit [Online] https://webarchive.nationalarchives.gov.uk/20140402164155/http://www.civilservice.gov. uk/networks/gsr/resources-and-guidance/rapid-evidence-assessment (archived at https://perma.cc/P5NS-JU6D)

 References

Aguinis, H, Shapiro, DL, Antonacopoulou, EP and Cummings, TG (2015) Scholarly impact: a pluralist conceptualization, *Academy of Management Learning and Education,* **13** (4), pp 623–39, DOI: 10.5465/amle.2014.0121

Barends, E, Rousseau, D and Briner, R (2014) Evidence-based management: the basic principles, *Center for Evidence-Based Management,* Amsterdam [Online] https://www.cebma.org/wpcontent/uploads/Evidence-Based-Practice-The-Basic-Principles-vs-Dec-2015.pdf

Bell, E, Bryman, A and Harley, B (2019) *Business Research Methods*, 5th edn, Oxford University Press, Oxford

Brown, T and Latham, G (2018) Maintaining relevance and rigor: How we bridge the practitioner–scholar divide within human resource development, *Human Resource Development Quarterly*, **29** (2), pp 99–105, DOI: 10.1002/hrdq.21308

Costley, C and Pizzolato, N (2018) Transdisciplinary qualities in practice doctorates, *Studies in Continuing Education*, **40** (1), pp 30–45, DOI: 10.1080/0158037X.2017.1394287

Day, A (2008) *How to Get Research Published in Journals*, Gower, Aldershot

George, S and Hayden, D (2018) The role of line managers in HR and L&D, *CIPD Factsheet* [Online] https://www.cipd.co.uk/knowledge/fundamentals/people/hr/line-managers-factsheet#8031 (archived at https://perma.cc/5NUA-F7CS)

Gubbins, C, Harney, B, van der Werff, L and Rousseau, DM (2018) Enhancing the trustworthiness and credibility of human resource development: Evidence-based management to the rescue? *Human Resource Development Quarterly*, **29**, pp 193–202, DOI:10.1002/hrdq.21313

Maxwell, J (2019) The value of qualitative inquiry for public policy, *Qualitative Inquiry*, DOI: 10.1177/1077800419857093

Miller, D, Hartwick, J and Le Breton-Miller, I (2004) How to detect a management fad – and distinguish it from a classic, *Business Horizons*, **47** (4), pp 7–16

Nutley, SM, Walter, I and Davies, HTO (2007) *Using Evidence: How research can inform public services*, Policy Press, Bristol

Renkema, M, Meijerink, J and Bondarouk, T (2017) Advancing multilevel thinking in human resource management research: Applications and guidelines, *Human Resource Management Review*, **27** (3), pp 397–415, DOI: 10.1016/j.hrmr.2017.03.001

Research Excellence Framework [REF] 2021, Research Excellence Framework, [Online] https://www.ref.ac.uk/ (archived at https://perma.cc/CZG4-LAGJ)

Robson, C (2016) *Real World Research: A resource for social scientists and practitioner-researchers*, Wiley, Oxford

Titchen, A (2015) Action research: genesis, evolution and orientations, *International Practice Development Journal*, **5** (1), pp 1–16 [Online] https://www.fons.org/Resources/Documents/Journal/Vol5No1/IPDJ_0501_01.pdf (archived at https://perma.cc/737C-CJ5L)

Tkachenko, O, Hahn, H-J and Peterson, SL (2017) Research–practice gap in applied fields: An integrative literature review, *Human Resource Development Review*, **16** (3), pp 235–62, DOI: 10.1177/1534484317707562

Trullen, J, Stirpe, L, Bonache, J and Valverde, M (2016) The HR department's contribution to line managers' effective implementation of HR practices, *Human Resource Management Journal*, **26** (4), pp 449–70

GLOSSARY

Terms that may be useful in your research methods assignments or dissertations

a posteriori **analysis:** Analysis and reasoning from known facts or past events rather than by making assumptions or predictions.

accidental sampling: Use of a speculative 'convenience' approach to attracting potential participants in a research study.

action research strategy: Research strategy concerned with changing activities or processes that involves close collaboration between practitioners and researchers.

analysis: The ability to break down data and clarify the nature of the component parts and the relationship between them.

anonymity: The process of concealing the identity of participants in all documents resulting from the research.

applied research: Sometimes referred to as Mode 2 research. Research to develop knowledge that can be used to solve problems, predict effects, and develop actions and interventions that are applicable in particular organisational contexts.

CAQDAS: Computer aided qualitative data analysis software.

case study research strategy: An approach to research that utilises a group of research methods to investigate a complex phenomenon where the boundaries between the situation and its context are not clear.

categorical data: Data whose values cannot be measured numerically but can be classified into sets (categories) or placed in rank order.

categorising: The process of developing categories and subsequently attaching these categories to meaningful chunks or units of data.

census: The collection and analysis of data from every possible case or group members in a population.

central tendency measure: The generic term for statistics that provide an impression of those values that are common, middling or average. These are expressed as: the mean, the median or the mode.

chronological: Arranged in date order.

citation: Attribution of the source of ideas, words or expressions.

cluster sampling: Probability sampling procedure in which the population is divided into discrete groups prior to sampling. A random sample of these clusters is then drawn.

code book: A listing of the definition of each code in a dataset.

comparative research strategy: The comparison of two or more cases to illuminate existing theory or generate theoretical insights as a result of contrasting findings uncovered through the comparison.

concept: An abstract idea.

confidentiality: Concern relating to the right of access to data provided by participants and in particular the need to keep these data secret or private.

consent form: Written agreement of the participant to take part in the research and give his or her permission for data to be used in specified ways.

contextual data: Additional data recorded when collecting primary or secondary data that reveal background information about the setting and the data collection.

convenience sampling: Non-probability sampling procedure in which cases are selected opportunistically.

correlation coefficient: Number between –1 and +1 representing the strength and direction of two ranked or numerical variables. A value of 0 means the variables are perfectly independent.

correlation: The extent to which two variables are related to each other.

credible: Convincing. For example, the authentic representation of research participants' experiences.

critical evaluation: Consideration of the validity, reliability, strengths, weaknesses and applicability of something being reviewed.

cross-sectional research: The study of a particular phenomenon across a range of cases at a particular time (a 'snapshot').

data protection: Control over access to data that respects individuals and their rights around privacy and use of their information.

data: Facts, opinions and statistics that have been collected together and recorded for reference or for analysis.

deductive research: Reasoning process where theory informs research into the problem, situation or issue of interest.

demographic data: Social statistics of a population.

descriptive statistics: Generic term for statistics that can be used to describe variables.

dispersion measures: The spread of data within a dataset. Two principal measures (the range and the standard deviation) express how the values for a variable are dispersed around the central tendency.

empirical literature: Literature from original research such as scientific experiments, surveys and observational studies.

empirical: Something that is observable by the senses.

ethics (research ethics): The application of fundamental moral ethical principles underpinning what are accepted as appropriate behaviours applied to research.

exclusion criteria: Additional characteristics of potential research participants who, while they meet the inclusion criteria, make it unlikely that the information they provide will be relevant for the specific research questions.

experiential data: Data about the researcher's perceptions and feelings as the research develops.

exploratory data analysis: The use of relatively simple statistical techniques to understand the data.

focus group: A facilitated group interview, composed of a small number of participants, in which the topic is clearly defined and interactive discussion between the participants is recorded.

framework: Description of the underlying structure of relationships between variables or concepts.

frequency distribution: Table for summarising data from one variable so that specific values can be read.

gatekeeper: An intermediary between the potential participants and the researcher.

generalising: Applying findings based on a sample of the population to the wider population.

grey literature: Sources such as government white papers and planning documents that are available in the public domain but not as a result of a specific publishing house.

grounded theory: Progressive identification and integration of categories of meaning from data. Theory development occurs after the data have been collected.

hermeneutics: The study of the theory and practice of interpretation.

histogram: Diagram for showing frequency distributions for a grouped continuous data variable in which the area of each bar represents the frequency of occurrence.

hypothesis: A supposition based on facts that has not been evidenced. A testable prediction that will contribute to answering your research question.

inclusion criteria: Criteria that describe key features of the target research participants that will make them eligible to provide information relevant to the research questions.

independent groups t-test: Statistical test to determine the likelihood that the values of a numerical data variable for two independent samples or groups are different. The test assesses the likelihood that any difference between these two groups occurred by chance alone.

independent variable: Variable that causes changes to a dependent variable or variables.

inductive approach: Research approach involving the development of theory or generalisations as a result of the observation of empirical data.

inferential statistics: Analytical procedures to describe and make inferences about the phenomenon being researched.

informed consent: Position achieved when intended participants are fully informed about the use of research to be undertaken and their role in it and where their consent to participate is freely given.

interpretivist: A research approach that is concerned to understand how we as humans make sense of the world around us.

interval data: Numerical data for which the interval between any two data variables can be stated but the relative difference between them is not meaningful.

interviewee bias: An attempt by an interviewee to construct an account that hides some data or when they present themselves in a socially desirable role or situation.

interviewer bias: Implicit or explicit attempt by an interviewer to introduce bias during an interview or where the appearance or behaviour of an interviewer has the effect of introducing bias in the interviewee's responses.

Likert scale: A fixed choice response format for measuring attitudes to a series of statements that explore different dimensions of a topic. It was developed by Likert (1932).

line graph: Diagram for showing trends for a variable.

literature review: Detailed and justified analysis and commentary of the merits and faults of the literature in a chosen area, which demonstrates familiarity with what is already known about the research topic.

longitudinal study: The study of a particular phenomenon over an extended period of time.

matrix: Data supplied or displayed in the form of rows and columns.

mean: The average value calculated by adding up the values of each case for a variable and dividing by the total number of cases.

median: The middle value when all the values of a variable are arranged in rank order, sometimes known as the 50th percentile.

method: The techniques and procedures used to obtain and analyse research data.

methodology: The theory of how research should be undertaken; the philosophical framework within which research is conducted; the foundation upon which the research is based.

mixed methods research: An approach to research that makes use of aspects of both positivism and interpretivism.

model: Representation of a phenomenon that makes use of theoretical concepts.

mono method: Use of a single data collection technique and corresponding analysis procedure or procedures.

multiple bar chart: Diagram for comparing frequency distributions for categorical or grouped continuous data variables that highlights the highest and lowest values.

multiple line graph: Diagram for comparing trends over time between numerical data variables.

multiple methods: Use of more than one data collection technique and analysis procedure.

narrative: A spoken or written account of connected events.

negative correlation: Relationship between two variables for which, as the value of one variable increases, the value of the other variable decreases.

negative skew: Distribution of numerical data for a variable in which the majority of the data are found bunched to the right with a long tail to the left.

nominal data: Data that refer to descriptions.

non-parametric statistic: Statistic designed to be used when data are not normally distributed. Often used with categorical data.

non-probability sampling: Selection of sampling techniques in which the chance or probability of each case being selected is not known.

non-response rate: The number of non-returned questionnaires as a percentage of the number distributed.

normal distribution: Special form of the symmetric distribution in which the numerical data for a variable can be plotted as a bell-shaped curve.

null hypothesis: Testable proposition stating that there is no significant difference or relationship between two or more variables.

observational study: A study in which individuals are observed or certain outcomes are measured. No attempt is made to affect the outcome.

ordinal data: Data presented in an ordered fashion and the numbers assigned to the outcomes indicate the order of importance.

parametric statistic: Statistic designed to be used when data are normally distributed. Used with numerical data.

participant-researcher: Person who conducts research within an organisation for which they work.

participant: The person who answers the questions, usually in an interview or group interview.

peer reviewed: Analysed and considered by experts on the topic for accuracy and quality.

pie chart: Diagram frequently used for showing proportions for a categorical data or a grouped continuous or discrete data variable.

pilot test: Small-scale study to test a questionnaire, interview checklist or observation schedule, to minimise the likelihood of respondents having problems in answering the questions and of data recording problems as well as to allow some assessment of the questions' validity and the reliability of the data that will be collected.

plagiarism: Passing off someone else's work or ideas as your own. This is treated as a serious offence in academic institutions.

population: The complete set of cases or group members.

positive correlation: The relationship between two variables for which, as the value of one variable increases, the value of the other variable also increases.

positive skew: Distribution of numerical data for a variable in which the majority of the data are found bunched to the left with a long tail to the right.

positivism: An approach to research that usually attempts to establish cause and effect relationships.

practitioner-researcher: Role occupied by a researcher when conducting research in an organisation, often her or his own, while fulfilling his or her normal working role.

primary data: Data collected from original sources with a specific research project in mind.

probability sampling: Selection of sampling techniques in which the chance of each case being selected from the population is known and is not zero.

professional standard: A consensual expectation of practice or behaviour in an occupational or professional field.

pure research: Sometimes referred to as 'Mode 1' research. Gaining knowledge to describe and explain phenomena and develop and test generalisable theories. See also – applied research.

purposive sampling: Non-probability sampling procedure in which the judgement of the researcher is used to select the cases that make up the sample. This can be done on the basis of extreme cases, maximum variation, minimum variation, critical cases or typical cases.

qualitative data: Non-numerical data or data that have not been quantified.

quantitative data: Numerical data or data that represent the dimensions of what is being studied.

quota sampling: Sampling procedure that reflects as far as possible the diversity of the wider research population in the same proportions.

random sampling: Probability sampling procedure that ensures that each case in the population has an equal chance of being included in the sample.

range: The difference between the highest and the lowest values for a variable.

ranking question: Closed question in which the respondent is offered a list of items and instructed to place them in rank order.

rating question: Closed question in which a scaling device is used to record the respondent's response.

ratio scale data: Numerical data for which the difference or 'interval' and relative difference between any two data values for a particular variable can be stated.

raw data: Data for which little, if any, data processing has taken place.

reflexive: The process of 'self-reference' where the researcher examines the interrelationship between his or her actions and the research context and outcomes.

regression analysis: A procedure for estimating a relationship between a dependent variable and one or more independent variables.

reliability: The extent to which data collection technique or techniques will yield consistent findings, similar observations would be made or conclusions reached by other researchers or there is transparency in how sense was made from the raw data.

representative sample: Sample that represents exactly the population from which it is drawn.

research design: The framework that guides decisions about the collection and analysis of data.

research ethics: The appropriateness of the researcher's behaviour in relation to the rights of those who become the subject of a research project or who are affected by it.

research objectives: Clear, specific statements that identify what the researcher wishes to accomplish as a result of doing the research.

research philosophy: Overarching term relating to the development of knowledge and the nature of that knowledge in relation to research.

research population: Set of cases or group members that are being researched.

research strategy: The general approach taken to answer research questions or achieve research objectives.

research: The systematic collection and interpretation of information with a clear purpose to find things out.

respondent: The person who answers the questions usually either in an interview or on a questionnaire (also referred to as a participant).

response rate: The number of complete questionnaires returned as a proportion of the number distributed.

sample: Subgroup of part of a larger population.

sampling frame: The complete list of all cases in the population, from which a sample is drawn.

scale: Measure of a concept, created by combining scores to a number of rating questions.

scatter graph: Diagram for showing the relationship between two numerical or ranked variables.

science: Seeking knowledge to describe, explain, predict and understand.

secondary data: Information that was previously collected by someone else and for other research purposes.

self-selection sampling: Non-probability sampling procedure in which the case (usually the individual) is allowed to identify their desire to be part of the sample.

semi-structured interviews: Interviews for which the themes and questions are worked out in advance but the flow and the order may change.

significance testing: Testing the probability of pattern such as a relationship between two variables occurring by chance alone.

snowball sampling: Non-probability sampling procedure in which subsequent respondents are obtained from the information provided by initial respondents.

stacked bar chart: Diagram for comparing totals and subtotals for all types of data variable.

standard deviation: The way in which values for a variable are dispersed around the central tendency.

statistical analysis: The collection and investigation of data to uncover patterns and trends.

stratified sampling: Procedure to generate subgroups based on common characteristics to enable random sampling to occur proportionally from each subgroup.

symmetric distribution: Description of the distribution of data for a variable in which the data are distributed equally either side of the highest frequency.

systematic sampling: Probability sampling procedure in which the initial starting point is selected at random and then the cases are selected at regular intervals.

t-test: Comparison of means between two groups.

table: Technique for summarising data from one or more variables so that specific values or instances can be read.

thematic analysis: An analytical method in which patterns of meaning are identified in a dataset.

theme: An idea that recurs in, or pervades, the subject of analysis.

theory: A logical model or framework of concepts that describes and explains how phenomena are related with each other and which would apply in a variety of circumstances.

transcription: The written record of what a participant said in response to a question, or what participants said to each other in conversation, in their own words.

triangulation: Data validation through cross-verification from more than two sources.

validity: The extent to which a data collection method accurately measures what it was intended to do. Also the extent to which research findings are really about what they profess to be about.

variable: Individual element or attribute upon which data have been collected.

variance: Statistic that measures the spread of data values; a measure of dispersion. The smaller the variance the closer individual data variables are to the mean. The value of the variance is the square root of the standard deviation.

visual data: Pictorial or graphic data.

The authors acknowledge the contribution of Dr Lynn NS Lansbury, Learning Support Tutor, University of Portsmouth, for additional entries to the glossary.

INDEX